The Spectre of Capital

Historical Materialism Book Series

The Historical Materialism Book Series is a major publishing initiative of the radical left. The capitalist crisis of the twenty-first century has been met by a resurgence of interest in critical Marxist theory. At the same time, the publishing institutions committed to Marxism have contracted markedly since the high point of the 1970s. The Historical Materialism Book Series is dedicated to addressing this situation by making available important works of Marxist theory. The aim of the series is to publish important theoretical contributions as the basis for vigorous intellectual debate and exchange on the left.

The peer-reviewed series publishes original monographs, translated texts, and reprints of classics across the bounds of academic disciplinary agendas and across the divisions of the left. The series is particularly concerned to encourage the internationalization of Marxist debate and aims to translate significant studies from beyond the English-speaking world.

For a full list of titles in the Historical Materialism Book Series available in paperback from Haymarket Books, visit: www.haymarketbooks.org/series_collections/1-historical-materialism.

The Spectre of Capital

Idea and Reality

Christopher J. Arthur

Haymarket Books
Chicago, IL

First published in 2022 by Brill Academic Publishers, The Netherlands
© 2022 Koninklijke Brill NV, Leiden, The Netherlands

Published in paperback in 2023 by
Haymarket Books
P.O. Box 180165
Chicago, IL 60618
773-583-7884
www.haymarketbooks.org

ISBN: 978-1-64259-988-6

Distributed to the trade in the US through Consortium Book Sales and Distribution (www.cbsd.com) and internationally through Ingram Publisher Services International (www.ingramcontent.com).

This book was published with the generous support of Lannan Foundation and Wallace Action Fund.

Special discounts are available for bulk purchases by organizations and institutions. Please call 773-583-7884 or email info@haymarketbooks.org for more information.

Cover art and design by David Mabb. Cover art is a detail of *Construct 25, May Morris, Honeysuckle / Alexander Rodchenko, Hard Currency*, wallpaper and paper mounted on linen (2006). Collection of the Victoria and Albert Museum.

Printed in the United States.

10 9 8 7 6 5 4 3 2 1

Library of Congress Cataloging-in-Publication data is available.

For Morag

Contents

Preface IX
Abbreviations XII

Introduction 1

PART 1
Object and Method

1 Capital and Social Form   9

2 Capital and the Actuality of the Ideal   19

3 Systematic Dialectic   27

4 The Two Dialectics of Capital: Analytic and Synthetic   36

5 With What Must the Critique of Capital Begin?   46

PART 2
The Ideal Constitution of Capital

DIVISION I
Capital in Its Notion

6 Commodity   69

7 Money   91

8 Capital   150

DIVISION II
Capital Relation

9   Circulation   201

10   Production   217

11   Reproduction   256

DIVISION III
The System of Capital

Introduction to Division III   265

12   Capital as a System of Capitals   267

13   The System of Industrial Capital   274

14   The Dual Ontology of Capital   329

15   Absolute Capital   338

16   Capital and Its Others: Labour and Land   352

17   The Spectre   368

18   Review of the Presentation   372

19   Beyond Capital and Class   388

Appendix 1: Commentary on the Hegelian Origins of the Logic of the Value Form   395
Appendix 2: Tables   408
Glossary   432
Select Bibliography   441
Index of Names   446
Index of Subjects   447

Preface

This work is devoted to the explication of the idea of capital. But it is unique in that it argues that capital is itself 'Idea' in much the same sense that Hegel advanced in his philosophy. For him an Idea is not a mental entity, but the full *actualisation* of a concept, of its 'truth', one might say. So capital, as such an Idea, is continually making itself *present* in reality. This book aims to show that capital is the spectral subject of modernity.

The term 'spectre of capital' I coined in a journal article of 2001.[1] It echoes the *Manifesto*'s 'spectre of communism'. But communism was a real movement aimed at abolishing the existing state of things, ruled by capital. However, just how 'spectral' and how 'real' is capital itself? Paradoxically it is both. Although it has purely a *spectral presence*, it is without doubt a real social power, and it retains this in the face of any critique such as that presented here. (Thus, in the phrase in our title – 'Idea and Reality' – the 'and' should not be taken contrastively; it is indicative of identity.)

The method followed in my presentation of capital, as a social form, rests on the logic proper to the peculiar character of its object. For a presentation of the inner logic of capital, the protocols of 'systematic dialectic' are required.[2] This systematic-dialectical presentation draws on Hegel's philosophical logic. It is unconcerned with recovering the grand narrative of his philosophy of history, and then relating it to historical materialism. Rather it is focussed on his *logic of categories*. Here this is taken to be architectonically homologous with the social forms of capital.

Systematic dialectic is deployed to articulate the forms of this social order, namely capitalism. My method of logical development of form is rooted in the observation that the movement of exchange is *analogous* to the movement of thought, in that there is generated a realm of pure *forms*, which stand in logical relations to each other, any content absented. Thus the presentation is informed by 'value-form theory'. This is a relatively new approach to the critique of political economy. It affirms that value relations play an active part in determining the shape, and purposes, of material production. The developed form of value (commodity, money, capital) is the characteristic social form of present economic relations.

---

1 See Arthur 2001.
2 For an overview of the literature on systematic dialectic see Arthur 2002. Path-breaking books in the field were Reuten and Williams 1989, and Smith 1990. Relevant earlier works were Sekine 1984, and Eldred et al. 1982.

Hegel is a natural reference for value-form theory because his logic is well suited to a theory of forms. Moreover, Hegel's systematic development of categories is directed towards articulating the structure of a totality, showing how it supports itself in and through the interchanges of its inner moments. This presupposes that the totality is structured by internal relations; this is so by definition in the case of a logic of categories. I argue capital *is* such a totality. A theory of active social form, specifically the value form, requires a systematic-dialectical presentation, then.

So the scope of this project is restricted to a theory of a purely capitalist society. More than that, it is restricted to its 'pure theory', or principles, as distinct from the stages of development of capitalism, on the basis of which an empirical study of an existing capitalism may be carried out in a historically informed manner.[3] Moreover, it is even more restricted in that its entire attention is directed towards the *concept of capital* itself. Indeed, I take the concept of capital so narrowly that even rent is excluded because I regard it as an impurity from the theoretical standpoint that elucidates only those forms which are necessary to capital as a concept, or, as I shall call it, the Idea of capital.

Despite this narrow focus, an important result is demonstrated, namely that the logical tendency of the Idea of capital is to complete itself through its own immanent development, and therewith to posit all its presuppositions; it is self-grounded, self-determining, and self-reproducing. The qualifications required to this bold thesis are addressed in the course of the argument itself as appropriate.

Such a study as this is the necessary prolegomenon to any adequate scientific study of capitalism. However, it is purely a conceptual exercise, developing a system of *categories* that stand in quasi-*logical* relations. So this book is not a work in economics, but of philosophy. For example, the 'capital concept' presented here is far from a properly articulated economic one. The same goes for 'production' and many other themes touched upon.

This is because the peculiar logic of the object has itself a conceptual character. The very possibility of a pure theory, and of the reality of the capital Idea, depends upon an ontological claim about the way capital itself abstracts from its material underpinnings, and constitutes a realm of pure forms. I hope to vindicate this large claim in part by developing the categories of capital within a systematic-dialectical framework. At the same time, it is a critique of the economic categories it presents. A critique of political economy is understood here not as a criticism of bourgeois apologetic for capital, but as a critique of the capital system itself insofar as its own forms lack truth.

---

3 On such 'pure theory' cf. Uno 1980.

In developing my ideas, I have been fortunate to be a member of the *International Symposium on Marxian Theory* research group, founded by Fred Moseley in 1991.[4] Beside Moseley himself, I thank especially, for their patient commentaries on my work-in-progress, long-standing members: Riccardo Bellofiore, Martha Campbell, Roberto Fineschi, Patrick Murray, Geert Reuten, and Tony Smith. (These thinkers are also those who have produced the most significant works in English on the critique of political economy.)

For commenting on the original manuscript of this book, I thank especially Geert Reuten and Tony Smith. They have saved me from many an error; but, of course, they bear no responsibility for the book itself.

[4] The *International Symposium on Marxian Theory* has published a number of conference volumes as follows: Moseley (ed.) 1993; Moseley and Campbell (eds) 1997; Arthur and Reuten (eds) 1998; Campbell and Reuten (eds) 2002; Bellofiore and Taylor (eds) 2004; Moseley (ed.) 2005; Bellofiore and Fineschi (eds) 2009; Bellofiore et al. (eds) 2013; Moseley and Smith (eds) 2014.

Abbreviations

ASV	absolute surplus value
C	commodity, also C′ and C″
c	constant capital
GRP	general rate of profit
I	individual
K	capital, also K′ and K″
lp	labour power
M	money, also M′ and M″
m	increment of money
mp	means of production
P	particular
PP	price of production
RP	reproduction price
RSV	relative surplus value
S	singular
SP	simple price
sv	surplus value
TP	transformation procedure
TFRP	tendential fall of the rate of profit
U	universal
URP	uniform rate of profit
v	'variable capital' (or the revenue of the wage worker)

Introduction

Although I start from Marx, I go beyond him. So my book aims to reconstruct Marx's work in the spirit of a systematic-dialectical logic. I do not take a position here on 'what Marx really meant', still less on 'what Hegel really meant', nor yet on 'whether Marx got Hegel right or wrong'.[1] What I aim at is entirely substantive, even though I draw heavily upon my readings of Hegel and of Marx. Insofar as I appropriate their ideas for my purposes it is easy to discern the readings I favour; but nothing hangs on this. Insofar as I attribute to capital in part an ideal reality with a problematic relationship to the material it subsumes, I wish this theory to be assessed in its own terms. Its plausibility does not depend on whether, in borrowing from Hegel and Marx, I have read them correctly. Even if I have read them incorrectly – and I freely admit to revision at various points – it is the fruitfulness of the 'incorrect' readings for understanding capital that is to be judged. What I present here should be understood, then, as my own view, not as Hegel's or Marx's.

This book exemplifies the 'homology thesis', namely that the logic of capital may be exhibited by reference to Hegel's logic. In particular, I take the architectonic of both orders to be in part the same.[2] (For example, see the Table at the end of this Introduction.) This does not *require* me to take a position on 'what Hegel really meant'. Tony Smith argues that Hegel's metaphysical language disguises a sophisticated social ontology.[3] But, for me, it is precisely 'the metaphysical Hegel' that is of interest in that capital models in its form the all-pervasive generation of its moments from itself. The presentation of capital in an ordered manner is, then, a question of actualising it in a sequence of *logical levels* of complexity, which I argue picks up nested internal relations.

This account is unusual in the tradition of 'Hegelian Marxism' in that it does not rely on a view that Hegel provides a *method* of general heuristic value, but rather it shows that even the most objectionable feature of Hegel's idealism, its apparent pan-logicism, is significant because this false ontology is abstracted from an inverted world in which the value form achieves priority over its material bearers, and the ideal logic of capital imposes itself on human beings.[4] (For more on my use of *this* Hegel see Chapter 18.)

---

1 For the aporias of Hegel's philosophy, see Arthur 2000.
2 Cf. Sekine 2020, pp. 40–1.
3 Smith 1990.
4 For a similar argument see Bellofiore 2014, especially p. 172.

If on occasion I appear to be paraphrasing passages from Hegel and Marx, then the sense to be attributed to such words is to be understood only in the context of my own presentation. Nonetheless, because I draw very much upon Hegel's categories, for the benefit of specialists, I give a commentary in an appendix showing in detail how and why my own terms, and their arrangement more especially, derive from my reading of his. I also provide in the *Appendices* three charts (organised in triads) of logical categories: (i) Hegel's *Science of Logic*; (ii) Hegel's *Encyclopaedia* Logic; (iii) The logic of capital (as I understand it) drawing on, but reconstructing, these versions of Hegel's system. In addition, I provide (iv) one of the value-form categories, based on (iii).

Throughout I freely use Marx's categories without any attempt at an exegesis of *Capital*. But, where I do not give my own glosses on the terms concerned, it may be assumed that I intend to follow Marx's use. (Among the Appendices is a *Glossary* listing unusual terms, and terms used here in very specific ways.) My most obvious differences from Marx are as follows: a) I postpone discussion of the labour theory of value until the form of capital is adduced; b) I provide a 'political' theory of the source of value in labour; c) I provide my own solution to the so-called 'transformation problem'; d) where the overall structure of *Capital* is concerned, I order my main divisions differently (see the Table on 'the system of industrial capital' in the *Appendices*); e) I take rent to be fully capitalised, but in any case I view it as supplementary to the core Idea of capital, to which I limit myself. I also note significant departures from the conceptual apparatus of *Capital* in my text.

If I rarely cite directly passages from Hegel, and from Marx, still less do I refer much to secondary literature. This is partly for reasons of space, and partly because I do not wish to attribute views to those who may not hold them (or may not now hold them). However, a selection of relevant books I have found stimulating may be found in the *Bibliography*.

This book is divided into two Parts. Part 1 is 'scene-setting' in that it justifies the approach to the critique of political economy taken here. With this background established, Part 2 proceeds to a systematic-dialectical presentation of the forms of capital, rising from abstract to concrete categorial forms of it, as 'Idea'.

The 'bridging' chapter, *Chapter 5*, is the most difficult in the book. Its upshot is that the presentation proper must begin with the commodity, but with an entirely 'negative' characterisation of it: as absence of use-value. It would be possible to omit this chapter on first reading, and to move to the 'affirmative' development of the value form in Part 2. However, I regard it as central to my unique take on value-form theory.

Capitalisation

In this book (and especially in Part 2), I capitalise initial letters of certain terms of art, fundamental to the presentation. (Note that in German all nouns have such capitals so Hegel could not call special attention to any one of them in this way. But, although German does not allow this honorary capital orthographically, I can.)

The central cases are 'The Concept', 'The Idea', and 'The Absolute'. These are virtually personified in Hegelian logic. So, in order to indicate its peculiar status 'The Concept' is capitalised. On the rule of parity, if 'The Idea' takes a capital so too should 'Nature' and 'Spirit'. Likewise, to maintain parity with 'the Concept', 'Being' and 'Essence' take their own capital. However, there is a complication here to be noticed. It is very common in Hegel's triads that the term standing for the *whole* also appears as the *first* term of the triad. This is so with Being, Essence, and Concept. For example, under 'Essence' there is the triad: essence/appearance/actuality. The reason for this is that the general principle of moving from the abstract simple determination to the concrete one is at play in every triad. Thus the triad of essence begins with 'essence' itself taken in its simple immediacy and then dialectically developed through its opposite to their unity. Only the whole triad expresses the nature of essence. It is convenient here then to mark the 'Essence' that is the topic of the whole Doctrine of Essence with a capital, and to give the 'interior' use of the term without a capital. Yet I do not follow this same rule with Being and Concept. I regard the founding opposition of the whole Logic, Being and Nothing, to be of such importance as to be worth flagging with capitals. The first moment of the Concept is 'the formal Concept'. Here, the reason given above for writing Concept with a capital would also apply. But to distinguish more clearly 'the formal Concept' from the Doctrine of the Concept, I take advantage of the presence in English of a similar term, 'The Notion', to achieve this (for more discussion see *Commentary on Hegel* below). Moreover, second in importance only to the founding triad is the triad of Universality, Particularity, Singularity; hence these moments together are given the dignity of 'the Concept'; as also Individual.

Here then is the full list of capitalised categories:

(Doctrine of) Being;
Nothing;
Being;
Nothingness;
(Doctrine of) Essence;

(Doctrine of) The Concept;
Notion;
Universality;
Particularity;
Singularity;
Individual;
The Absolute;
Idea;
Nature;
Spirit.

'One' is a special case (mostly employed in Chapters 5 and 6). Where the context demands it, for example 'a One', it is dignified.

Where there are contexts in which these words are used in non-technical ways, they do not take capitals. Note that the economic categories are not usually capitalised, unless they are qualified with a logical category that is so, for example 'Value-as-Concept'.

Paragraph Numbers

In Part 2, I provide the strictly dialectical presentation of my system of categories. From here on, much of the text is broken up with paragraph numbers. These indicate the logical relations of the categories concerned. At the beginning of Part 2, I give a list of its contents organised in these paragraph numbers.

Table of Correspondences

Hegel *Encyclopaedia* §18
I. Logic: the science of the Idea in and for itself,
II. The Philosophy of Nature; the science of the Idea in its otherness,
III. The Philosophy of Spirit; as the Idea come back to itself out of that otherness.

Arthur
I. Value Form: as the science of Capital in its Notion,
II. Capital Relation: Capital and its other,
III. Capital as systemic unity.

Hegel *Encyclopaedia* § 83
Logic falls into three parts:
I.   the Doctrine of Being,
II. the Doctrine of Essence,
III. the Doctrine of the Concept and the Idea.
That is, into the theory of Thought in:
I.   its *immediacy*: the concept implicit and in germ,
II. its *reflection* and *mediation*: the being-for-itself and show of the concept,
III. its *return* into itself and its developed being-by-itself: the concept in-and-for-itself.

Arthur
The dialectic of the value form falls into three parts:
I.   Commodity,
II. Money,
III. Capital.
That is, into the theory of Exchange in:
I.   its *immediacy*: value implicit and in germ,
II. its *reflection* and *mediation*: value for-itself, the showing-forth of value,
III. its *return* into itself, and its development of itself: self-valorisation.

Hegel: *Logic*
I.   The Doctrine of Being
A.   Quality
B.   Quantity
C.   Measure
II. The Doctrine of Essence
A.   Intro-reflection
B.   Appearance
C.   Actuality
III. The Doctrine of Concept
A.   Subjectivity
B.   Objectivity
C.   The Idea

Arthur: *Dialectic of the Value Form*
I.   Commodity
A.   Exchangeable commodities
B.   Quantity of commodities
C.   Exchange-Value of commodities
II. Money
A.   Value-in-itself
B.   Forms of Value
C.   Money
III. Capital (General Formula)
A.   Price
B.   Metamorphoses of commodities (C–M–C′)
C.   Capital (M–C–M′)

PART 1

Object and Method

∴

CHAPTER 1

Capital and Social Form

The question of social form is central to the proper understanding of economic systems. It is only in virtue of differences in social form that Marx can insist that there is no such thing as 'economics' in general, but that each mode of production has its specific and peculiar laws of motion. Before directly addressing the logic of capital, then, let me summarise the general context in which it is placed, a peculiar social form of production.

In order to explain the specificity of the social form of capitalist commodity-production I employ the triad of categories: *sociation*, *dissociation*, and *association*.[1] All economy begins with some particular mode of *sociation* of those productively active. In our society this is disrupted by the *dissociation* consequent on the social division of labour, immediately labour is private. It becomes posited as social labour only through a most peculiar form of *association*, namely the process of exchange of products. Let me elucidate.

By *sociation* is meant the universal, ahistorical reality that, in order to be active economically, people engage in social relationships and social practices.

By *dissociation* (the negation of sociation) is meant the historically specific reality of the separation between economic agents predominant in the bourgeois epoch; 'separation' here does not mean a geographical distance, but a *social* barrier. Dissociation has four dimensions: first that useful objects are held by persons as their private property and hence are not immediately available for satisfying the needs of others; second that production is carried out in enterprises likewise in the hands of private owners; third that labour power is separated from its object in that the most important means of production are held as the property of members of the capitalist class; fourth that production and consumption are separated, production is carried on by enterprises and consumption by households.

By *association* is meant that the opposition of sociation and dissociation is mediated in the form of exchange whereby consumers acquire the objects they require, production units acquire inputs and dispose of outputs, and through contracts of labour people find work and capitalist enterprises find workers. It is important to understand that when dissociation is negated through asso-

---

1 Here I draw on the terminology of Reuten and Williams 1989, although I do not pretend to follow their definitions exactly.

ciation this is on the same ground; that is to say, the basic element of privatised appropriation of goods is retained, but in mediated form. Thus association does not replace dissociation; rather it replicates it through developing its conditions of existence; sociation now takes the contradictory form of their unity.

Since the exchange relation provides the first moment of association it is the conceptual starting point of the presentation of the bourgeois epoch. The presentation proper will thus start with commodity exchange. Since exchange is a voluntarily undertaken transaction, not indicated by any central authority but rooted solely in the private purposes of the agents concerned, it is on the face of it extremely unlikely that any coherent economic order could emerge at all, still less one characterised by some beneficent 'hidden hand'. The problem is to determine the form of social cohesion that unifies a system in which all decisions to produce and to exchange are private.

So far, I have not mentioned capital, the theme of this book. The point is that capital is a social form that emerges from the contradictory relationship of dissociation and association. Exchange is the historically specific condition of existence of this relationship, and of the capitalist system in general. This condition must be reproduced by the movement of the system of capital itself. Exchange, for example, must extend its reach, rather than die away. Only *generalised commodity production* requires universal exchange as its necessary foundation.

The main thesis to be explored is that capital itself achieves the reproduction of its own conditions of existence. Although the form of capital is shown to be the overriding moment in the system, the drive that provides the impulse for reproduction, I cannot start with it right away, because it is far too complex a determination. Rather this presentation of capital (in Part 2 below) deliberately starts with the most indeterminate characterisation of the whole, namely what is implicit in the commodity form. The argument develops precisely because of the need to overcome the inadequacy of this characterisation, measured either immanently, for example by its self-contradictory implications, or by reference to its failure to be self-subsistent. In this way thought is impelled onward to conceive a more concrete totality; only when the presentation reaches the whole is the starting point grounded in its connection with the whole and thereby validated as a true determination in this relative sense of being inadequate on its own but valid as one of the determinations that come together in a mutually grounding interchange to constitute the concrete whole. The whole is mediated in its elements, and these elements ground themselves in the whole. Commodities are the starting point; I do not at first raise the question of where commodities come from, whether they are produced or non-produced goods, or, if they are produced, under what relations of production. But the development of the argument itself eventually *grounds* them as results of capitalist production.

A notable feature of the presentation to come is that I do not thematise labour until after conceptualising the general form of capital. To begin with I analyse the commodity form itself, and only at the end give reasons for picking out as systematically important those commodities that are products of labour. In this way, by exploring to the full the dialectic of form, and letting the form itself reach the content it demands, I do something very different from those who are always in a hurry to address the material content. However, under definite historically emergent conditions, the value form comes to acquire a ground in labour, or, conversely, labour comes to express itself in value.

To sum up: the sociation-dissociation contradiction is the presupposition of the entire epoch, and hence of our presentation below; it is association through exchange that gives this contradiction 'room to move'; *exchange* is a primary mode of social synthesis in the bourgeois epoch, and it reproduces the dissociation of social production into autonomous units; the first concrete category is therefore this mediation, and we study its further development; this first category of *movement* determines goods as commodities, and hence the first *object* of analysis is the commodity, a unity of use-value and exchange-value; this doubling is a relation in which form dominates matter; the value form is therefore the *theme* of the categorial dialectic.

An important foundation of this book is that the argument is shaped by the protocols of value-form theory. This sets itself against those who neglect the relevance of the form of value, as if this form passively reflects the material metabolism of production. On such an account, money veils – or even distorts – the real relations of production; value itself is often simply *identified* with labour in such interpretations of Marx's theory of value. By contrast, value-form theory affirms that the *money form* has an active role in directing economic life; it is not merely a mediator of more fundamental forces. It follows that theory must accept the reality of *formal determination*, distinct from – albeit working alongside – causal determination. It is the value form that determines the dimensions of the so-called 'production' of value.

For example, when it is claimed that the magnitude of value is a function of socially necessary labour time, it may be considered that the former is 'caused' by the latter. However, such a view fails to account for the very existence of such a relation. It is only the social form of commodity exchange that determines why, and how far, such a function can exist. Moreover, the actuality of value presupposes a fully developed capitalist social formation. Two things follow. First, that the ideality of the value form develops from commodity to money to capital in accordance with a dialectical logic of totalisation; second, the material pole develops in response to formal determination, but predicated on what is materially possible for the available human and natural resources.

My aim is to reconstruct the inner nature of capitalism through interrogating the founding category of value. The truth of value becomes real only in the totality of its forms. While the dialectic of the value form appears at one level as a self-referring system, at another level it depends on a material ground from which it is estranged. Conversely insofar as social labour finds expression in this system of estrangement it appears only as an abstraction from itself, as reified labour. The material and ideal moments of the economic system are never coherently unified. I come back to this at the end, but it must be borne in mind throughout.

I argue (in Chapter 5) that the starting point of a systematic presentation of the idea of capital is the pure form of exchange, from which both use-value and labour are absented. Since it is common for these to be considered superior foundations for 'economics', we address them in the remainder of this chapter. (After all, nothing is exchanged unless it has use-value for others, and nothing is there at all unless someone makes it!)

I begin with 'use'. In Marx's terminology, the nature of commodity exchange is analysed using the categories of 'use-value' and 'exchange-value'. It should be explained that in his usage 'use-value' is identified with the material body of the good concerned. It is the various properties inherent in it that allow it to have various uses, but rather than focussing on such *relations* Marx employs the term *substantively*, such that it is possible to speak of a commodity as 'a' use-value. Putting the point this way heightens the sense of paradox when it is contrasted with its 'value', because, again, this too is to be taken, not in a relational sense in which it stands for an exchange ratio, but substantively again, such that the commodity is 'a' value. Now, while speaking of a commodity as 'a use-value' might be deemed a somewhat peculiar locution, there can be little objection, in that the material body of the commodity taken under this description is clearly something present to inspection. By contrast, to speak of 'value' as such (as I do in Part 2) could be taken as highly objectionable.

To proceed, in *exchange* a practical abstraction from the material properties of goods leaves a *pure* form, namely the form of value, within which they are determined as commodities for both parties. Value contains not an atom of matter; it is in effect an ideal social form opposed to the material characteristics that give the commodity some sort of use-value. Here we presuppose the objective validity of the 'abstraction' predicated on exchange relations.² Whatever may be true before and after exchange, in the sphere of exchange itself the commodity is entirely abstracted from its character as a use-value.

It is of great importance here that this abstraction is not effected by consciousness but is objectively constituted in the real process of exchange. This is a *practical* abstraction from the character of the commodities as use-values, which latter is 'absented' for the period of exchange. The commodities acquire as a new determination the character of values; and the bodies of the commodities concerned play the role of *bearers* of this determination imposed on them while passing through this phase of their life cycle. They become subject to the *value form*.

What is at issue in the constitution of the value form is by no means the same sort of abstraction as natural science employs when it studies mass, for example, and treats bodies under this description regardless of their other properties. For mass is indeed a given property of the bodies concerned, inhering in each. But there seems no limit in the *form* of exchange itself to *what* people might take to exchanging.

At first sight, then, it seems an empty mediator, tailor-made to registering various heterogeneous relations. The advance of value-form theory is the insight that the value form develops to the point at which, with self-valorising value, it is constituted as a *self-relation*, and 'takes over' the world of production and consumption given to it.

The exchange determinations are dimensionally incommensurable with use. Notice that to say 'we *abstract* from use' is very different from generating the abstraction 'utility' from heterogeneous use-values, by disregarding the *particularity* of use. Exchange is certainly not an *actualising* of the 'common property' of utility.

Moreover, the thing must be realised as an exchange-value *before* it can be as a use-value. It might be said that exchange is underpinned by the comparative preferences for A and B by the parties, but in this case what is actualised is some weight of such preferences in the minds of the exchangers rather than an identity *in the commodities* A and B. The latter identity, namely of A and B, is the *value* in exchange of *them*, whatever external conditions shape the ratio of exchange. Moreover, exchange could not be based on *their* identity as use-values, or it would have no point; rather they must be different, so that one

---

2 Alfred Sohn-Rethel (in his *Intellectual and Manual Labour*) deserves credit for thematising abstraction in exchange. For the process he used the term 'real abstraction' (Sohn-Rethel 1978). Better is to say that exchange effects a 'practical abstraction' on the commodities exchanged. This last notion was advanced by Reuten and Williams 1989, pp. 63–4.

person's preference may be for A and one for B. The non-identity of the commodities as use-values is set aside then in their identity as exchange-values.

While it is a fundamental condition of commodity exchange that a commodity bears the character of 'use-value for others', its use-value is 'suspended' for the duration of exchange. However, this 'absenting' is equivalent not to destruction but to 'distantiation', so that use-value *remains* potent at a level immediately removed from exchange determinations; the body of the commodity appears in exchange, but simply as a 'bearer' of value, its use-value having been substantively *displaced*. (Nonetheless we show later that use-value has its own economic determinacy.)

Value and use-value are immediately contraries. Where value *is*, use-value *is not*: if use-value *is*, value is nothing: there are two different regions of being in which what is present in the one region is absent in the other. It is a feature of the structure of commodity relations that use-value and value exhibit such duality (yet eventually interpenetrate).

To sum up: exchange brings about a *sui generis* form without any given content, because *all* use-value is absented, not merely all *determinate* use-value but the *category* itself. It is presupposed *to* exchange and actualised *after* exchange but simply not present *in* exchange.

Now I turn to the second important issue, the place of *labour*. For me labour is not the starting point of my presentation of value theory. But is not value theory centred on the capital relation? And does not that imply it concerns itself not merely with capital but with that which stands in an essential relation to it, namely labour? The short answer to this is that capital is related to *waged labour*, a form of capital itself; a longer answer is given throughout this book.

So why is labour not the starting point for a systematic-dialectical presentation of capitalism? It is true that historical materialism takes the mode of production to be the central determinant of all social formations. It is also true that the immediate producers, and their work, seem central to that. Nonetheless it is impossible to *specify* the mode of production without attending to the social relations within which work is carried on by producers. But are not such relations nothing but *their* relations? That depends. I take the position that capital is structured by inhuman relations which posit human agents simply as their bearers.

The 'original' unity of social production is here radically disrupted through various kinds of separation or dissociation. If one searched for the common social substance of the economy, it is no longer to be found in social labour. So, either there is no social substance at all, or unity is now established by an *alien* social substance-subject. This is capital. Capital is founded on the exploitation of living labours. But these labours are brought into connection, (a) only through an alien mediator, (b) only as abstract. 'Abstract labour' is in truth a value-formed determination. (See my treatment of this form in Chapter 10 below.) It should not be identified with some naturally given physiological identity of labour. In sum, if labour is structured by the requirement to produce saleable commodities, and that is solely the aim of capital, then it is logical to begin our investigation with the conceptual development of the form of the commodity into that of capital.[3]

Since, in the *Preface*, I said this is a work of pure theory, it is necessary to distinguish it from the view of 'pure theory' advanced by Kōzō Uno, and his followers, Tom Sekine, and Robert Albritton. They make the methodological stipulation that, for the purpose of pure theory, labour is to be taken as completely reified. (This assumption is to be relaxed as a less abstract level than pure theory.) For me, however, not only do I take capital to *constitute* itself only through overcoming its other, labour, but that necessity of its constitution is precisely the basis of my vindication of the labour theory of value. (Of course, capital has a *tendency* to reify labour, and part of my theory for simplicity takes this tendency as *completed*.) So the defining characteristic of capital is not the same here as in the Uno tradition of 'pure theory'.

I accept that the alienation of the social substance of labour consequent on exchange remains as the unspoken standing condition of the very possibility of, and necessity for, the dialectic of capital. In no way does this value form merely express a pre-existing unitary substance, namely social labour. Yet in order to ground itself in the real material world, capital takes possession of labour and then substitutes its own principle of unity on these divided labours. The big question is how far this alien world can effectively reproduce its own preconditions, thus making itself absolute.

The *ultimate* object of our theory is the capitalist form of social material *production*; but it does not follow that in the presentation it is necessary to evolve general categories of production and then further specify these in terms of capitalism. Because of the importance of exchange in shaping the character and direction of social production, the presentation starts with the *form* of exchange, bracketing for this purpose the origin of the objects of exchange.

It is characteristic of the dialectical development of concepts that initial simple abstract definitions be replaced by successively more complex and concrete ones. My initial abstract definition of 'value' is that it is 'the power of exchange' inherent to a commodity. It may be claimed that reference to labour should be included even at the most abstract level of determination of the Idea

---

3 Cf. Uno 1980, pp. xxiv–xxviii.

of value, because the entire value-form problematic springs from the social division of labour with its consequent contradiction of a labour that has to be simultaneously private and social.

The plausibility of this argument is undermined by the peculiarly abstract character of the value form itself. Insofar as it resolves the contradiction through an exchange system socially associating the products of dissociated producers within a universal form, it overshoots the parameters of the original problem. The commodity form is so empty of given content that it not only allows the exchange of heterogeneous goods produced in private enterprises, but the inscription of all sorts of other heterogeneous material. So it is illegitimate to argue that exchange-value is simply the form of association of private labours. The fit of form and content here is too loose. It is noticeable that Marx bridges the gap peremptorily, by introducing a stipulative definition of value as the objectification of labour. This leaves non-products as surds in the value form.

The most abstract level of analysis of the value concept is therefore that of a *pure* form of association, namely association through exchange, devoid of 'content'. Hence it should be possible to present a value-form derivation of money and capital without simultaneous reference to the commensuration of labours. But later the requirement of concretion yields the theoretically argued identification of products of capital as the only content adequate to the self-determination of the value form. Then I argue that the social ontology of living labour within capital gives good grounds for asserting a version of 'the labour theory of value'.

At the level of the immediate process of production the various concrete labours find their place in the structure of total social labour. Although they are denatured and posited as bearers of capital's motion, it still seems all capitalist economic determinations are reducible to exploitation of labour. But in the capital system the various capitals are structured by total social capital, and are posited as profitable, only within the rhythms of social reproduction. In this context capital's *own* determinations appear to subsume and supplant those of labour. My thesis requires recognition of a *dual ontology* of economic life; at ground level there are material relationships, but ideal ones supervene on the material (see Chapter 14 below).

It is impossible to start with labour and show the commodity is a form it takes on, because this form is an alien *imposition* on labour. It is *through* exchange that abstraction imparts itself to labour, making it abstract human labour, because it is the form of exchange that establishes the necessary social synthesis in the first place before labours expended are commensurated in it.

The method of presentation must engage with the value form first, and then provide reasons to narrow the focus of the inquiry to products, rather than start from 'labour value', and then inexplicably allow the scope of the commodity form to include non-values. (Just stipulating that non-products do not count as values merely begs the question.)

In dialectical terms, to presuppose at the outset that the items exchanged are labour products marks a dogmatic beginning. This could be justified externally by appeal to the broader concerns of historical materialism with modes of production. But for a dialectical presentation a beginning without imposed conditions is needed. Only after developing the forms of circulation is there ground for picking out as systematically important those commodities that are products of labour. (This I do in Division II below.)

Addendum on 'Simple Commodity Production'

If the object of analysis is *the capitalist economy*, circulation of commodities is to be considered the circulation of *capitalistically produced* commodities. Their value, and the relevant determinations of labour, are concretely constituted only in the capital relation. I reject then the model of 'simple commodity production'.[4]

In such a model, exchange at 'value' is supposed to take place because otherwise people would switch into the less onerous occupation. Notice that this 'law' presupposes everyone knows what labour is expended by others; this is a very doubtful proposition historically. Even if it is accepted as an idealising assumption, nothing like an objective law is operative. For the other necessary assumption is that the *only* consideration affecting the choices of individuals is avoidance of 'toil and trouble'. This *subjective* hypothesis has little to do with the fact that there exists in capitalism an *objective* law of value which makes exchange at value *necessary*. If the law relies on merely subjective judgements, then other subjective considerations to do with the trouble of learning new methods, or the preference for one occupation rather than another, may be operative also. Even if the fishermen noticed their working day was longer than that of the hunters with whom they exchanged, they might simply prefer life on the river to the darkness of the forest.

Key is the objective rationality of the system of capitalist competition, not an ideal type of 'rational economic man' read back into the natural state. There is

---

4   The myth that this 'model' is used in Marx's *Capital* I treat in Arthur 2005b.

a stark contrast between the peasant saying 'Time costs nothing' and the capitalist motto 'Time is money'. It is only in modern industry that competition within a branch, and the mobility of capital between branches, brings about the development of a common measure. When all inputs, including labour power itself, have a value form, and production is subordinated to valorisation, then an *objective* comparison of rates of return on capital is possible and competition between capitals allows for the enforcement of the law of value. Only because capitals need a rule to allocate profits, according to the necessity of their form, is a rule of equivalence in exchange imposed to secure this; only because capitals are constituted through exploiting labour is this rule correlated with the amounts of labour extractable; and only because capitals are inherently time oriented in virtue of their form is the measure of such amounts of labour socially necessary labour time. The theory of surplus value *grounds* the law of value.

Summary

Before presenting the logic of capital (in Part 2) a number of contextualising chapters are required (here in Part 1). This chapter sketches the peculiarities of the social forms upon which the capital system is established. Centrally, there obtain a set of *dissociations*, such as that between units of production held in private hands. In order to remedy this, the form of exchange creates the requisite *association*, but only in a contradictory way, for, nonetheless, dissociation is retained. Exchange mediates this opposition.

For goods to be exchangeable they must bear some specific use-value. However, exchange gives rise to a radical *abstraction* from the heterogeneity of the goods exchanged, when they are identified with each other as exchangeable. Moreover, all putative characteristics of the exchanged commodities are rejected as possible supports for orderly exchange; in particular 'utility' and 'labour' cannot account for the almost infinite range of things that may be exchanged. The commodity form is, then, *pure form*.

However, it is anticipated that the pure form may well have real effects through a process of *formal determination* of the economic metabolism. It is further anticipated that, through a dialectical development, this elementary form logically results in the form of capital, and, indeed, of capitalist production. But, only once the general formula for capital is developed, is it appropriate to turn to the *grounding of value* in the production process.

CHAPTER 2

Capital and the Actuality of the Ideal

The method followed in my presentation of capital's social form rests on the logic proper to the peculiar character of the object. For a theory of active social form, specifically the value form, Hegel's dialectic of logical categories is relevant. To the objection that an idealist science is hardly appropriate to a materialist critique of political economy, I reply that the value form has itself an objectively 'ideal' character insofar as it may be presented as a logic of *pure* form, forms as pure in their own way as those presented by Hegel.

The systematic dialectic of form is rooted in the observation that the movement of exchange is *analogous* to the movement of thought, in that there is generated therewith a realm of pure forms, which stand in logical relations to each other, any material content absented. Of course, the *exchange* forms have their own specificity, in that sense not *identical* with Hegelian *thought* categories. But, nonetheless, in virtue of their origin in practical abstraction, they, and their relations, are *homologous* with the pure thoughts adduced by Hegel. It is of the first importance to see that I am *not* applying Hegel's logic to a given material, rather I find that exchange itself *generates* pure forms *parallel* to Hegel's logical categories. I argue that the analogy with Hegel's turn from logical truth to the reality informed by it is that the pure forms of value sink into the world of production, circulation, and distribution.

Much more is at stake than method. Hegel's so-called 'logic' is really an (idealist) *ontology*, its categories define what is required for the real world to gain its actuality. In the same way, my own investigation is ontological, its categories define what makes capital a real power in the world. It is in this context that I can answer the big question: how can Hegel's ontology serve as a guide in the critique of capital? It can, precisely because in an important respect capital is ideal. The abstract beginning of the presentation itself parallels capital's abstracting from production, when it throws commodities on the market unmarked by their origin.

Hence, in my view, a significant homology obtains between the movement of exchange, generating a system of *pure forms of value*, abstracted from the material specificity of commodities, and the movement of thought, generating Hegel's system of *logical* categories, abstracted from the real material world. Here, because of its importance in shaping the character and direction of social material production, below (in Chapters 6–8) I analyse first the value form *as such*, 'bracketing' entirely the origin of the objects of exchange.

The main reason why I must give a more complicated account than Hegel's is that the pure forms I address are borne by material objects, commodities in the first place. Thus, whereas Hegel simply derives the category of universality logically, I have to say that the equivalent value category must be borne by money, which stands in a *logical*, rather than *material*, relation to commodities. It makes present their universal aspect to them, namely their *identity* with each other as values ideally posited through exchange.

The ideal realm, as it is constituted here, is not a true opposite of the material, because it is a peculiar 'fold' in material reality induced by the *practice* of exchange, which entirely absents use-value. This fold contains an inverted world in which socially objective abstract forms, *sui generis*, appropriate material 'content'. It is not the case that productive activity takes appropriate form in value. Rather, the value form shapes this given material into *its* adequate basis. This interpenetration of the ideal mediation with the material ground of the economy means each pole has its own peculiar effectivity on the other.

Certainly, in our case, all depends on material exploitation; yet the ideality of the value form has an immediacy of its own, once constituted in its separation from matter. If it is said the real underlying 'essence' is to be contrasted with the superficial 'appearance', this is too one-dimensional a picture. Rather, the interpenetration of the material and the ideal means that living labour and capital are yoked in an unhappy marriage of material and ideal, each *equally* real, and each having autonomous effectivity in their combinations.

If I grant production is a more fundamental determinant, when I say the object of our theory is the capitalist mode of production, this is to align it with the general thrust of historical materialism, and in addition, to acknowledge that capitalism is a specific form of production, preceded and succeeded by other forms. However, capitalism is peculiar because practice has displaced this material ground, as the most fundamental of a hierarchy of determinations constitutive of the social whole, and it has substituted for it the seeming hegemony of abstract forms. While still effective in its own right, material production narrowly conceived cannot claim unproblematic dominance when there is also the effectivity of purely formal determination, of the value form, narrowly conceived.

I argue that the categories of Hegel's logic may be deployed in understanding the nature of capital because material practice has generated a model of Hegel's logic of the concept. This idea is the most novel, and difficult, aspect of what I propose here. There is no 'given' object realm of which one forms a concept, namely the concept of value, rather value *is a concept* given to us from practice, having been generated 'behind our backs'. Value is a concept *objectively presented* to us in the circuit of capital. It is not through some externally applied method that the nature of capital is identified and defined; capital defines its own identity through the circuit of the determinations of its concept that it itself presents.

To be sure there is here a lack of analogy with Hegelian identity of (our) thought and being, in that theory remains at a distance when it *corresponds* to the dialectic of the value form. However, since the dialectic of the value form is conceptual in nature objectively, its being and *its own concept* may be considered objectively identical.

In order to establish the *special* relevance of Hegel's logic to this project, it is necessary to grasp the *ontological* foundation of the capitalist system. This foundation is the *reality* of that abstraction in exchange predicated on the *identification*, as 'values', of *heterogeneous* commodities. This 'practical abstraction' has a substantive reality quite independent of any methodological point about abstraction in theory construction. It produces an 'inverted reality', in which commodities simply instantiate their essence as values. The use-value character of the commodities concerned is 'suspended' for the period of exchange. They must be realised as values before they can be realised as use-values. So the value form of the commodity creates a split, between value as the *identity* of commodities premised on equivalent exchange, and their material *diversity* differentiating them from each other as use-values.

Here the problem to be explored is why and how a categorial logic drawn from Hegel's idealist philosophy is relevant to a critique of political economy. In my opinion what has to be understood as subjected to an idealist inversion is not only Hegel's 'Idea' but *capital itself*. It is because capital is upside-down, so to speak, that an upside-down philosophy applies to it. How does a domain of material reality become inverted? Well, in the first place it is because the logic of exchange imposes the same universal form on all goods, namely the value form, which then develops to capital as the form of self-valorising value. I hold that there is a peculiar affinity between the articulation of Hegel's 'Idea' and the structural relations of commodities, money, and capital. Moreover, since the human bearers of the structure of capital are reduced to personifications of its categories, *the* capitalist, *the* wage-labourer, and so on, we find the same kind of *self*-acting forms as those in Hegel's logic. They cannot be forms of *thought* as they are in Hegel. Nonetheless I believe that the capitalist system does indeed consist in part of logical relations.

Hegel's logic starts with an abstraction from everything determinate. The 'pure thoughts' spring from the evacuation of contingent empirical instantiations to leave the category as such. We see the same process in practical terms when a commodity acquires a value form which disregards its material body.

Just as Hegel's logic follows the self-movement of thought as it traverses the categorial universe, so the dialectic of exchange sets up a *form-determined system*.

There is a sense in which the forms *apply themselves* to the material to be formed, rather than the form naturally being taken on by the supposed content. However, this means that the form and the material content are not fully unified, but retain a structure of abstract contraposition: the content is inscribed in the form while retaining much that cannot be grasped in it. Because of this, I argue that capital is both material and ideal.

Here the formal structures are indeed 'self-acting', not just in the sense of being categorially connected by our thought process. Immediately, such formal determination posits commodity value as nothing more than the abstract possibility of place, a pure algebraic variable, a determinable with no particularly necessary determinate content. Although there is no *given* 'content' that could express itself in exchange-value, the latter reflects its form into itself, we shall see, itself *as* content. So anything and everything can in principle become a bearer of value.

The relationship between Hegel's logic and the value form is much closer than that of an external identification of its logical structure, or a methodologically motivated application of its norms of adequacy, or an expositional strategy that finds it convenient to move from simpler to more complex structures. I believe that in some sense the value form and Hegel's logic are to be *identified*. There is a significant homology between the practical movement of exchange, generating a system of *pure forms of value*, abstracted from the natural specificity of commodities, and the movement of thought, generating Hegel's system of *logical* categories, abstracted from the real material world.

Commodities brought to market are incommensurable as use-values because their particular qualities are adapted to different uses. What happens in the formation of exchange-value is the negation of this difference of use-value. It is not necessary for the parties to the exchange to know what they are doing in this respect. But as a consequence of this *practical* abstraction from the specificity of the use-values concerned, which is 'suspended' for the period of exchange, the commodities acquire, as a new determination, the universal form of exchange-value. Theoretical priority must be accorded to 'form analysis', because it is the practice of exchange that establishes the necessary social synthesis in the first place, before labours expended may be commensurated in it.

What is at issue in the value-form abstraction is by no means the same sort of abstraction as natural science employs, when it studies mass, for example, and treats bodies under this description regardless of their other properties. For while mass is indeed a given property of the bodies concerned, inhering in each, value has a purely social reality. Whereas in the case of mass 'the principle of abstraction' may quite properly be used to say that two bodies, balancing each other on a scale, share the same mass, in the case of value this principle operates in reverse, so to speak: because we equate commodities in exchange, we in practice impute to them the same value *as if* value were a property *inherent* in them. But the fetishism so posited is an objective phenomenon, not a confusion of social consciousness.

I go further than just drawing attention to methodological lessons from Hegel's systematic ordering of categories, as do others. I draw also on his ontology. Hegel is the great expert on how an ideality builds itself up, moment by moment, into a self-actualising totality, an 'Absolute'. If then, as I believe, capital has in part an ideal reality, then if it can be shown to incarnate Hegel's blueprint it may be self-sustaining in the same way. Hegel's logic can be drawn on in such a study of capitalism because capital is a very peculiar object, grounded in a process of practical abstraction in exchange in much the same way as Hegel's dissolution and reconstruction of reality is predicated on the abstractive power of thought. Abstraction is 'out there'.

It is striking that the dialectic of capital is pretty much parallel to the dialectic of Hegel's logic. It is as if Hegel, in his philosophy, absolutised the specific dialectic of capital, although his factual knowledge of fully functioning capital was gained second-hand, in his readings of classical political economy and the English newspapers. (This 'elective affinity' is more striking than the parallel of Protestantism with 'the spirit of capitalism', as suggested by Weber.)

Initially the presentation follows Hegel in first treating the Ideal (in our case the logic of the value form) as opposed to the Real (in our case the material metabolism of the economy). However, he shows that the Ideal subsumes the real, 'idealises it', so to speak, such that the Ideal *makes* itself Real, indeed quite as real as the material sphere. In its unity with the Real, the Ideal shapes the former according to its own logic. So the Idea as the unity of the two aspects is objectively present, not merely a thought in the head. But my presentation is complicated by the fact that the homology of form relies on commodities and money to *bear* the ideal. These are perfectly *real* themselves, whether their putative ideal aspect is, or is not.

When I argue that the object of critique should be the *Idea* of capital, I do not mean by this 'ideas *about* capital', but that what confronts us *is* itself Idea in the Hegelian sense of an identity of concept and reality.

For Hegel's absolute idealism the major point of reference is not the individual thinking being. Instead of the ordinary mind solving problems with this method of advance, Hegel likes to think of the categories arising and dissolving out of their own instability; insofar as they are thought, it is by some 'objective mind'. This 'objectivist' tendency of his logic is further strengthened because its truth is meant ontologically as much as logically. The coherence of the logic is at the same time the coherence of reality.

Hegel drew on previous systems of categories such as those Aristotle and Kant articulated. But his view of system is *peculiar* in that he claims 'the Concept' is the self-acting author of its own forms. I say the same of capital. Just as Hegel holds that thinking itself, devoid of personality, is 'the productive subject', so I take capital as a productive subject devoid of personality. It is the activity of the subject that is *constitutive* of objectivity. Thus it finds itself in its *own* world. So here capital is the constitutive subject that builds a world for itself, but on material foundations, including human labour, that are potentially destabilising of it. The counter-subject, labour, is trapped in the capital relation, which is played out in a counterpoint such that it is the very same movement that engenders both the self-constitution of capital and the self-negation of labour.

I aim to show that, epochally, capital has made good its claim to be Absolute through its wealth and power. In subsuming all otherness as a moment within it, capital seems a self-identical totality because the totalising logic of the value *really* imposes itself in such a manner that material and social relationships become inscribed within it. But I shall argue that capital as an *ideal totality* cannot account for what is in excess of its concept of itself, the concrete richness of social labour, not to mention that of Nature.

Finally, I must explain that a *specific* domain of reality, namely capitalist commodity exchange, can yet give rise to the most abstract categories, homologous with those of Hegel's logic, the most abstract part of his *universal* philosophy. Whereas Hegel abstracts from everything through the power of thought, exchange abstracts only from what is presented to it, a delimited sphere of use-values. So we have in the dialectic of capital one that is less general than Hegel's in its *scope*, but within its own terms equally *absolute* insofar as it is founded on all-round abstraction to leave quasi-logical forms. Hegel's philosophy is encyclopaedic, and it has hundreds of categories accordingly. Capital, compared with the universe as a whole, is characterised by a poverty-stricken ontology, in which the qualitative is generally less prominent than the quantitative.

Because capital has a poverty-stricken ontology this has consequences for my use of Hegel. To put it bluntly, what is presented below may be rightly characterised as a 'bare-bones' Hegel. What is lost is the conceptual richness of Hegel's categories, as well as their wealth of reference. Nonetheless, even in the schematic version deployed here, they function well enough to elucidate the value form and its inner dialectic.

The identity of the presentation with the inner dialectic of capital itself is vindicated in that capital has a certain conceptuality to it *in reality*.[1] The relation between forms has a logical character, despite their need for material bearers. This is why the presentation traces the unfolding of the capital Idea *itself*, not of *my* conceptualisation of capital. Thus I do not *apply* the logic to capital. I follow *its* logic.

This also explains why the forms adduced must be grasped as *simply logical*. For example, let us consider the category of 'substance', which I use below when I term money 'the value substance' (§ 23). (This case I have found in experience is a category to which objection is made.) If I were to *apply* it, I would immediately have to ask, what kind of substance is that of value? Is it material or spiritual or what? But it is not *any kind* of substance; for it is the elucidation of the *pure form* here incarnate. It is true that these forms of value are socially *constituted* through practice, so for short one could speak of value as a 'social substance', for example. It is also true the forms become present in the ideal realm; so for short one could speak of value as an 'ideal substance'. However, that is wrong if it presupposes it could have been a material substance. In truth, in this realm there is only 'substance' without any such attribute, other than its equally *logical* ones. (But to be borne in mind is the sublated material realm with its material substances underpinning use-value.)

So the *self-presentation* of capital takes shape as the Concept presupposing and positing itself, in an ideal activity which we unfold *as if* theory conjures up the categories itself. Moreover, the peculiarity of my domain of enquiry means that in the development of its categories I use only some of Hegel's own. It also leads me to introduce new categories.

The most general guideline in evolving these new categories, and in the presentation of the whole system of categories, is that the presentation should be able to establish a clear order of succession, from the simplest to the most complex, from the most abstractly indeterminate to the most concretely specific. Each category will unify a manifold. But insofar as it appears external and imposed on the elements, and they, conversely, appear only contingently available to it, the category is not securely grounded, and hence the real as it is grasped under this aspect appears unstable and liable to dissolution. So, we follow in the method of presentation a Hegelian procedure in ordering categories according to their relative abstractness, and in motivating transitions between them according to the criterion of the relative insufficiency of the currently established categorial framework to guarantee on its own basis the self-reproduction of the system.

---

1 Cf. Adorno 1976, p. 80.

Insofar as the real is self-reproducing, the presentation should be able to exhibit its categorial articulation in such a manner as to show how this is achieved through certain inner necessities of its structure, in other words, to show how the logic of the system tendentially ensures its reproduction. It should also be possible to indicate the degree of dependence of the system on empirically given contingencies. Thus that money is a necessity for capitalist development may be demonstrated; but the role historically played by gold in this connection clearly presupposes the contingencies of its existence and suitability.

The ultimate object of the theory is the capitalist form of social material production; but it does not follow that in the presentation it is necessary to evolve general categories of production and then further specify these in terms of the form of capital. It is proposed here that, because of its importance in shaping the character and direction of social material production, the value form (as the germ of capital) should be analysed first; and the transition made to production in accordance with the determinations *immanently* required for the reproduction of capital according to the necessity of its concept.

I begin with the same perception as that of everyday consciousness, namely that in the bourgeois epoch nearly everything is capable of taking on commodity form, so we avoid the arbitrariness of concentrating from the outset only on products of labour. My approach has the advantage of starting with commodities in general, while arriving through the dialectic of the systematic presentation itself at the justification for a focus on production as the prime site of economically significant relationships.

Summary

The actuality of the Ideal results from the way the *practical* movement of exchange parallels that of *thought*, insofar as it generates a system of pure form. So the method here is *not* the application to our specific domain of one of universal truth, such as Hegel's logic. Rather, our domain itself generates a system of self-moving forms. Thus it is anticipated that there will be a homology between the economic forms and the categories of idealist ontology. Capital is an 'upside-down' reality instantiating an 'upside-down philosophy'. However, that we deal with a specific domain means only some of Hegel's categories need be taken up, primarily those of quantity, for capital has a poverty-stricken ontology. The material basis of the economy has effectivity; but this is regulated through its formal determination by its Idea.

CHAPTER 3

Systematic Dialectic

The method employed in the presentation of the forms of value below may be unfamiliar; it is therefore worth spelling out. What it is not: it is not an inductive method generalising from empirically given instances a hypothetical law of the phenomena, to be further tested in experience; it is not a hypothetico-deductive system in which an axiom is made the basis of a sequence of inferences that formally follow from it, the result being, as it is said, already 'contained in' the premises; it is not a transcendental argument for the conditions of possibility of a form of experience taken as established. It is the logical development of a system of categories, or forms of being, from the most elementary and indeterminate to the richest and most concrete; it is self-evident that the result cannot be 'contained' in the premise, for the latter is poorer in content than the former. But this is precisely the key to the argument; the impulse to move from one category to the next is the *insufficiency* of the existing stage to prove its necessity and prevail against the contingencies to which it is subject. Upon examination, it is seen that the form under consideration is not able to sustain itself on its own basis; it depends on conditions of existence that seem to be contingent, such that it could easily vanish.

The movement of thought is thus from the 'conditioned' to the 'unconditioned'; each stage 'takes care of', with the minimum of new elements, the problem perceived with the previous stage, but in turn is found insufficient. The presentation ends when all the conditions of existence needing to be addressed are comprehended by the entire system of categories developed. The forms incorporate within themselves, and produce through their own effectivity, these conditions; this means that the totality so grounded is judged self-sufficient. Moreover, the originating form gains actuality and truth only when grounded in the totality to which it gives rise through the dialectic outlined.

I argue that the peculiar character of the object under investigation requires a systematic-dialectical presentation. I reconstruct Marx's *Capital* in this light. In the present chapter, having briefly sketched the difference between historical dialectic and systematic dialectic, I go on to treat the latter in more detail.

There are two different types of dialectical theory in Hegel. Famously there is a dialectic of history. Hegel believed there is a logic of development underlying world history. But there is a second sort of dialectical theory, found in writings such as the *Science of Logic* and the *Philosophy of Right*. This may be termed 'systematic dialectic' because it is concerned with the articulation of categories designed to conceptualise an existent concrete whole. In discussions of dialectic generally it is most often taken to characterise a *historical* process; indeed, it is frequently reduced to a type of efficient causality. A contradiction is said to 'produce' a resolution in much the same way as a cause 'produces' an effect. But, in treating a *given whole* and demonstrating how it reproduces itself, the ordering of the categories is in no way determined by the recapitulation of a historical sequence; it is articulated synchronically on the basis of purely systematic considerations. So the expositional order of these categories does not have to coincide with the order of their appearance in history. In sum I distinguish between *systematic* dialectic and *historical* dialectic. *Historical* dialectic is a method of exhibiting the inner connection between stages of development of a temporal process. *Systematic* dialectic is a method of exhibiting the categorial articulation of a given whole.

Science in treating such a totality must elucidate a set of categories, capturing the forms and relations constitutive of it in an ordered presentation. While categories mark ontological unities, and are thus required to render reality intelligible, they must themselves form a coherent whole; they must take shape as a system. The categories must be systematically related to one another in such a manner that their presentation shows how each category gains systemic meaning by virtue of its positioning with respect to the other categories and the whole. The object here is a *totality* where every part has to be complemented by others to be what it is. Taken in isolation, in abstraction from its systematic placing, a category is imperfectly grasped.

Since all 'moments'[1] of the system exist synchronically, all movement must pertain to their reciprocal support and development. While this motion implies that moments become effective *successively*, the movement winds back into itself to form a *circuit* of reproduction of these moments by each other. Because of this character of a totality the theoretical system traces a logic of mutual presupposition in the elements of the structure and hence of the *necessity* of certain forms and laws of motion of the whole under consideration.

If what is *concretely* true is so only as *totality*, science in treating such a totality must take the shape of *system*. Hence the *presentation* of the totality in thought takes the shape of a *systematic dialectic of categories*. The task of systematic dialectic is to organise such categories in a definite sequence, deriving one from another logically. Although it is natural to read a systematic exposition as one in which later categories are developed from their antecedents – at least in the sense that the latter must be analytically presupposed – this cannot

---

1 This is cognate with the moments of a lever, not with a moment in time. See *Glossary*.

be the whole story; for a dialectical presentation rejects any dogmatic founding category. The progressive development is therefore not securely established on a *given* presupposition. There is, however, another consideration. Since the categorial progression cannot be validated as a deduction, it can only be a *reconstruction* of the totality. The whole, as the most concrete, complex, and complete reality, sustains all the elements that make it up. Thus theory retrogressively justifies the logical sequencing from this viewpoint. Insofar as Hegel's dialectics finish with something 'absolute', its absolute character grants validity retrospectively to all the stages of its exposition, and their dialectical relations; if 'the truth is the whole', the moments of the whole gain their validity within it; if the lower categories lead on to the highest, the reason is that the lower categories are merely abstractions from it. It is the whole alone that is self-subsistent.[2]

Since the presentation employs a non-deductive logic, this approach raises the question of the *logic of transition* in the exposition. At each stage it seeks the sufficient condition for a further stage of development of the Idea. There is a problem, requiring an innovative solution generated through a 'leap' to a new form, but with the minimum new notional material. Resolving that problem gives rise to a new one, and so on. Generally the basis of the advance is that each category is deficient in determinacy with respect to the next and the impulse for the transition is precisely the requirement that such deficiency must be overcome. Interrogation of the category reveals its limits and leads to the determining of a further category to complete it; successive categories are always richer and more concrete. The justification of the whole movement is *retrospective* when the sequence of categories is shown to 'hang together', in designating the forms of its self-reproduction.

If it is presupposed that the whole system of categories is complete and internally self-sustaining, then it is possible to reconstruct its order precisely through moving sequentially from categories deficient in such respects (that is in being inclusive and self-sustaining) to ones less so, until the system as a totality is thereby exhibited as such. Moreover, the method of presentation articulates the categories in such a manner as to show how the logic of the system tendentially ensures its completeness. The presentation ends when all the conditions of existence needing to be addressed are comprehended by the entire system of categories developed.

Thus in a dialectical argument the significance of any element in the total picture cannot be concretely defined at the outset. As the presentation of the

---

2 See Smith 1990, p. 49.

system advances to more complex and concrete relationships, the originating definition of a concept shifts accordingly, normally towards greater determinateness. Thus the dialectical method remains open to fundamental reorganisations of the material so far appropriated, as it gets closer to the truth of things in the perfected system. Such a system is complete only when it returns to, and accounts for, its starting point. Because any starting point is severed from the whole, as abstracted thus it is necessarily ungrounded.

While every category depends on its antecedents for its constitutive moments, the problem of the beginning is resolved if the richness of the granted content presupposes analytically the simpler, more abstract, antecedent categories. To reiterate, the progressive introduction of new categories cannot be deduction (for the beginning is not to be taken as an axiom), it can only be a reconstruction of reality which takes for granted that what it is headed for is logically complete. So the sequence of categories has to be read in both directions, as a disclosure, or presentation, progressively, and as a grounding movement retrogressively. What constitutes progression is an arrangement of categories from abstract to concrete; successive categories are always richer and more concrete. In the dialectic every category needs to complete itself in another. All stages are deficient with respect to the final fulfilment of the dialectic in a systematically ordered totality.

Indeed, the progressive/regressive sequencing depends upon the presupposition that there is a whole from which a violent abstraction has been made so as to constitute a simple beginning, which, in virtue of this negation of its positioning in the whole, has 'lost its footing', so to speak; and thus there arises a contradiction between the character of the element in isolation and its meaning as part of the whole. The treatment of this moment as inherently in contradiction with itself, on account of this, is given if it is assumed throughout the dialectical development that the whole remains immanent or implicit in it. This provides the basis for the transitions in the development of the categorial ordering. There is an impulse to provide a solution to a contradiction – a 'push' one might say – and there is the need to overcome the deficiency of the category with respect to its fulfilment in the whole – a 'pull' one might say.

For the most part these elements exist in combination. Since dialectic is generally regarded in the former sense as the positing and resolving of contradictions, I stress here the importance of the fact that the final goal is the fully comprehended whole and that any given stage *en route* is always deficient with respect to it. The impulse to move from one category to the next is the *insufficiency* of the existing stage to comprehend its grounds, or conditions; each stage 'takes care of', with the minimum of new elements, the problem perceived with the previous stage, but in turn is found insufficient. (It is important that the transition involves a 'leap' to a qualitatively new categorial level. A dialectical development has nothing in common with a vulgar evolutionism predicated on extrapolating an existent tendency.)

A key term of art in a dialectical presentation is 'sublation'. It comprehends simultaneously three linked determinations: elevation, abolition, and preservation. It is the characteristic figure of a dialectical transition towards a greater truth (only the whole is – strictly – true). The primary meaning of sublation is abolition, for example, of a category, or, more commonly, of a pair of categories, for example, Nothing and Being. These last are sublated in my presentation by the more *concrete* category 'the Being of Nothing'. So, in this instance, 'Nothing' and 'Being' are not really abolished but preserved in the more complex category to which they have been elevated. What is, then, abolished is their *abstract opposition*. In establishing the 'truth' of our central concept, namely 'value', the presentation therefore develops from less true to more true forms of it; only the self-supporting whole of the capital system realises the whole truth of value, including precisely its articulation as a set of such forms.

In applying systematic dialectic according to a rigorous scheme, a problem emerges as to contradiction and closure. According to Hegel the Idea of the modern state achieves final harmony, resolving all opposition. Marx, on the other hand, thinks capitalism is riven with unsurpassed contradiction, between use and exchange, capital and labour, forces and relations of production; Marx from the outset, and throughout, is always critical of capital, accordingly.[3]

So how is it possible to argue, as I do, that capital has the structure of the Hegelian Idea? While I do indeed hold this, I also admit that, in the last analysis, capitalist society cannot achieve the self-transparent unity of the Idea. How so? At the outset of my whole system, I show it originates through the exchange abstraction, which introduces a division between the logic of the value form and the useful purpose of the products of social production. This separation is never healed, no matter how much adequacy of each side to the other is achieved; so there remains throughout my exposition a context in which the capital system is always to be understood as alienated from human sociality, and its material basis. On the other hand, it is incontestable that capital has the logic of the concept, for 'the general formula for capital' is marked by 'teleology' (a category basic to Hegel's Concept); it has its own aim, namely accumulation.

The solution to this problem is precisely to underline the split between form and matter. Thus I hold it is acceptable for me to consider that the *form* of capital itself follows the logic of the Concept, even though the opposition between

---

3   This contrast between Hegel and Marx is emphasised in Smith 1990.

capital and labour can never be harmonised; even though in truth the value form and the material inscribed within it are never fully identified. Nonetheless, capital *acts as* an autonomous power. It is not just a mistake by us to treat it *as if* it were standing over against us dictating our possibilities. Moreover, insofar as it has successfully subsumed labour under itself, it is *effectively* the ruling Idea of our epoch.

Since I am following the dialectic of capital, all concern for freedom pertains to capital's freedom, all ends that count are capital's ends, all vindication of individuality pertains to the individual capitals. Human ends have no more significance in this respect than the ends of plants and animals have to us omnivores; they are just material to be manipulated through capital's cunning of reason. If this dialectic is *immanent* to *capital*, it is capital's vindication of *its* freedom and individuality that is exhibited; to this human ends are properly subordinate, human beings are merely the *bearers* of the economic movement.

Our ends are important *to us*; moreover, they exist at the limit as the possibility that capital is not as self-sufficient as it thinks it is, and that it will collapse in the face of the action taken by the people figured as 'in and against' capital. In fact, this acknowledgement of the human is thematic because class is integral to my concept of capital, as we shall see. But *within* the dialectic of capital this is seen only as a limit to be overcome.

In the remainder of this chapter, I address the issues of contradiction and closure; and of the deployment of the same categories at different levels.

I have said that every higher category is truer, because more comprehensive, than earlier, more simple and abstract, ones. It seems then that systematic dialectic necessarily has an *affirmative* character. To be sure, any dialectic of the Hegelian type resolves all contradiction in the Absolute. The affirmative dialectic of capital shows it becoming absolute in the sense of conquering and shaping production and consumption. But if one traces the logic through which *capital affirms itself*, it is difficult not to identify with its standpoint. There is the risk that the exposition of a reified system of self-moving abstraction appears itself as a reified dialectical theory unrelated to human practice.

Such a dialectic would show how capital subsumes under its forms all elements of economic life, becoming absolute in the sense of conquering and shaping the use-value sphere itself. If it were absolute, it would effect its own *closure*. However, the *critical* aspect of this dialectic shows that on the use-value side capital faces two 'others' of itself that it cannot plausibly claim to be merely aspects of its own self. Its external other is Nature, which capital is degrading at frightening speed, thus undermining its own material basis. Its internal other is the proletariat, capital's own creation, which is potentially capable of overthrowing it. The dialectic of capital remains open, in this sense.

The points I made just now do not invalidate a method of exposition based on systematic dialectic. One can use the notion of a drive to overcome contradictions in order to motivate transitions from one category to another, whether one assumes, with Hegel, that a final resolution within the terms of capitalism is available, or whether, with Marx, that capital cannot overcome its contradictions.

It is characteristic of systematic dialectic that the same category may be deployed at many levels of the presentation as it moves from abstract to concrete. What sense then can be given to the notion of its proper place in the dialectic of forms, given such a 'nesting'? This is at the category's *initial* introduction, for two reasons, firstly because this is the place where the dialectic is immanently *compelled* to introduce it, secondly because, if it is adequate to the task set at that level of abstraction, it is no more than adequate; hence the need for its sublation by more concrete categories. If it is carried forward to more concrete levels, then it will certainly still be true but less and less informative at such levels just because it abstracts from the new more concrete determination. Moreover, is it really the same category at more concrete levels? In truth, the new context redefines it – indeed, unfolds its true significance.

For example, this is true of 'value', which moves, in the presentation below, from a relation to a property to a substance (with money) to a subject (with capital as self-valorising) to an Idea (the capitalist system). Only at the end is it fully actual. In the same way the abstract notions of bad and good infinities sequentially laid out at the start (when endeavouring to fix what it is to have value) become much more concrete when capital turns the false infinite into a 'genuine' infinite in the spiral of accumulation.

Following this line of thought we could argue that all categories achieve their truth only in the entire system of categories when they inform each other. It is the result that is privileged if anything. The truth of earlier categories being preserved in the whole development, a certain amount of repetition is permissible because they will still characterise the more concrete level. For example, the dialectic of 'one and many', introduced below in treating commodity exchange, may also be illuminating in treating competition of capitals.

The category of 'commodity' is introduced as an abstract form of that which is present in exchange. A dialectical development demonstrates the necessity for it to double into commodities and money. A further argument identifies its 'concrete content' with the product of labour. However, these arguments are not simply expositional, such that the more concrete definition abolishes the more abstract one. Rather, what is traced in the presentation are the *ontological levels* of existence of the commodity. This means the abstract form persists *in its very abstractness*. This is why non-products may take commodity form.

Moreover, the form swallows its own tail when that which is derived from it, capital, *itself* takes commodity form; we speak of costs of capital, money markets, capital markets, and so forth. (In a strange twist it is common to speak of 'financial products'! – a hopeless confusion of categorial levels.) This explains some complications. It explains why bourgeois economists are unable to grasp the difference between a product and capital. Everything is treated as if its movement were that of commodity circulation. Yet this confusion is not due simply to stupidity, it is due to the way capital presents itself on the surface, when reducing everything to commodity form.

A dialectical presentation of the capital system going from the more abstract to the more concrete, is tracing its *reality*, it is not merely as a method of *arriving* at the reality, having rejected its most abstract expression in favour of concreteness. Categories, therefore, must be rigorously ordered from abstract to concrete, but not in the usual way, by 'adding in' further determinations; rather, it is through the immanent movement set in train by the requirement of reconstruction of a self-subsistent whole. The interconnectedness of the whole is presupposed, each and every moment is conditioned by others, only the whole is *unconditioned* if it reproduces in its own movement its interior moments and its material conditions of existence. All its presuppositions must be posited. Validation, then, is always retrospective; but this method of vindicating the necessity of what-will-have-become-of-it is nothing to do with a teleological history; it is simply a demonstration of the logical place each form has in supporting the totality; in analysing how it maintains itself I begin by identifying its most abstract moment, and then positing this presupposition.

As we saw, one consequence of the method of rising from the abstract to the concrete is that the more abstract categories still have application at the more concrete levels. But, naturally, they are not then sufficiently informative about the forms concerned, which require defining with an adequately concrete category. This means the temptation is usually to introduce a value form too *early* in the logical progression of categories, because the more abstract category still applies, as we said, but *only abstractly*; hence failing to elucidate the logical complexity of the form concerned.

A striking example of this led me to revise Hegel's *own* logic. When one sees that he has 'Measure' in the doctrine of Being, and when one knows money is the measure of value, there is the temptation to equate the two. But, although money certainly functions as measure of value magnitudes, it cannot be reduced to a form of 'Being'. The logic of Being is sufficient only to articulate simple commodity relations; and there 'measure' equates with exchange-value. But, in order to introduce the doubling of the commodity into the relation of commodities and money, the logic of Essence is imperatively indicated. I take care of the more concrete form of measure, found in money, in *this* context, terming it measure proper.

Summary

At the methodological level *systematic dialectic* emphasises the need for a clear order of presentation, which, however, is not a linear one, for the starting point is not empirically or axiomatically given but in need of interrogation. Ontologically it addresses itself to totalities and thus to their comprehension through *systematically* interconnected categories, which are sharply distinguished from *historically* sequenced orderings; the presentation of the totality in thought is a systematic dialectic of categories. The presentation does not reflect a sequence of historically *changing objects*. It is the progressive development of the forms of *the same object*, namely capitalism. It goes from a highly *abstract* initial concept of it to more and more *concrete* levels of its comprehension. While the presentation follows this order all categories are grounded only *retrospectively*; for they gain truth only through their position in the whole system. The logic of transition depends on the insufficiency of the form under consideration to adequately sustain its claim to truth. It must be grounded in a further development of form, and its conditions of existence secured. Care must be taken to identify exactly the level of abstraction at which each category must be introduced, and to avoid characterising a concrete form in an overly abstract way.

CHAPTER 4

The Two Dialectics of Capital: Analytic and Synthetic

The value form of the commodity is not an axiom, or an empirical given, upon which all else depends; as an abstract beginning, it gains actuality and truth only when grounded in the concrete totality to which it gives rise through a dialectical development.

To begin at the beginning. Should one follow the method of *rising* from abstract determinations to the concrete whole? The concrete as the unity of diverse determinations is then the result, not the starting point. Or should one begin with something concrete, such as the commodity, because wealth presents itself to us immediately as 'a heap of commodities'? Confusion on this point is resolved by taking account of two different meanings of 'abstract and concrete'. Marx speaks, in his Preface to *Capital*, of the power of abstraction, by analogy with the microscope, because it yields 'the economic cell-form', the commodity. Here the 'abstract' means that which is taken apart from the whole that supports it, and within which it gains its meaning; it is *separated* off from it. But, especially if the commodity is not understood as mediated in the whole, it may be taken in immediate *experience* as 'concrete' in the sense of tangible. However, a more usual sense of the 'abstract' is that which results from the most general way of thinking about anything, achieved by leaving aside all its specific characteristics so as to generate a simple immediacy for *thought*, namely a pure category not susceptible to analysis (as is the concrete of course). If this distinction is accepted then my systematic presentation has, correspondingly, *two beginnings*: analytic, and synthetic.[1]

In its first sense, 'abstraction' means to separate something from the whole that produced it and within which it has sense, by analysing the whole into parts. Capital is the object, but this is *analysable* into the movement of money, and money mediates commodity exchange. This makes the *analytical starting point* of the systematic presentation the commodity, as the 'cell' of the economic organism, abstracted from the context that gives it meaning. This same commodity, we will say, is 'posited' once it is grasped as the immediate product of capital.

---

[1] Cf. Banaji 1979, p. 40.

This beginning has the apparent advantage that the commodity can be hefted in the hand, so to speak. However, this advantage is only apparent, because one cannot tell *what it is* one has in one's hand: that it is a product of capital, for example. One cannot tell from the taste of wheat from what mode of production it comes. Even if the concrete context of its acquisition defines it as a commodity, it could be produced from plantation slavery, share cropping, yeoman farming, or a gigantic capitalist agri-business. Its *social* character remains opaque.

In the second sense, 'abstraction' signifies stripping away from the concrete all its determinacy, leaving it characterised only by a simple category. In the case of the commodity, we first distinguish its specific usefulness and its universal exchangeableness. Once all its bodily qualities, supporting its use-value, are left out of consideration, there remains only its social standing as a commodity exchangeable with others. It has, beside its use-value its exchange-value. But that the commodity *has value* is not branded on its body. Turn and twist it as one may, no value can be discerned in it. So this commodity form is a *pure* form, and it is the synthetical starting point from which the concrete as a unity of many determinations is to be reconstructed by unfolding what is implicit in it. It is a methodological premise of the systematic-dialectical logic required for this enterprise that it moves from abstract to concrete. Although the analytical starting point, namely 'the commodity produced by capital', appears as a concrete one, I shall argue that the *practical abstraction* imposed in exchange from every given feature of it leads to a systematic dialectic of 'pure form' comparable with the 'pure thought' of Hegel's logic.

Yet the form of exchange-value may be empty in itself, merely registering the effect of external contingencies. How can it be the form *of value*? Thus the synthetical starting point is the highly speculative presupposition that commodities are intrinsically valuable. This beginning must be treated with suspicion, thoroughly interrogated, and *shown* to be both the real basis of the whole system, and the result of its movement. The systematic exposition shows how the truth, therefore, is only the whole.

There is no doubt the commodity *exists*; the problem for theory is to explain its *prevalence* in this mode of production. On the other hand, it is a *conjecture* of theory that the capitalist economic order is rooted in, and may be developed from, the presupposition that *value* obtains. Here 'presupposition' means that it is taken in advance of the argument to establish it. Only as a *result* is this presupposition 'posited'. The value form is the abstract starting point for a *systematic-dialectical* development of the concrete whole of capitalist production articulated in terms of the totalising concept of 'value'. The synthetical starting point, value, is shown to exist only as a result of the full development of capital, which, as self-valorising value, produces above all itself, but in so doing makes real its abstract moments. Likewise, that value is an abstract moment of capital is consistent with its presence in this very abstraction when commodities are thrown on the market as a mere heap of exchangeables.

Just now, and in what follows, I deploy a key dialectical figure, that of the 'positing of the presupposition'.[2]

The dialectic of positing the presupposition has two referents and the presuppositions are accommodated in two different ways accordingly. These referents are a) the analytical dialectic, and b) the synthetic dialectic. In the movement of positing the presupposition, I distinguish 'conditions of existence' in the first, from 'grounds' in the second. I propose to treat 'condition of existence' as a term referring to an original 'given' later 'posited' by the system; and I distinguish it from 'ground' which is the mediated result of the dialectic of form, as a development of a category to its positedness in its further forms of existence.

So, beside the search for the mechanism that reproduces conditions of existence already obtaining and appropriated by capital, I treat the *transformation* of the forms of value itself as a grounding movement. Here something unobservable and highly abstract (namely 'value') is to be grounded in the course of its presentation at successive levels of concretion. This argument will culminate in a claim that capital is a self-grounded system exercising power over its human bearers. Thus when money grounds exchange-value, it makes true something which at the prior level (simple exchange of commodities 'at value') cannot be true, and hence must be sublated. However, this move to money *preserves* what element of truth is there at the outset, namely the notion that commodities have a value to be realised. Similarly, credit money replaces gold, which is inadequate to the truth of money, but it preserves the ambition of gold, namely to make actual the unique universal equivalent.

I now show how the two aspects of the systematic presentation work together, first treating them separately so far as it is possible.

1   Analytical Dialectic

The analytical phase begins with the object of enquiry, namely capital, as an uncomprehend whole, and then analyses it into simpler elements. The most striking result of such research is the realisation that capital is money in move-

---

[2] This figure was brought into the discussion of Marxian method by Bellofiore and Finelli (1998, p. 50). For 'posit', see the *Glossary* below.

ment, so we first must understand money, but then money has meaning only in relation to commodities, so we must begin by determining what a commodity is: this is the analytical starting point of the presentation. Indeed, the most common meaning of 'presupposition' refers to that which is analytically necessary to something. It is in this sense that we say that capital presupposes money, and money presupposes commodities. Such a chain could be interpreted in two ways: as purely logical, or as also historical, in which latter case each stage is a causally necessary condition of the next. But here we treat the matter logically.

The *presentation*, then, reconstructs the whole capitalist system, by first defining what a commodity is, then going to money and finally to capital understood as a unity of circulation and production. This systematic dialectic is a movement of theory designed to present the whole in its inner determinations. The presentation begins with the commodity as simply given; but at the end it is comprehended as the result of capitalist production, in its prevalence as the general form of the product.

But the analytical starting point is supplemented throughout the presentation by further episodes of analytical reflection that identify necessary conditions of existence of the form under consideration. While there is no self-positing movement of the sequence of such preconditions there is a specific phase of the systematic dialectic that shows how each is dialectically incorporated in the developing system, as they are posited as moments of it.

For example, it is a necessary condition of capitalism that 'free labour' comes together with the general form of capital so as to generate the capital relation. So it is seen that for capital as a general form to prevail socially, it must appropriate wage labour. This condition of its existence presupposes a further precondition, namely the availability of 'doubly-free labour'. Such labour is that of freed slaves or serfs, now lacking immediate connection with any means of production. This last is the work of history, but in the systematic presentation it is treated initially as simply given. But the upshot is that I show capital in its own movement recreates this condition of its existence. Free labour was historically produced but now is subsumed by the capital system. (It is important that, although the presence of free labour is a necessary condition of existence of capital, it does not necessarily *lead* to capital, as can be verified historically.)

There are many such conditions encountered by capital, and then subsumed, reproduced, and transformed. Such conditions of existence theory takes up at the appropriate point in the reconstruction of the capital system. When it is shown that they are endogenously reproduced by the system their origin is sublated. We say the presupposition is now posited. This means it is different from an *assumption* which remains as an external condition of the process, e.g. capital assumes the availability of infinite natural resources.

2   Synthetic Dialectic

While the prevalence of the commodity is an empirically given fact, that it is a value is not. Thus we take it as a presupposition in need of grounding that the economy is ruled by a law of value. Then we ask what social forms make that possible.

Forms of value are synthetically developed in the presentation, but their reality is normally problematic. For example, I show that exchange-value is grounded in the form of immanent exchangeability. But that latter form is simply an assertion of the presentation, itself problematic, until it, in turn, is grounded when money posits commodities are values in themselves. In this case, too, the presupposition that money has this power must be posited. This is accomplished when it is grounded in a more concrete form. The *ground* actualises an inadequate form of value that cannot at the outset be considered as self-sustaining, allowing it now to subsist, albeit as an abstract moment of a more complex form. The presentation is in large measure a grounding movement from less adequate to fully adequate social forms. Ultimately the only adequate ground is the whole system, which supports its interior moments.

It is noteworthy that my retrospective method of following a retreat through a grounding movement seems necessarily caught up in such a dialectic of presupposition and posit. Every significant move takes shape as a 'leap' to a new form of existence of the category concerned.

For example, if we consider the transition from C–M–C' to M–C–M' (C = commodity; M = money), I do not seek to show that there is a *tendency* for the movement C–M–C' to become that of M–C–M'. I say that, since M–C–M' more permanently grounds value than does C–M–C', let us turn to consider this ground of its existence; this itself is grounded in turn when the further development of the dialectic posits it as a mediating moment of capitalist production.

3   Interpenetration of Analysis and Synthesis

The two movements just discussed intertwine because the synthetic movement is forced to take up the analytically necessary conditions of existence of capital to show that value is actual; but it is capital as the form of self-valorising value that powers all the positing of presuppositions in the resulting whole.

The commodity as a *given* existent lies at the origin *uncomprehended*, but it is finally understood as the characteristic product of the system. In this system the product of labour takes the social form of a commodity. Implicitly it is assumed to be produced by capital, which is the only mode of production in which the commodity form of the product is prevalent rather than secondary. So, although capital analytically presupposes the commodity, it then posits it as its own, sublated in it.

By contrast, that the commodity is implicitly a value is certainly *not given*, but is a highly dubious assumption which cries out for a grounding movement. This is supplied by the synthetic dialectic which develops this abstract category to more concrete forms of existence.

Throughout, the grounding movement of ideal forms is interlaced with the positing of analytical conditions of existence. Indeed, the two provide mutual support. For example, we shall see the logical contradiction in the general formula for capital is resolved systematically only when surplus value arises through the subsumption under this form of labour power as a given precondition. Conversely, the prevalence and persistence of labour markets is explained by the dominance of capitalist exploitation which ensures the reproduction of the workers' propertylessness. Such a circle characterises a self-grounded totality.

Such preconditions are not 'deduced' in the ordinary way; they are taken as given, but introduced into the dialectical development of value, and surplus value, as *necessary* supports of the actuality of the whole, each at the appropriate point in the argument. They are reproduced by the system itself in its whole movement. However, living labour, and land, in their original materiality, are *subsumed* by capitalist relations but retain their 'otherness', however shaped into a foundation adequate to capital.

I begin with the commodity. In a material sense there is production of commodities by means of commodities; but in no way does *the commodity* become self-positing therein. Rather its prevalence is the doing of capital. But capital is self-valorising value, so *value* is hence the totalising concept, once it is fully actualised as capital; capital is self-actualising. But value only becomes author of its own action *once* it becomes capital, a subject that reproduces its own abstract presupposition, sheer value. Value is the logical *presupposition* of capital for our theory, but its actuality is sheer conjecture until finally *grounded*. Although the *capital* system 'produces' value, it cannot do so except on the basis of material conditions of existence that it cannot produce, but only 'subsume', and make its own only by doing violence to their own ends (particularly those of living labour).

So the commodity requires that it be (i) produced as a use-value, when the product of labour takes generalised commodity form, (ii) produced as a value, which means in accordance with the law of value. So under the first we run up against analytical conditions of existence, e.g. free labour, machinery etc., and with the second we run up against an endless deferral of the actuality of the abstract form because only the self-grounded whole actualises the systemic order of categories.

It is an important methodological point in my presentation that the movement of the presentation from abstract to concrete in truth models exactly such a hierarchy of form in the object itself. In market exchange the commodity is presented to it by capital in abstraction from the real ground of its value, and hence it functions there immediately as the bearer of a pure form. As the presentation develops capital 'recollects', as it were, that as a concrete whole it was the ground of all the pure shapes of its abstract moments, commodity, money, profit and so forth. Likewise the presentation develops capital initially as a pure shape, but then it is shown to gain a material 'filling', as it appropriates the real economic metabolism.

The encounter of theory with the 'cell-form', the commodity, is immediate, and no special power of ours is required to select it as our starting point. What is not immediate, in the appropriation of the commodity by theory, is that it is the bearer of an ideality sufficiently free from the material 'content' as to support a self-grounding movement of pure form. This is what our presentation is to accomplish. A rigorous proof of this is required because the market could chaotically register the effect of forces generated outside it, and impacting upon it.

A peculiar methodological difficulty I have is that I operate simultaneously with the most abstract logical terms, and with historically determinate ones. It is a general theme of historical materialism that very little is accomplished by ahistorical categories such as 'mode of production'. If, then, we follow the method of rising from abstract to concrete we must beware of such a beginning; rather the beginning is to be made with a historically determinate abstraction. This would be very general with respect to this particular mode of production, but sufficiently specific to mark it out from others; 'the commodity as the general form of the product' is such a determinate abstraction. However, there is a complication: all round abstraction is precisely what is historically determinate in our case. The commodity, on analysis, dissolves under the force of abstraction – including abstraction from use-value – to leave an empty form. So, we follow in our presentation of the system two orders of categories at the same time, those articulated in the logical structure, and those material determinations predicated on their interpretations in value terms. Along with the system, its moments are shown to reproduce each other, and hence are results of the system they support.

It is senseless to select one moment and claim it is the independent variable presupposed by the rest. Every element presupposes its support in the whole. One can ask *historical* questions about how a moment became present. The most interesting such question is the historical conditions of 'free labour'. But one does not *need* to answer this, because, from a systematic view, it is reproduced *now* by the system of which it is the presupposition. Its 'origin' is *in* the system itself.

I finish this chapter by recapitulating the *taxonomy* introduced. Here, I shall underline that the relation of 'positing the presupposition' has a different result, according to whether the context is analytical or synthetic.

Systematic-Dialectical (SD) presentation table

	Analytical dialectic	Synthetical dialectic
Starting Point	*Commodity*: its prevalence is a *given* to be posited as result	*Value*: the pervasive totalising form posited as grounded on itself through SD
Movement	*Uncovering* of necessary *conditions of existence* (CoE) then posited	*Development* of *grounds* sufficient to posit the starting point
Sublation	CoEs are sublated when posited as 'idealised' by SD	Presuppositions are sublated through the grounding movement of SD
Positing the Presupposition	CoEs are posited through the SD	*Grounds* posit sequentially the actuality of what they presuppose
Result	All CoEs are *subsumed* in the system as it reproduces itself	The whole grounds its moments when developed in a hierarchical system of determinations

a) The development of the dialectic requires the presupposition of certain *analytical conditions of existence* of the system (such as the material possibility of surplus product). These are initially taken as given, and then introduced to the presentation at the appropriate place. Capital appropriates these under its peculiar forms. As such they are 'idealised', they have a new meaning in the contribution they make to capital accumulation. In a sense, then, they provide a necessary condition for capital's actuality. But equally they are *sublated in it*, especially if capital takes charge of reproducing them (for example, preserving labour's propertylessness in the capital relation, and increasing its productivity).

There are two sorts of necessary conditions of existence: (i) *material* conditions, such as the capacity of workers to produce more than they consume; (ii) *social* conditions, such as the presence of free labour. In the case of material conditions capital thoroughly penetrates, and forms, them into adequate shapes of its material existence. In the case of given social forms these are very often shown to be *posited* as a result of the movement of the whole system. Their historical origin is therewith *sublated*; they become moments of capital itself, which in this respect is now unconditioned. An example is that once capital moves on its own basis, free labour is produced immanently.

b) In the case of the *synthetical* development of *new* social forms, the presentation of capital takes the shape of a *grounding movement*.[3] Here the term 'ground' refers to the need for an abstract form, lacking in truth precisely on that account, to be posited when it is sublated in a more concrete form. This ground is *not* a given, but it is shown to be a new level of development of the system itself. In the development, the more concrete grounds the more abstract (money grounds immanent value, we shall see). In this case the overly abstract (hence relatively untrue) form becomes posited as the presupposition of the more concrete. But, here, in contrast to the previous case, it is not *the ground* that is sublated. What is sublated is the originating form now taken up into the more concrete form which grants it therewith the truth apart from which it would be lacking.

So the outcome of positing the presupposition here is the reverse of the analytical case. When money grounds exchange-value it is not sublated in it. Rather value is actual only as money. Money presupposes value in some indeterminate sense, but it posits this presupposition, not in its original indeterminacy, but now as comprehended as that which will have been actualised in what grounds it, which thus determines it, makes it true when fully transformed in the upshot. In the end the whole grounds the sequence of forms by taking up these presuppositions into itself so as to posit them in their truth (whereas abstracted from the whole they are lacking), but, insofar as it *is* the sequence of its own production, it is identical with what was to be grounded, not some supra-reality. The unifying principle is the movement of negativity which generates the system, I shall argue below.

In both cases there is a positing of presuppositions; but the outcome has a different meaning. In case (a), the required condition of existence is given, and once appropriated by capital *it* is sublated in it. In case (b), the more abstract form is posited, by that which gives it grounds, *as* presupposed. Only thus does it have any standing (or it lacks ground to stand on, so to speak). The ground actualises the truth of what is posited by it as the *logical* presupposition (not *material* condition of existence) of the concrete form, but it is the earlier form that *becomes* true only when taken up by the later.

---

3 This aspect of systematic dialectic was first adumbrated in Reuten and Williams 1989, p. 22.

In sum: the uncovered condition of existence, once appropriated and transformed by capital, *is sublated in it*; but the ground is *not* sublated in what it grounds, rather the grounding movement yields the reverse; when the presupposition is grounded, the more developed form sublates the previous form.

Finally, I stress that there is a difference between 'developing' and 'subsuming'. One can speak properly of the *development* of form where 'home-grown' forms like a banking system are concerned. These capital brings forth as its own, so to speak. The revenues of financial and commercial capital, while distinct from those of industrial capital, are not distinct from those of capital as a whole, of which they are *interior* moments. Quite different are those material conditions of existence of capital that it *encounters*, and then subordinates to its purposes, *subsuming* them under peculiar value forms. Such conditions of existence are naturally or historically *given* to capital and then brought within it. An example of a natural condition is the fertility of the soil. But whatever transformation the capitalist mode of production may effect on the earth, its externality remains permanently.

Summary

There are two beginnings to the presentation of the systematic dialectic of capital: the analytic, and the synthetic.

Capital is analysable into the movement of money, and money in turn mediates commodity exchange. The analytical beginning is, then, the prevalence of the commodity form as the given mode of association. This condition of existence of capital is reproduced by capital itself such that the presupposition of the commodity form of wealth is posited by it. Other conditions of existence analytically necessary to sustain capital are uncovered as the presentation develops, especially the availability of 'free labour': this presupposition is also posited by capital itself as a result of the reproduction of the capital relation.

If the commodity is further analysed into the duality of use-value and exchange-value, the latter is taken as the presupposition of a synthetic movement that grounds it as the result of capitalist production. However, while the prevalence of the commodity form of the product of labour is a given, the supposition that the commodity is 'a value' (distinct from, and opposed to, use-value) is highly speculative. To make it a truth, a grounding movement is required for it. Each stage grounds the claims of the previous one, but in turn stands in need of a ground. Only the whole system adequately grounds it interior moments, and therewith *makes them* into its own presupposition, now adequately posited as such.

CHAPTER 5

With What Must the Critique of Capital Begin?

It is presupposed at the outset that exchange is a primary mode of social synthesis in the bourgeois epoch; it constitutes and reproduces bourgeois relations such as the dissociation of social production into autonomous enterprises. So the dialectical exposition proper begins with the most abstract indeterminate notion, but nonetheless the essential and originating one, which initiates the process of social synthesis in the bourgeois epoch, that of exchange. The only presupposition made at the start is that dissociation is overcome through exchange. Goods therein take the form of commodities.

It might be objected that starting the presentation with the notion of simple commodity exchange is dubious because we never see this: all trade is mediated by money. Even if it were true that barter relations once existed, this supposed historical beginning has no relevance to the purely systematic presentation here to be developed. So it must be admitted that the presentation starts from a *virtual* relation, for logical reasons, namely to begin with the most *elementary* relation possible. (Money is clearly a very complex form; it is hence *to be developed* in the course of the argument itself.)

As I said in the previous chapter, there are in effect *two* beginnings: the commodity is *analysable* into the complexities of use, on the one hand, and the utter simplicity of its exchangeableness, on the other. Hence the 'synthetic' beginning of the value-form logic is as simple as that of Hegel's, once use-value is left aside.

The founding moment of the idea of capital is that there is a realm of ideality set up by the exchange of commodities. One might say that exchange results in a practical *abstraction* from the given nature of the commodities. But this is not quite correct, for it could imply that what is generated through exchange is the category of 'utility' (an abstraction from the specificity of use-values, but not from the genus itself). It is essential to the possibility of a commodity entering exchange that it has a specific use-value (however qualified this imputation). In a practical abstraction it would be logical for the result to be that the commodity retains use-value, but in the abstract, sheer 'utility', all difference of use-value (which gives sense to the exchange in the first place) being ignored. For example, it might be possible to argue that two baskets of goods selected in a supermarket that happened to cost the same overall price must therefore be 'equal' in utility, or someone would change their basket from the less 'valuable' to the more 'valuable'. (This is an illusory equation, a shadow form cast by money; but it shows the need for a proper value theory to oppose value to use-value altogether.)

However, exchange is more radical than that in its constitution of the commodity, not only is its specific use-value disregarded but the genus use-value itself is abstracted from. The very fact that it is a use-value is suspended as it crosses the space of exchange; if when used the commodity is not being exchanged, when exchanged it is not being used. Hence, rather than the notion of 'abstraction' I prefer that of 'absence' consequent on a peculiar 'negation'.[1]

An objective transcendental negation is brought about in the exchange of commodities through a total absenting of all the bodily characteristics of the goods exchanged.[2]

It is a very peculiar case of a determinate negation. That determines something as other, but in principle both are presupposed to occupy the same field. Thus 'This is not green' has sense if it is coloured – perhaps it is red – but not specifically green. But I hold that what happens when commodities are taken as identical in exchange is a *complete negation* of use-value, not just of specific use-value. Thus the commodity is defined as 'Being-in-exchange' in opposition to *all* the bodily features that sustain any conceivable use-value. It is because of these considerations that I say that the practical judgement effected by exchange is that of an '*infinitely negative judgement*' on the material character of the commodities that underpin their use-value. In a formula, the commodity as Being-in-exchange *is* not-use-value.

The resultant judgement on the commodity is 'this *is* not-what-it-is'. In denying all possible predicates of the commodity that might give it use, it seems that *nothing is said* of it. But I shall contend this is yet a determinate negation yielding a determinate result because of its origin in a definite practice. Conversely exchange does not exclude any given object; anything whatsoever might be exchanged.

The obvious response to this is to say, then, that exchange is an entirely external operation *on* commodities to be grounded in the motives of the exchangers, and that the notion of commodities having exchange-value *intrinsic* to them is moonshine. However, my presentation seeks a grounding for value, beginning from the very unpromising start that accepts it cannot be grounded on anything given in the commodities prior to exchange.

Before proceeding further with my characterisation of exchange as resulting in an 'infinitely negative judgement' on commodities, I must address its distinc-

---

1 For the category of 'absence' see Bhaskar 1993.
2 This notion is similar to that of 'transcendental abstraction' employed in Reuten and Williams 1989.

tion from the existing logical term, discussed by Hegel, of 'negatively infinite judgement'.

A positive judgement is 'a rose is red', to which corresponds a negative one 'the rose is not blue'. Conceivably the rose could have been blue, but happens to be red. However, what if the predicate is qualitatively other than the range of predicates which it is possible to ascribe to the subject? Hegel, under 'negative judgement', considers also the 'negatively infinite judgment' such as 'this lion is no table' which leaves *untouched* all possible predicates of 'lion', 'table' not being one of them.

However, Hegel's negatively infinite judgement is not at all the same notion as my 'infinitely negative judgement' which absents *all* relevant predicates (including 'uselessness'!). My own, superficially similar, term is a generalisation of Hegel's in that, instead of a judgement that some one grammatical predicate stands to the subject as qualitatively other than the categorial status of that subject, I am considering a case in which every possible predicate attached to the commodity is qualitatively other than its being as result of exchange. The judgement comprehends an infinite number of such negations.

A transcendental sphere is therewith constituted throughout the space of exchange, an ideality which reduces the absented sphere of use-value to its sublated origin; nonetheless, the notionally absented field is yet required as the material bearer of the ideal one. Thus a new ontological level is posited beyond that of use-value. In a sense this transcendental negation creates its own space within which to effect a contrast with all real being of goods.

The point is that the commodity as such is identical with the sum of its material properties so that to constitute it as something other than this is to manifest sheer absence, but this all-round negation is yet determining. The usual case of determinate negation says if something is not-white it must be black, and conversely black is made determinate in being not-white. But here there is all-round negation resulting in the real being of the commodity getting wholly displaced (yet, although displaced, use-value is still *presupposed*, but in sublated form).

There is a subtle difference between the following two claims.
(i) 'Value is not use-value' means merely that value is a diverse determination, having a different character to that of use-value, possibly a contrary one in the sense that both cannot be realised at the same time.
(ii) But 'Value is not-use-value' is an infinite judgement, which is the *affirmation* of a *negative* predicate; it affirms *through* denying, so the 'is' makes a positive claim, not a negative one merely, as in the first case.

In sum this primordial practical judgement defines what a commodity *is*. It is negative because it says that, as 'Being-in-exchange', it is defined as what *is* not-use-value. It is infinite because the whole basis of its utility is absented, not merely specific use-value.

(When I speak of the infinitely negative 'judgement', this deploys a different sense of 'judgement' than that I use later when I discuss the judgement *of worth*, namely 'this commodity is worth $x', characteristic of a determination *within* the value-form analysis. The latter is a case of the well-known propositional judgement, in our case uttered easily enough in the marketplace. In this chapter, however, the so-called 'judgement' is a practical one, which obtains *objectively*, not as a form of *thought*. It generates an ontological divide between material and ideal realms, underpinning the original separation between use-value and value.)

Thus the commodity form is a *pure form* imposed on goods without expressing anything given in them. The judgement 'this is *not* use-value' is an abstract negation rather than a determinate one. But I take it to be determinate when it is read as the *definition* 'this *is* not-use-value', albeit that means we are left with an empty place-holder devoid of content.

In the beginning the movement of exchange *negates* the use-value of the commodity while it crosses the space of exchange, meaning here that its 'real being' is absent. Hence one can say *what* it is only by expressing the infinitely negative judgement that it is absolutely *other* than all the real physical properties of the commodity (corresponding to real, or imaginary uses). But *what* is it that is left as a result? In the space of exchange, there is posited a *bare singular* thrown back from the emptied field of predication. It is identical *with itself* because, abstracted from all determinate *predicates*, it becomes determinate only if it reflects itself *into* itself, becoming simply a faceless 'One'.

It follows that the other commodity in the space of exchange is equally One. It would seem then impossible to distinguish them. However, we shall argue below that there is a numerical difference in that they are poles of the exchange relation. Accordingly they *affirm* themselves as other than their other. But in our presentation the relatedness is as yet an empty form they inhabit. The infinitely negative judgement, which strips away all material being, results in an impermeable singularity.

At the same time, the negative unity of the absented predicates affirms itself simply as the *pure form* of predication. But this is an empty form, in that anything and everything real may in principle be exchanged. The dialectic to follow will show how this empty form gains self-subsistence. Yet, qualifying nothing but the void, all the affirmative categories generated constitute ideal forms absolutely other than their bearer, the One.

The negativity arises in the first place from the practice of exchange. Later we shall see how capital itself takes charge of the movement of negativity. Only then does the present discussion gain retroactive vindication. It might be true that this notion of 'empty being' is itself an empty thought. But my value-form dialectic aims to show how this singularity fills itself out, through absorbing the use-value field originally opposed to it. It becomes 'full of itself' insofar as it subjects the alien field to itself. At the start this form is so pure that the items inscribed within it are not even seen as products; so, in my view, it is only through a long argument that products are to be discovered to be the appropriate content of the commodity form.

Now the argument in detail begins by presenting Tables of categories with a commentary upon the dialectic of these forms. (The following discussion is a more discursive treatment of the movement to be traced at the beginning of our dialectical presentation proper in the next chapter.) This Table shows the regional absences and presences summarising our view.

Absence and presence in exchange

	'production'		exchange		'consumption'
A: real being (use-value)	present	⇒	absented	⇒	present
B: ideal being (in exchange)	absent	⇒	present	⇒	absent

The focus here is on exchange; terms in quotation marks are overly concrete for this level of the exposition, but are used to help give a more accessible 'picture' of what is going on. Line A is understood as originating the dialectic, through absenting real being (use-value) during exchange, and line B is derived from A as a quasi-inversion of it.

At A, then, 'production' and 'consumption' (or, more abstractly, the presenting of goods for exchange and their removal) are presupposed to exchange as realities, and a wealth of use-values gets transferred through exchange from one hand to another. While use-value is here presented *to* exchange it is suspended for the period *of* exchange; this absenting of use-value while commodities cross the space of exchange constitutes them as all that is not use-value, sheer absence. This line, therefore, is characterised by 'the positing of absence (of use-value)'. Immediately, the exchanging commodity is simply predicated as 'not-use-value' but this absence 'makes space' so to speak in line B for the emergence of 'absence' into positive presence (as illustrated in the middle column above).

The Table gives expositional priority to the use-value line, from which we seem to derive a ghostly inverted echo under it. (Using the term 'value' somewhat proleptically) this inversion is itself inverted when value *posits* itself against use-value, we shall see. At this level the immediate motor of exchange appears to be – not value but – the exchange of one commodity for another of a different kind having a different use. Thus a condition of existence of exchange is the universe of use-value. (However, the further development of the dialectic of the value form will *posit* this condition of its existence in the production of commodities for exchange.)

The movement from A to B is a switch to an inverted world; insofar as line B is itself a determinate negation of the whole of line A, it is here taken as a reality axed around *presence* (of absence grasped as resulting from the negation of use-value). The 'ontological inversion' is the moment of 'negation of negation', but whereas the first negation (of the presence of use-value) is brought about *by* exchange, the second negation is effected *in the space of exchange*, a space predicated on absenting the 'real being' of the commodity as use-value (even as an abstraction, utility). So, instead of returning to the starting point, and recollecting that the commodity is, after all, use-value, within this space there is posited a pure Being-in-exchange: we cannot say *what* this Being-in-exchange is, only *that* it is. It makes itself *present to us* through *displacing* the real being of commodities, and positing 'absence as presence'.

Notice that the movement *across each line* is characterised by ontological reversal, but that *from line to line* by ontological inversion. The difference is that the reversal maintains the original presupposition, and posits in the same 'universe', so to speak, the opposite. But the ontological inversion supplants the entire 'universe' together with its existing regional presences and absences such that *all* is presented as other than it is, as standing on its head. Now why should there be any inversion of line A into line B at all? It must be emphasised that this 'perspectival switch' from A to B is as such only a presentiment of the reality of the 'topsy-turvy' world of capitalism; as such it seems merely a shadow cast by exchange.

To give the shadow substance requires a long development, in which new, more concrete, categories are brought to birth, precisely through the consideration, at each stage, of the *insufficiency* of the shape under consideration to prove that it has *made itself present*.

Thus this argument can follow somewhat the same lines as that of Hegel's onto-logic, his attempt to constitute the universe out of the self-movement of thought; however, in this case it is the self-movement of capital that has to be shown to constitute its universe.

Let us examine more closely the movement of exchange as we now understand it. Although commodities pass *across* this space, nonetheless something is posited *in* this sphere. When a commodity is exchanged it has duality, as 'Being' *in* exchange, hence as 'non-being' *outside* exchange.

One use-value is replaced by another use-value, but the very same Being persists *in* exchange. In proportion as the Being-in-exchange develops into a reality, the 'real being' of commodities itself retroactively becomes merely its shadow, its other being, its *non-being*. The reality that was absented is still latent, but absenting its absence to reach Being-in-exchange leaves the commodity as a use-value facing it as sheer otherness, something of which this Being knows nothing, where it is not, its non-being. This is shown in the next Table.

Being-in-exchange and its other

'production'	exchange	'consumption'
(use-value) non-being ⇐	Being ('in exchange')	⇒ non-being (use-value)

Commodities are hence posited, when taken as use-values prior to exchange, as the 'non-being' of 'value', before they are present in exchange as Beings (of 'value'), only to be 'devalorised' as they pass beyond it to be used. 'Non-being' might be thought a strange way to refer to the visible reality, use-value; but what is meant is that there is *nothing of value* in it as such a visible reality, that one can never find 'value' there. (Considered as something destined *for exchange* its 'Being' in exchange may be ideally anticipated, but here is only a potential.) But the use-value space is no longer defined as real from value's point of view, having been reduced to its non-being.

It is necessary to beware the error summarised in 'what is not exchange-value is use-value hence if value is Being, the Nothing must be use-value'. Rather, defining itself negatively, value simply is the *absence* of use-value, leaving Nothing, so to speak. Hence, both Being *and Nothing* are founding moments *of the value form*. Although what is other than value is use-value, this latter is now posited simply as the non-being of value. But 'non-being' is distinct from 'Nothing', which as *absented* use-value is a moment *of* value. Once constituted, value is then one of the two aspects of the commodity, each determined as not the other. Thus I distinguish between a structure characterised by the *correlative* moments 'Being' and 'non-being', and the unstructured immediacy of 'Being' and 'Nothing', as the starting point of the value form.

However, if and when value succeeds in making itself real, and appearing in finite form as characteristic of all commodities, then, from the standpoint of ordinary empirical understanding, the two determinations appear as contraries, becoming determinant in turn in the life cycle of the commodity. *Now* what is not use-value is value and what is not value is use-value. But *originally* value *is* not-use-value, parasitic on it rather than established alongside it.

Yet, in developing the value form, use-value (as the non-being of value) seems to be set aside to begin with. However, it is important that use-value comes back in all the time insofar as the body of the commodity is *first* required simply as the *bearer* of value, and *later* use-value is treated as having its own economic determinacy. This is especially the case with the use-value of labour which is a necessary condition of existence of capital.

Consider the inversion of absence into presence exhibited earlier in the relevant Tables above ('Absence and Presence'; 'Being-in-exchange') covering the columns: 'production'; exchange; 'consumption'. What I need now to do is to focus on what is occurring in 'exchange' (the central column), a sphere taken in its own actuality. This means leaving use-value aside (for now), and showing that Being-in-exchange is made present in this sphere. Bearing this distinction in mind allows me to articulate the original *separation* between use and exchange with the origin of the systematic-dialectical *development* of exchange determinations themselves, considered later. (See the Table below in §11.13: 'Dialectic of Being-in-exchange'.)

I shall argue that, because absence (of use-value) is here a determinate absence, having been determined as such by exchange, it has *presence*; thus what is present is not a mere void but has some sort of *Be-ing*, albeit a negative Be-ing, namely *Nothingness*.

Since the categories 'Nothing' and 'Being' are reminiscent of Hegel's logic, let us turn aside to consider this. One significant disanalogy is in the *starting point*. The practical absenting of the bodily shape of the commodity in the movement of exchange is rather like the process Hegel took as presupposed by his science, but not a part of it, when thought clears the ground of all determinacy, and all dogmatic assumptions, to arrive at pure being as the starting point of his logical dialectic. However, my 'clearing' is more radical in that the founding category goes behind Being to Nothing.

Hegel *starts from 'Being'*, passes to 'Nothing' and back again, resolving this instability in 'Becoming', and collapsing this to *'Dasein'* (usually translated as 'determinate Being', or, literally, Being-There). On the basis of the absenting of use-value, I start from sheer *'Nothing'*, but then make a transition to its possible inversion as 'Being'. But if Hegel rises from Being in an 'upward pointed' spiral of determinations, its shadow side, logically equally possible, is a 'downward pointed' spiral from 'Nothing'.[3]

---

[3] See Arthur 2002a, pp. 163–6, drawing on Willett 1990.

So if we deconstruct Hegel's dialectic, a certain 'prejudice-for-truth' is revealed. Occluded is another possibility: a world of falsity, where everything is inverted. This 'downward' spiral would be the concretisation of nothingness, the apotheosis of the false, insofar as 'Being' is demoted to the other of 'Nothing'. Such a hellish dialectic, in which, contrary to the vision of 'the whole is the true', the whole is the false, is precisely the case in capitalism, we argue. Since the downward spiral, concretising 'Nothing', reflects Hegel's upward spiral, concretising 'Being', all the more determinate categories of the downward spiral develop in parallel to the upper, with the understanding that they qualify the 'Nothing'.

It is important to Hegel's onto-logic that the stages gone through, in developing the Absolute Idea, are *constitutive of it*, not abandoned husks of its immature shapes. They are *preserved*, albeit as sublated moments of the self-comprehending Absolute. This is why even the most primitive, 'Being', is itself a way of referring to the Absolute, albeit very abstractly; for the Absolute certainly *has* being; indeed, in a way, it is nothing other than the fullest expression of 'Being'.

As a *dialectical* development, this concretisation of 'Being' is equally always constituted at each stage with reference to its opposite, at the start sheer 'Nothing'; but in Hegel's dialectic 'Being' encloses this 'Nothing', albeit Nothing is carried along 'within' the whole development. For Hegel 'Nothing' is reduced, in effect, to the lack of determinacy of his 'Being', and a signal that the latter requires concretising until it has achieved plenitude in the Absolute. For me, 'Nothing' is at the origin, and encloses 'Being' in the building-up of the shadow world of Nothingness.

Now in the presentation proper, my dialectical development moves forward in parallel with Hegel's in *affirming* the necessity of further categories. But, whereas Hegel is reconstructing a positive reality, my categories have a hollowness at their heart. If this is overlooked the dialectic seems purely affirmative.

It follows from the argument thus far that the scaffold of *categories*, which lies incarnate in economic *form*, certainly develops itself into a world. However, these pure forms are not forms *of* anything at all but are to posit themselves as their own presuppositions. To say that Nothingness is at the heart of capital is to say that value is pure form, not the form of a given content. This it produces from within itself, we shall see: itself *as* content.

In our case it is not *thought* in its abstractness that yields the beginning with Nothing. Rather, the practical movement of *exchange* absents the realm of use-value to leave nothing; as determinate this has its own Being. What has become absent through such a process leaves a *trace* structured by the specific process that brought it about, albeit it is nothing.

In considering the Being-in-exchange, a key movement is that of 'presencing', the making present, of this Nothingness. In truth, I see this as the motor of the whole dialectic to come. It presents, not a static array of categories, but the process of their *becoming present*.

What is prior to the project of reconstructing the inner dialectic of capital, is the external force (exchange) that took hold of goods – against their will so to speak – and transformed them into commodities, comprehensively negating their use-value. *Within* the space of exchange, then, this absence leaves us with an immediacy, namely 'Nothing', as the point of origin of the dialectic of capital. However, it must yet *prove* itself as *present to* its world, through inverting its constitutive context. It achieves real presence if it can be demonstrated to develop into a power over reality. But if this 'Nothing' is not able to affirm itself as Being-in-exchange, it loses any actuality. Unless Nothingness *makes* itself present it remains a philosophical fiction.

Although exchange and circulation set up an 'ideal world' of pure forms, empty of content, which then take hold of production, this is consistent with, indeed depends upon, the acquisition of *emergent powers*. In virtue of the mechanism of emergent powers it is possible to suppose that, if there is at the base level a determinate absence, then a more complex practice might *re-determine* this as a pseudo-positive *presence*, albeit an 'empty presence'. Yet, it will be argued, this spectral objectivity prevails over the material of economic life. So our presentation will show how capital *makes itself present*, a real power in the world, albeit what is made present is this void behind it, which seizes reality only to make of it something other than it. Nothingness *becomes* present only as pure negativity, which sets up the positive only to supersede it continually.

A final word is required to warn the reader that the presentation to come employs a peculiar language. Not only is it inspired by Hegel's logic, it mimics his idiom. In Hegel's case the self-movement of thought is understood objectively; it is not *his* thoughts that are presented, it is a matter of 'thought thinking itself'. One thought of itself gives way to another. My own presentation take shape in the same manner. I speak of the *commodity* becoming money, of *money* becoming *capital*, without any reference to human agency. This is because I take these social forms to be self-acting, and giving rise to one another through an inner dialectic. In the earlier stages some 'ventriloquism' may be suspected; am I not really directing this movement from behind the scenes? However, it is not I but the Idea of capital that ensures the forms are reproduced immanently. Yet, to show that, I must naturally develop first this Idea *through* following its self-production as presented here. So, if a reader finds the form of argument in the next chapters 'occult', I beg indulgence for this; for I argue that it is philosophically justified. As to human agents, they play a virtually negligible role in the logic of the systematic presentation; it is assumed that, notwithstanding contingent idiosyncrasies, they act in a general way in conformity with the logic imposed upon them by capital. (Recall Marx's famous '*Charaktermasken*'.[4])

Following this logic is what I aim at in *my own* 'presentation'. In what follows therefore the presentation of the matter follows the dialectic of the subject's own presentation of itself. The systematic dialectic simply records the logical development of this presentation in its unfolding. While the initial steps in my own dialectical presentation are apparently reflections on commodity exchange externally undertaken by theory itself, later it becomes clear that theory just reproduces capital's *self*-presentation. But theory is still distinct from the object. My presentation indeed follows capital in its movement; but I have the bigger picture in mind throughout, which gives me a standpoint for critique of capital's drive to realise itself.

Thus the dialectic of capital is one of 'self-moving social form'. The original *displacement* of the material process of production and circulation by the ghostly objectivity of value, is complemented when self-positing capital takes *possession* of it. Capital emerges as a 'spectre' that *haunts* the world of commodity production and circulation.

Summary

I begin with the observation that the commodity has diverse, even contrary, determinations, namely use-value and exchange-value. The question arises as to the nature of the relation (if any) between them. Is it such as to allow a well-founded judgement asserting that there is an order to them? For example, someone might claim that the greater the utility of a commodity the greater its value. Moreover, it may be that the social form of exchange is adopted as a practical convenience, but does not admit of any regular determinant of exchange: the form is simply empty. My thesis is that in a developed capitalist economy there is a most peculiar historically unique connection between the two determinations, namely that exchange-value is *constituted* by the negation of use-value. This allows me to assert that practice has carried through an 'infinitely negative judgement' on the material commodity, generating a peculiar social form of ideality, within which form commodities are inscribed.

---

4 See Marx 1976, p. 179 (the translation is loose here).

I admit this all-round negation is a paradoxical form of 'judgement', not least because it is socially *constitutive* in creating a fold in materiality that flows over into a wealth of ideal determinations. However, despite its practical character, it is yet *logical in form*; hence it is relevant to compare it with Hegel's logic. Moreover, whereas Hegel talks vaguely of a preliminary clearing away of all determinacy, I provide the precisely articulated logic of that move in the infinitely negative 'judgement', albeit I reach 'Nothing' (not 'Being'). The 'Nothingness', to be posited here as 'the presence of absence', is the origin of the capital system as a *historically determinate* social actuality. In the rest of this book I show that further exchange determinations (money especially) *ground* this imputation.

In the next part, I begin the presentation proper of the dialectic of the value form.

PART 2

The Ideal Constitution of Capital

Part 2: The Ideal Constitution of Capital

On the page opposite begins a list of the paragraphs comprising the bulk of this second (and final) part.

The strictly logical presentation of the value-form categories (in Chapters 6–13; 15–16) is organised in paragraph numbers that reflect the logical level of the categories concerned. Because the logic has a triadic movement, the numbers concerned naturally run in threes. However, the logical level of the category concerned is indicated also by the addition of a further number (thus, by adding 1, 2, and 3, '§ 1' divides into '§ 11', '§ 12', '§ 13'; '§ 2' divides into '§ 21', '§ 22', '§ 23'; and so on); where the system becomes very fine-grained the more extended number is broken up with points ('.') and slashes ('/') (e.g. the category of 'monetary medium' is placed at '§ 23.31/32'); these points and slashes have no substantive significance; they are used simply as an aid to scrutiny.

Interpolated into the presentation are *'Remarks'* not strictly necessary to the argument. Note that the format rule followed is that a *Remark* is one paragraph, and only one paragraph, long, before the main text resumes. In very rare cases a longer interpolation is headed *'Remark on …'*.

PART 2: THE IDEAL CONSTITUTION OF CAPITAL   61

The Presentation of Value Form Categories

Division I Capital in Its Notion
§ 1 Commodity
    § 11 Quality of Being Exchangeable
        § 11.1 Being Present in Exchange
            Nothing; Being; Nothingness (the Presence of Nothing)
        § 11.2 Exchangeableness: Something and Other; Spurious Infinity; True Infinity
        § 11.3 An Exchangeable
            One; Many; (Relative) Totality (Attraction / Repulsion)
    § 12 Quantity of Commodities Exchanged
        § 12.1 Pure Quantity (Infinite Unity of All Exchangeables)
        § 12.2 Number of Commodities Exchanged in a Transaction
        § 12.3 Ratio of Exchange
    § 13 Exchange-Value as the (Specifying) Measure
        § 13.1 Rule of Pro-rata Exchange
        § 13.2 Series of Exchange-Values (i.e. of Specific Measures)
        § 13.3 Infinite Unity of Measure Relations

§ 2 Money
    § 21 Value as Immanent Exchangeability
        § 21.1 Exchange-Value Reflected into the Commodity
            § 21.11 Positing Reflection
            § 21.12 External Reflection
            § 21.13 Determining Reflection
        § 21.2 Reflex-Determinations of Value
            § 21.21 Identity (Value Is in the Commodity)
            § 21.22 Difference (Value Is Not in the Commodity but Different from It)
            § 21.23 Contradiction (Value Is and Is Not in the Commodity)
        § 21.3 Value Grounded in the Value Form
    § 22 Value as Appearance
        § 22.1 Value as Existent
            § 22.11 Value as (Relational) Property of a 'Thing'
            § 22.12 Form and Content
            § 22.13 Value as Law-like in Its Appearance
        § 22.2 Forms of Appearance of Value:
            § 22.21 Form I Simple Form

§ 22.22 Form II Expanded Form
§ 22.23 Form III General Form
§ 22.3 Correlation of Immediate and Reflected Totalities of Value
§ 23 Value as Actuality: Money
§ 23.1 The Modalities of Equivalent Form: Possibility; Contingency; Necessity; Form IV: Total Form of Value
§ 23.2 Money as Absolute Form of Value
§ 23.21 Exchangeability-in-Immediacy; Form V: Money Form of Value
§ 23.22 Immediate Exchangeability; Form VI: Laying-out of Money
§ 23.23 Reciprocity of Form-Determinations of Money
§ 23.3 Value as Substance (the Substantiality of Value Exists in Money)
§ 23.31 Value as Substance in Immediacy
§ 23.31/1 Substance-in-Itself; Its Oneness (Its Self-Identity)
§ 23.31/2 Substance-for-Itself as a Dimensionally Extended Body of Value
§ 23.31/3 Money as Finite Mode of Value:
§ 23.31/31 Immanent Magnitude
§ 23.31/32 Monetary Medium
§ 23.31/33 Measure Proper Is Given in Units of Money
§ 23.32 Value Substance Actualised in a Realm of Finitude: Commodities
§ 23.32/1 Money Is the Real Measure of Value of Commodities
§ 23.32/2 Commodities as 'Values'
§ 23.32/21 Value as the Substance of Commodities
§ 23.32/22 The Transubstantiation of the Commodity
§ 23.32/23 The Commodity Posited as 'a Value'
§ 23.32/3 Value as Absolute Relation of Form and Content
§ 23.33 Infinite Unity of Value Substance: Form VII: Substantial Form
§ 23.33/1 Interchangeability of Commodities as Values Predicated by Money

§ 23.33/2 Money as Comparator (Unitary Measure of Value)
§ 23.33/3 Merging of Values in a Mass of Value Measured in One Sum

§ 3 Capital
  § 31 Price (Subjectivity of Value)
    § 31.1 Value as Notion
      § 31.11 Infinite Value Notion
        § 31.11/1 Universality of Value
        § 31.11/2 Particularity as 'Amount'
        § 31.11/3 Singularity as 'an Amount'
      § 31.12 Finite Value Notion (Schematised in Money as 'Measure-Making')
      § 31.13 Value Brought Back to the Infinite: Fungibility of Money.
    § 31.2 The Value Judgement (Money Assumes the Role of Measure-Taking)
      § 31.21 The Judgement of Worth, 'This Commodity Is Worth \$x'
      § 31.22 Standard of Price; Money of Account;
      § 31.23 The Unfolding of the Judgement of Worth
        § 31.23/1 The Formal Judgement (Qualitative and Quantitative)
        § 31.23/2 The Categorical Judgement;
        § 31.23/3 The Judgement of the Concept
    § 31.3 Transitivity of Price
      § 31.31 Syllogism of Abstraction: If A Is Worth \$x, and B Is Worth \$x, Then A = B
      § 31.32 Syllogism of Equality: If A = B, and B = C, Then A = C
      § 31.33 Syllogism of Syllogisms:
If A = B & B = C Then A = C;
If C = A & A = B Then C = B;
If B = C & C = A Then B = A (the System Is Closed).
  § 32 Exchange and Circulation (Objectivity of Value)
    § 32.1 Immediate Exchange (Money as Ideal Measure) C–C'
    § 32.2 Sale Is Purchase (C–M) ≡ (M–C)
    § 32.3 Metamorphoses of Commodities and Money
      § 32.31 Sale and Purchase (C–M) + (M–C')

      § 32.32   Metamorphoses of Commodities C–M–C′ (Finite Teleology)
      § 32.33   Metamorphoses of Money (Monetary Circulation: Infinite Teleology)

§ 33 Capital as Concept and Idea
    § 33.1 Money as Money (Value as 'Individuated')
      § 33.11   Money as End of Exchange
      § 33.12   Money as Means of Payment
      § 33.13   Money as Funds
    § 33.2 Money as Capital
      § 33.21   Money as Its Own End
      § 33.22   'Life Process' of Capital: General Formula for Capital
      § 33.23   'Generation' of Increment of Money
    § 33.3 Capital as Idea
      § 33.31   Accumulation
          § 33.31/1 Transformation of the Monetary Increment into Capital
          § 33.31/2 Rate of Accumulation as a Measure of Capital by Itself for Itself
          § 33.31/3 The Infinity of Capital
      § 33.32   The Formal Determination by Capital of Its Real-World Existence
          § 33.32/1 Subsumption
          § 33.32/2 Valuation
      § 33.33   Idea of Capital Realised in Contradiction

Division ii Capital Relation

§ 4 Capital in Circulation
    § 41 The Temporality of Capital Accumulation
    § 42 Ideality and Reality of Circulation
    § 43 Capital Posited in and through Its Otherness
      § 43.1 Merchant Capital
      § 43.2 Money-Lending
      § 43.3 Industrial Capital

§ 5 Capital in Production
    § 51 Industrial Capital in Its Notion: Genesis of Value in 'Time' (Production) and 'Space' (Exchange)
    § 52 Capital Relation Proper

PART 2: THE IDEAL CONSTITUTION OF CAPITAL   65

       § 52.1 'Abstract' Labour
       § 52.2 Formal and Real Subsumption
       § 52.3 Constitution of Capital via a Dialectic of Negativity; Alienation of Labour
   § 53 Self-Valorisation of Capital
       § 53.1 Value Added
       § 53.2 Genesis of Surplus Value
       § 53.3 Wages of Labour

§ 6 Reproduction of Capital
   § 61 Simple
   § 62 Extended
   § 63 Results of the Immediate Production Process

Division III The System of Capital
§ 7 Capital as Universal and Individual
   § 71 Capital as Subject
   § 72 Individual Capitals
   § 73 Capital as One Idea

§ 8 The System of Industrial Capital in Its Double Determination
   § 81 Capital as such Reflected into Itself
       § 81.1 The Rate of Surplus Value
       § 81.2 The Metamorphoses of Capital
           § 81.21 Fluidity and Fixity of Capital
           § 81.22 Three Circuits of Capital
           § 81.23 The Circuit in Its Conceptual Unity
       § 81.3 Simple Price and the Rate of Profit
   § 82 Difference of Capitals
       § 82.1 Competition: Absolute and Relative Surplus Value;
       § 82.2 Organic Composition of Capital;
       § 82.3 Uniform Rate of Profit and Prices of Production
   § 83 Systemic Unity of Total Social Capital
       § 83.1 General Law of Accumulation
       § 83.2 Reproduction of Total Capital via Departments of Reproduction
       § 83.3 Reproduction Prices and the General Rate of Profit;
           Addendum A Note on the Neo-Sraffian System
           Addendum A Note on the Tendential Fall in the General Rate of Profit

§ 9 Absolute Capital
    § 91 Absolute Capital in Its Notion (*ex nihilo* Money)
    § 92 Externalisation of Inner Moments of Capital Circuit
        § 92.1 Finance;
        § 92.2 Commerce;
        § 92.3 Industrial Production Proper
    § 93 Capital as Absolute Idea
        § 93.1 The Absolute as Individual
        § 93.2 The Elliptical Movement of Capital
        § 93.3 Capital as Absolute Idea

§ 10 Capital and Its Others
    § 101 Capital
    § 102 Internalisation of Capital's 'Others'
    § 103 General Conditions of Existence of Capital

DIVISION I

Capital in Its Notion

∴

CHAPTER 6

Commodity

Introduction

I now begin the presentation proper of the systematic dialectic of capital. It presents *the ideal constitution of capital*. This divides into: I Capital in its Notion, II The Capital Relation, III The System of Capital.

Division I corresponds to Hegel's logic, and its forms are pure forms, characterised by internal relations, such that as a whole it may be considered a simple immediacy compared with the subsequent division. Division II, developing 'the capital relation', takes forward the logic of the value form as it mediates itself in its relation to the material economic metabolism, especially in relation to wage labour. Thus these two divisions deal with capital as such, but to articulate the grounds of this notion I investigate, in Division III, 'the system of capital' as it informs the entire world of circulation, production, and distribution. (Although 'use-value' is largely absent from the first division, in the second and third divisions, use-value considerations are especially important to the systematic presentation of capital.)

As a preliminary to its detailed presentation, here is the plan of Division I, namely Capital in its Notion:

§1   exchange in its immediacy: value implicit in *commodities*;
§2   in its mediation: the reflection and showing-forth of value in *money*;
§3   in its return into itself (circulation) and its development of itself (accumulation): *capital*.

'Capital in its Notion', then, divides into three: Commodity; Money; Capital. Their presentation corresponds to the main 'Doctrines' of Hegel's logic. In other words, what it is to be a commodity follows the logic of 'Being'; the necessity of money follows the logic of 'Essence'; the development of capital follows the logic of the 'Concept'.

Notice that I use up the categories of the logic simply to reach the category of 'the General Formula for Capital'. Why is this? Now the logic is only *part of* Hegel's system of philosophy, and it is precisely that part in which, because thought deals only with itself, there are no obstacles to its free movement; it is in its native element. But this is certainly not true of the other domains Hegel attempts to 'logicise'; here there is always to be reckoned with otherness, contingency, finitude, and alienation. The Absolute wins its freedom *in the real world* (not in self-contemplation), and it does so only *through* overcoming obstacles. It must engage in 'the strenuous labour of the negative', in which it becomes lost to itself, and becomes what it is only through emerging from this otherness having recognised itself in it.

If one maps the capital system on the *whole* of Hegel's philosophy, the first move is to ask: where does value move freely in its own element? If there is such a sphere this is where the pure forms of logic are likely to find their correlates. The answer is surely the sphere of *circulation*; in such phenomena as the exchanges of commodities and money, value deals only with itself in its various expressions.

A crucial turning point in the presentation is when the general formula for capital includes the emergence of a monetary increment, but where circulation alone cannot explain its source. Then we leave 'the sunlit sphere of circulation' and enter 'the hidden abode of production'. In other words, capital must transform materials, and for that it needs labour, which remains opposed to capital even under conditions of 'real subsumption'.

In my opinion, then, the analogy with Hegel's turn from the Absolute Idea, to the reality informed by it, is when the pure forms of value sink into the world of production, circulation, and distribution. In Hegel's philosophy the pure forms of conceptuality become Absolute Idea insofar as they are understood as at the same time to shape the world; thus Hegel's philosophy turns from Logic to the reality of Nature and History. Indeed, strictly speaking, the 'Idea' is not part of the Logic for it is present only when the 'Concept' is united with the real material of the world so as to 'fill out', as it were, the *pure* forms of thought. From the point of view of reality in its comprehensive articulation the categorial system of the *Logic*, despite its inner complexity, is *as a whole* a simple immediacy. The Idea then mediates itself through determining itself to concrete difference in Nature and back to its unity in difference with itself in Spirit.

How does this movement between these spheres inform my account? It requires the logic of the value form in its purity to be taken as an abstract immediacy negatively related to the material inscribed in the value form. The parallel to Hegel's turn to Nature is the turn to the material process of production. Just as Hegel claims Nature has its truth outside itself (in the Logic) so here production has its truth outside itself insofar as it is formally determined by the imperative of capital accumulation.

The cases are analogous in that it is a question of seeing how the Idea (of capital in my case) informs the world. But these new forms are 'mixed' in that they pertain both to logic and a specific reality, which in my case is the economic metabolism. So in the later parts of my presentation there are to be found only formal analogies with Hegel's *Realphilosophie*. Thus for Hegel the Concept is paradigmatically incarnate in willing individuals; here it is in the many capitals.

In the logic of the value form proper, the three determinations of value, namely commodity, money, capital, map Hegel's 'Doctrines'. The logic of *Being* is one-dimensional; its categories are merely descriptive; just so the parallel categories define what it is to *be* a commodity. The logic of *Essence* is two-dimensional in that its categories consider how things are hidden behind appearances, yet it explains how this happens; the parallel categories trace how value originally implicit in commodity relations becomes actual in money. The logic of the *Concept* is three-dimensional in providing categories of reflexivity culminating in the self-positing Idea; the parallel categories show how money in motion returns to itself with more money. The 'truth' of value is achieved only in capital accumulation.

§1 Commodity

This first section thematises what it is to be a commodity. '*Being*' is the first domain of Hegel's logic; and its sub-categories here follow those of it, namely 'quality', 'quantity', and 'measure'. The commodity, as a Being-in-exchange, has (§11) the *quality* of being exchangeable, (§12) in a definite *quantity* practically required to make exchange determinate, (§13) which therewith constitutes one commodity as the *measure* of another, that is, gives it exchange-value. These determinations are dialectically related and are to be developed in a logical progression.

§11 *Quality of Being Exchangeable*

If being exchangeable is not merely the result of external determinants such as demand and supply, it will be taken here as an *immanent* determination of universal exchange such that something becomes *present* in the space of exchange. The systematic dialectic begins, then, by considering the *qualitative* determinations of the commodity, with this triad:

§11.1 Being Present in Exchange; §11.2 Exchangeableness; §11.3 an Exchangeable.

In more detail:

§11.1 Being present in exchange
  §11.11 Nothing; §11.12 Being; §11.13 Nothingness (the presence of Nothing);
    §11.2 Qualitatively determinate being; exchangeableness:
      Something and other; Spurious infinity; Genuine infinity;
    §11.3 Being-for-itself of an Exchangeable as one amongst others:
      One; Many; (relative) Totality constituted by attraction/repulsion.

§ 11.1   Being Present in Exchange

Being present in exchange is, first of all, to be *there*. But *what* is there? The presenting of goods for exchange, and their removal, are presupposed to exchange, and a wealth of use-values gets transferred through exchange from one hand to another. While use-value is here presented *to* exchange, it is suspended for the period *of* exchange; this absenting of use-value while commodities cross the space of exchange constitutes them simply as 'not-use-value', sheer absence. But this absence 'makes space', so to speak, for the emergence of 'absence' into positive *presence*.

This 'ontological inversion' is constituted by a moment of 'negation of negation', but whereas the first negation (of the presence of use-value) is brought about *by* exchange, the second negation is effected *in the space of exchange*, a space predicated on absenting the 'real being' of the commodity as use-value. So, instead of returning to the starting point, and recollecting that the commodity is, after all, use-value, within this space there is posited a pure Being-in-exchange: we cannot say *what* this Being-in-exchange is, only *that* it is.

It makes itself *present to us* through *displacing* the real being of commodities, and positing 'absence as presence'. This means leaving use-value aside (for now), when showing that Being-in-exchange may be made present. This is the burden of the following *dialectical development*. Thus the original *separation* between use and exchange lies at the origin of the *systematic-dialectical development* of exchange determinations themselves.

Remark[1]: Throughout the discussion I assume the dialectical principles that 'to determine is to negate' (e.g. a red rose is determined as *not* blue). And 'to negate is to determine', that is to say, all negation is determinate (e.g. if the rose is *not* red it must be because it *is* some other colour).

Now I consider the inner moments of 'Being present in exchange' namely: § 11.11 Nothing; § 11.12 Being; § 11.13 Nothingness (the presence of Nothing).

§ 11.11   Nothing

Because absence (of use-value) is here a determinate absence, having been determined as such by exchange, it has *Presence*; thus what is present is not a mere void but, since this absenting is effected by a real operation on the commodity, this is a *determinate* Nothing, hence a Being of a sort results, albeit pure empty Being.

---

1 Note that the format rule followed here is that a *Remark* is one paragraph, and only one paragraph, long, before the main text resumes.

Remark: Recall that in the previous chapter I distinguish Nothing *as a moment* of 'value' from the non-being *of* 'value' in general, a sphere where considerations *other* than 'value' are in play.

§ 11.12   Being

Consider this move from Nothing to Being. If Being is not to be nothing, something distinct from it, how is it *determined* thus? Clearly there is lacking in Being anything absent from Nothing that could make a difference. As totally indeterminate it amounts to nothing.

However, there is a purely logical difference here if Being is characterised simply by the presupposition that it is 'not-nothing'. It posits itself through its own negativity as not what is not, a double negation constituting a peculiar positive. The required difference between being and nothing is thus introduced here purely *formally*, sheer difference in formal status not sustained by any content of which it could *be* the form. (It is presented more concretely below in the dialectic of 'something and other'.) But to affirm itself thus is to make *present* Nothing, that is, to posit 'Nothingness'.

Note that I reach Nothingness after two distinct movements of negation of negation.

(i)   In the preliminary dialectic I begin from Real Being (the realm of use-value) and then absent it (the first negation) but arrive through the negation of the negation at the *Presence* of Absence (of use-value). I then consider this result as a new *immediacy*, so I redefine it affirmatively (without reference to the negation of the negation of Real Being), as 'Nothing'.

(ii) As an immediacy, this Nothing has itself *Being* (first negation) but, if Being here is merely not-Nothing without any *determinate difference* from Nothing then this subsists only if its (second) negation – namely not-not-Nothing – is not the original abstraction, Nothing, but the concrete presence of Nothing, which I term *Nothingness*.

§ 11.13   Nothingness

'Nothing' is used here to denote sheer absence, defined *abstractly* as the simply *negative* moment of the dialectic of exchange, understood as carrying out in practice an infinitely negative judgement on the commodity presented to exchange. By contrast, 'Nothingness' is my term for this 'presence of Nothing'. For what is thrown up in the space of exchange, positively, what *becomes present* there, is Nothingness. The 'presence of Nothingness' is indeed our first concrete category since Nothing and Being are mere unstable abstractions from it unless held together in it. To establish the reality of *Nothingness* requires a long development, in which new, more concrete, categories are developed, through the consideration, at each stage, of the *insufficiency* of the shape under consideration to prove that it has *made itself present*.

In order to establish the categorial place of 'presence', let us consider an interesting form in Hegel's exposition of the dialectic of Being, namely that of *'Dasein'*, of which the literal translation is 'being-there'. Translators differ on its rendering. Traditional is 'determinate Being'. As a *translation* 'determinate Being' is clearly wrong. *However*, given that Hegel puts it as a middle term between Being and Being-for-itself it is *structurally correct*.

But I feel Hegel should have distinguished *Dasein* as 'being-there' from this, by having it characterise Being itself, as it embraces the dialectic of 'Being and Nothing'; for what is *becoming present* is surely the Being there before us, the *Dasein*. Whatever view is taken of Hegel, I myself treat the middle of Being and Being-for-itself as 'Determinate Being', and I consider what is *there* is 'presence'.[2] *Dasein* in this sense is precisely an *indeterminate Being*, although, *as there*, as present, it has that bare determinacy, sublating sheer absence. It is distinct from properly 'determinate Being' because that has determinacy only in *its other*, I show below, so it is a moment of *difference* compared with the simplicity of Being-There.

If 'Nothingness' is to make itself *present*, it must be capable of determining itself to be-ing there, as a negative form of Hegel's onto-logic, an *empty presence*. *What* is there? *Nothing* is there. But Nothing *is there* all the same, that is, as Nothingness.

'Nothing' is an immediacy, which as *present* is equally Being as an immediacy. Their unity, an absence yet present, is Nothingness. It is an indeterminate Being, as when people say that they feel a (ghostly) Presence, without being able to say *what* is there. This becoming present of Nothingness is to be grounded in the further dialectical development.

The derivation of these categories is shown in the columns of the following Table.

Dialectic of Being-in-Exchange

as Absence	as Presence	as Presence of Absence
Nothing ⇌	Being ⇒	Nothingness

---

[2] 'Presence' is the first translation of *Dasein* in *Cassell's Dictionary*.

Nothing-ness is what *is present*; if it is the presence of an absence, it is yet the *becoming* of this presence, hence a 'presencing', in the sense of presenting. Nothingness is what is to be made present, or better: what *makes itself present*. Without such a positing the purely formal difference of Nothing and Being would collapse.

If Being is to be determinately present, and there is no *range* of determinables within which to establish a contrast, it can only be characterised as *pure* determinateness, a 'there-ness', *an empty presence devoid of all body*. As empty presence there is nothing to it; it is a *spectre*. Moreover, as an empty presence it cannot be fixed, but is simply the movement of ever *becoming* present; for it is unable to gain the metaphysical fixity of permanent presence. Nothingness makes itself present only as a permanent becoming, a shape of negative Being that builds a universe to inhabit. The economic forms appear positive but are in effect determinations of Nothingness making itself present in their shape.
Remark: This incipient ruling power is initially determined as a negative being in a very similar way to the characterisation of God as purely negative in negative theology.

The fundamental category is 'being present in exchange'; so what is present may be termed 'Being-in-exchange'. How is this to be further determined? If all the bodily characteristics of the commodity are absented through exchange, then it seems this leaves the 'Being-in-exchange' void of any determinacy whatsoever; yet, as posited, it is *there*.

This determinacy is achieved when it is determined in relation to its identical other. Without this dialectic of presence to another it has no 'standing', no ground to stand on. So its determinacy is granted simply when it is present to another. Nothingness cannot have presence purely abstractly, it must be posited, *made* present, which is achieved only when it is present to another such identical presence. The duplication of not-not-nothing collapses into itself unless it is refigured in the dialectic of 'Being-for-other' as other than its other. The not-not-nothing is unfolded into a relatedness of the said nothings.

In our case the pure form of relatedness is exchangeableness. (This grounds presence, and retroactively calms the wavering of 'Being' and 'Nothing'.) In Hegel's logic the movement of *thought* develops the category of 'determinateness'. However, if it is the movement of *exchange* which makes Being-in-exchange *present*, then that Being does after all have a relevant determination, namely the bare *quality* of '*exchangeableness*', which anything appearing in exchange has.

§11.2   Exchangeableness

If Being-in-exchange is not to be a function of external determinants but to be intrinsic to the commodity then it must be determined as in itself exchangeable. Nothing determinate is present *in* the commodity at this level of the dialectical presentation, yet there is *something* there, characterised by exchangeableness. (Later I distinguish from this 'exchangeability', which gives it a measurable sense: see §12.)

Being *determinate* requires the moments 'quality', 'quantity', and 'measure'. We began with the most immediate: to be what it is requires that something has a qualitative character; without such a quality it would not exist. The *operation* on the commodity is fixed as a *result* in this determinate quality of exchangeableness. This is its determinate being, albeit ungrounded as yet in the presentation. Since the movement here is not that of logical thought but the practice of exchange, what is homologous with the logical category of determinacy is here exchangeableness, because that is the fundamental determination which is presupposed of the being that is present in exchange as it stands opposed to its use-value character.

My dialectic does not enter *into* the commodity to find a ground for exchangeableness; rather I go *out* from it to the development of the value form to money and to capital, in order to show that in its logic value is *self-grounded*. The real being of the commodity is emptied of its own soul and becomes the *shell* of the fulfilled power of Nothingness making itself present.

Having said that, the issue arises: why this needless detour through Nothingness? Is it not observable at the outset that commodities combine usefulness and exchangeableness? The point is that I show that the *form* of exchangeableness has no *given* origin in the commodity itself; hence I avoid the fruitless discussion as to whether it is because a commodity is useful, scarce, or consists of 'embodied labour'. What has been gained through this presentation is that, in its *origin*, a purely social form is attributed to the commodity in and through exchange.

At this stage there is no reply to the objection that the commodity is not *in itself* exchangeable, because it appears in exchange solely because the *exchangers decide* to make an exchange. Thus to attribute exchangeableness *to the commodity* may be a hypostatisation. Indeed it is! That the dialectic of the value form vindicates its objectivity I shall show. I will show how this 'spectre' makes itself a real power in the world. Initially this world is that of exchange, and the further development of the dialectic will show how value might be grounded *in exchange itself* (rather than the peculiar concerns of the exchangers). Only at that point is the spectre conceivable as *making itself present*, rather than merely haunting a fetish form of consciousness.

I identify determinate being specifically with 'exchangeableness'. But how can *any* determination attach to Nothingness? There surely has to be *something* to *be* determinate. However, this is possible if determinateness is understood as *pure form*; this does not *attach* to the commodity but *inscribes* the commodity within the form.

Remark: It shares with Hegel's 'determinate being' the *purity* of form in that no content is yet adduced. Because the value form in its purity is devoid of content its analysis presents the greatest difficulty for our exposition. Nonetheless the logic of form must be thoroughly articulated before the material inscribed in the form is considered.

Commodities are distinguished from being goods in general by the *quality* of being exchangeable. (The denotation of the category is of course historically variable. Water was once a free good; now it is an expensive commodity.) Everything exchanged shares this quality. If that which is *there* becomes determinate in the space of exchange, to *be so determinate* requires it to be Being-for-another. So we now make a transition to the category 'something and other' because the something defines its quality only in opposition to some other quality which determines the first in and through the limit marking them off. Everything is what it is *because* it is *not* another thing. The 'something' is now determined through another, such that it is other than its other. In being-for-other, being present gains qualitative determinacy

But recall the Being-in-exchange is mere Nothingness. How can Nothingness generate a negative relation to something other when there is nothing about it to negate? How can such empty presence achieve any determinacy at all? The only such negation is hence otherness *as such*. The exchangeableness of something is vindicated simply in its opposition to some other equally so characterised. It *does* exist as determinate because of the simple fact that it is determined as what it is by its relation to another in exchange. Thus for this determination to have any meaning requires a dialectic of 'something and other', for something gains exchangeableness only if there is some other something with which it may *be* exchangeable. Since, in our case the constitutive movement is not that of thought but of *exchange*, the *relation of something and other* is present in the form of the *exchangeableness* of one commodity with another. (Although neither commodity has as yet been determined in such a way as would refer this imputation to something in it, which would account for it, nonetheless, as pure form its claim to reality is presupposed in practice.)

What something *determinate* faces is but another opposed something, characterised as sheer otherness, something that exists as being-for-another not merely being-in-itself. The latter is an empty abstraction. This otherness determines something by giving it a limit, a restriction. Yet, if so, the something thus determined by another has its 'being' within the limit that posits it as other than the other. *Something* determines itself in opposition to its other; something passes *into* its other through this relation of opposition; hence refers to *itself* in its other.

How does this dialectic apply to the commodity? How does something prove that it has exchangeableness? This requires the commodity to have others against which it may exchange. It is only insofar as a commodity is translated into a second commodity that its exchangeableness is demonstrated. But that this exchangeableness has yet been retained, and not dissipated in its realisation, is shown if the second commodity in turn is exchangeable against a third commodity, and so on. But defining a commodity in relation to another seems to generate an infinite regress. If one defines itself in relation to another, and this other in turn to yet a third, there is no stopping the endless regression. Every putative commodity validates itself in still another, endlessly, generating a *spurious infinity*. But a *genuine infinity* is posited when the other commodities are grasped only as complementary forms of the first in a closed system in which all commodities refer back to each other.

In sum, in the domain of the exchange form:
1) A commodity may be characterised as exchangeable only with reference to another distinct from it because exchange is a two-place relation.
2) A commodity proves its exchangeableness only when passing into this other.
3) A commodity is what it is, as exchangeable, only by reference back from the other in which it 'sees' itself. When the exchangeableness of a commodity manifests itself, it is translated into another commodity; therewith the truth of the commodity is determined as excluded from itself and posited as the second commodity; then, if the second commodity defines itself as the other of *its* other, it is brought back to the original commodity.

The commodity returns to itself having been presented *in* its other, but it is one and the same in both cases. Thus the commodity gains '*being-for-self*'. Every commodity is now characterised as in itself an 'exchangeable', and all commodities are systematically posited as *exchangeables*. (But, as yet, it is merely a presupposition that this genuine infinity is grounded in an intrinsic quality.)

§ 11.3   An Exchangeable

The commodity gains its 'being-for-itself' in this form, as an exchangeable. How is this category justified? When exchange 'absents' the use-value rooted in the material body of the commodity it does so by asserting that all commodities are identical as exchangeables, but, since this last is *not* a property inherent as such to commodities, rather one which is imposed on them, to hypostatise it, as if it were, is to posit some *imputed* universal – whether property or substance – already present within the realm of use-value; but there is no such commonality. *Only the very fact of being exchanged unites the commodities generically.* Since the range of exchangeables is unlimited, to characterise anything thus is not to pick out something belonging to the nature of the object but a reference to the operation on it. In fine, exchange does not flow from an *inherent* power of exchange *in the commodities* as such. Rather, the operation of gathering them into the class of exchangeables reflects itself into them.

Remark: But why is it not merely a metonymic figure? Why should we go beyond the relation of exchange to the presumption that the very Being of a commodity is to be exchangeable? At this level of the dialectic this objection cannot be refuted; as always in our presentation the leap to a new category has to be retroactively justified in the sequel in which the form proves itself to be objectively active. The problem here seems especially acute because we said at the start that a commodity is not exchangeable as such but only in relation to another; nonetheless we are now saying there is something about it that is already present before it enters into such relations and proves itself in and through its participation in them. We claim the commodity doesn't just *have* exchangeableness in such relations; it *is* an exchangeable, but this has yet to be *grounded*.

Moreover, the 'being-for-self' thus developed is problematic. It is 'one' which *excludes* other ones, the *many*, yet it is not distinguishable from them; in their mutual definition they are all one and the same, having no inner specificity. Their separateness is sustained therefore only by continual '*repulsion*' of one another, a process of reciprocal '*excluding*'.

The 'one' determines its being through the negative relation to other such ones, the 'many', yet its identity *with* its others necessarily connects it indissolubly *to* its others; this relation is a force of '*attraction*'. In the same way, because there is no difference between the commodities as exchangeable with one another, and all commodities are posited on this basis simply as identical bodies, this relation implies such 'attraction'. Thus the distinction here is wholly abstract, just *numerical difference*. (If two things are identical in all respects they may be said to be the same thing. However, if they are nonetheless countable as two, they are said to be 'numerically different'.)

Thus, as indiscernibles, on either side of the relation the same 'exchangeable' appears twice, but in virtue of the repulsion characteristic of a polar relation they are different 'exchangeables'. For 'repulsion' exists if they have numerically different bearers, in different commodities, even if they are posited as identical as such. This is at the same time a relation of 'attraction' between items lacking in distinction. An exchangeable commodity is valid only through another (attraction). But for them to be distinct exchangeables the requirement of numerical difference must be sustained (repulsion). However, while the exchange relation identifies the sides as substitutable, its polarity preserves the moment of repulsion at the same time. So here the dialectic of repulsion and attraction realises one commodity in another very abstractly, not another of *different* quality (except in use-value of course) but simply another identical to the first.

The category 'quality of a commodity' initially refers to the observation that everything appearing in exchange is characterisable as possessing exchangeableness. However, this is the *pure* category; there is also the more *determinate* category in which quality exists only in the *contrast* between one quality and another, and defines itself in opposition to another. The more *determinate* notion of quality is that for something to be present requires its being for another; this means that the determination of 'quality' requires its being limited by some other quality distinct from it. Now in our case, there is *no* such further determinacy to exchangeableness. The other which defines exchangeableness is simply itself, that is to say, the presence of exchangeableness requires its actual *doubling* such that it has its necessary referent in another, not in something qualitatively different in some respect but simply in otherness as such. A commodity is a commodity only because there are others that share the quality of exchangeableness.

The consideration there are many such exchangeables demands an investigation of quantity, as such, complementing the qualitative side. However, in our treatment, we must notice that ours is a very special case. Since there is no further determination of exchangeableness in a qualitative sense, i.e. there are no *kinds* of exchangeableness to be related, the *only* further determination is quantitative.

So it is not that commodities happen to come in quantities, it is of their very definition that they are only present as standing in quantitative relations. Here we simply note that the difference between commodities offered for exchange is not qualitative but quantitative (once all use-value considerations are set aside). The limit between them as different exchangeables is a pure notional limit as such: six apples are other than eight apples. But *as commodities* apples do not differ from oranges. That is merely a material difference of products or of use-value. (I underline that 'quality' is here strictly a category of *the value form*, it does not pertain to the variety of use.)

The many can be treated as ones because they are the same, indifferent to their number. Their unity is achieved as '*totality*'. The category of totality is not Hegel's term for this synthetical moment, but it seems to be the logical unity of one and many (as in Kant). However, it should also be noted that, here, this is not a fully-fledged totality centred on itself but simply a network of presupposing elements, what Hegel in other contexts terms a 'relative totality'. This depends on the coexistence of 'repulsion' and 'attraction' to hold the totality together.

The category of 'totality' will be posited more concretely with the doubling of the commodity into commodities and money; then the commodities both repel money from themselves so as to establish a universal equivalent and yet at the same time achieve an adequate expression of their unity only insofar as money is their common centre of attraction. Together, determined as 'one One', so to speak, *by money*, they constitute a totality.

The commodity is now established as 'one' among 'many'. But *the many*, determined *as a whole*, raise the question: how many make it up? But it does not matter! Since they are all identical as exchangeables, their quality of exchangeableness does not change into another quality no matter how many commodities are in play in this network. This means quantity is a determination 'external' to quality.

§12   *Quantity*
The last category of Quality is that of (relative) totality, the unity of one and many in that it is the many considered as one. Reduced to immediacy this gives Quantity. If its unity takes precedence this is continuous quantity; if plurality takes precedence this is discrete quantity. In the logic of quantity we begin with 'pure quantity', which may be glossed as 'infinite unity'. Then we continue with 'quantum', and finally a 'ratio' of quanta.
Remark: Throughout, we shall find that the category 'quantity' is a central determination of value, since the latter is primarily developed in quantitative relations rather than qualitative discriminations. The prevalence of quantitative determinations arises because there are no qualitative determinations of value. (This peculiar feature of the dialectic of the value form is not shared with Hegel's logic.)

§12.1   Infinite Unity of All Exchangeables
Immediately, the totality exists in itself as *pure quantity*. The quality of exchangeableness does not change into another quality no matter how many commodities are in play in this network. So there is an infinite unity of all exchangeables, for the quantity of exchangeables has no inherent limit. Every exchangeable relates to putatively infinite others. Only when it is determined to finitude does it require a *limit* so as to make possible *determinate* exchange relations.

§12.2 Number of Commodities to Be Exchanged in a Transaction

The infinite unity of all exchangeables is a pure quantity, but for exchange to occur quantity must appear in *delimited* form, as 'Quantum'. The *quality* of exchangeableness requires *quantitative* determination. The good has to take on a determinate shape, and has to specify itself in discrete units, each of which announces itself as an instantiation in *delimited* form of the good concerned. Only thus is a commodity *specifiable* as an item for exchange.

§12.21 Unit

There is a certain ambiguity here because such a determination may take shape differently according to whether it is discrete, or continuous. In the case of discreteness, the basic unit of quantum is 'one'. In order to be exchangeable a commodity must be capable of appearing as an *item* offered for exchange. In the case of continuousness, the unit is an arbitrary division, such as pounds of butter. However, normally this appears as an item such as a pre-weighed, pre-wrapped, pound of butter. So here 'amount' is taken to be a matter of 'how many?' rather than 'how much?'

Moreover, every One in the totality has to be determined as an exchangeable item, because it is as an exchangeable that the commodity achieves its 'being-for-itself'. Indeterminate bundles of stuff could exchange, but it is presupposed here that this universe of exchange is orderly.

So, the many, considered as determinate, consists of discrete 'ones'. Every 'one' has to be determined as an exchangeable item if exchange is to be possible. It is not enough for the commodities to be specified as having properties that make them exchangeable in a general indeterminate sense; a determination is required that allows for discrete exchangeables to be presented for exchange. A baker has to specify such a *unit* as 'a one-pound loaf' for example. Only thus does exchange become determinate.

Remark: This abstract identity of the commodity exchanging is conventionally reflected in the material concerned; thus every bag of apples offered for sale at the same price is assumed the same as all the others, but yet the buyer must beware. Identity in price does not imply a lack of difference in use-value, which may vary within the parameters specified, here 'a bag'.

§12.22 Amount

We have now established the commodity as 'one' among 'many'. But 'many' can be exchanged as if they are 'one'. As pure quantities, hence in that logical sense subject to mutual attraction, two instances of a certain commodity may be merged into one bundle; hence, as an *amount* of that commodity. The many collapse to one because of such attraction; hence the exchangeable 'item' can be extended to an amount of such items, treated as effectively one item, treated as itself One in the offer of exchange. A commodity must be delimited as an exchangeable, for instance 'a loaf', to be an example of a commodity, yet this limit is equally sublated since any *amount*, for instance of 'loaves', may be taken as together exchangeable since, if one is, all the many identical ones taken together are too.

The commodities, then, take determinate shape as a limited quantity, here concretised as unit and amount. Assuming 'amount' pertains to a discrete magnitude their unity yields the category of a *number* of units.

§ 12.23   *Number*

'Amount' therefore gains further determinacy as *Number*. An exchangeable gains determinacy in a *delimited* number of items, offered as a block, so as to shift many units as one, such as three pairs of socks. So commodities must be countable items. A baker does not sell 'bread' but a number of loaves of such and such a weight. Because it is rare for commodities to be exchangeable one for one, allowance has to be made for the commodities related to be numerous for a number of units of one commodity to exchange against another number of units of another commodity.

The striking thing about this quantification is that, although each of two goods exchanged has its own *conventional* index of magnitude (weight or whatever) in terms of which haggling goes on, these commodities seem unable to refer to any *common* index of exchangeableness because, *ex hypothesi*, as very diverse goods, their index of amount differs absolutely (moreover, it cannot be a physical dimension in any case; no one would exchange two pounds of gold for two pounds of iron).

The contradiction is that the bodily properties that give all commodities their material quantity are too peculiar to them to form the basis of a common measure; yet in a bargain a pure quantitative relation is fixed in spite of such absolute difference. Incommensurable as material bodies, the commodities are bargained over in the abstract, where the haggling is in terms of pure quantitative variation. Hence the quantity exchanged is a *pure* number, and yields a *ratio* of such numbers: 'I will give you six of these for four of those' is the quantitative form of the offer for exchange.

§ 12.3   Ratio of Exchange

Brought into unity with itself in this practical way, as self-related, 'number' passes over into *ratio*. Thus in our case, the number of units of one commodity, with respect to the number of units of another commodity, is the quantitative bearing on one exchangeable of another. Related to itself in such a ratio, the being-for-itself of quantity is achieved, in that the ratio is the manner in which a quantum relates to itself having passed through the other related quantum.

Such a ratio of quanta, as the being-for-itself of quantity, implicitly reinstates quality when it is independent of the different magnitude of its terms. The units of the commodities on each side are incommensurable since they remain as yet conventionally determined by convenient divisions of their material dimensions such as yards of linen, etc. There is no meaning here to the claim that both magnitudes must be magnitudes *of* a shared dimension, still less of a shared substance.

Nonetheless the key point about this is that the ratio subsists in abstraction from the specific units involved. So, in this way, if a ratio of exchange exists, it will be given in terms of bodily amounts, for example yards of linen, bushels of corn, but the incommensurability of these units does not affect the presupposition there exists a quantitative relation of exchange between commodities with respect to their proportionate exchangeability (even if this is nonsense in use-value terms, e.g. one fridge exchanges against half-a-car).

The next step is to make a transition from the category of ratio to that of 'measure'. In our case this is exchange-value.

§13   Exchange-Value

The form of exchange-value follows the logic of Specifying Measure, divided into: §13.1 Rule of Pro-rata Exchange; §13.2 Series of Measure Relations; §13.3 Infinite Unity of Measure Relations.

§13.1   Rule of Pro-rata Exchange

The transition from quantitative ratio is first to the category of 'rule'. There is simply an abstract notion of ratio developed above. But when a ratio remains the same no matter that the sides are proportionately multiplied, we have a quantity that retains its identity, or quality, regardless of this 'external' variation in the quanta so related. In rule the implicitly qualitative character of measure is made explicit in that a given term keeps its relation to its other *stable*, in that it follows the principle of proportionality. When there is the reiterated identity of its quotient, the terms of the ratio are regulated by rule because increase (or decrease) in a given number is always matched proportionately by an increase or a decrease in the other number.

In this case, if there is a stable *rate of exchange* that one commodity has against another, then a *rule* is operating. The key point about pro-rata exchange is that the ratio abstracts from the number of specific items involved. If, in this rate of exchange, two of A exchange against three of B, and four of A against six of B, then it is clear that a rule is followed.

How is this rule both quantitative and qualitative? If the same ratio can be multiplied up endlessly, in a sense it is a more determinate version of a notion of pure quantity. But the quantitative is still 'external' to the quality in that the actual numbers may vary on every occasion as long as the ratio conforms to the rate of exchange. At the same time the ratio can also be given in terms of a discrete item in the series, as has to be the case when a rate of exchange is concretised in a specific bargain. The category of 'quality' is again found here because the unity of the two sides of the rate of exchange gives the identity of self and other characteristic of the final category of quality, namely *being-for-itself*. I am not speaking here of the abstract identity of a ratio *with itself*, but of the rule by which one commodity passes into another in accordance with it.

Considered as a result, such passing over of the one to the other gives it a measure of its exchangeability: what it 'amounts to', so to speak, is specified in something other than itself. (Recall that I distinguish the quantitative notion of 'exchangeability' from the qualitative one of 'exchangeableness'.) As to these sides, notice that neither side is self-subsistent; each becomes determinate not in itself but only by external reference to another which determines what it amounts to, namely measures it.

The existence of pro-rata exchange is grounded if every commodity has 'exchangeability'. This form is determined as a pure form, indifferent to its bearers, but determining the exchange relation of each commodity with others. As quantitative this is a 'measure'. The measure of exchangeability of a commodity is defined here as its 'exchange-value'. This exchange-value of a certain commodity is different from that established according to other rules, or in relation to other commodities. Each rule has its own quality in this sense. It follows a different ratio than others but varying within itself in endlessly multiplied quanta as we have said. Exchange-value is necessarily given in a *specific* commodity. However, the rate of exchange taken by a commodity differs for every commodity related to the given commodity. So a commodity has many such exchange-values, so many measures, yielding a *series of specifying measures* given in qualitatively different ways.

Remark: Later (§ 23.31/3 and § 23.32/1) we shall show that money is the proper value measure, and hence that it is the real measure of commodities' 'value', concretising value in exchange. But I use it only at the level of Essence, because I presuppose to it the value category of 'immanent magnitude'. Here, then, I am concerned only with 'specifying measure', namely the elementary form of exchange-value.

The commodities set in the ratio of exchange are therewith brought into a certain ideal 'space' with a certain ideal 'metric'. Note that, thus far, there is simply a ratio of numbers, but without it being possible to say of what there is a common magnitude.

To sum: goods entering the circuits of exchange become determined as commodities; their quality as exchangeables requires a complementary quantitative dimension if bargains are to be struck; exchangeable commodities can only actualise themselves through a bargain in quantitative form. Conversely, the quantitative ratio practically uniting them in the bargain actualises their common character as exchangeables. The ratios of such quantities given in exchange is thus implicitly a *measure of exchangeability*, i.e. their value in exchange.

§ 13.2   Series of Exchange-Values

If we have a number of units of a commodity to be 'shifted' (to use the vernacular), and this quantity exchangeable with a number of units of another commodity, where these different units are in bodily terms incommensurable, but where, nevertheless, a relation of such quantities is established, there is a rate of exchange. If this remains the same when the numbers are raised proportionately, we have a *rule* of pro-rata exchange.

Now, since numerous commodities may relate in this way to one, the latter has a *series* of specific measures, of exchange-values, given in each other commodity in turn, which are co-existent. But there are as many such exchange-values as there are commodities capable of exchanging against a given commodity; this indefinite *series* of measures cannot here be measuring different qualities of the commodity because it has only one, namely exchangeableness; this itself is quantitatively determined as *exchangeability*. Thus if a genuine 'measurable' is to be posited it must exist in a form that is *indifferent* to the measuring rod by which it is measured, to all the specific exchange-values, which are all equivalents of one another as its measure. Yet, as such, they are in *unity*.

Remark: Why is Specifying Measure inadequate? A has measure specified in B, which itself, as in this very relation to A, has *its* measure specified in A. More broadly all commodities can be set as exchange-values of each other. But, if this *relative* totality of measure relations *seems* to determine them all as reflections of each other, equally they each, and all, *fail* to find a stable unit of measure, still less a *common* unit capable of ordering them. No self-subsistent form of measure is yet gained. One trick, resorted to by orthodox economics, is to give this decentred totality order by saying *we* (*nota bene*) may select one commodity to use as a measure of all the others; this is termed a numeraire. The crucial point here is that this is an external intervention by theory. The commodities themselves have not yet formed through their own movement their proper measure. (The money commodity is *not* a convenient numeraire, we shall see, but a practical *reality*.)

§ 13.3   Infinite Unity of Measure Relations

If a genuine 'measurable' is present it must exist in a form that is indifferent to all the specific exchange-values, which are all equivalents of one another as its measure. All these specific measures being valid, they are substitutable. So we reach the notion that there is some *unity* to them, that, although they are all different exchange-values of a commodity, they represent the same 'measurable' underpinning them, because exchangeableness is a unitary determination. So either there is some external contingency (e.g. preference schedules) producing them, or, all the exchange-values measure the *same* thing.

The different measures present various ways in which one commodity gains measure, specified in another, and another, and another, simultaneously; all the specific exchange-values possessed by a commodity form in truth a set.

Remark: In my presentation 'the series of specific measures' plays a role superficially similar to that of Hegel's 'nodal line of measures', in generating the transition to 'essence', so it is worth explaining our different strategies here. Hegel develops the category of the 'nodal line' from his consideration of the way in which quantitative changes in a thing eventually give rise to a qualitative change. Every new quality will have its own proper measure, it is assumed; hence successive such changes generate a nodal line of measures (whereas I just have brute qualitative difference of measures which in no sense therefore transit from one to another in an orderly way but simply *lie beside each other*). Hegel argues that these changing qualities have the same permanent *substratum*, indifferent to them, and to their measures. In this 'indifference' to measure Hegel sees 'the becoming of essence'. In our case I replace Hegel's diachronic line of measures with a synchronic series of measures in order to get to my own final term of the *unity of measure relations*.

When a commodity is considered quantitatively, namely in terms of its 'exchangeability', it has many measures, as its exchange-value is specifiable in terms of many qualitatively different other commodities. Moreover, the sheer externality of the measure means there is no preferred measure-giver; so all available commodities stand as measures; but this of itself means 'exchange-value' is not yet a totalising category, there is only sheer variance.

The presupposition that there underlies the series of exchange-values a totalising form is grounded if there is some common element in this series of measures, appearing phenomenally in various 'external' exchange-values: exchange-value as such, *indifferent* to all the specific 'measuring rods', so to speak.

Here at its introduction the category of 'measure' does not refer to the act of measuring something that *already* has a given magnitude which simply requires determining. (For such an act of measuring see below the section on 'substance': § 23.3.) So exchange-value as a relation is *constitutive* of the bringing of the commodity to the point at which it 'gains measure'. But this measure relation is not as yet reflected into itself such that the commodity is to be grasped as 'having a measure' *prior* to its expression in exchange-value.

Remark: We shall show that, as reflected into itself at the ontological level of Essence, the measurability of the commodity is finally secured only when it is related to a measure that *is* value in autonomous form, namely money. But such considerations belong to the categories of 'Essence', where I argue money is the real measure.

Here – at 'Being' – exchange-values, considered as a set of specifying measures, require grounding in the presence of something indifferent to any and all of them, namely value as essence. But such a form is yet to be posited. The various exchange-values are parametric equivalents, even though they are given in terms of incommensurable units, such as yards of linen, litres of wine, etc., because there is a quantitative identity of them in their unity even though there is yet no determinate algorithm generating them. They may be presupposed to represent a common metric although this is not yet posited.

However, in truth, as ideal in form, value has no determinate metric, but exists as *pure quantity*, which is measured virtually in terms of itself, not some external ruler. (But its monetary medium, say gold, we shall see, does provide a model of measure in a single metric, here ounces of gold.)

Although the unity of measures leads us to go beyond it to 'value as such', this presupposition is not secured, because the term 'exchange-value' may be simply a mental generalisation over what are disparate relations of commodities in practice. By abstraction from the set of specific measures I reach the notion of value as such. But the argument seems as yet *my abstraction*; I say that *if* there were a genuine unity to exchange-value then this points to immanent exchangeability as the essence of the commodity. But such a presupposed essence has to be shown as posited in *the movement of commodities themselves*.

Remark: Jumping immediately to the labour theory of value does not provide any measure because labours are heterogeneous and not immediately commensurable; certainly concrete labour has many dimensions: time, intensity, etc., while 'abstract labour' returns us to the same problem of finding the adequate measure. Moreover, nothing has yet been said about the *determination* of that magnitude by a theory of value. I am still here developing the categorial prolegomena to such a theory.

If the quantitative determination established in an exchange is not to be purely conjunctural, determined extrinsically in the contingencies motivating the agents bearing the goods to market (preference schedules, for example), it requires a dimension intrinsic to a commodity yet distinguishable from its appearance in commodities as immediately different. This dimension is such that, for each commodity, it obviously varies in proportion to its own index of amount; but it is itself, insofar as it has nothing to do with the variety of use-values, a unique quantitative determination, that is, *value-in-itself*.

If the unity of measure relations amounts to a *simple* indifferentness, this remains still at the level of Being because the measures here are merely external magnitudes. At best the unity is established only as a negative totality defined in *opposition* to the variety of measures. If this totalisation is effected simply by our thought, through an external reflection, we do not yet reach a new level of reality, namely essence. For this negative totality must result from the movement of the form itself, that *the negative itself* sets itself against the immediacies characteristic of being, and therewith posits itself as of the essence. Just as at the start exchangeableness makes itself present as pure form, so next we show that value makes itself the essence of commodities. Yet, although in this way value grounds exchange-values, it yet requires a grounding movement itself, through which it *makes itself* present. This is the burden of the next chapter.

Summary

The chapter confines itself to the 'Being' of the commodity, tracing its 'surface' forms, up to that of 'exchange-value', defined here as the measure of commodity exchangeability. To be a commodity requires the forms of quality, quantity, and measure, the latter being specified in the relation of one commodity to another. The starting point of the presentation of capital 'in its notion' is that the commodity as 'Being-in-exchange' is defined in opposition to all the bodily characteristics that support its potential uses; these are comprehensively 'absented'. But this negativity carried through in practice leaves an empty form. Nonetheless it gains a certain determinacy in its quality of 'exchangeableness', albeit there is nothing behind it. This quality is posited concretely in the relation of one commodity to another, in which it gains presence as the 'other of its other'. While there is nothing to distinguish them, the polarity of the relation secures their numerical difference. So the commodity, as 'an exchangeable', is now posited as one among many. The many taken in unity gives rise to the form of quantity, concretised as the number of items to be exchanged. If there is present a stable pro-rata ratio of exchange this is posited by the exchangeability of the commodity, which is given through this ratio a specific measure, or exchange-value. However, a commodity has as many putative exchange-values as there are other commodities. Thus there is present a series of co-existent such measures. This leads us to consider whether we may presuppose that, underlying them, is an *immanent* magnitude common to all of them. Such a distinction is one characteristic of the categories of 'Essence'. So, for the positing of such a presupposition the presentation must turn to that (in the next chapter).

CHAPTER 7

Money

Introduction

At the level of 'Being' the aim was to say what a commodity *is*, but if commodities are to subsist in an orderly universe then we must *presuppose* that, underlying them, there is something common to them, an *immanent* exchangeability. Exchangeability is a quality that necessarily has a quantitative determinacy. However, thus far it is here taken without considering how it achieves a definite magnitude in its own terms, but only in *contingent* exchange-values. The immanence of exchangeability takes the set of exchange-values as distinct specifications of it. (With the move to essence we have in effect a *doubling* of reality, ultimately to be registered in the doubling of the commodity into commodities and money.) This requires the reflection of exchange-value into itself so as to ground it in an underlying 'value'. But, if 'essence' must appear in a law-like fashion if it is to validate itself, then the 'forms of appearance' of value must succeed in positing value itself. The *actuality* of value is finally posited only in the money form of value. I show that, not only is money its measure, but that money constitutes value as grounded on itself in an ideal social substance. This chapter has the following structure: § 21 Value as Immanent Exchangeability; § 22 Value as Appearance; § 23 Value as Actuality.

§ 21   *Value as Immanent Exchangeability*
Immanent exchangeability I term 'value' now we have made the transition to the category of 'essence', so that we can speak of value as the *essence* of the commodity. I now develop value as of the essence of the commodity and consider the forms in which it is made manifest. At the level of Essence the immediacies of Being themselves pass over to a sphere of relation and reflection; here Value-as-Essence defines itself in opposition to the immediacy of exchange-value, reducing the latter to mere *existence* as defined in opposition to *essence*.

Let us review how we determine value as 'essence'. I take the 'abstract equivalence' of the measures to result in 'indifferentness' to all categories of Being. Behind Being lies Essence. Thus it might be that value *as such* lies behind the set of exchange-values. *If* it were *presupposed* that value is the essence lurking within the shell of the commodity then it *would* appear in exchange-value. But such an assumption has to be vindicated in the further development of the presentation. Exchange-value is the *immediately given* presupposition of value in the first place. Whence this value? The worry here is that 'value' is *my* abstraction; so the movement of commodities *themselves* must show that value determines itself to be of the essence of commodity relations. I show that value results from the reflection of exchange-value into the commodity.

This is achieved in the following triad:

§ 21.1 Exchange-Value reflected into the commodity,

§ 21.2 Reflex-Determinations of Value (Identity, Difference, Contradiction),

§ 21.3 Value grounded on the value form.

§ 21.1   Exchange-Value Reflected into the Commodity

If exchange-value is reflected into the commodity to posit it as in essence value, equally such value must *show* that it is present. However, there is an inherent ambiguity of the term 'show'. On the one hand it has a positive sense in such phrases as 'showing forth'. Yet it has a negative sense in 'make a show' of something. Both these are relevant, when immanent exchangeability both shows itself, and at the same time opposes itself to what is a mere semblance of the truth that resides 'behind the scenes' of the show, so to speak.

If it is presupposed that the commodity has something essential about it, then it has value *in itself* distinct from the relativity of exchange-value. But, when I presuppose that the commodity has an essence, initially the *distance* between essence and appearance appears unbridgeable because we took unity of measure to be *indifferent* to the contingent specifying measures. Although they are analytically presupposed, value is to be taken *apart* from them. Hence there seems no true unity of the two sides of the relation. So it seems that value is to be deemed *essential* and exchange-value thus inessential, a mere *semblance* of value, subject to extraneous influences, whereas value as such is the truth abiding within the shell of the commodity. Value posits itself *against* exchange-value, as it were. But for value to be counterposed to its presuppositions in this way neglects the fact that, at the same time, it has its real being precisely *in* them, that the sides *reflect* each other.

The development of the category of reflection is as follows:

§ 21.11 positing reflection; § 21.12 external reflection; § 21.13 determining reflection.

In 'positing reflection' essence and appearance presuppose each other; in 'external reflection' the value essence is taken as given, but it lacks immanent determination; in 'determining reflection' the supposed immanence of value makes itself explicit through its own movement.

§ 21.11 Positing Reflection

Essence posits itself immediately against what is inessential and in this way posits itself. Positing reflection is self-relating negativity in that essence is defined against the inessential semblance as *not* that immediacy. But, if essence is to be real, it must make itself manifest in *existence*. It requires the mediation of that immediacy from which it is reflected. Thus value, and exchange-value, simultaneously constitute one another as their opposing term, and undermine themselves insofar as each term has to presuppose the other's truth without good reason for doing so. Neither side can make itself the ground of the relation.

Let us consider the argument in more detail. When Being is reflected into itself to constitute an essence for itself, and Essence in turn shows itself in Being, this movement amounts to a new 'Becoming'. This absolute negativity is the constitutive moment. It is a positing movement wherewith one side of the commodity posits the other as its truth; something has founded itself on something else; both, though, belong to the same thing; there is here self-relation in this reflective movement.

The immanence of value implies an opposite, a surface being, *against* which value determines itself as essential, at first therefore as contrasted with what is inessential to it (contingent exchange-values). But something is essential only if it is *self*-mediated and thus contains its other within it. Yet what is distinct from essence, as other than it, has its own identity and immediacy. Hence the sphere of essence is – here and throughout – a still imperfect connection of *immediacy and mediation*.

The dialectic of such reflection is a hall of mirrors in which value itself is never fixed. If it is presupposed that exchange-values are valid then they express value-in-itself. But if exchange-value is *nothing* without value-as-essence, and yet value-as-essence is *nothing* but what appears as exchange-value, there results an oscillation from nothing to nothing. Each reflects the other but, from a logical point of view, it is the reflective movement of nothingness to nothingness, and back. The relation falls to the ground unless value-as-essence is itself posited distinctly from value-as-appearance.

In one sense the oscillation is conformable with our presentation of value as pure form developing itself from an empty presence. Given the wavering between the essential and the inessential, it is never clear which side of the value relation may legitimately be presupposed without waiting to be posited by what it itself presupposes. So the question arises as to whether we can find a form in which the mutual presupposing of value and exchange-value may be posited by fixing value as essence, i.e. making real a form of immanent exchangeability.

§ 21.12   External Reflection

If *we* suppose that there *is* such a value *essence* then it is unproblematic to say that it *exists* only if it reflects itself through exchange-value. However, if this positing arises simply from an *external reflection* on the set of exchange-values, which yields value in *abstraction* from it, this reduction means value-as-*essence* has not yet, in *its* movement, posited itself as of the essence. What is required, then, is that *value itself* posits exchange-value as its presupposition and, therewith, posits itself. We require a '*determining reflection*'.

§ 21.13   Determining Reflection

Initially it seems that exchange-value is *presupposed* as a valid form, and value is taken as what must underlie it, if it is to be more than semblance, thus *posited* as the exchange-value manifesting the commodity's intrinsic value. The unity of positing and external reflection is determining reflection in which something gives itself reality through its own activity of positing its presupposition as immediacy, thus ensuring it is mediated *within their very relation*. Determining reflection combines two opposed moments. In one the essential does not go outside itself because what is posited only refers back to essence; the posited is the inessential against which essence defines itself negatively; in the other moment, what is posited is reflected within itself, defined by, but not reduced to, its origin, for it must be *distinct* to be real.

Below, exchange-value is shown to be a *moment* of value. *As such*, it is not the mere semblance of value, but the immediate reality facing exchangers. To be sure, they may consider that the prevailing rate of exchange is all that value amounts to; they do not see exchange-value as the appearance of an underlying value. But equally wrong is to view exchange-value as an insubstantial veil of the underlying value; for essence *must appear*. This is true, even though the appearance of appearance necessarily has the form of immediate reality.

§ 21.2   Reflex-Determinations of Value

If value-in-itself underpins the superficial ratios of exchange such that the exchange-value measures are posited, this presupposition requires the commodity to reflect its exchange-values into itself. At the most abstract level, that of pure positing reflection, this is a movement of absolute negativity, from nothing to nothing and back again. The commodity defines its value, only through positing that its value *is* not what it is not (exchange-value), an essence that is purely empty. If, however, it had some *determinate* value relation, such that what it is not is some determinate *other* commodity, then we may take its essence to be posited through such a *determining reflection* in which the commodity itself determines that which is to count as its appropriate expression.

In the movement of reflection upon itself the commodity must achieve *identity* with itself as value. Yet value is *other* than its immediate being as a material body. Thus value is not after all immediately identical with the commodity but is *different* from it. So this requires explicitly the mediating moment of being-different-from-itself when value is made manifest only in another commodity. There results therefore the *contradiction* that value is, and is not, found in the commodity. The *value form* in which one commodity expresses its value in another commodity gives the contradiction an ideal *ground* allowing coexistence of the moments, we shall show.

§ 21.3   The Value Form
In the form of value, the value that cannot be identified with the use-value of the commodity is presented in what is not the commodity, namely the 'opposite' commodity, excluded by the first commodity, albeit formally similar to it. The other commodity now *counts* as the bearer of the value of the first commodity. This is the *ground-form* of value as essence. Next to be developed are its determinations.
Remark Here I analyse the way the value of one commodity appears as the body of another. The possibility of such reflection of one in another requires the relation of *two* commodities. The very existence of such commodities is taken as *given* at the start. But this is a condition that is secured when capital produces these commodities. In general, our exposition of the capital system tries to determine how far capital can reproduce its material conditions of existence.

The commodity cannot *relate to itself* as a value but only as use-value; if the value gains its being in something else, not the commodity, then this other seems after all to be what is essentially value. In the logic, such a contradiction may *subsist* as such if it has a ground supporting it. A ground allows the thing to have both an affirmative and negative nature and exist as their unity. For us, the ground which allows the commodity to be determined as value in both affirmative and negative senses is thus the value form. The claim of a commodity to be value-in-itself is secured only in what it is not, namely another commodity standing over against it as its exchange-value. Because its identity with itself is wholly mediated in this contradictory manner this is a long way from value existing for itself. The value that the commodity cannot contain in itself it yet can affirm once it is reflected in another commodity, therewith there is posited the presupposition that the first is value-in-itself. So value exists here only in the value form, namely in the relation of value to itself allowed by it.
Remark: We digress to remark on the peculiar character of the dialectic of capital, which, it must be remembered, does not exist in identitarian thought but in *objective* relations. As we have expounded it, the difference of a commodity

from itself is given by reference to *another* commodity which is determined as the *bearer* of the value of the first commodity. *In itself* the original commodity remains a material body supporting its use-value character. However, use-value considerations proper appear later in our presentation.

In its very constitution value is *opposed* to the bodily shape sustaining use-value. However, in the value form, we find the value not found in the body of A is borne by that of B. Analytically the ideality of the commodity, and its materiality, are abstract opposites that fall apart. But, within the value form, which exists in the relation of commodity to commodity, instead of falling apart, the opposing determinations of the commodity are reflected against one another.

In the *simple* opposition of value to use-value, in which it is understood that, when considering the commodity as value, it is not considered as use-value, there is missed the subtlety characterising my own approach, in which value is *constituted* as the *not*-use-value. Given that this opposition is *constitutive* in character, it underpins the otherwise arbitrary claim that the second commodity, as not identical with the body of the first, is hence a body in which value is to be *affirmed*, whereas in the body of A the value exists only negatively, as what the body of the commodity is not.

For us value is from the start logically *opposed* to use-value while yet related to it, just because it is constituted in this infinitely negative relation to the material properties of the commodity. Thus value is only present in A as *absence* and it thus achieves positive *presence* in what it is related to as not-A, namely B. Value is affirmed in commodity B *just because* it is negated in A. The value form as a whole sublates the contradiction that the commodity is, and is not, value.

If the value of commodity A *is* B this determinacy allows value to be both not-A (i.e. its determinate negation) and yet appear as B. Commodity B is *materially* not A, yet, *affirmed* as the value of A, it is thereby *formally* posited as 'not-A'. But commodity A determined as not-B reflects 'not-A' into itself. There cannot obtain an *immediate* contradiction within commodity A, but in its relation to commodity B this richer form allows the contradiction to subsist; it gives it space to unfold. For now the value of commodity A, as not-not-A, is *posited* through this negation of the negation.

Although commodity B must be a specific commodity it is also true that no particular one is required. For all that is required here is a purely numerical difference from A, so *any* relevant commodity serves if it stands opposite commodity A in the value form. The actual commodity B is specific as a use-value but here this use-value has no bearing on the manifestation of the value of A, its specificity being purely notional.

MONEY   97

Remark: Although a being may be grounded on its essential nature, it may yet have other conditions of existence not part of that essence. If, however, such conditions of existence are brought *within* the totality that it is, then, while every element may be conditioned by every other, the whole is *unconditioned*. In effect this is true only of what is *actual*. However, when all such conditions obtain the thing has immediate existence. For us, at this level, the only condition of existence required is that there be two commodities in relation. We do not yet know what other conditions of existence value may require, nor even the origin of the said commodities.

§ 22 *Value as Appearance*

I showed that value-in-itself appears as value-for-itself, when the contradiction that value is and is not 'in' the commodity is sublated by allowing the value of a commodity to appear in another, as value 'for-itself', as well as 'in-itself'. Value, grounded in the value form, is present as a relatedness. In developing the dialectic of the value form I pass first to Value as Existent (§ 22.1). Following the completion of the triad of 'existence' with 'law of appearance', I thematise the 'world in itself' and the 'world of appearance', under which find their place the logic of the so-called 'forms of value', namely the *expression* of value in simple, expanded, and general, forms (§ 22.2). Finally we consider the correlation of these two worlds made manifest in the *unity* of the value form (§ 22.3).

§ 22.1 Value as Existent

In its ground-form, value subsists as a *relatedness* of one commodity to another. This immediacy is now reflected into itself, such that it is underpinned by the presupposition that it obtains because – just as immediately – value is *existent*.

The forms of existence of value are: § 22.11 value as a relational *property* of a '*thing*'; § 22.12 form and content; § 22.13 value as law-like.

§ 22.11 *Value as (Relational) Property of a 'Thing'*

Up to now we have been considering value as arising in the *relation* of two commodities. This is more securely grounded if the relation springs from something that *exists as value* such that the relation springs from a relational property of the existent, here nominated as generally as possible as 'thing'. This remains an immanent determinant, even if at the outset this is no more than a placeholder for a *determinate* existence of what *has* the property. However, we now presuppose that the form of value springs from a *relational property* (that is only *apparent in* its relations, of course). We thus posit value as what a 'thing' *has* (just as a coat keeps us warm because it is 'a warm coat'). But a property of what? – Not exactly of a commodity because its material properties are relevant only to use-value. Thus in our logic of pure form there is nothing to which such a property attaches other than value-in-itself.

The question addressed here is: what is it for value to *exist*? If we say there is an entity that *has* value, this leaves such a thing as a formless substrate. In truth, the latter is in effect non-existent; all that exists is the movement from value-in-itself to its appearance and back again. The thing that 'has' value is no-thing, simply value as a relation metonymically substantiated into its bearer; albeit the material commodity bears this designation. Value is its own substrate and this movement from value-in-itself to value-for-itself just is the structure that determines value as existent. There is an identity between the putative 'thing' and its putative 'property' in this reflection.

But how does form relate to what has this form? For value to relate to itself as such requires its *double-sidedness* as a form. It cannot exist as essentially value with no determinate relation to how it appears phenomenally. If the commodity is supposed to contain value-in-itself this cannot be posited as such if it has no determinate relation to how the thing-in-itself appears to other things.

If the relatedness of the value form is considered all-important then it might seem that to *form* belongs everything determinate, in contrast to the relative *indeterminacy* of that which *is* formed. The latter is so indeterminate it has no reality except that of putative *bearer* of its property. So if form is taken as the determining principle then this is what *makes* the commodity a value. What is left over from form is simply a *'thing-in-itself'* posited by form itself but in effect nugatory.

Moreover, since any determinacy of the form comes from the context of the commodity's interactions with others in apparently contingent ways, it seems there can be no *law* intrinsic to the commodity expressed in such relations. On the other hand form cannot be simply a contingent addition to the thing; it requires the form so that what is essentially value reflects itself therein, such that it appears to other commodities and for itself. Both moments are essential to the value form. We now explore further the developing relation of these sides to show how value gains *determinate existence*.

§ 22.12   *Form and Content*

If we take seriously the idea that the form of value has *something* of which it is the appropriate form then we might construe this element to be value as the *matter* of the form. But this gives form to *matter* in a purely external way (a verbal 'fix', so to speak). Matter is the *passive* side over against form as the *active* side. The form gives shape to something material but which is essentially alien to it. If a blackmailer sells his negatives we have one relationship – of power – taking shape as another – the commodity form. (Later we shall argue that such cases are significant economically when labour power and land take commodity form, without their being genuine commodities.)

If the *activity* of form translates itself to its matter, such that we have a unity in which what is formed is just as much determining as is the form, then the form becomes determining *through* its other, now become a *content*. The value content is such because it has implicitly its form as its essential complement.

The value form is explicitly active in determining the commodity as exchangeable against another commodity, but the value content is implicitly determining of what the commodity is *in itself*. But it is perfectly possible, because of the very character of form as the *external* shape of value, that the form be *empty*. Indeed there may be no value content at all. Thus, on the one hand, if the form *is* inwardly reflected, it *is* the content; on the other hand, as *not* reflected inwardly, it is an external existence that is indifferent to the content.

Another consequence of this uncertainty is that the mere commodity form of an object does not guarantee that the value contained is adequately expressed. Its expression may vary from value because of other determinations affecting its appearance. When form internalises itself as content adequate to it, and content perfectly appears as form then both sides are in effect formed as value, but as different moments of the *law* which expresses their correspondence.

Remark: This presupposition of the identity of form and content is not yet *posited*. This is accomplished only at the level of 'absolute relationship' (see § 23.32/3).

Note here that we are not dealing with the *original separation* between the ideality of the value form and the material content bearing it, and regulated by it, but with establishing the complementarity of value-as-form with value-as-content. This doublet, as such, still allows for the possibility of inessential form (e.g. a gingerbread man). In such a case the phenomenon is not determined as an *essential* existence, rooted in a law intrinsic to the thing, but is 'determined by another' (for example supply and demand).

§ 22.13   *Value as Law-like*

Law makes the existent *essential* existent instead of a mere combinatory of essence and existence. If value is to take the shape of a content adequate to its form, and content appear in the form proper to it, then this must be *posited*. Then both sides are formed as value but as different moments of it, wherewith the inner value is expressed in its *proper* form of appearance.

If law acts as a force, there is not just a contingent fit of form and content, but a *necessary correspondence*. Both sides are forms of value because they are fully unified in a law of their relation which informs them despite their distinction. Each, as it were, *contains* its other. An *adequate* relation of form and content allows value to appear in law-like fashion. But if there is *no* content, there is no such law, and value relations are subject to contingency; but the *possibility* of a mismatch, between form and what is formed, should not be generalised such that the value form is *necessarily* fathomless.

Remark: Note that reference to 'law' here does not mean any determinate principle is yet provided, merely that for the first time in the logical development of categories we speak of value as characterised by some sort of law-governed exhibition of itself without at present knowing what exactly governs this. What is at issue at this point of our presentation is simply the development of the *form of law*, as a requirement of the actuality of value, that the relation of content and form is law-like, but as yet without any determinacy – certainly without any knowledge of magnitudes. The point is simply that for value to be essential to the commodity there must be determinacy in the relation of content and form.

§ 22.2 The Forms of Appearance of Value

I showed earlier that value presented itself in the *relatedness* of a commodity to another. Thence I treated the determinate existence of value as a unity of content and form. More specifically I argued that for value to appear properly required a law-like relation obtains between them. So this is presupposed here. However, thus far, value-as-essence is not yet disentangled from the mutual positing of the two sides. It does not yet achieve *self*-groundedness. It is not present *for-itself* in a shape distinct from a 'property' attributed to every commodity when related to others. We shall next see that the actuality of value may be dialectically developed precisely from the form of value itself.

I now turn then to the forms of *appearance* of value. In the ordinary way there is nothing wrong with thinking of a unitary *essence* expressing itself in different *appearances*. The problem here is that *no* unitary essence is yet posited, although there needs to be if value is to be present in the manifold commodity relations.

Remark: This problem does not arise if one holds that immediately social labour time has already been *given* as this unitary essence; then quite naturally one reads the development of forms of value as realisations of this given *identity* in commodities, and there are *no* defects of form, because all forms are adequate expressions of value, and all that is required is to show how the money commodity emerges as a numeraire.

What is needed here is to identify value as the essence of commodities precisely in order for it to be posited as present in a context in which we appear to have pure relatedness of externally given commodities which share no inner essence. The lack of a *given* inner essence is here to be made good by the positing of *value as essence* in the dialectic of this relatedness itself. Since 'essence must appear' in order to exist at all, the development of the category of 'appearance' is not a *consequence* of essence but its *constitution along with essence itself*, as two worlds of value correlated with each other. We now develop the forms of appearance of value. We shall employ the dialectic of 'force and expression' in this.[1]

§ 22.21   *The Simple Form of Value*
At first sight it seems the simplest expression of value implicit in commodity-relations exhibits value adequately.[2]

> **Form I** *The Simple Form of Value*
> z of commodity A *expresses its value in* y of commodity B

In this elementary form of value, if value appears in accordance with its *law of appearance* then both related commodities take specific forms of value, such that the commodity in 'relative form' (A) expresses its value in its 'equivalent' (B). The commodity in relative form is the 'active' pole of the expression, because that is the commodity whose value is to manifest itself, and the commodity in equivalent form is the 'passive' pole, because it serves merely as the material shape of the value of A. It is important to notice that the commodity in equivalent form appears there not as a value (because *its* value is not being expressed) but simply in its bodily shape.

Because the first commodity plays an active role, and the second a passive one, it is impossible for the same commodity to play both roles at the same time. These forms rather *exclude* each other as polar opposites. This means that the alternative expression, 'The value of yB is zA', is materially opposed to 'The value of zA is yB', because in that case B is the active force that makes manifest its value. Both opposed expressions are abstractly possible; but once one commodity has taken the active role it cannot coherently be put as pass-

---

[1] See the *Commentary on Hegel* in Appendices for its source.
[2] It is unfortunate that Marx uses as an abbreviation the formula '*x of commodity A = y of commodity B*'. The problem here is that a *relation of equality* is reflexive and symmetrical. But the expression of value is neither reflexive nor symmetrical. And Marx knows this! In his discussion he explicitly denies the expression of value is reflexive and symmetrical. (For a thorough discussion of the logic of relations here see Arthur 2004.) Only much later in my exposition do I show that *prices* are reflexive, symmetrical, and transitive.

ive equivalent at the same time, because value needs a simple unitary way of expressing itself throughout the whole value space; in effect A and B would then be unstable disruptive forces in this field until one is fixed in relative and one in equivalent form.

Ideally value is determined in opposition to the heterogeneity of use-value. But value must *appear* if it is to have any actuality. Immediately a commodity appears as a use-value, but, because the value of a commodity is defined in *opposition* to its own use-value, it cannot appear therein. Paradoxically the claim that A is a value requires A to *exclude* this value from itself and to posit it as the body of B. Even if B is itself potentially a value, *its* value expression is as it were stifled at birth so that the body of commodity B figures as the actualisation of A's value.

It is not that commodity A has a *given* essence simply expressed in the equivalent but that value as essence *comes to be* in this expression, and is figured rather at the equivalent pole as what appears in the *shape* of B. The 'peculiarity' of the commodity in equivalent form is that its *sensuous* body counts as the phenomenal shape of a *supersensuous* world of value. So here the world of value predicates itself on use-value in inverse fashion. In essence value *is not-use-value* (of A); it is a *supersensuous realm*; but in its appearance it is a *sensuous reality*, the body of B.

The reason for the peculiarity of the equivalent form is that the body of B, as *not* that of A, *acts as* value because the value of A is *defined* as not-use-value-A. The value of A cannot be found in its own body. Turn and twist it as we may, value is not found in its sensuous body; if it has value at all it must be a supersensuous determination. But the supersensuous world of value absent in the body of A is made present in the sensuous body of the equivalent commodity. (However, the identity posited in this relation requires further grounding.)

The deficiency of the simple form is that in it a commodity is related only to one other, which means that value has not yet achieved the universality of its expression implied by the presupposition that, underlying the web of exchange relations, there is some force that regulates them, that the many exchange-values which a commodity may have nevertheless exist in a unity.

This 'accidental' expression of the value of A in B is therefore defective because it is not all-encompassing. Moreover there is nothing special about the commodity B that would grant it a rôle as a privileged interlocutor of A. One could have taken A's relation to C, or to D, under review, because A might just as well express its value in any other available commodity. B lacks the requisite comprehensiveness to present the world of value in autonomous form to A. There is equally possible the form: 'The value of x of A is expressed in z of C'. Similar expressions of the value of 'x of A' hold for all existent commodities.

§ 22.22 The Expanded Form of Value

Taking these other alternatives into account gives rise to the more comprehensive 'expanded form of value'.

Form II *The Expanded Form of Expression of Value*

z of commodity A *expresses its value in*
$\begin{cases} \text{y of commodity B} \\ or \text{ x of commodity C} \\ or \text{ w of commodity D} \\ or \text{ so on and so forth} \end{cases}$

At first sight it seems this expanded form presupposes that the value of A remains unaltered in magnitude, whether expressed in units of B, C, or D, or in innumerable other commodities. But this is not at all plain since all these commodity equivalents are incommensurable. Notice also that the connector here, significantly, is 'or', not 'and' (when reversed in the general form it will be 'and'). Why in the expansion of the simple form is it the connector 'or' which links the various equivalents? When expanded the simple form cannot result in a heterogeneous bundle of use-values because the parameters of the problem under consideration demand that the form of essence be unitary. Hence B, C, D, and so on, are *alternative* 'units' of value logically implicit in commodity relations. These are *alternative* ways to express the value of A. This expression is therefore deficient because of the inability of any one commodity to exclude the others from being value as essence. The lack of a unitary essence is a defect of this form. Of course, if value as essence were already given then the deficiency could be interpreted only as a lack of common measure. But such a common essence is not yet constituted.

§ 22.23 The General Form of Value

If the expanded form of value is *reversed* we therewith reach the *general form of value*, to wit, 'The value of B, and of C, and of D, and so on, expresses itself in A.' Notice that B, C, D, and so on are here linked with an 'and' not an 'or' (as in the expanded form), because B expressing its value in A does not exclude C from so doing. It is instructive to consider the meaning of this reversal more closely. To begin with let us distinguish two things that might be meant by reversal.

'Reversal' may mean that we move from the perspective of commodity A expressing its value in B to that of commodity B taking A as its equivalent, the two expressions being considered side by side, so to speak, as covering the same content but different formally in that the 'sense' of the expression runs in a different direction. Nothing significant is changed if a whole set of commodity A's equivalents is reversed such that A is the common point of reference.

Another meaning of 'reversal' takes it that what is reversed is the original expression of commodity A's value in its equivalents, such that this origin is *preserved* in the reversed expression, along with the positing 'activity' of commodity A. The two expressions are not side by side but dialectically determined as *related* through opposition, through *developing* the meaning of A's determination as value. I adopt this second point of view.

The significance of this dialectic of reversal is rooted in the asymmetry of the poles of the value expression. I take the activity of the commodity in relative form as expressing its value through exerting a force on its opposite. This dialectic of '*force and expression*' is powered by the contradiction that the force is supposed to *belong* to the thing just as it is, yet an unexpressed force is no force at all; however, to be expressed it requires its *solicitation* by other things. These others must themselves therefore be forces. While a force proves itself only in its expression, in its effect on something, the nature of the latter is the necessary complement of the force. Gravity attracts apples but not rainbows. The force requires 'solicitation' by that which suffers its effect. The first force and the soliciting force are therefore two moments of a whole relation and share a common content.

Just so, if commodity A expresses its value in a definite amount of commodity B, at the same time it is *enabled* by B to reflect on its nature as value. B solicits A to recognise it as the means whereby value may be realised. It follows that commodity A, just insofar as it posits commodity B as its own equivalent, conversely posits itself as the relevant referent of B's proper expression of itself; it presupposes it is the value equivalent of B. If all the commodities in equivalent form solicit a value expression of A in this way, this allows A to posit itself as *their unitary equivalent*. The dialectic moves from commodity A determining commodity B, C, D, etc. as the expression of value, because it cannot be found in the body of A, to commodity A determining *itself* as containing the value essence, when it reflects all the original alternative equivalents into itself. Abstracting out this reverse movement gives the general form of value. To remind ourselves, this is:

Form III *The General Form of Value*

$$\left. \begin{array}{l} y \text{ of commodity B} \\ and\ x \text{ of commodity C} \\ and\ w \text{ of commodity D} \\ and\ so\ on\ and\ so\ forth \end{array} \right\} \text{\textit{express their value in} } z \text{ of commodity A}$$

In this form the commodity A solicits all the *other* commodities to solicit *it* as their unitary form of value. Thus A, while now the *universal* equivalent, does not simply assume the rôle of *passive* equivalent, as it would do if we considered an *original* one-sided relation of B, C and D, to A. It preserves its active rôle because it *attracts* the other commodities to express their value in it as a *unitary* form. It determines itself thus as *essentially* value, becomes value-for-itself, rather than having merely implicit value as in its original position. So value not only must *appear*, when the value of commodity A appears as *what it is not*, namely commodity B; if it is to be *actual* it must appear as *what it is*, exchangeableness as such, and that is what is present in the universal equivalent.

Remark: For the sake of continuity with Marx's discussion I use the term 'universal equivalent'. This may appear out of place because I follow a strictly logical development of categories in which value as universal is to be discussed when I reach value as Concept. Strictly speaking, before that I should use the expression 'common'. However, the locution 'universal' may be justified here if we bear in mind that the term is used at the level of the doctrine of essence to mean no more than what a class of items have in common as opposed to their singularity, a way of speaking that is congruent with the level at which we are currently working.

As its reversal the general form is a more complex form than the expanded form, implicitly preserving it, more precisely dialectically sublating it. The defects formerly noticed (that the simple form is not general and the expanded form lacks unity) are overcome here because A is the unitary form of value of all commodities, their *universal equivalent*. As the outcome of the *dialectical* (not *formal*) reversal, A now *contains* in sublated form the opposition of relative form and equivalent form within itself, *actively* determining itself to the position of value in autonomous form, and attracting the other commodities to it accordingly. For the opposition of active and passive poles is itself sublated in the general form. Now there is *reciprocity of forces*.

It is not a question of different owners offering competing determinations of value such that 'the value of A is B' is countered by 'the value of B is A'. These different, indeed contrary, locations of the appearance of value cannot coexist within a consistently framed universe of value. The solution is that commodity A determines itself to the position of universal equivalent by a process of negation of negation (which differs from a flat contradiction). First value is located not in A but in B (i.e. *not-A*), then seen not in B but in *not-B* (i.e. in *not not-A*) i.e. A. Likewise this dialectical understanding of the form of value shows that the simple form and the expanded form are not false starts to be discarded once the general form is found; they are moments in the fully-developed form, sublated in it.

Originally the activity of the commodity A in *relative* form seems to generate the resulting peculiarity of the equivalent form; after the reversal of the expanded form, the general form allows commodity A now to be active as the universal *equivalent* form, and to posit *itself* as two worlds of value, reflecting value back to the generality of commodities just because it is itself value in a peculiarly immediate form.

The general form is an advance on the simple form in which the positing of the equivalent as value is the result of the activity of the commodity in relative form, hence not *self*-posited. With the general form, reached through the dialectic of force and expression, the original commodity A, now the universal equivalent, retains its active rôle in expressing itself through its relations to the other commodities, but now instead of positing them as its equivalents it posits itself as theirs; moreover, just as it is, so it counts as value *incarnate*. In no way should the general form be read as a set of simples, neglecting the logic of the reversal, because in the simple form the equivalent is *passive*, but the *universal* equivalent actively determines itself to the position of value in autonomous form.

The singularity of the universal equivalent *makes* commodities socially commensurate in a homogeneous value space for the first time. By this form, commodities are, for the *first* time, *really* brought into relation with each other as valuable.

The dialectic of the value form has now generated an important result. In the simple form the notion of the peculiar role played by the equivalent is already implicit, but it is still difficult to keep hold of the polarity of the expression. But now we see the expanded form and the general form are massively different in their practical implications. To reverse the expression alters its whole character. Before, it was A that endeavoured to express *its value* in *alternative* equivalent commodities: now the other commodities all express *their value* in a unitary form, namely in A. Other commodities are validated as value by it.

The peculiarity of the equivalent form is raised to a higher power in the universal equivalent form because it seems to *posit itself* as immediately value, as value-for-itself, a locus of intrinsic value. This gives it a 'fetish-character'. The fetish-character of the commodity is distinguished from 'the fetishism' of commodities, in the following way: a thing acquires a *fetish-character* when it has socially imputed to it a power it (really) has only as a consequence of its objective positing as such, but where the social determinations are hidden in the objectivity of the form; *fetishism* occurs when that power is taken in social consciousness as natural to it.[3]

---

3 Cf. Bellofiore 2014, p. 177.

The fetish-character of the commodity has 'objective validity'. The gold fetish is a very clear example. But what is decisive here is the ideality of the form not the particular material that is posited as the bearer of the form by the relations within which it is inscribed. Yet the role of gold as value in autonomous form is objectively posited and therewith effectively functions as such because it bears this *form-determination*. This fetish-character becomes outright fetishism when gold is taken to be by nature uniquely valuable.

In origin, developed from the simple form, the universal equivalent is a mediated immediacy; but the mediations giving rise to it vanish. Taken equally immediately by social consciousness, gold, just as it is, seems immediately given as inherently valuable. Such a naturalisation of a *socially* constituted objectivity is full blown fetishism. Notice the other commodities are not so fetishised in consciousness because everyone knows commodities need to prove themselves valuable by their ability to draw money in exchange. But, insofar as this occurs, and they bask in its reflected glory, they may also be taken to have been valuable before this social acceptance. (See § 23.32/23.)

§ 22.3   Correlation of Immediate and Reflected Totalities

The general form of value is a *unity* of form. To begin with we have this contrast between the sensuous appearance (body of A) of a supersensuous world of value *behind* the body of the commodities (such as B, C, D, and so on). If the relations of B, C, D, etc. to A are in accord with their law of appearance then this 'supersensuous realm' is a '*first intelligible world*' of value. ('Intelligible' here can be understood in Kantian terms as what gives sense to the manifold of value-bodies by granting them this essential meaning.) There is now given a split between the level of the *sensuously* accessible surface of things and a kingdom of laws at the level of the *supersensuous*.

Remark: This law-like connection is not the mere conjunction of variables in the nomological conception of law characteristic of empiricist ideology, but their essential relation.

So the first world of value comprises the law-like *expression* of value in the body of A. But in a second step it emerges that, as the universal equivalent, A in its *sensuous immediacy* is a '*second intelligible world*' of value which contrasts with the supersensuous world of value that was originally posited behind B, C, and so on.

The presence of the second world follows from the realisation that if value *is* now A, then this equivalent itself is not just the effect of a force expressing itself in it, but is itself value in another shape, namely immediate value. Instead of (or as well as) value reflected back from the equivalent, the equivalent reflects value onto itself. Because commodity A as a sensuous reality is at the same time value, a second world of value is posited at the level of sensuousness, complementing the supersensuous one. These two worlds of value stand in an *inverted* relation to each other: in the first one value is opposed to the bodily appearance of commodities, whereas in the second one value is identified with a specific body, that of commodity A. The second value world co-exists with the first in that the material body of the universal equivalent does not just *reflect* into a visible world the hidden original supersensuous world of value; it now, just as it is, counts as value in *immediate* shape.

Because the originating moment is preserved in sublated form, we find the realm of value *doubles* into *reflected and immediate totalities*. In the universal equivalent, value, originally defined in opposition to the body of A (hence a supersensuous reality), *is* now A (a sensuous reality). This is outright *identity of opposites* (whereas, in the simple form, value, defined as not A, is given in B, so it is supersensuous and sensuous at the same time, but in relation to two *different* commodities). The two worlds of value, the sensuous and supersensuous, are here immediately one; the very same commodity (that in universal equivalent form) contains both worlds. They are *essentially related*. Value is a sensuous supersensuous 'thing', in which one pole – value as the hidden essence – is made manifest in law-like fashion in the other pole as a sensuous reality, but equally the latter itself makes present the immediacy of value.

In sum it is the very same world of value that is divided into the reflected totality and the immediate totality, they are *essentially* related, or correlative. However, these moments are unified in form not only because the universal equivalent contains them both, but each contains the other; for each is senseless unless incorporating reference to its other.

This insight is verified by considering what happens if each of these shapes of value is taken without its other. If it is said that value is exhausted only in the full range of partial equivalents, then it is obvious enough that this chaotic manifold lacks the synthesising unity established through reversal whereby they are given a universal equivalent without which they are not *formed* as values. What is less obvious is that the converse also holds. If the universal equivalent claims to *be* value over *against* the other commodities as mere use-values, it too collapses to formlessness. It cannot be value *for itself* unless there is something posited as value *in itself* to which it *gives form*. Each side is the opposite of its opposite and includes it, rather than bounded by it, so there is here an infinite identity of value.

It may seem as if the original combination of use-value and value in the commodity were here externalised through a *doubling of the commodity* into commodities embodying use-value and the universal equivalent commodity embodying value. But value is a form which *relates* the two. Nonetheless there is *a doubling of value* here, with the reflected totality of value and the immediate totality coexistent. In sum, each totality on its own being mere formlessness, value exists only in their unity.

But how is this unity of form *really* held together? That is what we next show. This section has developed the opposition of essence and appearance to the point at which we now see there is nothing in essence that is not in appearance, and nothing in appearance that is not in essence. With the general form the diverse commodities are posited through the universal equivalent as a unity in essence, just as much as the universal equivalent is itself posited as the essence of the value presupposed in them. The unity of essence and appearance is 'actuality'.

§ 23   *Value as Actuality: Money*

The general form of value supersedes shapeless essence (value-in-itself) and unstable appearance (the indefinitely large set of particular equivalents in which value may or may not find expression for itself). But it will be shown in this section that value in-and-for-itself is actual only when money incarnates the universal expression of value. This is the way value itself appears in actuality as the law-like phenomenal existence of the value of commodities. The triad of *Value as Actuality* is as follows:

§ 23.1 The modalities of the equivalent form (covering possibility, contingency, and necessity), including Form IV total form of value; § 23.2 Money as the absolute form of value, Forms V & VI; § 23.3 Value as absolute relation, Form VII.

§ 23.1   Modalities of the Equivalent Form

Form III above is merely 'a' general form of value, because it is not yet determined *which* commodity is *the* universal equivalent. For 'commodity B' could follow the same route as 'A' did above, such that *it* ends up as the focus of a 'general form'. Hence the universal equivalent posited in the intermediation of commodities has not *yet established its own ground* to stand upon. A commodity functions as universal equivalent only if it alone successfully solicits the other commodities to recognise it as the *only* appropriate expression of their value. Value must appear in a *unique* universal equivalent to be actual.

In developing the category of Value-as-Actuality I turn first to consider the modal categories: formal possibility, contingency, necessity. (Then I move to value as unique equivalent in an absolute relation, finally as 'substance'.)

Actuality makes manifest essence in such a way that essence consists simply in being that which manifests itself. So value not only *must* appear if it is to be actual, it must appear *as what it is*, exchangeableness as such, namely that which is made manifest through the value form, the universal equivalent. However, because the difference between the commodity in universal equivalent form and the others is no difference, it seems arbitrary that one commodity rather than any other occupies this position. While the relation of identity and difference between those in relative form, and the universal equivalent, is perfectly intelligible as an abstract form, it requires a ground in a *real differentiation* between the commodities concerned.

If there is nothing to *distinguish* one commodity from another as value, the unfolding of the form of value generates two empty abstractions in the general form, namely the indeterminate identity supposed to be secured in value-for-itself and the manifold values-in-themselves. These empty abstractions *require* grounding to be effectively determining of their unity rather than merely formally correlative. The two worlds need to be one; but *oneness* is actual only if it is centred on a *unique* universal equivalent.

Notice that the putative universal equivalent posited in the intermediation of commodities has not *yet established its own ground* to stand upon. It is a *mediated immediacy* which contains in sublated form the process of its own production, in the dialectic of the forms of value, immanently. It functions as universal equivalent only if it successfully solicits the other commodities to recognise it as the *only* appropriate expression of their value. Indeed, the general form of value breaks down into a set of simple forms if the universal equivalent is not capable of carrying within itself its logical genesis through the reversal of the expanded form, such that it counts as the commodity actively projecting its value.

The supersession of this difference must not be a *semblance* of unity but a *determinate* actuality. To say the identity must be determinate is to say the universal equivalent must be a *unique* universal equivalent. Only then is value a manifest reality in which the 'utterance' of value is value itself. If we have merely the aforementioned empty abstractions their reflection into each other is the movement from nothing to nothing and back again.

Correlation is a still imperfect interpenetration of opposites because they do not reach identity. As I shall show shortly, they actually become one only if organised as a centred totality by money. Without it, the universal equivalent is not a true synthesis of essence and existence. The reflected and immediate totalities of value remain stuck in this movement from nothing to nothing unless there is something different about commodity A that allows it both to establish its negativity *itself* (rather than through an *external reflection* upon the relation), and moreover to *exclude* other commodities from running through this reflective movement to establish value-for-itself in their body.

Beside the world in which A is of the essence, there are *other worlds* in which this same commodity A is only one of those in relative form, showing its value essence in some other universal equivalent.

Let us lay out formally the problem (using abbreviated expressions):

Form IV *The Total Form of Expression of Value*

1) *The total expanded form*
   The value of zA *is* yB or xC or wD etc.
   or The value of yB *is* zA or xC or wD etc.
   or The value of xC *is* zA or yB or wD etc.
   or etc.
2) *The total general form*
   The value of yB and xC and wD etc. *is* zA
   or The value of zA and xC and wD etc. *is* yB
   or The value of zA and yB and wD etc. *is* xC
   or etc.

In this 'total form' there are two complementary moments: the total expanded form yields through its reversal the total general form. Implicit then in exchange relations are a manifold of potential value expressions. There are many potential points of origin such that we have multiple expanded forms. Since in each of these the expression 'The value of A is B' is matched by an alternative expression 'The value of B is A' in another, they are exclusive of one another. A commodity in one instance is in relative position and in the rest is a partial equivalent. Likewise the multiple 'general' forms involve putting a commodity in equivalent form once but relative form in all others. All these general forms are potential ways to actualise value. But, once again, these forms exclude one another.

A commodity cannot possibly be in both forms at once if value is to achieve its essential *unity*. To speak proleptically, commodities cannot form prices of each other. This would be absurd. For value to be actual requires there is not merely the logical possibility that a commodity be the *unique* equivalent but that this uniqueness is effectively grounded. Only thus is value a reality. In these sets of potential value-expressions, many *alternative* worlds of value presented, but, although these many universes of value are all possible, they are not compossible. Yet I have not given adequate *grounds* for granting one of them *actuality*.

Determining reflection is not achieved in the dialectic of essence and appearance because as late as its final category of *Correlation* all we have is *pure positing reflection*, albeit the universal equivalent is supposed to be sufficient to make a value system self-referring.

The Total Form exhibits the *systemic relationality* of commodities; but there is no ground making determinate any one of its moments. This principle of uncertainty pervades this form, until one moment gains necessity, and by reaction upon them determines the actuality or otherwise of the rest.

Consider the transition from this impasse to money. The defect of the general form is that the universal equivalent form can be assumed by any commodity. Yet there cannot be more than one universal equivalent if value is to be a unitary sphere, therefore some principle of selection must make just one possibility actual. Logically there is nothing to distinguish commodities. But the problem was solved *historically* by social custom. Gold was chosen to be the universal equivalent although something else could have been. At all events the *singularity* of gold brings value relations to a focus and creates a homogeneous value space (leaving other potential spaces unactual).

So the first section of Value *as Actual* determines the conditions of existence of the *unique* universal equivalent, namely money. However, the *logical* transition to it is not at all an easy one. The steps in the argument follow the modalities of value: namely possibility; contingency; and necessity.

(i) it is *possible* formally that any commodity can serve as the unique universal equivalent;

(ii) since any commodity could have served thus, whichever it is, its status as unique seems merely *contingent* (on having been excluded for this purpose by the other commodities arbitrarily, or chosen by external fiat), not essential.

(iii) Thus to actualise value, the one that is selected must make itself *necessary* to the system.

The existence of money depends on the existence of other commodities as its correlates, but if it *acts* as *exchangeableness-in-immediacy* then this mediation vanishes. While these commodities are its analytical presuppositions, as value-for-itself money posits itself as *not* posited. Gold as value-for-itself presupposes that there are commodities to *be* valued by it, but only *with money* are commodities posited *as* values in themselves. The upshot is that it is not commodities that are immediately values, and hence posit money as their mediated reflection; rather it is money that is determined as value in immediate shape, and thus reflects value into such commodities as prove themselves to it. Value, as a unitary essence, is posited once money *constitutes* this unity of form in *practice*. (Moreover, only if the form of value is practically constituted does any material content become socially recognised, and commensurated, in it. Without money products do not confront each other as commodities, but as use-values only, *not as values*.)

However, for value to be actual requires not merely that there is the logical possibility that a money commodity be the *unique* value equivalent but that this uniqueness is effectively grounded. But is not the presence of money simply *presupposed* at this point? More especially, if it is gold *how* does it achieve its unique position here as *the* universal equivalent? By its own act! Money is always already the attractor of commodities because it is the only way of presenting their value.

This point needs more discussion. It is of no moment to enter into a historical treatment of gold's emergence as the money commodity. The key issue for a systematic-dialectical presentation of this 'fact' is why gold is money when it is *present*. In the systematic presentation of its rôle even the mediations *logically* presupposed in its development vanish. The money form of value links back to the simple form, having been developed from it by a series of metamorphoses that it must run through in order to win its finished shape. However, the presence of gold money retroactively denies any other commodity the *opportunity* to 'run through' the dialectic of form to become money.

Remark: But whether an object takes one form or the other is indeterminate logically. Those familiar with recent physics may consider the potentials by analogy with uncollapsed quantum states, such that when gold 'collapses' to money the others must immediately 'collapse' to saleable commodities.

The derivation of money flows from the requirement that value appear in autonomous form. It is of course true that logic alone does not designate the commodity that is to be the unique universal equivalent, since there are no formal properties distinguishing one commodity from others, once the material specificity of use-value is disregarded. All can aspire to the role of universal equivalent. What is crucial is that the many possible 'universes' of value, starting from every commodity that may end up excluded from others so as to serve as universal equivalent, evaporate when gold is excluded by the other commodities in practice to condense the value sphere around its singularity. The upshot is not that a particular commodity becomes money because all other commodities express their values in it, but, on the contrary, that all other commodities universally express their values in a particular commodity because it is money. The virtual movement through which this process has been mediated vanishes in its own result.

This brings me to the *logic of exclusion*. It seems that *commodities* exclude one of their number to serve as their unique universal equivalent. But if the money commodity is excluded *by the others* the '*fact*' that it is money only obtains through *their* activity. Thus gold does not yet exist as money on its own account; it remains, in effect, *contingent* on that *condition* of its existence.

But if we bear in mind that the dialectic of force and expression ends with the universal equivalent *actively* asserting itself as value-for-itself, then it seems better to ask how the *activity* of the money-commodity *excludes itself* from the other commodities, even if expositionally it appears otherwise. The actualisation of value consists in how value *acts*, and gold is money because it acts as such, attracting other commodities to exchange for it because it is value in immediate shape as the unique universal equivalent. At this point in the presentation, gold *effectively* occupies the place assigned this form, namely the form that is necessary to make a reality of value. Money maintains itself as value in autonomous form *against* the other commodities. As their centre of attraction it prevents any other commodity taking its position just because it *already* acts as value in immediate form in virtue of fulfilling the money functions, accordingly attracting other commodities to find a value equivalent in it.

It seems as if the other commodities excluded gold 'in the first place' but the boot is on the other foot once it becomes active on its own account. The alleged 'effect', namely the exclusion of the money commodity by the other commodities, becomes the cause of itself when money posits the presupposition that it alone 'was' excluded virtually, by actually excluding any other claimant to its throne.

The *reflection* of commodities and money into each other is not merely a 'positing reflection' of value as in a mere correlation of relative and equivalent poles of value, for this lacks sufficient determinacy in that the position of the commodities could be reversed. Nor is it adequate to its existence that a certain commodity is given a privileged rôle through some 'external' stipulation, for example a state issue of a 'legal tender'. What is required to give value its self-subsistence is a 'determining reflection' in the required sense, in truth a self-determination whereby a commodity posits the presupposition that it is money just by acting as money. Once in actuality gold is exchangeableness in immediate shape, it posits itself as its *own* presupposition, instead of being posited *by its presupposition*, namely the commodity manifold.

So, instead of depending on conditions external to it, namely that the commodities have excluded it from their number, money maintains its exclusivity through positing these commodities as its own presuppositions, that is, positing that it always already is virtually excluded from them. That gold is money is so because *it is*, having sublated its virtual conditions through its own activity. As a *fact*, money appears as unconditioned, having always already sublated its condition, which now appears as what is conditioned when money gives commodities their validation as values. The *activity* of money as a fact means the vanishing of the virtual mediation of its existence by commodities. It is taken at 'face value'.

The nature of money itself posits the other commodities as opposed to it. Having sublated its virtual origin in the dialectic of the forms of value, it is not a passive *measure* of commodity value, but it stands opposed to the mundane existence of commodities as their absolute other, as the judge of their worth; they exist as recognised commodities only by its grace. As such it is the God of commodities.

The point is not to show how a *process* of exclusion occurred, but to show that the logic of money is itself exclusionary. So, although it could be silver, not gold, *in the imagination*, in *actuality* the money commodity is what it *is*. This seems a mouse of an argument, but this is a point where dialectic must acknowledge its limits: if money is gold, and how gold became so, is not a logical point. But the demonstration of what money *is*, in relation to commodities, is a *logical* investigation.

Certainly dialectic cannot retroject its systemic logic into a *historical* force, wherewith the necessity of money to the present system makes itself into a speculative requirement that people originally act so as to fix a commodity as money. Money is necessary to the systemic constitution of value. But, if absent, it requires some contingent process to bring it out, because it cannot bring itself about before it exists; but once it does exist it becomes necessary to the system it supports. The logical derivation of money is a retrogressive grounding movement of value.

Yet if one thinks about an immediate relation of commodities to each other as mere barter there is a problem, for it is hard to see anything contradictory about the persistence of barter relations. Barter is a well attested phenomenon historically and anthropologically. It has no *necessity* to develop into a money system. However, my presentation rejects a quasi-causal story about commodity exchangers having as a result of the structure of their situation a tendency to invent money.

Remark: The systematic-dialectical method of understanding the logical necessity of money contrasts with that of a *myth of origin*, which traces the development of money from an imaginary primitive shape of exchange in accordance with a quasi-causal narrative wherewith each stage produces its successor. A thought experiment purports to show how traders would, in the absence of money, be led *over time* by the nature of their situation to evolve it. The method takes as its starting point owners of commodities making offers for 'sale', and seeks to demonstrate that there would be a tendency for such traders to accept as an intermediate asset the more exchangeable commodities, one of which eventually becomes generally accepted as the sole bearer of purchasing power. This function of money having been established, the other functions follow. A difficulty with these fables is that a wrenching of gears has to take place from the obvious reading of 'more exchangeable' as 'more generally required' to the nomination of gold, which is merely a luxury. This slippage papers over a radical traverse, namely that a money economy is not continuous with barter economy, but is characterised by a radical *opposition* between commodities sold for consumption and money, which is never sold but only buys. That is its peculiar 'use'; moreover to retain this use requires that in being used it be not 'used up'; it must be imperishable. Because of this last point, if I were to indulge in a myth of origin I would derive money from its function as store of value. A family would not trade away their means of subsistence but only their luxury items, one of which, namely gold ornaments, is by nature imperishable. It is thus a perfect asset for 'saving for a rainy day' to then facilitate the acquisition of badly needed means of subsistence. Those in the fortunate position of having surplus means of subsistence could trade such perishables for such permanent 'wealth' as gold. It is a small step from permanent wealth to the money function of store of value. However, I do not press this fable because I have argued here that a systematic derivation of the necessity of money requires analysis of its *present* position.[4]

Thus the derivation of money is not based primarily on a 'forwards' argument but rather a 'backwards' dialectic, in which it is assumed that value is to be socially validated, and then money is shown to be (at this stage) the most adequate actualisation of value. Once the category of 'money' is granted then value is *better grounded* than it is in simple commodity relations. If at the start one imputes value to a single commodity (through an analytical abstraction from the world of exchange relations) one immediately creates a contradiction between use-value and value because value has a purely social reality. Since in isolation commodities lack a form of value distinct from their bodily forms, such a commodity can appear only as a particular use-value, yet at the same time is required to realise the universal *negation* of use-value, for that is how value is socially constituted. If value *cannot* appear in an isolated commodity, then one can say a 'demand' has arisen for this contradiction to be superseded through the said commodity finding a way of distinguishing itself as a value from itself as a use-value, to express this value as *other* than itself therefore. This it does in calling on another commodity to be its equivalent as value. In this simple relation we see the germ of money which as a special commodity excluded from all others is 'value-for-itself' and reflects back on them an adequate value form in their price.

---

4   For the real history of the emergence of money see Seaford 2004.

If the unique universal equivalent is in its very notion a determinate unitary form the *presupposition* of it must be similarly determinate, rather than a commodity that theory chooses arbitrarily as an example. Without such determinacy value as a unitary essence has signally failed to stabilise itself. *How* is this uniqueness achieved? By means of the *becoming necessary* of gold, as always already the attractor of commodities because it realises their value. 'Necessity' means value is actual if the universal equivalent necessarily exists, that is, produces itself as that object. In a systematic presentation, the form of necessity may well contain alongside it that of contingency. For the actual *bearer* of the universal equivalent may be contingent on the suitability of available commodities such as gold and the specific history of its adoption. If for some reason gold failed, another commodity could be used in this role and become necessary to the system.

It is important to notice that the whole argument is driven *conceptually*: for the concept of value to be meaningful, money is required. If the validating of the value inherent in commodities is only accomplished in the dialectical movement to a higher category, to money, it is also true that the commodity as such retains its contradictory character. The resolution of contradictions does not abolish them, nor discard them, but *grounds* them. Furthermore, money as a commodity itself turns out to embody a contradictory unity of use-value and exchange-value at a higher level.

Value having left behind its determination in the relatedness of commodities I speak hyperbolically of value now taking the form of *absolute* value, in the next section.

§ 23.2   Money as Absolute Form of Value

Money, as the unique universal equivalent, is necessary to the actuality of value. In this section I show how in its own activity money makes itself necessary by taking on the position of 'absolute value' over against commodities.

Remark: Strictly speaking at this stage I am not speaking of value as absolute in the sense of unconditioned. I simply go beyond the notion of value as an external relation to that of something substantively presented as independent of exchange-value, and in this sense 'absolute value'. A key move in value theory is to get beyond the notion of value as an immediate external relation (possibly conjunctural), that is, as exchange-value merely, to that of 'value as substance' which relates simply to itself.

To recapitulate, Essence is a first cut at a less abstract sphere than Being; it is a sphere of polarity, of *relatedness*, to begin with the relation of essence and appearance which is to be finally unified in absolute relation. The basic contradiction of a logic of essence is that a thing is supposed to be identical with itself yet in appearance always different from itself. Something really essential must show itself as *what it is*. All the oppositions are shown to be capable of being refigured as internally related mutually complementary moments of a unitary whole.

The dialectic of force and expression is the logic characteristic of the forms of appearance of value we saw, and it results in the relationship of the universal equivalent to the other commodities, soliciting them to solicit it as *the* expression of their value. However, for value to be actual requires that the universal equivalent be unique. But Form III does not *ground* this requirement of unity in essence of commodities insofar as it is a case of *pure* positing reflection. If it is hard to see the simple form of value as more than barter, it is equally hard to accept any commodity can be money if the dialectic of force and expression results in a merely *relational totality* in which all commodities form 'exchange-values' of each other. This last is absurd because value must be a *unitary* essence of commodities. It must be actualised only in a unique equivalent, namely money. It seems possible for *any* commodity to emerge as the unique universal equivalent, and hence the actual universal equivalent is so only contingent on its conditions of emergence whatever they are; these seem to be *externally* determining conditions, not part of what money *is*.

I then argued that the virtual exclusion by commodities of one of their own to serve as money is now reversed when we grasp money in its own action excludes itself from commodities. This means that money presents the moment of their essential unity as values to commodities when acting as their unique universal equivalent. Money, through *its own activity*, secures its hegemony over the commodities that seem to be its conditions of existence.

Now I resume the systematic presentation, and I explore how money posits itself as 'absolute value', used in the sense that it is without qualification, that is to say, not considered as the value *of* something. This movement is no longer the reflection of value in otherness, but as money it is simple self-reflection held within itself. What we now show is that this relatedness becomes 'Absolute' in the sense that these two totalities of value pass into one another so as to posits value as their identity. Money is *value in absolute form* because it exists in seeming autonomy from the commodity relations originally supposed to be characterised by value. Determined *as* 'absolute', it simply exhibits itself as what it *is*.

Immediately the Absolute is already determined with a form, absolute form to be sure. But this has two constitutive moments, namely absolute identity and absolute totality. The identity exists here in the *determination* of its identity. But the absolute *identity* of form is complemented by the *exposition* of the absolute totality. This form is determined in two senses then; taken negatively, the inwardising movement, when the absolute folds in upon itself to actualise its self-identity; and, taken positively, the 'exposition of the Absolute' whereby, as totality, it lays itself out, or unfolds itself, into its difference within itself. If the former is its intension, the latter is its extension.

This means that, on the one hand, money is the self-identity of value, and 'swallows up' so to speak all commodities, as they depend on it for recognition as value; on the other, the exposition of value is accomplished when money is laid out on commodities. The categories of 'identity' and 'exposition' are termed 'form-determinations' of value here.

The form-determination of value as essential identity, in the above sense, requires complementing with another form-determination that *also* contains the whole of value, namely that to which the form extends itself, the commodity manifold. Thus we see now that the commodity manifold counts as a determination of that form itself. So in virtue of the interchange of these determinations, commodities *themselves* have value form. Thus the moment of difference presented in the 'laying out' of money on commodities is not nugatory, but an essential complementary form-determination of value. These two complementary form-determinations of money are exchangeability-in-immediacy, and immediate exchangeability.

Remark: This category of 'form-determination' is distinct from a category I use later, namely 'formal determination'. The hyphenated term, form-determination, indicates a *determination of* form, whereas formal determination is the process whereby something is *determined with* the relevant form. In the first case commodities and money are form-determinations of value. In the second case, something is given a value form in addition to its bodily form. At an abstract logical level such a process of formal determination ('valuation' and 'subsumption' are central cases I treat later) simply inscribes reality within the form; but in a stronger sense the material inscribed in the form is *transformed* in its very materiality, a central case being the real subsumption of the production process under capital, we shall see.

The triad of Absolute Form is:
(a) Absolute Identity: money as exchangeability-in-immediacy; Form V the Money Form of value (§ 23.21);
(b) Exposition of the Absolute: money as immediate exchangeability; Form VI the Laying out of money (§ 23.22);
(c) Reciprocity of these form-determinations of money (§ 23.23).

§ 23.21   *Exchangeability-in-Immediacy; the Money Form*

Form v *The Money Form of Value: exchangeability in immediacy*

20 yard of linen
1 coat
40 lbs. of coffee } *express their value in* an ounce of gold
10 lbs. of tea
Half a ton of iron
etc.

Note Here are given examples of commodities, rather than variables A, B, C, etc. because it is important to the money form that a *specific* commodity *is* the universal equivalent, and in being so excluded itself excludes all other *specific* commodities from its place.

At first, absolute value has the form-determination of *absolute identity*. If we recall the two totalities of value, the immediate, and the reflected, are implicitly one unity of form, this means value has self-identity in their relation. In effect it is a relation of *reflexivity*. Money does not require the expression of value different from it. It actually *is* value.

So I now turn to analyse this Money Form of Value, where value achieves its self-identity as exchangeability-in-immediacy.

Remark: Recall that 'Exchangeability-in-immediacy' is not the same notion as 'Immediate exchangeability'. I reserve the latter below for the use-value of money as purchasing power. Here with 'exchangeability-in-immediacy' I have in mind the role of money as the sole vehicle of the realisation of value.

In analysing this absolute form of value it is illuminating to tie the discussion back to the original emergence of value as a *being-for-self* and its dialectic of one-many-totality, in which commodities are held together through attraction but repelled so as to be numerically different from each other. However, the totality may itself become one, a sort of 'one One'. Thus a definitive resolution of this opposition between repulsion and attraction is not a static equilibrium but implicitly a positing of this notion of the 'one One', a unitary principle in relation to which the many ones are its mere 'extension'; it is thus their 'realised ideality'. This universal attractor, money, does not *absorb* all the many ones because it remains rooted in the primal repulsion; it stands in a relation of exclusion to the ones it yet represents. Money as the 'one One' brings all attraction and repulsion into a unitary focus. There cannot be two monies because value as the *identical* essence of commodities can only be actualised in a self-identity which is what the money form of value is.

It is a concretisation of the *relative* totality established when commodities are systematically interconnected as values. With money the relational totality is refigured as a *centred* totality with money playing the organising role as the universal attractor. Money, figured as this One, holds together the many commodities as its 'filling' or 'extension'. Thus we can see commodities as simply the *extension* of the category of 'exchangeable'. The imputed value dimensionality of commodities is *concretely* actual in their relation to the universal equivalent *excluded* from them, namely money. However, money has this dialectic within itself: just insofar as it is excluded from commodities as their posited value, it *attracts* them to realise themselves as commodities in exchanging against it. Equally the 'universal attractor', money, *contains* the mediation of 'repulsion'; without any commodities opposed to money there could be no determinate value form.

Remark: I noted earlier that Hegel avoided introducing the category of 'Totality' as a third to 'one' and 'many' (§ 11.3). I speculate that this was because he thought of Totality as properly centred, as making possible 'totalisation'. At the level of 'Essence', as superior to 'Being', the notions of attraction and repulsion may be concretised as the intension and extension of the value form with money and commodities assigned these places. Such a centring could not be established at the earlier stage of '*being-for-self*' because it requires the complexity characteristic of Actuality.

Money does not *represent* the given value of commodities; rather it *presents* it to them. It is not a re-*presentation* of something given in commodities, but it is the only way in which value is made *present* concretely (rather than as some unreal abstraction). Once value is thus presented explicitly 'for itself' (rather than as a mere immanence) in money, it posits the commodities as values 'in themselves'. Although gold seems a 'representative' commodity, it becomes through its form-determination *antithetical* to commodities, excluded from them so as to present in objective shape what they must *exclude from themselves*, namely their supposed value, which they cannot bring to light in their own 'stuff' but only in the material that stands over against them, money.

In money value becomes One, identical with itself, yet full of itself through its ability to lay itself out on commodities.

§ 23.22 Immediate Exchangeability: The Laying Out of Money

Form VI: *The Form of Immediate Exchangeability* or *The Laying-Out of Money*

an ounce of gold *is immediately exchangeable for* ⎧ 20 yards of linen
and 1 coat
and 40 lbs of coffee
and half a ton of iron
and so on ⎫

Remark: About 'and' in the Table: I am not yet talking of real exchanges for which a large number of bits of money may be required.

The exposition of the Absolute Content for us is the second form-determination of value as absolute. We saw that in the money form of value money distinguishes itself *from* commodities as exchangeableness-in-immediacy. However, there is an asymmetry here because money is exchangeableness in *immediate form*, whereas the commodities require the mediation of money to realise their value. But equally money goes beyond its own immediacy when it is active in valuing commodities, bringing them under its hegemony. Now we turn to the movement whereby money lays itself out *on* commodities; it therewith proves itself to be immediately exchangeable (as is shown in the reverse of the Money Form V, namely Form VI above). In Form VI we see that money, being *immediately exchangeable* with any commodity, *lays itself out* on commodities. If money-in-itself is exchangeableness-in-immediacy then money-for-itself is 'immediate exchangeability'.

Whereas Form V showed money as the centre of attraction *for* commodities, Form VI shows how money actively determines itself *to* commodity form. Yet, in being laid out, money remains *at home with itself* as value when it becomes determinate in commodity form. These are posited as themselves shapes of value. Money as value in autonomous form does not just hold itself aloof from commodities in this negative relation to all determinacy, as if money were an indeterminate and empty form. It fulfils itself, gives itself a filling, when it demonstrates its immediacy as value is made actual *in* them as complementary forms of value that it is immediately exchangeable with.

Remark: Form VI is very different from Form II, the expanded form. In the latter, as I had occasion to stress, the commodities on the right were *alternatives* to each other, signified by the use of the connector '*or*'. As a result the commodity on the left could not express its value adequately because it got lost in this endlessness. Here, however, money *comprehends* this infinity under its own form-determination as the value *universal* that may be laid out on all commodities alike; thus it takes the connector '*and*'.

Money *demonstrates* that it is value incarnate by its *purchasing power*. It shows that as immediate exchangeability money may be turned into any kind of commodity. While commodities gain validity only if sanctified by money, money does not have any special commodity opposed to it; whatever it is laid out on is accidental one might say.

That money has no material use-value of its own (ignoring gold ornaments) is paradoxically the very condition of its being a permanent possibility of *all* use-value! As a use-value it is an individual commodity, but at the same time it is posited as universal. Gold is *the universal commodity*, not just an instance of the type. It has absolute singularity. This may seem a dizzying exercise in metaphysics; but the practical proof that this dialectic of presupposition and posit has generated a new objectivity is that the universal equivalent commodity now has an entirely new, objectively perceptible, social use-value. As *immediately exchangeable* in a way other commodities are not, money is the singularity of general *material* wealth. It is the universal commodity that potentially has the use-value of any desired commodity.

Remark: Implicit in the money form is price – which I come to later – but, since price *is given in* money, money has no price itself, it *is* price. But has money *value*? This claim overlooks three very interesting circumstances. First of all, the whole point of the value form is to allow a commodity to express its value in another because it cannot express its value in its *own* body. But money *does* express value in its own body because money fixes the peculiarity of the equivalent form which we discussed earlier, namely that its *body counts as value*. It has no need to express its value in some other commodity, because as value-for-itself it does not need an expression of value-in-itself as do the other commodities. Secondly, reading a price-list backwards does not return to the indeterminacy of the expanded form but to money, as immediate exchangeability, having universal power of exchange (as other commodities do not). To ignore this is to go back behind money to the bare *commodity* status of gold, losing the peculiar status it has *as money*. (See Form VI.) Thirdly, that leaves only the vulgar notion of 'the value of money' rooted in worries about the contingency of money's purchasing power, given inflation. But this relation has nothing to do with a measure of value, but of power of purchase. It remains the case that money *is* the measure of value, so therefore cannot *have* a measure. This point is indirectly supported by the great difficulty of finding an absolute measure of purchasing power. Any basket of commodities, selected as a standard, is arbitrary from a logical point of view. This is hardly surprising, if we remark that in this purchasing power relation we consider the *use-value* of money not its *value*. (Note that in the expanded relative form we did not consider a *basket* but a list of *alternative* expressions of value.)

§ 23.23   *Reciprocity of the Form-Determinations of Money*

Exchangeability-in-immediacy and immediate exchangeability are logically complementary determinations of the activity of money; as the former it attracts commodities to express their value in it; as the latter it lays itself out freely on commodities. Form VI is then simply the complementary form-determination to Form V, the money-form. The two moments are required to constitute value as a *unitary* form. The one is indeed a condition of the other. They are reciprocally determining. Money has immediate exchangeability just because it is exchangeability-in-immediacy; conversely something that is immediately exchangeable is perfect to serve as universal equivalent.

Money is active in two directions; *negatively* as excluding itself from commodities to be their universal attractor, *positively* as immediate exchangeability with them. But despite these complementary roles what is really effective is their unity, exchange as a whole.

Taking Form V and VI together in this unity of value as actual, we see at the same time the activity of sublating the immediacy of value into mediated shape (i.e. in Form V money as exchangeableness-in-immediacy becomes in Form VI mediated in its exposition of itself) and also the sublating of this mediation (Form VI) back into immediacy (Form V).

I term money the *absolute form* of value because whether the money is placed to the right of the value expression (as it is when functioning as exchangeability-in-immediacy), or to the left (as when it is exhibited as immediately exchangeable with the commodities on which it is 'laid out'), these are to be understood as simply pure form-determinations descending from the same unitary actuality. The very same money divides itself between these roles. Their 'overturning' one into the other is shown when we see in one single transaction that it may be read in *both* directions, *from* money or *to* money. The mutuality of these two reduces them to aspects of the same relation. Absolute Form achieves its unity once the centripetal and centrifugal movements, *to* money and *from* money, are taken as one unity.

These two roles being mutually conditioning, in a whole of intermediation, we may conclude that it is the very same substance that appears in these complementary form-determinations. The absolute form of value is absolute because it is the *form of itself* not of some other stuff. This *pure* determination is borne by money. 'Content' is produced by form out of itself. Value-as-content taken in unity with value-as-form is value-as-substance. Under the determination of finitude it posits itself as content in the value of commodities. While *itself* substance, it exists in what is formed as value by money, namely commodities, as *their* ideal substance, lurking within the material shell. (But later I shall argue that the material determinations flowing from the *production* of commodities does really determine the *magnitude* of value.) The unity of the form-determinations of money is thus explicitly posited in the category of 'Value as Substance'. (Thus I take money to be value *as substance* as opposed to searching for the substance *of* value.)

A form that exists on its own account is substance, here *value as substance*.

§ 23.3   Value as Substance

Value is one substance, but it holds *within it* the relation of money and commodities. So this value substance divides into:

§ 23.31 Substance-in-immediacy; this is the infinite homogenous substance embodied in money; substance related to itself yields money as measure proper;

§ 23.32 Value substance as absolute relation of the money form and the commodity form of value: here substance is in finitude with money as the real measure of commodities; indeed money constitutes commodities as values in the very process of giving their magnitude of value;

§ 23.33 The *substantial* form of value gives rise to the infinite unity of all values.

I first discuss value as substance-in-itself as it is incarnate in money; most important here is that money gives value measure proper, makes value *measurable*. Value takes its *own* measure in its peculiar monetary medium; then as equivalent to itself it serves as the *real measure* of the value of commodities. Along with this, money imputes to these commodities a peculiar form: that of *being values*. Thus the one homogenous substance-in-itself here descends to the finite realm. Although identical in substance with others, every value in commodity form is posited as a *shape* of the value substance, value as a 'thing'. Finally, the moments of the substantial form of value exist in infinite unity.

The presentation of money as *'the value substance'* is a very different use of the term 'substance' from that view which considers labour as *'the substance of value'*. The latter use of the term equates with 'stuff' or 'material', with what value is 'made of', so to speak. Here, in the development of the value form, the dialectic generates forms *of value itself* that become more concrete and complex. So, as *commodity*, value seems to 'inhere' in it, so to speak, as a quasi-*property*. But, as *money*, the inverse is true: value is itself a *substance*, of which the particular body bearing it (e.g. gold) is merely a transubstantiated outer shell. So I never speak about 'the substance *of* value' at all, because I consider value as *itself* a substance, and there cannot be a substance of a substance.

When I treat value as 'substance' this is a technical sense of 'substance'. It is not to align it with common or garden substances such as matter or mind. For here we are constructing a scaffolding of pure categories. Thus 'substance' here exists simply as *pure form* within this dialectical development of the value form. It retains the basic definition of substance as that which exists on its own account; but it is not further specified as a kind of substance whether physical or spiritual. It is here simply the *logical* form brought to life by the peculiar constitutive role of money. If it were to be objected that the category is a metaphysical importation from philosophy unsuited to a science, I would reply that it is just such a metaphysic that the value form initiates, and supports, *in practice*.

In the development of the value form from relational property to substance there is an inversion. At the level of the commodity, as exchangeable, we have to say *its* social *form* attributes value *to it*. It is a thing *of value*. So the commodity qua social form may change *its* value. But once the inversion is posited it is value that prevails and changes *its shell* from one commodity to another. (But it is also the case that the more elementary forms are preserved as potential ways of expressing value if required.)

The difficult thing is that our context remains the bifurcation between material and ideal realms. *Within* the ideal realm value exists on its own account. Yet it cannot exist at all without the material realm that underpins it, for example commodities and money. Both realms are present and interpenetrate. Taken ideally, the material commodity is presupposed as the 'shell' of value, because practice posits this when it is now taken ideally as ontologically secondary to value itself.

Remark: Substance here is *an ideal social substance*, thus immaterial. The qualification is not generally repeated but must be borne in mind. It is also important to mark carefully the distinction between the 'value substance' and the material substance, if any, of the bearers of value.

§ 23.31   *Value as Substance in Immediacy*

The substantiality of value exists in money. The unity of the two form-determinations, namely exchangeability-in-immediacy (Form V) and immediate exchangeability (Form VI), is grounded when money is understood to constitute value as a unitary social substance. The ontology of a substance is clearly more concrete than that of a relation, even though we shall see this ideal social substance contains internal relations, e.g. between its Oneness and its finite modes of existence.

Substance is unconditionally present in actuality. In itself value is one infinite homogenous substance. Yet it does not simply absorb commodities as if they are merely its accidental shapes. Rather, value achieves actual substantiality only through the articulated determinacy of the two poles of the value form, money and commodities. Especially important in their relation is money's function as measure of value I shall show. Before money relates to commodities as their measure, I first analyse further what it is for value to be in itself an ideal substance.

Substance in itself has as its *primary attribute* the qualitative one of *self-identity*. It is One. But, in its complementary attribute, *extension*, it is intrinsically quantitative and hence *this* means that value as substance is implicitly therefore *notionally* divisible into different amounts of itself. Such amounts taken in *their* self-identity – as 'bodies' of value – are realised in the finite modes of substance.

The triad of *Substance-in-itself* is thus divided as follows: § 23.31/1 Substance-in-itself; its Oneness (its self-identity); § 23.31/2 Substance-for-itself as a dimensionally extended body of value; § 23.31/3 Sums of money as finite mode of value.

§ 23.31/1   Value as One Substance

Value as one substance is incarnate in money, and it is important that a perfected value system requires one, and only one, money, and that money is One. I shall argue that sums of money are potentially swallowed up again, that is, summed! This is because the defining characteristic of value considered as substance is that it is one.

Money *as* absolute *substance* is identical to itself; it has a reflexive relation to itself. More precisely, it *is* not merely self-identical, as in the identity of absolute *form*, but *posits itself* when considered as self-reflexive. The identity of form is merely the void into which all determinate value is absorbed; but the present, more articulated, notion of identity allows for its determinacy equally to manifest itself.

Moreover, the *oneness* of substance is not merely the reflex-determination of identity, which is posited as such only in its difference from difference; here such identity has become *reflected into itself*. Exchangeability-in-immediacy is identity only as negatively determined against commodities, hence not really reflexive. Value as Substance is taken to be self-identical and supports the relations of commodities and money. Value *is* a substance, incarnated in money, and we shall argue that it is the substance *of* commodities.

§ 23.31/2   Substance-for-Itself as a Dimensionally Extended Body of Value

The extended body of value is quantitatively of an indefinite extent, *notionally* divisible into ideal 'bodies' with determinate magnitudes. This quantitative dimensionality of value is a moment of difference compared with the immediate oneness of value as substance. But here difference is always internal, so even if value is attributed notionally to an extended realm of bodies, such value bodies are held within the one value substance, or identical as value. The value substance attributes identity and difference to itself, *implicitly*. Where notional difference is to be marked it is thus a matter of indifference where it is so. But, given in *finite modes* of existence, as sums of money, it gains 'measure' proper.

§ 23.31/3   Sums of Money as the Finite Mode of Value

I make a transition to the finite modes of existence of value, in the first place to sums of money, by the consideration that money is divisible into quantitative 'bits' of value. If we combine the oneness of substance-in-itself with this attribution of dimension, there results the category of finite amounts of value. Taken in *their* self-identity the finite modes of the existence of value are *discrete* sums of money.

Determined to finitude the sole infinite value substance takes the shape of an extended realm of finite value 'bodies', which may be incarnated phenomenally in coins and notes. These are formally determined as each the substantive presence of value. Since the only *quality* of value-as-substance is that it has a *quantitative* dimension, these value bodies appear in finite mode as unit and number, as 'bits' of money. Value exists as a sum of money in these finite determinations.

Notional differences *between* such bodies are secured by an extended realm inhabited by pieces of gold, and so forth. Value is real as the ideal substance of such bodies. The finite mode of value, found as discrete value 'bodies', has actuality in *measure*. So the positing of money as the value *measure* also falls within the finite mode of substance. A value body has a magnitude which at the same time is self-identical as a definite sum of money; this is distinct from other existent sums despite their unity in the one value substance; there are *separable* notional value bodies, e.g. existent in separate accounts. A sum of money is an extended magnitude, e.g. a number of coins, which yet counts as one. Although *one* sum, this value has a definite *magnitude*.

Value bodies exist on their own account, grounded on themselves, despite virtually 'falling into the abyss' of indeterminate unity. But at this level value lacks true singularity, despite the self-diremption of the value substance into determinate 'bits' of money whose destruction is without question a destruction of value. The necessity of value to inhabit a use-value shell pins the fate of value to that incarnation; money 'down the drain' is a loss of value. However, as the bearers of money the gold pieces secure materially the *notional* apartness of value bodies; the 'cost' being that value vanishes with its bearer.

When I say that a moment of substance is oneness, I take the latter as its essential determination. But the moment of difference also exists in that the determination of oneness lies in its quantification, that money comes in *finite amounts* of itself, hence there exist masses of value, which require a proper measure. In sum money makes value *measurable*.

Value as measurable comprehends these moments: § 23.31/31 value as an immanent magnitude; § 23.31/32 the monetary medium of the magnitude of value; § 23.31/33 the value measure proper; extended 'bits' of value become actual only as *discrete sums of money*; the most immediate function of money as a sum is to serve as measure proper; value itself takes form as measurable.

§ 23.31/31   *Immanent Magnitude*
The value substance is one substance, now taken as finitely divided into bits, each of them 'one' distinct from other such ones, and all incarnating value as *immanent* to them. Because value has a quantitative character we have then the category of value as an immanent *magnitude*.

I shall show that, although it is insubstantial in the ordinary sense, the positing of value as equal to itself gives it a further determination, namely immanent magnitude, which itself is insubstantial unless complemented by a medium through which it is enabled to take its own measure, and that of others. If magnitude is the only determinate 'quality' of value, other than its basic definition as exchangeability, then it has to have a notional pseudo-quality, which provides an extended body for it to appear in, its medium of presence, and this in turn then makes possible value as measure. With one, and only one, money, a single dimension of magnitude is given with which to compare commodities. *Remark*: I take 'immanent magnitude' to be a category of Essence. In 'Being' I use only thin 'surface' categories of quantity, number, ratio, rule and specifying measure. These simple categories are developed in the context of immediate commodity relations. Here *magnitude*, by contrast, is present as a magnitude of something *immanent*, which has 'depth' in a 'value-in-itself' indifferent to its exchange-values, and which varies in its own self, as a substance that comes in *amounts* of itself.

Although it seems that measure presupposes a dimension within which things gain their metric, in this case the grounding movement is the reverse. It is the practice of measure that *constitutes* the dimensionality of value. Without it, the magnitude of value is *mere immanence*, implicitly quantitative but without any metric of its own. Money as measure introjects the form of magnitude onto this immanence. Substance in its immediacy has no metric, hence takes the measure of itself merely notionally.

§ 23.31/32   *Monetary Medium*

Value notionally has immanent magnitude, but this is formless unless there is a medium of value that crystallises it and gives it phenomenal measure.[5] So for value to obtain finite mode a *monetary medium* is required. This must model value as magnitude, namely it must be both homogenous and yet be materially divisible into amounts of itself in order to give the value dimension a metric.

One thing which distinguishes the money form from the purely general form is the requirement that the commodity excluded from the rest has to *embody* adequately the conceptual character of value. It is to be 'a value-body', to give body to the logic of value. So the purely formal requirement there be selected a universal equivalent has to be supplemented on the material side by suitable physical characteristics of the money commodity. To model the ideal immanence of value as an extended magnitude, the monetary medium, and its own measure, must provide for homogeneity, additivity, divisibility, imperishability, transportability, and so forth. The use of gold is merely a stepping-stone toward perfecting this.

Moreover, it must be a suitable vehicle for the functions of money such as measure, medium of circulation, and store of value. Although money is to be used, it is important to its functioning as value incarnate that its use should not entail its being 'used up'! It requires an immortal body. (Gold is nearly perfect; its defect is its susceptibility to abrasion.) To begin with, my presentation abstracted from the specificity of use-value; but the logic of the form of value results in specific use-value requirements for money! Thus the money commodity is the *actuality* of value.

I am making a great deal of the term 'monetary medium', but the monetary medium is required only because of the significant difference, to which I have adverted often before, between Hegel's logic of pure thoughts and the generation through the practice of exchange of pure forms of value. These forms require at all points material bearers, such as commodities, and their practically achieved connection with one another. This is why the value essence is not given immediately within commodities but presented to them from the outside, so to speak, in the money commodity (or its replacement). In the same way, for value to be present as a magnitude requires that a suitable medium for its measure be given. However, there remains a more concrete problem. A commodity is valuable in virtue of its relation to money; yet to ask the question 'how valuable?' requires further determination of the value substance. All

---

5   I follow Reuten 2019, pp. 43–5, in bringing to the fore the form of 'medium of value'.

along the quantitative character of value is presupposed hence value always has a putative magnitude; yet as an *ideal* substance it lacks any empirically graspable *unit* of magnitude. This is the problem solved when there is a monetary *medium* appropriate to the task. If it is a commodity, such as gold, it must model appropriately the metaphysical qualities of value; above all in this context, it has to have its inherent measure of amount, for example weight, to act as a proxy for a magnitude of value. Thus when I characterise money as the measure of value, we suppose value is an ideal substance present in amounts of itself, but whose measure requires the presence of a real medium of the ideality of value.

Value requires complementary determinations, the ideal magnitude without which the monetary medium would not be measuring anything substantial, and the material medium without which the ideal potential for value to be measurable cannot be real.

§ 23.31/33   *Money as Measure Proper Given in Units of Money*
Now that I have posited value as a social substance, it comes in amounts *of itself*, not merely amounts relative to some arbitrary relations. Value I now say has an *immanent magnitude* expressed in a sum of money, which is the unique mode in which a *real measure* of the value of commodities is properly given, I shall argue. Money posits the presupposition of a unitary measure that was unfulfilled at the level of mere exchange-values of commodities, which failed to unify the commodities in a single order. I may now speak of money as the value measure proper and, if it takes shape in a medium with an index of amount, it has a workable metric. Money as measure proper *grounds* the imputation that value exists as a magnitude immanent to commodities. The monetary medium is not a suitable measuring-rod for pre-existing magnitudes; rather it gives a space for value to constitute itself *as* a magnitude.

While 'specifying measure' refers to the various exchange-values one commodity has, given in amounts of *others*, 'measure proper' (measure-for-itself) must specify its measure in *itself*, just as a foot rule is the material embodiment of the length of a foot. Once there is given a proper measure in money this then measures the value of commodities. Now the commodity is no longer bogged down in its specification in numberless 'measures'; money alone has the function of measure of value, and in this manner ordering commodities in the same conceptual universe of value.

In sum: value with a finite metric granted by monetary units now exists as *measure proper*, as an immanent unity of identity and magnitude, not the merely contingent exchange-values of commodities. Value gains a measure of itself in sums of money. There is here a non-logical premise, namely that gold has been specifically selected for this role of proper measure of value. However, my 'logical' argument demonstrates *what money is* and how it acquires its functions.

Value, as one homogenous social substance, is a continuous magnitude in its notion, but when it appears in finite mode it gains measurability in *money units* which give it a discrete magnitude. Under certain circumstances the value may be assessed to many decimal places. However, for practical purposes, especially when coin is the means of payment, 'rounding' is required. So, as coin, money takes the finite mode of a countable unit.

When elucidating the notion of a measure of value it is important to set aside all examples of physical measure, such as the ruler. In these cases, the measure is applied to something already inhabiting the relevant dimension; there are lengthy things prior to the application of the ruler to measure their length. Even in the case of a measure which seems discrepant such as the length of mercury in a tube there is yet a functional relationship between that and the heat measured, which exists independently.

In the case of value, however, there is no question of finding a measure congruent with the value dimension, because there is *no* value dimension prior to the existence of measure. Value is a mere *immanence with no metric*, unless and until money creates in practice the requisite dimensional status of magnitude. The money measure unifies the immanent magnitude and the monetary medium so as to posit the value presupposed to it.

Since value has not an atom of matter to it, it is a purely social substance. It follows that value in autonomous form, namely money, has not an atom of matter, and it is itself a purely social substance. Confusion arises if this socially imputed substance is conflated with its contingent bearer, especially if the latter is gold, a commodity. However, it is necessary that money inhabit a material medium, whether the latter is gold, paper, or simply money of account. This is because value as an immanent magnitude requires phenomenal expression in numerical shape to gain a metric. Gold is a material substance, but as money it seems transubstantiated, posited as merely the golden shell of an ideal substance. However, in truth, there is consubstantiation here, because the material reality of gold still subsists; abrasion, and so forth, may sabotage its money functions.

Of all the functions of money, that of measure is most essential because it is categorially connected to the positing of value as substance. This 'measure proper' is the *ontological* foundation of the act of measuring in that it refers to the thing *being* measurable in a certain dimension. It is only in this sense of 'measure' that 'everything has its measure'. The basic function of such money is to act as the *real measure* of the value attributable to a commodity. In the next section, treating the act of measuring, I characterise money as being the real measure of value (of commodities). (This presupposition that value has magnitude is as yet purely formal so there is nothing said here about the determination *of* its magnitude, merely that it is taken as a determination *with* magnitude.)

§ 23.32   *Value Substance Actualised in a Realm of Finitude: Commodities*
To begin with in this section, substance was treated as absolute, the one homogenous value subtending all quantitative variations in magnitudes of value. This *value substance* is incarnate in money. Now, however, with the treatment of *finitude*, we show that each and every commodity is valuable. Here value as a social substance takes shape in two different ways. Clearly money attributes value to commodities when it declares them all 'of value'. Less obviously, money 'attributes' value to itself when it takes shape in *finite mode* as sums of money. Even though it *is* value in form, now the form determines its proper content as reflected within the form itself as its various amounts. Money attributes determinacy to itself just so as to equate commodity values to it.

When the form of measure was first raised, within the discussion of the simple 'Being of exchange', there was 'nothing' *to* measure. Measure was merely the ratio in which one commodity stood to another. In other words, we dealt with 'exchange-value' not 'value'. But now value is posited *as essence*, it is considered an ideal social substance with a 'mass' that is notionally 'a measurable'; but it is only given a metric in the reflection into itself of money magnitudes. Money is the form of 'measure proper' insofar as it gives the value substance a measure in sums of money. Now the form of money as measure of itself is won, we move to its use as the 'real measure' of commodity value.

The triad of value as a substance in finitude is as follows: § 23.32/1 Money as the real measure of commodity value; § 23.32/2 The commodities as values; § 23.32/3 Value as absolute relation of form and content.

§ 23.32/1   The Money Form of Value: Real Measure
The finite mode in which the attributes of value appear phenomenally is that of finite *amounts*. The finite mode of value is made possible because the monetary medium allows money to appear as a finite amount, in a sum of money, really distinct from others albeit identical in substance to them. The presence of money in such finite shapes allows the application of the measure of value to be determinate. A sum of money is not merely self-identical, but is self-equivalent; it is equal in value to itself. When money attributes value to itself it is making a difference within itself which is no difference but simply the absolute attribute of identity as quantitative measure, namely self-equivalence. It must take

its own measure when placed in the realm of finitude prior to equating itself with that of the commodity. It is only because of this that it serves as the real measure of value.

Moreover, because the money magnitude is equal to itself, it does not need a relation to something other than itself to secure this status as value. To speak of the value *of* money as if it were measured in something else is absurd. A commodity is immediately identical with itself as a *material* body, and does not need a relation to posit this, but as *value* it does, namely its relation to money. In contrast, value in money form is reflexively equal to itself, whereas the commodity as value is not, because the latter requires an equivalent form outside itself.

It may be objected that in saying money is self-equivalent as value is to offend against the principle that money has no price. However, this self-equivalence is not a price form just because it is not a value expressed in something other than itself. It is necessary to find a path between two mistakes. Money is not equivalent to itself in value because like all commodities it is always already a value, differing from them merely as the numeraire. That is one mistake. Conversely I reject the view that all value is relative, hence the notion of inherent value is to be avoided. Another mistake. The peculiar social form of money is that it is taken *as if* value were *peculiarly* present in it, as value in the form of its own equivalent.

Before we can say 'how valuable' a commodity is, it is first necessary that there be the form of 'real measure' of value that is practically operational. This requires that the magnitude of value present itself phenomenally in a material medium. But the term 'material' here is misleading if it is taken to imply the necessity of a commodity money such as gold. The latter can itself be 'idealised', from a real weight of gold to a number in an account. It is simply an amount of itself as a finite measure. Such a *presentation* of value as magnitude is all that is required, if this measure has universal application. In their finitude, commodities are a genuine plurality of things of value, not merely the notional plurality of sums of money. Yet to serve as real measure, such notional sums must be posited in finite mode, whether as coins or as simply a number in an account. But commodity monies are imperfect bodies both materially (e.g. they may be indivisible), and because of their 'honorary' status, which may be swept away by revolutions in their conditions of production.

Space as such cannot have *a* length, it simply 'makes space' for things within it to have a definite length. So here the value space contains commodities with definite value. Money constitutes the commodity manifold as a space of commensuration by valuing them in practice, insofar as it takes finite form 'within its own space' so to speak, as a measuring-rod. But what happens in practice is the inversion of the normal order. While a measure of value presupposes the value dimension, in effect by valuing commodities *as if* there were such a homogenous dimension of value, we bring into existence the very condition of such measurement ideally. The presupposition is posited in our practice.

Money, as equal to itself, is its own measure, because it is *measure proper*. However, with money as the real measure of value there is possible its application to finite empirical measures *of* commodity values posited as also participating in the value substance but in a different way. There is: (i) immanent measure posited in an amount of money given in its own units; and (ii) applied measure, when taking the measure of a commodity by reference to its monetary equivalent. In the latter case no longer is there merely a ratio, as when we first treated exchange-value, but a real measure presupposing a *substantive* community of commodities and money as value. In this unity commodities may be said to have the same value in abstraction from their relatedness.

Money, as the *real* measure of value, has a dual character. Ideally, it constitutes the dimension of magnitude of value such that a ratio of exchange can be said to express a law, whether descriptive (the 'going rate') or normative (a 'fair' exchange), rooted in a common value space. But, to fulfil this function, it must on the material side incarnate the relevant substantiality of value. Without the medium, magnitude would not be articulated in a determinate dimension, while unless value took determinate shape as a quantity then the rule would be barter, even if gold were to be set aside as an intermediate good. If the value substance takes shape in a medium with an index of amount, there is a workable system of measurement.

Money has the form of a measuring-rod of value because of its self-equivalence (just as a ruler is identical in length to itself). As such it is *real measure*; and this allows the many commodities to be commensurated in it. Having established the capacity of money to be the value measure, I now consider the act of measurement through which money attributes value to commodities. These exist in an extended manifold, and insofar as they are posited as things of value by money they become *real value bodies*, I shall argue. Here it is important to distinguish the merely notional finite moment of the value substance in itself, from the development of these moments in *exteriority*, in which a 'body of value' is really present in distinct commodities, an extended realm of finite 'values' in the plural.

Remark: It is as if space exists because a ruler unfolded itself from some infinitesimal singularity and brought into being the dimension it measures. Here the money commodity as a singularity of value unfolds from itself the dimension (infinite in reach) *within* which commodities find their place as finite beings of value.

In the previous section it was shown that value as a substance is itself determined as an extended realm of value 'bodies', so to speak, when a sum of money is present *alongside* other such sums. However, value as a unitary substance continually recalls such sums to their identity as value; their distinctness is merely *notional*; they easily fall back into the abyss of absolute substance.

Now in this section I consider the *application* of the money measure to the finite realm of commodities. What happens when money measures the value of commodities is that it *attributes* value to them just in the very act of subjecting them to measurement, I argue.

Remark: If the measure function of money simply provides the *form* of commensuration, how the actual magnitudes are *determined* is another question; the real magnitudes may be contingently determined for all we know, such that there is nothing to measure really. (In my view the magnitude of value remains indeterminate until conceptualised as the result of capitalist competition.) But if there is some determination of magnitude it is nugatory unless the money form provides the dimension of magnitude in the first place. (Here we are concerned with the ontological basis of measure relations, rather than articulating the logic of a judgement of worth; that we reach in value as the concept.)

Ontologically the practice of measurement is important as the immediate vehicle of the forming of commodities *as values*, I argue. This *constitutive* role of money means that *logically* its function as measure has to be thematised prior to its other functions. Of course, the prevalence of gold money, throughout the pre-capitalist era, makes it seem continuous with other commodities, for example in having a use-value. But notice that the use-value of gold, *qua* metal, is quite different from its use-value, *qua* money, in fulfilling monetary functions.

§ 23.32/2   Commodities as Values

This theme is discussed in three sections as follows: § 23.32/21 Value as the substance of commodities; § 23.32/22 The transubstantiation of the commodity; § 23.32/23 The commodity posited as 'a value'.

I shall first discuss the positing of the presupposition that value is the ideal social substance *of* commodities. But it is substance posited as existent on its own account, subsisting on its own ground. Thus, secondly, this leaves the matter of the commodity as merely the transubstantiated shell of the value substance. Finally, we conclude that the commodity is 'a value'; ideally the bodily shape of the commodity is merely the *bearer* of value.

§ 23.32/21   *Value as the Substance of Commodities*
Because money in finite mode is equal to itself, it is able to function as measure of value. However, money not only *gives* value its measure but through its application it enables commodities to gain the quality of *being* measurable. In the ordinary way this is not an issue; a thing has weight prior to its relation to the given measure of its weight. But value is not a substance with a given dimensionality, requiring only a numeraire to set up a system of measure. In this case practice *imposes* the pure form of measure on commodities. Value gains an immanent magnitude only when the *form* of measure is practically applied and grounds the required dimension.

So value appears immediately as sums of money, and through the mediation of money a specific value is attributed to a commodity. The commodities in the plural are posited as all embodying 'value', while the oneness of the value substance is affirmed in the homogeneity of money, and the notional character of its presence as a finite sum, as explained later. Insofar as money is the encompassing moment, value is posited as the ideal social substance *of* commodities, a substance radically other than their bodily substance, being an ideal imputation.

Value as the *ideal substance* of commodities is not the content of the *material commodity*. But the set of commodity values *are* a content with respect to money as their common form.

§ 23.32/22   *The Transubstantiation of the Commodity*
The measure relation of commodities and money secures the genuine finitude of value-as-substance in that commodities are posited as 'of value'. Value is incarnate in the material shell of the commodity, therewith acquiring a bodily shape.

By contrast, if a sum of money is also a body of value, this is so merely notionally insofar as money is present merely as a number in a ledger (a debit card in notional dollars adequately replaces coins and bills): this number is a number 'of' *nothing*. Money embodies the *actuality* of value itself, and it posits the commodities *as* value magnitudes in the very act of 'measuring' them 'as if' they were always already given as having a definite value. The order of dependence works retroactively; at some point the 'as if' passes to 'as is' when all the conditions of existence are present for value to actualise itself.

It is necessary to distinguish the value attribute of extension (sums of money) from commodities as bodies of value, with reference to the *irreducibility* of the real extended realm of commodities to oneness. But ideally they are of one substance, namely value. Separate sums of money are merely notionally existent in extended fashion in that all such sums collapse to one sum if brought back to unity. While substance, as one substance, attracts all sums of money into its all-embracing identity, the moment of distinctness is here vindicated when every commodity is posited as having its own value.

Commodities and money, as finite things, are *shapes* of the same infinite value substance, abstracted from any material shell, as in money of account. With the descent of value to finitude each separable commodity contains value. Sums of money in accounts merely are ideally *counted* as finite modes of value, but a heap of commodities are real values in finite mode materially presented. Now there is a genuine plurality of values, not merely a set of items defined in relation to each other and to money.

Marx often uses religious metaphors; advisedly so. Especially germane is the Christian doctrine of the Eucharist. On one view the communion wafer retains merely its *appearance* as a natural body but is *substantially* the body of Christ. This is a case of *transubstantiation*. On the rival view the body of Christ is indeed really present, but it does not displace the material body of the bread which persists throughout the sacrament. The two substances exist at the same place and time. This is *consubstantiation*.

In capitalism value as an ideal substance posits the transubstantiation of gold, which appears as if the golden shell merely veils the presence of the ideal substance, just as in the case of the doctrine of transubstantiation. In the case of commodities proper there is consubstantiation because the material bodies also are relevant to their exchangeability, as it is necessary to give sense to consumption. The formal determination of commodities as value requires value to become earthly if it is to redeem their souls, so *value appears to them as gold*, which has the special use of immediate exchangeability with commodities; baptised as 'values' commodities are yet consubstantial since they retain their ordinary use-value as well. The commodity, then, has an earthly and a heavenly nature, but the latter is redeemable only through the grace of the Jesus figure, money, value incarnate, having acquired a bodily shape capable of intercourse with such finite souls.

All commodities, including gold, have a body and soul, so to speak. But as money gold is transubstantiated if the bodily shell is treated as inconsequential because its *material* use-value is never realised. In contrast, ordinary commodities are entangled in a contradiction; for their nature is internally polarised between use-value and value. (This creates problems for their joint realisation, as I show below: see § 42.)

In the following sections I leave aside the issue of material substance for now and simply consider commodities as of ideal substance.

§ 23.32/23   *The Commodity Posited as 'a Value'*

Only in finite mode does the ideal substance take on *determinate shape* as a set of independent existents. But commodities as material beings have themselves separate material existence. They are suitable *bearers* of the requirement that value is determined as a *realm* of values in exteriority. Each commodity is posited as 'a value', truly existent as a discrete item. Such values are plural even though they have a common substance. But money is never properly plural because its finite mode, a sum of money, allows one to speak of sums of money (but not a sum of monies) only as notional divisions of the one unitary value substance. That has the attribute of extension, meaning here a dimension of magnitude, which is the only determinate quality value has that is distinct from its infinite self-sameness. (I have less money, not fewer money.)

In commodities value is posited as existing phenomenally as the shaped value substance such that each individual commodity is posited as such an individual existent 'value', and together are hence a realm of 'values'. So commodities have true *separateness* as shells of value to balance off the *commonality* of value substance.

But its value substance, arising from transubstantiation, is wholly distinct from the material body of the commodity. Although appearing as a thing *of* value the commodity *counts as* 'a value'. This is a case of *objective* metonymy. To call a commodity 'a value' is not just a figure of speech. (Compare 'a use-value', which is.) This is because the commodity has a 'fetish-character', which has objective validity; within the value form the commodity is posited as a value among values. Earlier (§ 22.23 *The General Form of Value*) I showed that a peculiarity of the universal equivalent form is that it has a fetish-character. However, we see now that ordinary commodities are also socially posited fetishistically as things capable of initiating relations with each other.

Value is imputed to commodities, as their (ideal) substance, when they are posited as values through their monetary mediation. One consequence is that we have superseded now the view of commodities merely *related* in the value form; they are now imputed with the ability to act as values on their own account. Moreover, it is characteristic of the value form that human relations appear as relations between the commodities they produce and exchange, these things become posited as effective in their own right.

Remark: Later I shall treat the alienation of labour, in which the powers of labour are objectively displaced to these 'values', relations of labours appearing as relations of things. As the commodity acquires a life of its own, so living labour is reified in such thing-like form.

§ 23.32/3 Value as Absolute Relation of Form and Content

Money as absolute form of value seems to reduce commodities to vanishing moments. But, as form determined to finitude, value must posit itself in a subsistent 'content'. When money attributes to commodities the value substance, it is posited in them as the content complementing the money form. In every commodity, value becomes a self-sufficient unity of substance, being formed as value by money, and through that posited as in itself ideally value. It is 'a value'. The material body of the commodity serves as the shell of the value that is its true substance as a commodity. The absolute relation of money and commodities instantiates fully the logic of form and content touched on above much earlier. Now money as absolute form produces a content from within itself in the shape of commodity values. However, value as pure form posits itself as a content lacking in material determinacy. (Only later shall I discuss how capital as subject takes possession of its *material basis*, and how the magnitude of value is therewith determined.)

Remark: In order to keep the categories straight, notice that two uses of the term 'form' are here employed. In its broadest sense 'form' comprehends the entire sequence of categories deployed through this discussion of the value form (which last contrasts with the bodily form of the commodity), and which comprehends all the logical categories predicated of value in the exposition, including value-as-form and value-as-content. But in a narrower sense, that in which, within this discussion, I oppose form and content, then money is *the* form of value and the value attributed to commodities is the content. Moreover, this notion of the determinacy of form is different from the imposition of a social form on material given to it, which we reach later with the notion of the 'formal determination' *of* the material inscribed within it. (See *Glossary*)

The absolute relation of form and content is posited when money attributes value to commodities as the adequate content of the value form, although as yet this determination is purely notional.

Remark: I distinguish this category of 'absolute relation' from the earlier 'essential relation', i.e. 'correlation', which is the culminating category of the dialectic of appearance. A relation is essential if it makes its poles what they are (e.g. relative and equivalent forms of value). A relation is absolute if the poles turn out to be an internal opposition within an overarching identity; they descend from the same source so to speak. In a sense, absolute relation is no relation because both sides are sublated moments of the whole.

In the *absolute relation* form is not detachable from a supposed content, nor can there be a content indifferent to its form. Form passes over *into* content, and the content express itself *in* the form. The highest point of absolute relation of form and content shows the activity of the form determines itself only to shapes of itself. The supposed content is simply the self-presentation of the absolute so always already *actual* (rather than lying *behind* a superficial form). Here we see the passing over of form to content and content to form; yet as both are movements within the absolute relation its self-determination arrives only at forms of *itself*. Thus there is an 'absolute' character to the content. The 'content' is commodities that *are* formed as values through the activity of the money form; and they become themselves a form-determination of value just as money is. Posited as values they take money as what always already formed them as such.

When we first introduced 'form' this stood opposed to that of which it was supposed to be the form in that the latter was an abstract thing-in-itself, a mere *bearer* of the 'property' value (technically 'existent' but not 'substantial'). 'A value' amongst values is a category of actuality. It is more concrete than the earlier existent thing with properties. This latter is simply based on value as a *relational* property of the commodity, which might lead thought to jump metonymically to the notion the commodity is 'a value', just as it is 'a use-value'. But there is no ground for this in the given body of the commodity, nor yet was value itself a 'body of value'.

Earlier we also saw the doubling of form allows form to be inwardly reflected so as to be a content, but form also, as mere immediacy, may be allowed an external existence indifferent to content, hence the form of value may be empty when non-products take commodity form or the law of value is distorted. Here, with money as the absolute form of value, the reciprocity of content and form presuppose a 'fit'. But this requires further grounding.

So the relation of the money form of value to the commodity form of value is nothing other than form posited as its own content in commodities. The bodily shell of the commodity 'contains' a value body shaped as such by the money form. If, in the commodity, value is content, this does not mean *the commodity* is the form of that content for the form is *money*. What we have in the bodily shape of the commodity is not merely the shape of its material stuff but also the bodily *shape* of the value substance as posited by the commodity status of the material object. Commodities are now self-identical values (just as much as self-identical use-values).

Remark: The sense of 'content' in this paragraph, in which it flows from form, is different from that sense in which the development of capitalism depends upon its material 'content' (which I reach later). In the latter context, social capital, in the entirety of its form-determinations, is the driver of the system, but it is enabled by the productive forces, and the magnitude of value is a function of the socially necessary labour time as it reduces.

§ 23.33 The Infinite Unity of the Value Substance

At first (§ 13) the value of a commodity existed only in terms of another, which served as its specific measure. Then, through the dialectic of the forms of value, I reach money as the real measure of the value of commodities because money is posited as value in autonomous form, as absolute form, as the value substance capable of sustaining its own proper measure (§ 23.31).

When applied to commodities money not only measures value but as absolute form in effect shapes commodity value into its content. As an absolute relation of form and content the two turn into one another, being in effect two determinations of the same substance. Commodities count as 'values', as all embodiments of value. Now we bring together the notion that value is yet *one* substance, with its existence in finitude in such 'values'. Once the value measure is related to the commodity manifold in this function it brings coherence and order to it. The commodities have genuine discrete existence as 'values' in the plural.

Now, under the category of 'the infinite unity' of value-as-substance, I address the three dimensions of this underlying unity of value, namely: § 23.33/1 The value of commodities is one substance, hence lacks true individuation; its modes are fully subsumed in it; nonetheless value must appear in finitude as numerically different bits; § 23.33/2 The function of money in making possible the comparability of commodity values; § 23.33/3 The merging of values in a mass of value measured as one sum, i.e. the additivity of sums of money.

I refer in this discussion to Form VII: the substantial form of value.

Form VII: *The Substantial Form of Value*

a units of A	*is worth*	z of money
b units of B	*is worth*	y of money
c units of C	*is worth*	x of money
d units of D	*is worth*	w of money
etc.	*is worth*	...
A & B & C & D ... together	*are worth*	the sum of z + y + x + w ...

NB Thus, A & B & C & D *together* are worth n, a single sum of money, where n is the *sum* of z + y + x + w ...

§ 23.33/1 Identity of Commodities as Values

As values, all commodities are *identical* in substance (a qualitative moment). Commodities are, as it were, 'shapes' of the one substance. The form-determinations of value as substance, namely money and commodities, are complementary. If money as a sum of money is a finite mode of the value substance in immediate shape, once valued by such a sum a commodity is also posited as a finite mode of value, 'a value', so to speak. What is of the essence at this point is that the *interchangeability* of commodities follows from this unity in substance. 'Difference' here is no difference; for commodities of equal value are notionally *substitutable*. (Thus we may anticipate that the *exchange* of commodities, whether with money or other commodities, appears as *value exchanging with itself*.)

§ 23.33/2   Comparability of Commodities as Values

If value is embodied in commodities of definite worth, one commodity may be *compared* with another in magnitude (a quantitative moment). Values differing merely quantitatively are implicitly different only within their common substance.

Now, as shown in Form VII, money enables commodities to be compared in value terms even if they are not in use-value terms. Money situates all commodities in a homogenous value space, infinite in extent, showing how one commodity may be worth twice as much as another, for example. Money makes commodities *comparable in value*. The value of a commodity appears as less than, equal to, or more than, the value of another, as they are systematically co-determined as a system of values in a unitary value space.

§ 23.33/3   Merging of Values

The identity in substance of what is comparable in magnitude is not merely notional when we see that the value of commodities may be merged, and that their amounts are summable as shown in Form VII. This in principle is infinite additivity and shows there is something above and beyond existent finity. This we shall argue is the very *concept* of value, of which all possible finite values are determinations.

Value, although taking finite mode in sums of money or as embodied in commodities, is not fully individuated. Sums of money must be numerically different one from another, but notice that this difference is purely notional. For this numerical difference in sums of money is equally sublated in a combined sum of money when the different amounts *merge* into one amount. 'Bits' of money are ideally attracted into one, but they are notionally distinguished by a notional repulsion materially effected by the bearers of value. Two different accounts, each containing 10 dollars, achieves the necessary separation of amounts of value by purely formal means. But notice that if I have 10 dollars in an account, and I enter a further 10, I do not have two '10s', as if the account were a cash-box; I have a single sum of 20 dollars, so here the moment of *pure magnitude* takes precedence over that of numerical difference; even so I can re-divide the amount by withdrawing, say, 12 dollars.

Commodities come in incommensurable physical amounts. But their money values are not merely commensurable, such that the *relative* worth of commodities may be compared; they are *additive*. Most importantly, a set of commodities, each valued by a sum of money separately, may be treated as *one*. A basket of different commodities, which are heterogeneous in use-value, is capable of being taken as a unity with itself as a single value because the separate values are *additive*. All values merge to form one value by simply summing the separate magnitudes. As a homogeneous amount of value what they are worth *together* may be stated as one sum of money. Nor is the summing achieved by abstraction as when one cat and one dog make two animals. Values are not distinguishable from one another except in magnitude, hence there is no need to abstract from qualitative difference in order to sum them; conversely pure magnitude is not sufficient to separate them, for ideally they merge to form one magnitude. But as embodied, for example, in coin, value is peculiar in that the magnitudes are both ideally one, yet materially many numerically.

Thus in Form VII, the commodities in the left column may be aggregated in terms of the values on the right. The oneness of money, explained in § 23.31, trumps the differences presupposed in § 23.32. Quantitative difference, being subsumed in this identity, is sublated in the infinite additivity of sums of money. Values merge into one mass of value. All that is necessary to make a transition to value as Concept is that the infinite unity of the value substance become explicitly posited by value itself. (This opens the way to the emergence of subject out of substance.)

Since we are totalling, the question arises implicitly as to the sense of valuing the total economic output including gold (if only gold is money). This is possible because gold can appear on the 'left' side of the measure relation with the other commodities, i.e. *really* present like them, and, on the right, figures *notionally* as the measure of all, including itself. With respect to the current status we have ascribed to commodities, as a pole of the absolute relation of value, they are certainly self-*identical* (a *qualitative* moment) as values, but only the money commodity is also *self*-equal (a moment of *magnitude*) because the measure function is the prerogative of money; commodities cannot 'stand outside themselves' so to speak, in order to take their own measure, the money commodity must supply their measure, just in virtue of being self-equivalent, as we argued earlier. The substantive form of value establishes that gold is valuable in itself if it is money; as such it measures itself; and the entire sum of commodities, including gold, may be given a measure in the standard unit of gold. The infinite unity of the value substance underpins such practical totalisation.

Remark: This practical fact that all 'values' may merge into one sum of money confirms that value is *one substance*, not a class of independently existing substances. Value *is* a substance, incarnated in money, and is the (social) substance *of* commodities. Since value is a substance we can properly speak later of its 'metamorphoses' (how a substance, here value, changes shape in finite mode). Moreover, money as capital allows value to appear as a substance that can be *accumulated*.

Although unity in substance is a presupposition of the extended realm of value bodies *in-formed* by it, it is not a question of its explicit self-determination as it will be with value as subject. The implicit unity of substance discussed above has to become the *explicit* unity of the all-embracing concept if we are to grasp the logical form of capital.

More precisely, 'the Concept' is ontologically required for our presentation to advance from the consideration of a self-subsistent *substance* to that of a self-determining *subject*.

Logically money incarnates the homogenous value substance; yet commodities are the shell of differentiated values, each substantively value. A *unified* concept of value requires this difference to be a self-difference.

The transition to the Doctrine of the Concept employed here is similar to that used to vindicate the transition to the Doctrine of Essence. There, the infinite unity of the measure series suggested the presence of an underlying essence. Now the infinite unity in substance of all commodities as it is constituted by their proper measure, money, suggests that the indefinite set of values may be treated as potential instances of a universal. We shall show this formal possibility becomes actual in their real movement, for example the metamorphoses of commodities.

Here the additivity of value means that the total amount of value present may be limitlessly large yet never ceases to be the incarnation of value as one homogenous mass. Notwithstanding the existence of sums of money as distinct, they are all notionally brought together insofar as they are of one substance. All sums may themselves by summed. Taken to the limit such magnitudes transcend themselves, not in the meaninglessness of an infinite sum, but in the unitary *concept* of value distinct from any and all instances. Thus value *as such* is distinct from *any* such quantity.

I next move to consider how such a presupposed Concept posits itself. 'To determine is to negate'. Thus if a commodity is worth say four pounds, it is *not* worth, e.g. five pounds. But as concept of value, money negates all these negations and is grasped as their *negative unity*. To actualise the oneness of value means to go beyond specific sums, even an infinite sum, to register the negative unity of all these possible sums in a higher form, the unitary value-concept capable of determination in infinite ways. This supplants the occult notion of the abyss of one substance by an explicit positing of the universal and its determinations.

In substance values are present only in a *passive* unity. But to *think* them in their identity is to presuppose a pure concept. From this I shall reach capital. Value is a self-sustaining substance that becomes subject as self-activating capital.

Addendum on Commodity Money

This chapter may appear odd to some, because it commits itself to commodity money, namely gold. The reason for this is related to the method employed in the presentation, which must proceed one step at a time in a perspicuous order. (The prevalence of gold money historically is *entirely irrelevant* to it.) It is necessary that there be money, but surely it is not necessary that money be *a commodity*. Yet in presenting the development of the value form at this level I proceed to a money commodity when seeking to actualise the universal equivalent form. Why is this? The methodological reason for it is that each stage of a systematic dialectic supersedes the previous one with a *minimum* of new material. In stabilising the previous determinations, the new form requires only the minimum *sufficient* conditions for this, not *necessary* conditions. Thus I do not seek to show that gold is *necessary* to a capitalist economy (notwithstanding the occasional flight to gold).

At this level of commodity relations it suffices to solve the present problem by positing a money commodity. The logical development of the *necessity* of money and its functions is required, and is carried forward, even if gold is here its *contingent* shell.

The monetary medium allows money *really* to confront commodities; this is what makes commodity money seem the obvious bearer of such reality. Although in the medium of gold the function of measure is effected materially, this is not essential. The key requirement is merely that the medium has a metric, that it makes present in finite form value as an amount of itself; it is clear this may be done formally with inconvertible bank notes. The reason for this is that the medium provided by it simply has to make money visible so to speak.

Nevertheless, for value to make itself present requires *some* medium or other, even when commodity money is abandoned. But at *this level* of the presentation we consider only commodity money since that is the resource available. Gold money is not a necessary condition for capital but money of some kind is. In order to give the measure its operational actuality some believe it must be a product of labour, because it must be of the same nature as what is measured, just as weight may be measured in a balance by standard 'weights'. But this is unnecessary. Here we are considering measure as *pure form* corresponding to our presentation of value as pure *immanence*. It is certainly *not* the case that a measure of value must *itself* be something *of* value.[6] (For a start, how would this value itself be measured?) To give value in a monetary medium requires simply that its essential character as quantitative be made phenomenally present in the *forms* of unit, amount, proportion, etc.; what the *bearer* of these forms is does not matter as long as practice designates them as socially acceptable tender.[7] The pure form of measure requires simply a linear metric such that four dollars are worth twice two dollars. Indeed, the perfect money bearer should approximate as closely as possible to an immaterial being.

Gold is no longer money; however, even in Marx's day gold did not circulate but was simply represented in accounts. Today we have various forms of credit money, centrally non-convertible bank notes. In circulation inconvertible paper may *function* as money; this it does, not by being a *representative* commodity, nor by being a *representation of* value, but by serving as the *presence* of value. How is such money to be understood? There two possible alternatives to gold: bank money created *ex nihilo* and state-issued paper.

It is not possible for the presentation to give an account of bank money at this point for the simple reason that banks are capitalist institutions, and we have not as yet developed such an institutional framework, *nor even the very concept of capital itself*. The systematic development cannot have credit money (properly capitalist money) come in straight away, when it is only later in the argument that it may be developed after earlier in the presentation commodity money functions 'virtually'.

If it is said that something with a socially objective status outside the body of the commodity whose value is expressed is required, but that it may be left indeterminate on this level whether that is commodity money or credit money, would that be adequate to the purpose of positing money? However, such a

---

6 Campbell 2017 shows Marx's *Capital* allows for the possibility that a fully functioning money need not have intrinsic value. She says the fact that money does not have to have *intrinsic* value, to function as measure, is an important step towards credit money.

7 Reuten 2019, pp. 103–5, pp. 108–9, argues that 'bank account money' as 'socially acceptable tender' is derivable prior to the state and 'legal tender'.

move leaves money as '*our* abstraction', as *externally* generated. The form of 'external reflection' lacks immanent determination.

So the *determining* reflection *immanent* to the movement of commodities themselves is needed. We require a minimum sufficient condition. Indeterminacy is certainly minimal but not a *sufficient* ground to support the *objectivity* of value, whereas a commodity is already there and merely has to be reassigned to generate the dimensionality of value. It does not mend matters if one were to suppose that some *external* agency *imposes* a 'money', for example, a 'legal tender' consisting of state-issued paper. This is logically consistent with the confines of simple circulation. However, such a supposition disrupts the *immanent* development of the money form of value, which I have undertaken.[8]

Finally, let us note an important defect in commodity money. Now, initially, a certain commodity, gold, is presented as the bearer of money. Although a commodity, it is posited as *counting* as money. However, this means barter is still not transcended. In a perfected system of generalised commodity exchange all commodities enter circulation by sale. But gold enters as a produced commodity with a potential value, which remains *unexpressed in price*. In order for money to oppose itself to commodities *as money*, not as any sort of commodity, this defect has to be overcome.

Later such defects of gold may be addressed when the means to remedy them have been developed. We first must develop the concept of capital, and then the specific form of banking capital. On this basis I develop properly capitalist money, namely *ex nihilo* credit money (see § 91 in Chapter 15).

Summary

This chapter begins by promising to show how is posited the presupposition that value lies immanent in commodity relations. The centrepiece of this argument is the development of the money form of value. We show that if value-as-essence is to be grounded it must find an appropriate form of expression in its world of appearance. This world is unified in 'Form III the general form of value' in which the unique universal equivalent instantiates value in autonom-

---

8   My position – that money and banks should not be brought into the exposition early – contrasts with Reuten 2019, which gives a systematic argument for the necessity of money and banks, by saying that money is a necessary condition of existence of 'one-dimensional value' (p. 43), and that this in turn presupposes the actual creation of money *ex nihilo* by banks (p. 103). (One advantage of this position is that the exposition avoids a stage of gold money, which is not a *necessary* condition of capital.)

ous shape. This necessity is secured by the social acceptance of a suitable money commodity (at this stage of the presentation). Money as the absolute form of value unites two form-determinations of money: 'exchangeabilty-in-immediacy', and 'immediate exchangeabilty', in value as an ideal social substance. This substance is presupposed as an immanent mass of value, but its magnitude is grounded only in the money measure, which provides a suitable monetary medium for this purpose. As measure proper, money is the real measure of value of commodities. But this grounds the imputation that commodities are themselves now posited as 'values'. Despite the fetish-character of such a form it has objective validity, it is argued. The merging of such values in a single sum of value is the highest point of the form 'value-as-substance'. The implicit infinite unity of substance is sublated in 'value-as-concept', explicitly put, in the next chapter, on the capital form.

CHAPTER 8

Capital

§3 Capital

This chapter shows that value as substance (money) becomes subject (capital). In the pure dialectic of the value form I outlined, first I dealt with what it is to be a commodity; and concluded that to be a commodity is to have value intrinsic to it. Then I showed that such a presupposition is posited only with money; money is the actuality of value. Through this it is determined that value is a substance, capable of magnitude, incarnate in a monetary medium modelling the immanent quantitative characteristics of value present as an amount of itself.

Money gives value its proper measure. As its own measure a sum of money is equal to itself, and in this capacity it takes the measure of commodities, therewith positing the presupposition that a commodity *has* value. Moreover, this imputation effectively presupposes that, beyond its bodily shell, lies its *true substance*, value in some definite amount.

But this duality of value, as unitary form (money) and formed content (values of commodities) is itself sublated when the summing in money of a basket of commodities brings back the infinite unity of value to itself, when the notionally separate values merge. Thus these commodities are both immediately of specific value yet in principle subsumed by a unitary value substance. Below it is shown that *capital* is brought into being on the basis of the circulation of commodities and money such that value gains its unity with itself in practice, as self-valorising value.

Capital in its concept divides into

§ 31 Price: Subjectivity of Value

§ 32 Exchange and Circulation: Objectivity of Value

§ 33 Capital as Concept and Idea.

§ 31 *Price (Subjectivity of Value)*

There are some difficult conceptual issues involved in the exposition of value as 'the concept'. While unity is always to the fore, the determination of finitude must allow value to appear as discrete instances of itself. In the treatment of real measure, I kept such discreteness at a virtual level in that there the real presence of a piece of gold is not required; I merely give the notional measure of the commodity in a notional amount of money. This constitutive function of money posits the presupposition that commodities are values. I shall show that it underlies the rationality of sale.

An offer to sell at a definite price is rooted in a judgement of worth. Such a judgement requires the *practical* application of the value concept to the real empirical manifold of commodities. Here the virtual measure of commodities must become phenomenally present in an *alienable* piece of gold or at least as a number equated in the accounts of traders. Value, as 'the concept' present ideally, must be applied in the real world. Or, conversely, commodity values must be brought under their concept. For this to be possible the value present in the monetary medium must really appear in finite form as a fixed amount of itself capable of being exchanged for a commodity.

The price list looks exactly the same as the substantial form of value (see Form VII above). The difference is that in the earlier treatment the point was to exhibit the function of money as real measure of the value of commodities. But the sum of money represented was to be taken *ideally* in its measure function. No *actual* money need be present for this function to allow for comparability of values. Now the price list is to be understood as an offer for sale. (So price requires undertaking a judgement of worth, with the claims about 'worth' being 'subjective' unless and until an agreement for purchase is concluded, we show below.) In this case there may well be several similar items for sale, which means that the money used to purchase them must likewise appear in plural form. To sell three hamburgers at a dollar a piece requires not the notional measure of 'three dollars' but three distinct dollar bills presented. Conversely to sell one hamburger for a dollar requires simply *any* of the numerous dollar bills in circulation (not a token only valid for one of my hamburgers). Price is logically 'subjective' because it may in principle be assigned prior to actual sales. As such it is a purely notional form of value. Only when price is agreed between the parties do commodities and money get on the dance floor, so to speak; this objective process of exchange and circulation embodies a new logic, which I shall treat in 'the metamorphoses of commodities'.

The discussion of value in this chapter is somewhat difficult (but, nonetheless, important). because it relies on a distinction between '*the* Concept' (with a definite article) and ordinary concepts. *The Concept* is a logical figure that may be abstracted from ordinary concepts; it comprises the moments: Universality, Particularity, and Singularity (UPS). It is the very truth of ordinary concepts, indeed of everything of which we form a concept. As such, determinate concepts (for example 'dog') may be viewed as determinations *of* The Concept. Consider the proposition 'Fido is a white dog'. Here 'Fido' is singular, 'dog' universal, and 'white' particular.

Remark: Analytical philosophy has only a crude idea of the concept. It conflates particularity with singularity. Thus a typical dictionary of philosophy says that things are particulars and their qualities are universals, so that 'redness' is a universal predicated of all red objects. But things are not particulars, they are singulars and each red object is a particular shade of red. Presumably it will be replied that each shade is itself a narrower universal corralling its instances. But in this move their more universal character as simply 'red' is lost. The tripartite division of the concept is preferable because it adequately represents this complexity.

So far, so good. However, *value* is present at *both* these levels. Value-as-Concept comprises UPS. But the determination of this all-embracing universality is nothing more than its *quantification*. Thus there are many 'values' present, each of which has 'a' finite magnitude (and may be brought to judgement accordingly), so is contrasted with the 'infinity' of *the* Concept.

Hegel's term *'Begriff'* used to be translated as 'Notion', but now is always rendered as 'Concept'. This leaves Notion available for a special technical use in my system. I use it, in discussing price, to stand for what Hegel terms 'the subjective or *formal* concept' in the very first section of the Doctrine of the Concept. I think this is justified because in English 'Notion' carries such a subjective connotation; and a special term is required if we take seriously Hegel's point that it is *merely* formal, in the same sense that is self-styled 'formal logic', namely devoid of all content. For Hegel, of course, the concept proper *does* comprehend its content. I shall come to that.

I now pass to a detailed presentation of value as *Notion, Judgement* (required for assigning price), and *Syllogism* (transitivity of price). In this I shall try to employ the following terms. Value as pure Notion divides into Universality, Particularity, and Singularity. Value as finite divides into universal, particular, and singular. These divisions are, so to speak, the particularity of the Notion itself. But notice this means the movement of Particularity is doubled: keeping within the immanence of the pure Notion, it determines itself to Singularity; while unfolded into a finite realm it determines the existence of a wealth of singulars. Thus I distinguish the *formal* moment of Singularity, which pertains *to* the Notion itself, from the *application of* the Notion to finite singulars, of which there are many. (To put the point another way, it is necessary to distinguish the 'ontological' dimension of Singularity from the 'ontic' realm of singulars.) *A* singular is made possible because the concept in its singularity determines itself to many singulars that are each some particularisation of the universal.

But Singularity, as *a moment of* the Notion, is that through which the concept asserts its *unity* with itself as a totality of form. This is distinct from the moment of Universality, which is the moment at which the Notion asserts its self-sameness, in the sense that the moment of Particularity both negates the universal and yet is equally brought back to the universal. Yet if there is *one* Concept (here taken as logically distinct from the many concepts abstracted from the realm of finitude) the moment of Singularity is taken as *characterising itself*. It is that moment of selfhood which makes it possible to say that the concept is *self*-determining when the universal determines itself to the particular.

It is common to give the logical triad as Universality, Particularity, Individuality. However, my 'third' is Singularity; for I reserve the term 'Individual' for a special use later (for example § 33). (Note that Hegel's third term here, '*Einzelnheit*', is more properly translated as 'Singularity' in any case.[1])

Thus I give the English terms different roles. It is necessary, I believe, to introduce a distinction between two different senses of the projected third to universality and particularity. In the sense in which there is something to *contrast* with the other moments I prefer the term Singularity. But that there is a need for another term becomes apparent when it is understood that each moment of the triad is reflected into the others; so each is, for example, a particular moment of it. Crucial to my argument is that if we take the three moments in their *unity* a special term is required, for which I use 'Individuality'. The concept *posited* 'as totality' is clearly different from the moment of singularity in which it is positively determined as *one* particularisation of the universal. For the totality of the Concept is characterised by the 'negative unity' of its moments.

As concrete, the unity of the concept is not present in the universal moment alone but in its unity with the other specific determinations. This, as distinct from them in its identity with itself, and taken as the totality of its moments, I term the Individuality of the Concept.

Remark: For Hegel, this part of the Doctrine of the Concept has relevance to the form of 'constituted' subjectivity, proleptically tracing the abstract moments of the activity of the real Individual. This sense of 'subjectivity' is not obviously present in price, which seems set externally. Nonetheless, the moments of the Notion treated here are precisely those through which money as capital in its *own* movement unfolds itself.

The *Price Form* divides into the triad:
§ 31.1 Value as Notion,
§ 31.2 Judgement of Worth,
§ 31.3 Transitivity of Price.

---

1 I endorse the trenchant remarks on this in the translators' *Introduction* to *The Encyclopae-*

§ 31.1   Value as Notion

Whereas the function of money as measure is purely formal, the price list (while generated by subjective judgement) notionally proposes a real *transfer* of value if two subjective judgements coincide such that a bargain is *concluded*. So then money must be really (not simply virtually) active. Value as Notion divides into:

§ 31.11 Infinite Value Notion
§ 31.12 Finite Value Notion
§ 31.13 Value Brought Back to the Infinite

§ 31.11   *The Infinite Value Notion*

In its Notion value as Universality is all-pervasive; as Particularity, it is present as its amount; and as Singularity as *an* amount. It is important here that *the infinite* value notion does not admit of *singulars* which 'fall under' their concept, in the same way as Fido is dog-like. Although there are particular amounts to which value determines itself these remain purely notionally different; for any such amount is indistinguishable from any other identical such amount; if A and B, singly, are each worth a dollar, then to present that fact does not require two distinct dollars; it is simply the very same notional dollar, deployable infinitely. (Singular dollars we treat under the finite notion.)

Moreover, the general claim that a commodity is valuable can only be made determinate, not as what *kind* of value it is, but only as *how* valuable it is. What kind of universal is it that has no determinable qualities? It is practically specifiable only in amounts of itself. It is not that we have a class of value bodies of which the universal would be 'value as such' in abstraction from them.

The Notion is the universal form that validates commodities as values. This is logically prior to the *judgement of worth* wherein the value *of* commodities is reflected in a determinate sum of money. Once we have such a notion of value the next problem is how exactly this posits itself in finite form, i.e. predicates a specific value to commodities.

The moments of the Infinite Value Notion are:

§ 31.11/1 Its Universality
§ 31.11/2 Its Particularity as Amount
§ 31.11/3 Its Singularity: An Amount

---

dia Logic; I further endorse their scathing comments on that tradition in English philosophy which speaks of singular entities as 'particulars'; Hegel 1991, p. xix.

§ 31.11/1   The Infinite Value Notion in Its Universality

This is the simple pervasiveness of value across the whole conceptual space. It develops from the oneness of the value substance (incarnate in money) now explicitly put.

Here, under value as notion, we treat value as universal. Yet earlier in the systematic development we already introduced the idea of a 'universal equivalent'. How do these two uses of the term 'universal' differ? Money as the universal equivalent gives the form of value to a contingent collection of heterogeneous commodities determining them *as valuable*. Value itself, however, in its notion has its own *inner* determinations, its moments, when *reflected into itself*, rather than against commodities. The earlier use of 'universal', at the level of essence, is that which is *related* to what it subsumes in *form* and posits as a *content*. But the 'universal' proper, at the level of the concept is internally self-specifying in amounts *of itself*. So if we use the term 'universal' when treating the general form of value we are not getting ahead of ourselves because it is not the universal of the self-identical notion but the 'general commodity', so to speak, defined by its exclusion from the array of specific commodities. Money gives the general form of value *to commodities*. But, as value in *autonomous shape*, it has its *own* determinations, those of the Notion. Another way of situating the issue is to note that the difference between the general form-determinations of essence, e.g. substance, are supplanted at the level of the concept by the *explicitly* universal that particularises itself 'freely' (proleptically). But as conceptually universal it has UPS as its *internal* moments.

§ 31.11/2   The Infinite Value Notion in Its Particularity

In its pure *Notion*, value has no inner difference, so its only possible further determinateness is its quantity. This is that of amount, quantity as quality. As we saw under real measure a particular amount may be compared with others. But here we have particularity as such. Money *as* value in its particularity lies *a priori* behind the very possibility of such measure.

The poverty-stricken ontology of value modifies the Notion and its moments. What is problematic here is the moment of particularisation. This does not appear as *species* of a genus, but as a set of instances differing solely in magnitude, hence not essentially *different* from one another. Thus we shall say they are really unifiable 'as One', not merely as subsumed by their universal, perhaps a truly concrete universal albeit in a single register, that of amount.

Particularity has only one specific determination, namely amount, and hence its Singularity is *an* amount.

§ 31.11/3   The Infinite Value Notion in Its Singularity

This is *an amount*. Each such amount is conceptually indiscernible from any other identical amount and a certain sum of money meets any bill of that amount. Of course, there are many such amounts because particularity here is amount. But in value as pure Notion there is lacking the usual determinability in which amounts are genuinely plural, i.e. tokens of the type.

If the Singularity of the Notion is *an* amount of money this may be a purely notional determination. However, Value-as-Notion comprehends an infinity of potential amounts. To determine the Singularity of the Notion to an *actual* amount requires the form of the Finite Value Notion. This brings the infinity of the Notion into relation with worldly commodities. Money is the immediacy of the Concept but commodities are posited as true *singulars* recognised as *values by money*. (True reciprocal determining of money and commodities gains proper recognition in its *practical* endorsement in purchase and sale.)

§ 31.12   *Finite Value Notion*

Value in its finite determination (schematised in money as 'measure making') is manifest in a price list. A sum of money here has a dual character: first, it represents the absolute *Singularity* of money in its notional form; second, as a *singular* item, a coin for example, it acts – not merely as a value equivalent ideally – but as *practically* exchangeable with commodities.

Money, as measure making, requires that (i) it models the pure notion – hence one universal money; (ii) it appears opposite to commodities in finite form complete with its own measure dimension; (iii) it is incarnate in *singular* shapes.

Of central importance to my account of value is that *the Concept* plays the same constitutive function in our ontology as the equivalent category does in Hegel's logic. So it is wrong to speak of 'the concept *of* value' as if it were a *finite* concept; I speak of 'value *as* Concept'; yet I show it must *act as* a finite concept in its relations with commodities. Only with finite concepts is it possible that each of them covers a range of singular instances. In our case value is *the Concept*, which applies itself to the range of commodities conceptualised by *it* (not us) as values. (We shall have more to say about such application when we reach the judgement of worth.) However, the phenomenal existence of pieces of gold makes it appear as if 'value' were simply a *finite* concept covering an indefinite number of such instances. Worse, it makes it look as if money is a value among values, different merely in functioning as numeraire.

The difference in unity of commodities and money must be a self-difference within value as concept. *The* Concept is a sort of blueprint for finite concepts, but for us money does double duty, for ideally value is posited as a self-identical universal, but it acts in practice as if it were a finite concept abstractly opposed to its instances, just like 'mass' for example. So what is the relation between the money that *is* value as Notion, which *forms* commodities as values ontologically, and the finite amount of money which seems to equate itself, as a definite amount, with the value supposed to be borne by the commodity?

At the level of the Notion we observe, then, a *contradiction* in value between its being absolute Notion *defining* the monetary dimensions of the value space, and finite Notion existing as fixed amounts of money as if inhabiting an already *given* space.

What is to be grasped in this is the nature of the value concept; it is not like a universal of the analytical understanding, taking under review various values and *abstracting* the (finite) concept *of* value; value as *the Concept* transcends the whole commodity sphere and at the same time in-forms it with this determination. Hence its descent to finitude in 'bits' of money and commodity values contradicts the Concept because if makes it look *as if* value is a finite concept. Yet absolute *'reason' has* to descend to the categories of non-dialectical *'understanding'* when fixing equivalent exchange ratios, or when drawing up annual accounts *as if* capitalism were a natural system.

The great difficulty in making progress in the dialectical presentation at this point is to trace the twist whereby value descends to finitude, as it does in price, because, determined thus, value *acts as* a finite concept such that there are *singular* values. In order to 'apply' value as Notion to the realm of singular commodities so as to constitute them as values, a *mediator* is required which fuses the ideality of 'the Concept' with the empirically given manifold commodities. This is the peculiar service of money when it appears in phenomenal shape such as coin, *alongside* the commodities. The commodity manifold is incoherent unless it is informed with value. However, the presupposition that commodities are values cannot be posited except through money.

At first sight the commodity is thoroughly dualistic. On the one hand, as a material body it is destined for consumption. On the other hand, as an exchange-value it is posited simply as the bearer of an ideal substance, its value. But money presents the value of commodities to them in the shape of gold or some other material. What does it mean philosophically to say the material body of gold counts as value as such? Conversely, why must the *ideality* of value gain a quasi-*material* character?

Value exists *a priori*, as the pure transcendental form imposed on commodities in opposition to their empirical bodily shape. But for such a form to engage with commodities in actuality requires the presence of money. For in its sensuous material character it *schematises* the pure form of value in its implicitly quantitative nature. Only through the mediation of money are commodities effectively *inscribed* in the value form. Between the pure transcendental form of value and the material commodities, presupposed to be of value, lies the mediator money, which schematises value in that it has a crucial sensuous characteristic of presenting measure in a phenomenal metric to the various commodities; it is countable in unit and number, whether coins or simply money of account.

What is required is that value does not float in its universality above the commodities, but that it has sufficient phenomenal reality to enter into real relations with them, such as buying and selling them. Although I deploy Kant's term '*schematisation*' it is important to my presentation that the context of use is not really the same as that of Kant. For our problematic is *ontological, not epistemological.* In the Kantian account of the application of the categories to the empirical world, a mediating role is given to the 'transcendental schema'. Kant has a transcendental argument for situating his categories as *a priori* conditions of experience, and the problem which schematisation solves is that of their effective application in an empirical judgement. As *pure* categories they are unable to grasp any content. This *schema* has a dual character Kant says.[2] On the one side it is homogenous with the category, and with the phenomenon on the other, and so makes the application of the former to the latter in a judgement possible.

In the development of the value form there is no question of a transcendental argument. Nor is value taken as given *a priori*. Rather the dialectic of the value form shows how it is *practically* presented in a dialectic of presupposition and posit. Nonetheless it is equally true that I cannot avoid the figure of schematisation here. This happens because, throughout, the pure form of value is borne by material commodities, which in their bodily substance provide a 'shell' for the value substance. Up to this point no serious problem arose from this fundamental duality. But here we have to bridge the gap between the Value Notion and finite judgements of worth *on* single commodities. This requires the singulars to be subsumed under their concept. Money achieves this for the same reasons as the demands on the schema advanced by Kant. On the one hand money is the categorial existence of value as infinite form. Yet, on the other, in order to unify effectively the commodity manifold it is present there in phenomenal shape as a finite existence, supporting empirical judgements. Value is *materially present* (as contrasted with the transcendental presupposition of the unity of commodities in the same value space) only as money.

---

[2] The Kant passage is noted by Patrick Murray in his attack on 'third party logic' (Murray 1988, p. 159 and p. 255n34).

If the heterogeneous commodity manifold requires the transcendental form of value to effect its synthesis *a priori*, this means that commodities, to be determined as fixed values in the space therewith constituted, require their mediation by their value concept. The reality of value, however, is given only in its finite application. Thus the self-pervasive infinite value space crystallises into finite 'masses of value', that is, 'bits' of money that present the *Singularity* of the concept to commodities, positing them as 'values', a plural domain, as if value were a finite concept abstracted from them. But in truth value is a *sui generis* form *imposed on* commodities.

Value is the transcendental unifier of the commodity manifold for which money counts as its phenomenal *presence*. As universal equivalent, money gathers together commodities and constitutes them as values. On the ideal side money must represent the universal while at the same time having the plural numerical identity that makes possible its transfer.

Another way of putting this is to say that money as the unitary value concept has *Absolute Singularity*, because a specific incarnation of a sum of it is merely *notionally* a *singular* instance of a dollar. A dollar is always the same dollar and an immediate plurality of such dollars is not notionally possible, for, when brought together, they collapse to a specific sum. So to descend to the finitude of commodity values requires money to act *as if* the value concept were simply the concept *of* value, a finite concept with instances such that dollars exist in numerically distinct shape as standardised 'bits', exchangeable with commodities as if 'exchangeables' in the same sense as they are. Our *practice* of such exchange posits the finitude of value.

Albeit we have coins, only their material may be collected as a class, but the collection plate contains just *one* amount of money. Money is always single, corresponding to the singularity of its office, not a class name like 'animal'. However, with money as the presence of 'value' alongside commodity values, it is as if 'the animal' materially existed as singular, apart from, and beside, the various animals.

Value as Concept has a very different status to the ordinary concepts which are always 'the concept *of* something'. For example, 'weight' is *given* in its instances *prior* to their conceptualisation as 'weight'. The universal is derived by abstraction from them.

But commodity value is *not given*. It is only posited as such *by* their concept as it is objectively 'schematised' in money price.

§ 31.13   *Value Brought Back to the Infinite* in *the Fungibility of Money*
Because there are no singulars in the Notion, the singularity of the Value Concept is simply *immanent* within it, rather than 'applied' (i.e. amounts are

notional merely). When finite sums of money act, these 'singulars' are hence not fully individuated but merely notional because they present the Notion ideally, not in their own material uniqueness.

The ideality of price is shown in the phenomenon of fungibility. Money is *fungible* in exchange and circulation, when used as means of purchase and payment. When equating the worth of a commodity to a dollar it does not matter which material coin is taken as its equivalent; *any* such coin serves indifferently. It is a question of what is *acceptable* in exchange i.e. coins as singulars are substitutable *practically*.

When money serves to price the value of a commodity it is a matter of indifference which 'bit' of money is employed for this purpose; such 'bits' of money are qualitatively indiscernible. All serve equally well to price the value of a commodity. Moreover, as is well known, the loan of a dollar is repayable by another dollar, taken as *identical* with the first; it is not required to return the self-same original dollar coin in order to settle the debt. The fungibility of money indicates already that money stands in infinite unity with itself in that any and all 'bits' may come into play to serve the same purpose. By extension, all commodity values collapse into this infinite identity of value with itself. Because all units of money, and all sums of money, are qualitatively of the same substance, and because numerical difference is ideal, albeit incarnate in the monetary medium, money as legal tender is perfectly fungible.

Money appears as a finite amount of itself that can be set equal to every commodity, as if it were one among them; as if price were just souped-up barter. But in the form of price all sorts of commodities worth three dollars are worth an identical three dollars, which shows that money is their concept, whereas commodities are the real-world instantiations of value, each separately worth three dollars, and all together they are worth a multiple of this (that is, another *particular* amount, not a *class* of separate amounts).

I reject the analytic opposition between the universal as wholly abstract and the singular as concrete. The more dialectical view is that the universal is no mere abstraction, no mere abstract commonality, it is a *concrete universal* that comprehends within itself its particularisations.

While the universal thought-form comprehends its particularisations *in thought*, the value form comprehends its particularisations through the *objective relation* in which such money stands to commodities. This is why a material bearer of the value concept is required *alongside* the commodities it comprehends as values. For the 'inner nature' of goods to be value requires that this presupposition be *imposed* on them through the commodity form, and more precisely through their objective relation to money. Through money all commodities are held within the concrete universality of value.

Thus money 'conceptualises' commodities under a *universal* form, namely the price form; in which it must come in *particular* amounts; and if it is to *realise* multiple prices it must be present in *singular* existents such as coin.

§ 31.2   The Value Judgement

The form of price now posited, within it money assumes its role of measure taking. For money makes practically possible the *Judgement of Worth*.

In the judgement of worth we take commodities as values because money has reflected value into them. Now the reflection of this reflection is the valuing of what has been posited as value. Money as measure making is at the same time money as measure taking. The former determination makes commodities into measurable values, while the latter determines their magnitude (in the sense of registering it, what determines the value a commodity *has* remains to be addressed). It acts as their 'measure', once a standard measuring 'rod' is socially selected.

It is our practice of using money on the presupposition that the commodities are values that posits the reality of this ideality. However, for the value of the commodity to be brought to judgement, it must be *reflected* in the price as if money simply takes its measure. This is a finite determination such that the Value Notion now determines itself to finitude in the Judgement that such and such a commodity is worth a definite amount of money.

The moments of the value judgement are:

§ 31.21 Price expresses the *Judgement of Worth* that 'this C is worth $x'; thus I consider now *taking* the measure of value (contrasted with *making* it measurable);

§ 31.22 the measure requires to be concretised in a *Standard of Price*; (the realisation of price through sale is considered in § 32, but here I proleptically mention the qualities required for money to be alienable);

§ 31.23 the *Unfolding* of the Judgement of Worth.

§ 31.21   *Judgement of Worth*

The judgement of worth is exemplified by 'this commodity is worth x dollars'; or '*the* value of this commodity is x dollars'; that is '*the* amount' it is worth. Value as pure form unifies commodities but to be actual it must be capable of appearing in *finite* judgements of worth, for which the monetary medium is required to incarnate its metric. Money appears to be measuring the value already given in a commodity, but at a logically prior stage it *constituted* commodities as measurable values. So its dialectic moves from measure making to measure taking.

It is necessary that, at the level of *determinacy*, there are many singulars (not singularities). If value is the universal, how is it particularised? Given in the monetary medium, it is its *amount*. There are many possible amounts. For the further determination of these to Singularity we speak of 'an amount', contrastable with other such amounts. The next stage in determinacy is to *apply* these moments of the Concept to finitude, by registering *the* (singular) amount that this commodity is worth. So here we can make the judgement: *the* value of *this* commodity is ten dollars.

When we speak of a *definite* value, we use the *definite article*. But, if we generalise, we say: every commodity is worth *a* particular amount of money. Because then we have not limited ourselves to any *singular amount*, the *indefinite* article is appropriate. But to make a proper *judgement* on the worth of a certain commodity is precisely to delimit it.

§ 31.22 Standard of Price

Price presupposes that commodities are the bearers of value. I now consider, not the measure making role of gold, but its measure taking role, for which a *standard of price* is required. Thus if the monetary measure is gold, this still leaves the standard pound of gold to be determined. The index of magnitude of the standard then models the posited dimensionality of the immanent magnitude.

It is essential for systematic measurement that comparison of values is made according to the same standard. The provision of such a determinate standard of price, and the practice of its use, then generates the illusion that gold is just a numeraire. Money as a 'piece' of itself seems to be something that *has* value (which may be claimed of gold, just to confuse things) rather than being the necessary *form* of value. In price, money acts *as if* it were just a numeraire, and commodities acts *as if* they were inherently valuable. But in truth value *achieves* conceptual determinacy only through price.

The point here is not just that 'standard' is a more concrete notion than 'measure', but to grasp the dialectic of reflection whereby money is simultaneously *active* when making possible the status of the commodity as value, and *passive* when reflecting in price the value it is supposed to have; in this last respect money must have its own measure dimension, its standard of price, for which specific characteristics of the monetary medium are required. Money as making value measurable, and money as standard of price, are two different functions of money. Money as the real measure of value incarnates it in *notional* amounts of gold, as a homogenous material substance modelling the homogenous ideal substance. As the standard of price it gives gold its metric, e.g. weight not volume, pounds not grams. It is a measure of *metal*, so to speak, not value. It is its function as standard of price that encourages the illusion that gold is simply a numeraire; for what seems important is simply the metric space it sets up; but this forgets that there is the prior issue of the *constitutive* role that money fulfils at a more basic level in providing for commodities a space *of value* in which they may be posited as intrinsic values. (But my retrogressive logic means that the provision of a standard of price is not a mere convenience but a further step in the process of constituting the actuality of value.)

It is not a decisive objection to commodity money that gold may itself vary in value. Since two pounds is always twice one pound, it serves as a way of comparing the values of other commodities. The standard is the measuring-rod required by the act of measuring.

Remark: This function of valuation does not depend on any value its material 'has', if any. Thus it is common for there to be a discrepancy between an identical nominal, and variable real, value of metal coins; yet they continue to function as a standard of price indifferently. (Abrasion, clipping and debasement reduce the value of the gold content; but the ideality of money requires its emancipation from such material problems.) Mined gold is of varying purity. Social practice requires authoritative assaying and minting.

The fungibility of sums of money means that no *specific* material presence is required, so money of account is a perfect substitute for most purposes. Nothing more convincingly demonstrates the ideality of value than money of account. It is not the *matter* of money that counts but its ideality as value incarnate. Incarnating the ideality of the concept, money may be money of account, which is still at the level of *finitude*, correlative with the commodities, notwithstanding its loss of *materiality*. The account is not merely a *record* of money transactions. It *is* money in pure form because money is actually ideal. Because money is fungible it is replaceable by money of account.

Strictly speaking, a discussion of money of account presupposes the presence of banks. It is too early in the exposition to develop this theme. However, because it is important to comprehend fully the ideality of money, we are saying something about it.

When we develop the notion of value as of the essence of commodities, it is materially dimensionless, even though it is posited as a mass with magnitude. This magnitude can only be actualised as *pure Quantity*.[3] Hence the character of the monetary *medium*, which supplies in its own 'substance', so to speak, a definite metric, is *materially* irrelevant. This is obscured as long as something material, like gold, serves. *Ideally* money has the function of making present

---

3   Cf. Reuten 2019, p. 103, on money as pure 'quantifier'.

the quantitative attribute of value simply *as such*. This simplicity is perfectly realised in money of account. The denomination concerned must be merely formal, for example that of Central Bank issue (as long as that institution is trusted). Moreover, the detachment of money from any material bearer means that normally it cannot be destroyed (as can commodity money and notes), as long as records of accounts are properly 'backed-up'.

Remark: Money, in accord with the self-identity of the concept, is perfectly actualised in one, and only one, 'world money'. Although we here abstract from the state, and the existence of many states, a world market requires a world money. This was gold in Marx's day; but that was contingent upon the historical evolution of capitalism; in the twentieth century world money emerged as the US dollar, in which gold, oil, and other traded commodities, are priced, as are other national currencies. Note that it would be economically retrogressive to return to the gold standard for Central Bank money. However, this presentation is confined to the logic of form, in going from abstract to concrete; thus bank money, as a relatively concrete form, is not considered here until Chapter 15.

§ 31.23 Unfolding of the Judgement of Worth

Underlying price is *the judgement of worth* exemplified by 'this commodity is worth *x* dollars'. Money as measure taking presupposes a commodity belongs to the realm of measurables. This judgement is analysable as follows in the next paragraphs:

§ 31.23/1 Formal Judgement

§ 31.23/2 Categorical Judgement

§ 31.23/3 Judgement of the Notion.

This sequence progressively develops the character of judgement required in a perfected capitalist system.

§ 31.23/1 Formal Judgement

Qualitatively the judgement considers that something is inherently 'valuable'. However, it is inadequate to the concept to rest content with the indeterminacy of 'valuable'. Value is intrinsically quantitative here, so the supplementary question '*how* valuable?' raises itself. A definite price has to be determined. The specific judgement is rooted in the measure taking relation earlier discussed. But as we have seen, only money constitutes commodities as *measurable* values. *Formally*, almost anything can be given a price; here, then, to say 'this is valuable' because it is priced is to make a claim that is simply contingent. Thus the empty character of the value form, even when concretised in the money form, leaves open the possibility that price may distort value, or even fail to express value.

Earlier I noted that the doubling in the form of value allows form to be inwardly related so as to be a content, but form also, as mere immediacy, may itself be an external existence indifferent to content, hence the form of value may be empty (e.g. when non-products take commodity form or the law of value is distorted).

§ 31.23/2   Categorical Judgement

A judgement of worth has to be concretely contextualised, in that the merely formal application of the notion might give value to rainbows; so there has to be presupposed a class of objects giving a categorial 'fit' between the valuation and what is valued; the latter must be capable of being properly predicated with value, namely commodities. Underlying this question implicitly is a judgement of *reflection*. We say this is a judgement of reflection because it reflects something intrinsic to the commodity that means it is rational to assign to it *this* value rather than *that*; it is worth one dollar rather than two, for example. This is so even if in practice a price results purely from haggling, and is hence contingent.

However, the possibility of a *misapplication* of the judgement is always there. What exactly counts as a proper commodity? (I exclude labour power, for instance, but this is not obvious.) So at this stage what is to be posited as a commodity with value is still open.

The categorical judgement of value asserts that the aforementioned prices are not to be taken as empty attributions haggled over, but that the item priced is indeed a commodity in the substantive sense, namely the bearer of value, or, in short, *a value*, hence a *fitting* complement for money. This is a concretisation of the qualitative judgement. The judgement of worth is a *categorical judgement* insofar as no category mistake occurs (as when something not a commodity is 'valued'). In the categorical judgement both commodities and money qualitatively share the same *substance*. Money stands as genus, validating the specific values presented by the range of commodities. But since we are at the standpoint of finitude it is possible that a commodity may lose its value; but, if specific commodities do so, value itself survives in the shape of money.

§ 31.23/3   Judgement of the Notion

Even if the class of commodities is a determinate one, there still remains the question of the *validity* of a judgement of worth. It must be presupposed that, if value is actualised, every commodity has a value to be recognised in a valid judgement on it. However, this presupposition is here still far from posited. We have not yet elucidated the determinants of value and its magnitude. We are still at the level of a nugatory 'assurance' that any such judgement is more than subjectively based, but is properly *grounded*.

If a price reflects the 'true' value of the commodities, it presupposes that there is a good reason for the setting of an accurate price; there is something about the very being of the commodity to be expressed in a 'true' price. However, at this level of our presentation such a judgement is merely aspirational, for as yet we have not considered how the magnitude of value is actually determined.

In the judgement of worth we see value *doubled*: on the one hand it appears as singular, as 'a value', in the commodity, but its measure presupposes that value is a universal particularised in a sum of money, as a notional unity embracing all such commodities. The mediating moment here is that of *particularity*; to say the commodity is worth a dollar is to raise it above its purely singular status to the rank of a particular value, and money descends from universality to appear in a dollar as the incarnation of that very same particular value. Through this the unity of the value Notion is restored; instead of a singular *confronting* the universal, they are grasped as complementary moments of value.

In this judgement of the notion the synthetical role, uniting money and commodities, is that of the particular. Notice that the moment of particularity is doubled in that universality is particularised to singularity (a sum of money) but also to a realm of singulars (many commodities). The distinctness of such values is secured only with the distinctness of the use-value bearer; but while the wealth of use-value supports singular values it is not that the use-value is itself a particularity of the concept. (We shall later see capital is doubly particularised in the same way.)

There are *multiple* similar coats of the same value, where there is only *one* coat price. In the coat, commodity value exists consubstantially with use-value as if, like use-value, it existed naturally in this material form. As tied to a material shell these values are numerically distinct and can be destroyed both materially and through revolutions in market conditions.

As for money: gold presents itself as the *Absolute Singularity* of value because it is not, like other commodities, a single locus of value among others; it is *uniquely* posited as incarnating in itself value as substance. In a sum of money the value universal hence appears as its own instance. The double movement of particularisation results in both the presence of money as an amount of itself and the presence of single commodities, which in virtue of the parallel particularisation contain an amount of value. These moments are explicitly reflected against one another when a commodity is worth such and such an amount of money.

The commodity as always materially singular seems opposed to value because of its immediacy as a natural body. Money as *pure form* of value appears opposed to commodities. However, the link exists in the judgement of worth. Here value has particularised itself to a definite amount of *money*. Conversely, *commodities* are raised above their status as material singulars to that of particular embodiments of value. But there is no immediate *identity* in these particular shapes of value, only a *relation*, because one side of the equation is the value in ideal shape, as a moment of a universal concept, and on the other value is posited in single material shapes. Thus, when money, as the tangible concept of value, appears as a particular sum, it is not therewith constituted as *a* singular, it remains a *notional* particularisation. Conversely the commodity *is a singular* because of its material difference from others, and it is 'a value' only because it is valued by a particular amount of money. However, as 'a value' the commodity cannot be itself *immediately* an *instance* of the universal, just because it is *not* value *outside* the mediation of the price form. Albeit it is implicitly value, its actual *valuation* requires money.

However, the *application* of this notion to measure the value of commodities is fraught with doubt because this comprehends the relation of money to commodities in a broken-backed fashion. This is because, in and for themselves, commodities are use-values, and their positing as values depends on the interpenetration of this materiality with the ideality of value. The bridge is supplied when in the judgement of worth the particular value of a commodity is registered in a particular amount of money. Its value is *imputed* to it when it is inscribed within the value form and is granted a price.

But the move from materiality to ideality is a 'death-defying leap' with a fragile result. Despite the best efforts of its producer, a commodity may turn out to be worthless. Moreover, even if it is initially recognised on the market as 'of worth', its 'devaluation' may be precipitated by market movements. Where there is commodity money the same bridge is present when a piece of metal 'counts as' the incarnation (in the real sense of this term) of value in autonomous shape; but it may become demonetised. The nickel-plated coin 'counts as' money because social practice imputes it thus. An antique counts as wealth because its putative value is realisable. The expression 'count as' is a sign of the impossibility of a commodity having a logical *identity* with value; money price 'logicises' it through the particularity of the judgement of worth; thus we can account for it in a notional valuation.

§ 31.3   Transitivity of Price

I now pass to the logic of the syllogism, in which we show how judgements of worth are combined to exhibit more concretely the unity of the concept.

Following the thought just indicated, all these syllogisms are mediated by the identity of a particular price. From judgements of worth may be derived judgements of relations in which commodities stand to each other. So I here expand the value concept by considering the *relation of prices*.

§ 31.31   Syllogism of Abstraction

Money supplies dimensionality to value. Commodities are put as equal in value because money says so, not because a commodity exchanges against another commodity in a mere barter. Indeed, it would be quite wrong to say commodities are *already* of equal worth before money made possible such an equivalence relation. In money value is equivalent to itself, whereas the commodity as value is not, because it requires an equivalent form outside it. When at the start I treat such relations I conclude that it is a condition of such a relation having sense that the commodities share a common essence. This presupposition is now itself posited in their common relation to money.

So if the worth of two commodities is measured at the same price, then, by the principle of abstraction, we may conclude that they are identical in worth, i.e. worth the same as each other: if A is worth \$x, and B is worth \$x, then A is worth what B is worth, thus they are of *equal* worth. (A = B).

§ 31.32   Syllogism of Equality

If the price of A equals the price of B; and the price of B equals the price of C; then the price of A equals the price of C. Price is transitive. This syllogism takes the result of the syllogism of abstraction (A = B) and expands it into three such relations. The relation between commodities of equal worth is reflexive, symmetrical, and transitive. If A is worth what B is worth, and B is worth what C is worth, then A is worth what C is worth, and they all have the same price. However, *the transitivity of price* is so only formally; actual exchangers may be ill-informed about prevailing prices; so a specific commodity may sell at different prices. However, this syllogism anticipates the objectivity of a unified market with no arbitrage possible. (We discuss arbitrage later under the Idea.)

In considering the forms of value earlier, I argue that reflexivity, symmetry, and transitivity, do not obtain, because to say commodity A is worth A is not an expression of value since the value of a commodity cannot be identified with its immediacy, but only as mediated through another commodity against which it is reflected. Likewise symmetry does not obtain because 'the value of B is A' is not the converse of 'the value of A is B', because the relation has a definite direction. For the same reason transitivity cannot get off the ground. Only with price do we have transitivity. If one idealises a barter system, such that a relationship of exchangeability is set up across the system, which is reflexive, symmetrical, and transitive, then by abstraction one could say all these commodities have the same power of exchangeability. Although, strictly speaking, this is no more than an abstraction, the way is open to infer that such a system reflects an underlying 'value' *given* in the commodities by their very nature (e.g. simply in virtue of being products of labour). Money is then a numeraire selected from such products, just like a system of weights requires a standard gram. *But* this argument is fallacious. The network of *dyadic* barters would not realise the requirement of transitivity. Each ratio of barter would be contingent, occasional and vary in time unpredictably. A transitive order requires the imposition of a social form of systemisation. Money, as value in autonomous form, provides the necessary unity. Then the price system is in principle transitive, and posits the presupposition of community of value.

§ 31.33   *Syllogism of Syllogisms*

There also follows a syllogism of syllogisms, which permutates transitivity three more times to demonstrate that the whole system is 'in form' self-grounding. For, if the syllogism of equality has its premises and conclusion rotated, every relation of equality may serve as a premise or a conclusion; prices are systemically determined. The system is closed.

Syllogism of syllogisms:

if A = B, and B = C, then A = C
if C = A, and A = B, then C = B
if B = C, and C = A, then B = A

The triad of price registers the implicit conceptual unity of value, the proliferation of different price relations, and the systemic unity of all these relations. A self-sustaining system of truth is achieved when the premises of every syllogism are results of other syllogisms. This is obviously true if we shuffle the order of the syllogism of equality of price. Whatever two equalities are taken first, transitivity ensures the third. We have a consistent value space instead of a set of contingent prices, still less a mess of ad hoc barters. In the set of complementary prices, the concept of value is thus articulated as a unitary whole. It has universal range of reference, and singleness of form as the totality itself. *Remark*:   Money has *no price* because there is no possibility of reversing the price-equivalent form of value: it would be idiotic to say commodities A, B, C, D etc. form prices of the money commodity. The illusion that money has a price is based on the fallacy that all value equivalents can function as prices of each other. But the whole point of price is that it is conceptually unitary, enabling value to emerge as a homogeneous universal dimension of commodities. Only money is *immediately* exchangeable. It is for this reason that price expresses the value of a commodity (for instance a ton of iron) by asserting that a given quantity of the universal equivalent (for instance 2 ounces of gold) is directly exchangeable with iron. But it by no means asserts the reverse, that iron is directly exchangeable with gold. If the owner of the iron were to go to the owner of another commodity, and refer to the price of iron as proof that it was effectively money, they would get a dusty answer.

The culmination of the dialectic of price as a *formal* notion is the syllogism of syllogisms in which every relation serves as a support for every other. However, here we are still at the level of subjectivity. The syllogism is objectively realised by, or finds its truth in, the network of real exchange and circulation. Its elementary unit is the *bargain*.

In practice judgements may be discrepant, but if two judgements of worth *agree* then a bargain may be *concluded* between two exchangers. Clearly buyer and seller take the same price. This is, as it were, a practical syllogism. Price must be intersubjectively crystallised if exchange and circulation are to be possible. Prices remain contingently assigned until sufficient bargains are concluded to make a reality of an objective 'going rate'. Thus, although pricing is a subjective matter, the objective movement of commodities realises intersubjective prices.

§ 32   Exchange and Circulation (*Objectivity of Value*)

Having established the logic of a system of prices I turn to the objective sphere in which value is realised in exchange and circulation. When judgements of worth coincide, they may result in an exchange. To begin with, simple exchange of commodities C–C′; then exchange of a commodity with money C–M, which is necessarily reflected in the complementary moment M–C; finally, sale and purchase result in 'the metamorphoses of commodities and money'. Thus the divisions of value in objectivity are as follows.

§ 32.1 Immediate Exchange: C–C′

§ 32.2 Sale Is Purchase: (C–M) ≡ (M–C)

§ 32.3 Metamorphoses of Commodities and of Money

§ 32.1   Immediate Exchange

I begin with the simple exchange of one commodity for another. The social instantiation in exchange and circulation of a homogeneous sphere of value is not secured if agents have discrepant judgements of worth because no objective principle is at work. The 'action' of giving commodity A for commodity B requires the 'reaction' of giving commodity B for commodity A. However, just as logically correlated judgements allow a conclusion to be drawn, agreement in judgements of worth may allow a bargain to be concluded.

I underline that my use of 'immediate exchange' does not refer to barter but to a *notional* possibility of exchange *of values* on the assumption that the parties to it are able to grasp the judgement of worth of the commodities in money terms. Money is here the *ideal measure* of value but is not actually present in its own body, so to speak. Thus this exchange differs from barter, because here it is presupposed that, as true commodities, their exchange is mediated by their value. In the systematic bartering of goods there would eventuate no transitivity of exchange. The *form of commensuration* is required for such a transitive 'law' of equal exchange to obtain.

Even if it is presupposed that both commodities are of identical value and thus share common ground, this virtual 'attraction' remains too implicit to have effect. For, without its actuality as money, value remains a mere immanence without a metric, as I argued earlier. Only given the presence of money as 'value-for-itself' is a principle of unity explicitly put; that buyer and seller accept the same valuation in money expresses the identity of value with itself objectively. Money is the implicit centre of gravity of the commodity world but here remains out of sight.

The formula C–C' is thus misleading; for its existence is parasitic on a virtual reference to money price. Normally, then, a bargain is mediated by money in sale and purchase.

§ 32.2   Sale is Purchase

'Sale is purchase' is formalised as (C–M) ≡ (M–C). Here money is the *realisation of value* for one exchanger and the *means of purchase* for the other. But it is the very same transaction. Sale and purchase are here identical because every sale requires a corresponding purchase. So only one price is present. Even though there are two different points of view on it, they have an *affinity* in *abstractly reducing* to the same thing. We have here a more refined, but similar, case of the unity of action and reaction previously discussed: the offer for sale must be met by an offer for purchase. But, while the agents engaged in immediate exchange act in the same way, here seller and purchaser engage in very different operations. The two opposed designations of the same event exist in the identity of their difference. Sale is Purchase.

§ 32.3   Metamorphoses of Commodities and Money
The dialectic here develops through the following stages:
  § 32.31 Sale and Purchase (C–M) + (M–C')
  § 32.32 Metamorphoses of Commodities C–M–C' (Finite Teleology)
  § 32.33 Metamorphoses of Money (Infinite Teleology)

§ 32.31   *Sale and Purchase*

Two opposite movements, sale and purchase, exist at the same time in every transaction. We may consider the money price to be the identical 'hinge' of a transaction, so to speak. But what if this monetary hinge is unfolded so there obtains a sale *followed* by a purchase. This sequence I formalise as (C–M) + (M–C′). Instead of their *identity*, it is the explicit *difference* of Sale and Purchase.

§ 32.32   *Metamorphoses of Commodities*

While such sale and purchase may go on in an ad hoc manner, a new role for money presents itself if the very purpose of the sale is to acquire money for the succeeding purchase. Here an exchanger is looking for C′ but in order to get it they must first secure the necessary money from the sale of their own commodity, C. This relation is formalised as C–M–C′.

Here a new logic, and a new function of money, emerge. The new logic is the unity (not identity) of sale and purchase. For the one transaction is the means towards the end of the second. Yet the two transactions gain sense only as *one enterprise*, mediated by money, with a definite aim. C–M–C′ is a case of '*finite teleology*' because the C–M serves as a means for M–C′ which was the presupposed end now accomplished.

To be sure, the original sale may not have in view the subsequent acquisition of any *specific* commodity, but merely that of securing money for the sake of its immediate exchangeability when a new commodity is wanted. (As we know, that a sale need not be followed immediately by a purchase is an incipient cause of crisis.)

§ 32.33   *The Metamorphoses of Money*

If we consider what is implicit in C–M–C′, then we see it must be taken together with the point made earlier that every sale is a purchase. So we combine the difference of sale and purchase with their identity. This means the agent engaging in C–M–C′ must find a buyer for C and a seller of C′. In reality, there must exist a network of such transactions, as presented in the following diagram which shows successive exchanges; but while commodities arrive and depart money keeps on circulating.[4]

---

[4] The following two diagrams are inspired by those in Sekine 1997 (p. 59, p. 61), drawing on Uno 1980.

The metamorphoses of money I

```
                    circulation
                         ↓
Exchanges of agent W:   C–M–C'
                          ↘
Exchanges of agent X:   C'–M–C''      consumption
              production  ↘
Exchanges of agent Y:   C''–M–C'''
                         ↓
                    circulation
```

A commodity moves from the sphere of production to that of consumption across the space of exchange. W sells C and uses the money to buy C' from X who, in turn, uses that very same money to buy a different commodity from Y, and so on indefinitely. Money is a here a means of circulation. The striking thing shown in the figure is that money circulates endlessly; as the mediator of commodity exchange it passes from hand to hand yet never drops out of circulation, except temporarily. Here value seems to achieve a permanent presence. (But it is not *self*-present.)

However, the figure is incomplete in that it does not show whence money came nor whither it goes, it is also incoherent because the exchanges considered cannot be infinite in number since the number of agents must be finite. Clearly the 'bad infinity' must close with itself in a large, but finite, number of interchanges with all agents as sellers and buyers, and all commodities sold and bought. The first figure must therefore be supplemented with one showing the system as a totality.

The simplest possible case is that of three agents as shown in the next figure (overleaf).

W sells a commodity and uses the money to buy another from X who uses that same money to buy one from Y who uses it again to buy a commodity from … W! The second agent W is none other than the first agent W. The system is closed. (This objectively corresponds to the closed syllogism of syllogisms above.)

Money circulates and returns to its starting point wherever the supposed starting point is taken to be. This system exhibits infinite purposiveness throughout, for the *end* of one agent's transactions (M–C) is identical to the *means* of another's (C–M). Once the series of such transactions is brought back to itself the whole becomes an *organism*, every moment supports every other; this may be termed *infinite teleology*.

CHAPTER 8

The metamorphoses of money II

circulation

Exchanges of agent W:	C–M–C′
Exchanges of agent X:	C′–M–C″	consumption
production		
Exchanges of agent Y:	C″–M–C
Exchanges of agent W:	C–M–C′

circulation

Remark: A single act in which means are used to an end may be termed an instance of 'finite teleology'. If, however, the result is the reproduction of the agent, and the means, it may be considered an instance of infinite teleology even if the agent is not conscious of it. Thus the metamorphoses of commodities appears as a sequence of agents exchanging commodities. But if one ignores their aims, the system appears rather as one in which money circulates endlessly, implicitly therefore, it sustains infinite teleology. Insofar as money attracts commodities to exchange with it, money preserves itself in circulation as autonomous value.

Insofar as it is an organic whole the system maintains itself by the interchanges of its moments, as if this were its inner purpose. But whose 'life' is it that is being prolonged here? Inspection of the diagram reveals that while commodities arrive and disappear, money continues to circulate as if immortal. The universal moment of the syllogism, incarnate in money, has autonomised itself. It is the predominant moment of the whole insofar as it links up every circuit.

Originally it looks as if money is a means for getting rid of, and acquiring, commodities; but as the true *product* of circulation money is effectively its result. Unlike consumable commodities it has a permanent use in circulation, and is therefore wanted on its own account, because it is not tied to some particular commodity exchange but effects any and all transfer of commodities, and it persists infinitely, not tied to a finite purpose. So it is conceptually 'higher' then commodities as a form of value. As the true product of the system it takes precedence over the extremes it mediates.

Money has its own use-value (that of immediate exchangeability) so later we see it could be the end of an exchange. C–M–C′ is an example of *finite* teleology in that end and means are clearly distinguishable. *Infinite* teleology is a struc-

CAPITAL 175

ture of self-maintenance. It need not embody an explicit 'in-order-to' moment. Certainly in our case money is what emerges as the self-perpetuating ground and result of circulation, on the basis of, but in opposition to, the finite teleology characteristic of individual exchanges.

The aim explicit in the metamorphoses of commodities is still the acquisition of a use-value by every agent as in simple exchange, a case of finite teleology. But having served as means to an end money drops away. Or does it? In fact since every purchase is a sale the mediator money stays always in circulation, albeit further and further removed from the original purchase. But as simple monetary circulation it still appears as an emergent property of the exchange system; it does not *direct* it.

At this level the teleological drive appears to be coming from the commodities desired by the agents with money as their mediator. But this is true only for simple circulation. As we shall see later the circulation of capital is a different story.

If it recoils back on itself in the circuit M–C–M', money becomes the origin and aim of its circuit. In this way the implicit unity of the 'Concept' of value is grounded in the objective intermediation of its moments. Buying in order to sell reverses the teleological positing of C–M–C'. The mediator takes over from the extremes. Money now displaces use-value in setting the aim of exchange as its own. A system structured in this way is centred on the valorisation of value. It has *immanent* teleology. Money develops into the very *end* of circulation.

Remark: It is necessary to be precise about the referent for 'teleology'. While C–M–C' is clearly a case of teleological positing, the relevant agent is the commodity owner in the marketplace. The key shift in our development of teleology is with M–C–M', in which it appears as if the merchant, or some such, is the agent; but as we go deeper into the argument I shall develop the idea that capital as an 'automatic subject' becomes itself the driving force in the economy with the human agents reduced to its bearers.

In the discussion of monetary circulation I show it to be a case of infinite teleology, in that every moment, of sale and purchase, is both means and ends, that every moment contributes to, and is supported by, the stability of the whole system, and that the real product of it is money, in that this circulates permanently. However, for such a system to become one with an *immanent* teleological drive, requires the identification of such an explicit end. The question arises whether money becomes more than the eternal product of circulation but explicitly set as an end in itself.

Simple monetary circulation appears as epiphenomenal in the figure of C–M–C'. It could die away, perhaps. But, with M–C–M' we shall see, money *takes charge* of circulation, directing it in accord with the *immanent* teleology of capital. So the transition I now make to capital may be understood as another case of the retrospective argument in that capital *grounds* the rationality of monetary circulation.

Remark: In order to get the point of the next sections it is important to bear in mind that a systematic dialectic of value tries to develop what is immanent in the concept itself, with as little reference to external conditions as possible. I have just shown that money, as immediately exchangeable, serves circulation for the purpose of ensuring commodities are exchangeable through its means. At this point it is tempting to say, peremptorily, 'what if some crazy people decided to take money as their end, while trading in commodities as the means?' In this way the notion of 'capital' is established, once we add that this is pointless without a profit. This move is defective, just insofar as the transition depends upon an external intervention into circulation. For a systematic dialectic of value, it is necessary to show that there is something about value itself that rationalises this advance. Money has to be characterisable as the sort of entity that could properly take on the form of the subject of circulation, as its own end, giving an immanent account of the reversed teleological positing.

This means that the next section to be presented is the dialectic of capital. In this I make a transition to Hegel's category of 'Life', the homology of which we develop in the next section, with its *immanent* teleology, where an agent undertakes the business of throwing and withdrawing money into the system of exchange for the very purpose of accumulating more money.

(It is true that commodity owners seek to have means of payment on hand, as a fund, but such a money reserve is still in the service of the acquisition of commodities, albeit here money is significant as value in autonomous shape.)

The infinite teleology characteristic of the permanent presence of money in circulation passes to the immanent teleology in which money is not merely preserved but is used specifically to maintain and expand itself. So, in the next section (the 'life' of value) we combine the 'subjectivity' of the value notion with the 'objectivity' of circulation to show how value achieves an independent life, and is thrown into circulation so as to secure more money. Paradoxically this first requires that money assert itself *as money* against the circulation of commodities.

This relation of money and commodities is now to be further developed to capital-as-concept, which in principle opens the way to capital-as-subject if the determinations of the concept carry the import of *self*-determination.

Remark: Even the level of the (formal) Notion does not yet overcome the static dualism of Essence with its failure to fully unify immediacy (money) and mediation (commodities posited as values by money). The self-determining unity of the Concept is achieved only when value unifies them in practice as it moves in and through them. Then it is no longer, as at the start, merely a logical transition from one commodity to another in order to express the value of one commodity in another commodity, but a relation of substantial identity in which value is in truth *notionally* divided into the substance of various commodities, implicitly therefore capable of sustaining the reciprocal action of each on each. So the inadequacy of Essence is sublated when value is brought into motion in a sequence of exchanges which are ideally exchanges of value *with itself*; exchange of one for the other *retains* value in our hands. (This is the *fluidity* of the Value Concept.)

§ 33   Capital as Concept and Idea

The upshot of the previous section, on the metamorphoses of money, is that the category of 'teleology', exemplified when a commodity is sold for money with a view to acquiring a different commodity, is an example of *finite* teleology with the moments (means, activity, end) externally related to one another. In clear contrast to that is the *infinite* teleology of money itself as the continuing presupposition and result of the movement of circulation. I now consider the practice of using money to make more money; this end is internal to the nature of the form considered; as an end in itself such capital is characterised by *immanent* teleology.

Money as capital has the form: M–C–M', where M is money, C is the commodity bought, and M' is the money realised in its sale. Immanent teleology thus uses M as means to M'. This transition to this from C–M–C' is vindicated in terms of our method because value in that is simply a transitory effect of the movement of use-value. Value is more securely grounded if it is made the very aim of circulation.

However, we must not jump too quickly. What is it that is to set itself as its own aim? For money to be its own aim requires that it be *posited* 'for itself' rather than as mediator. This also points to money's functions as means of payment and store of value, for which its real presence is required. In this form money is separated from commodities and counterposes itself to their circulation. (But, of course, no moment of the concept can subsist on its own. The miser thinks he accumulates wealth but his hoard is just a metal dump apart from circulation.)

So I proceed one step at a time, by first developing the category 'value as individuated' where money is taken no longer as merely a mediator in the circulation of commodities but is considered simply as itself, *as* money, i.e. posited *against* commodities, so potentially as an end in itself. Then I show how money *as capital* gives value 'life'.

At this point in the presentation there is a notable shift in our categories. It will be recalled that earlier I gave the moments of the Notion as Universality, Particularity, and Singularity. However, I also noted that the category of '*Individuality*' I reserved for a more concrete form than mere abstract singularity. This is the place to introduce the category of 'living individual' as money takes on a life of its own so to speak. *Negatively* related to the generality of commodities it posits itself as self-identical rather than entangled with these 'others'. As thus individuated money as money is conceptually complex enough to contain the 'subjectivity' characteristic of the Notion.

Capital as 'Concept' divides into:

§ 33.1 Money as Money; § 33.2 Money as Capital; § 33.3 The Idea of Capital.

§ 33.1   Money as Money

The first moment of the Capital Concept is that in which value is individuated, taken in itself apart from its function of mediating commodity circulation. Before it is possible to discover the form under which money acts as capital it is first necessary to establish that money exists *as money*, that is to say on its own account. In the dialectic of this form of value, the individuality of value, *money as money* has three distinct moments: money as end of exchange; money as means of payment; and money as funds.

Remark: The first two of these are taken from Marx, the third replaces his category 'world money'. I do not include the category of world money because I deal with a purely conceptual account of capital. In such an account, there can only be one money because it incarnates the universality of value; a good case can be made that today the dollar is world money; but I abstract from problems caused by national currencies. Likewise I do not discuss bi-metalism. Experience shows a ratio of silver and gold has to be artificially set because the logic of money is unitary and such systems break down because of continual changes in the true value ratio.

Earlier we characterised an amount of money as the presence of the singularity of value. This was merely a formal notion; but to go through the objective exchange with commodities this singularity is concretised as the *presence* of finite sums of money distinguished from each other. In this manner the unity of the notion is present for itself as a sum of money, taken not as a vanishing mediator but as existing on its own account, as a bit of the value substance, value embodied, distinct from its role as value measure. This is not just a notional amount but has objectivity, 'this' amount is 'out there'. Taken for itself in this way it is value as *individuated*.

'Money as money' refers to the status of money as it is opposed to commodities, as having itself as its object rather than them. (Nonetheless it still enters into relations with them we shall see.) It is distinguished from money as measure, where it may be merely notional, and from money as medium of circulation, when it may be replaced by a representative. Money as money is the only adequate incarnation *of* value in the face of the other commodities, which *have* value.

It divides into three moments.

1) C–M, *End* of exchange, where the object is to secure, not a useful commodity, but value in autonomous shape.
2) M–C, *Means* of payment in which it must be present in order to make possible the acquisition of a commodity, especially in the case in which the latter is supplied in advance; this means of payment may come from the selling of another commodity; or it may be already present in the shape of a fund.
3) A *Fund* of money, a store of value built up so as to be available whenever payments fall due.

This dialectic of money as money is as follows. If one considers C–M, then, for the party concerned, M is the aim of the exchange with the sale of C in its service. For the other party, engaged in M–C, C is the aim with M as a means of payment in its service. (Thus the origin of credit money lies in the possibility that instead of regular means of payment a seller will accept an IOU in its stead, and then further circulate such an IOU.)

The Fund combines these two in that it is a potential means of all payment, yet, leaving aside newly-mined gold, it requires building up through previous sales. The purpose of a fund is to be a universal means, so to speak. Because such a store of value is perfectly universal it may be deployed for many reasons, not just to settle an IOU for goods bought, it can be used for rent, tax, or, crucially we shall see, as capital, when it becomes itself its own end. If the fund is simply a means to finite ends then it too may be satisfactory as a finite sum. To become capital, it must be taken infinitely, as an end-in-itself. The first point I shall consider, then, is the question: what exactly is it that is accumulated, when the aim of building up a store of value is present? As Aristotle first noticed, this object is very different from that of a store of use-value. Use-value is inherently limited, not just by spoilage considerations, but by the limits of need. One can only eat so much food a day. (We leave aside pathological cases such as Kane, with his artworks he doesn't even unpack.)

It is clear that all three of the functions of money as money are closely related. Money as the end of exchange may be destined to meet an urgent payment, or hoarded, while a fund of money is different from a miser's hoard only if the money resting there is intended for future circulation. These moments of money form a sort of syllogism in that 'end of exchange' is universality, because the 'end' is autonomous value in immediacy; means of 'payment' by contrast exhibits particularity for the bill to pay is necessarily of a specific amount; the 'fund' brings to the fore the moment of individuality because it is a notionally unlimited amount ready to be laid out on any finite end.

Gold, as a Fund, is taken in the presentation as always already there, flowing to or from the fund as required by the needs of circulation. But what about newly mined gold? How does it enter the system (when gold is money)? Money is never sold, it buys. Commodities are sold and do not buy. New gold is *produced* like any other commodity; so it *should enter* by sale; but it does not need to realise the value it 'has' because it is value incarnate. For what could it be sold? Itself? The only other way it could enter is by barter. But the other barterer is in truth *selling* because they do not want an ornament, they want gold for its *purchasing power*. For this function, new gold is fine. It seems then that new gold is *already* money, albeit not coined. It buys. Ideally an agent gets money – the social form of wealth – only through selling something he has produced privately. But the miner has refused that mediation and he has gained money immediately (although of course gold-prospecting is a risky business). Gold both *has* value (as a commodity), and *is* value, having been specially excluded from other commodities to be such.

Key is that in a perfected value system value must be excluded from commodities and exist as *pure form*; in this way it form-determines commodities as values if they are saleable. What happened with gold is that this ideal process of excluding value from commodities is achieved by excluding one commodity from others such that it *counts* as the immediate form of value regardless of its being also *of* value. This means it is the only commodity that cannot *realise* its value in a price form because it is precisely the instantiation of price. Indeed it has no value form at all *as money*. Money is *the* form of value so cannot *have* a form of value.

The problem is that a commodity should not be money because this means it embodies a sort of incoherence of form. For thousands of years people lived with that. It is simply a demand of theory that all commodities be sold so as to realise their value, so a money commodity is a surd in the system because *as money* it should be *simply* value incarnate. It follows that inconvertible paper is not a denaturing of money but the perfection of money because then gold can be sold. It is a contradiction that the value universal incarnate in money, opposed then to specific commodities and applied to them, *is itself a commodity*. But this defect cannot be overcome until credit money, with banks, are introduced to the presentation later. Then the universal liberates itself from the specificity of gold, to be realised in its purity. Thus newly-mined gold enters the economy as a fund (abstracting here from issues of minting) not originating in a previous sale.

The necessity of money to the actuality of value remains present throughout the presentation albeit that more restrictive conditions on its incarnation are introduced later. But the illusions surrounding gold are dissipated once the presentation develops purer forms of money, more adequate to its concept. In general, all dialectical transitions preserve the truth so far won, while discarding as inadequate its existing defective form. So a dialectical presentation does not build positively on truth, but moves negatively through correcting mistakes. In the present case, it is clearly an imperfection of the concept of value that there is within the system a produced commodity that is not sold. This is another very good reason for regarding credit money as superior to commodity money, but it is too early in our exposition to develop that.

Money as money is available, as such, for many deployments; it is therefore possible for it to be used as capital. But for it to be necessary that it develops to money as capital requires that it be *inherently* an end in itself, not merely that it be taken in the service of some external purpose. Money as a fund entails a tendency for agents to build it up; but this aim is *limited* if it is for contingently required means of payment. Even in the case in which money is preserved by investing savings in vehicles providing a hedge against inflation, this limited ambition means the money is not yet acting *as capital*. Money as capital has no limit in view.

The fund is *indifferent* to its potential uses, and thus it is here isolable as individuated value. This individuation thus acts as the presupposition of its embarkation on its own 'life', setting itself as its aim, not the circulation of commodities. Moreover, only if it becomes an infinite end-in-itself does it become truly 'Individual', rather than sinking back into a medium of circulation temporarily stored. Circulation acquires an end intrinsic to it when the point is to throw money into circulation in hope of drawing more money out of it. In the order of presentation of the value categories, originally money is wanted *as money* opposed to commodities. This is what we just treated. We now turn to the relation of money to commodities at a higher level when we consider money as *capital*. Thus the transition from 'money as money' to 'money as capital' is the next turn in our exposition of the value form.

§ 33.2   Money as Capital

Here we trace the *'Life'* of Capital, so to speak. The categories of 'Life' divide into:

§ 33.21 Money as Its Own End;
§ 33.22 Life Process of Capital, in Its General Formula;
§ 33.23 Capital Entails the Generation of New Value: M–C–(M + m).

§ 33.21 *Money as Its Own End*

When I discussed the category of teleology I showed that this is implicit in the selling of one commodity in order to gain means of circulation to buy one destined for use. It was further showed that money as this mediator of commodity exchange stays always in circulation. If such money were to be taken as an end in itself, money as money, not means of exchange, then circulation could support another aim, namely that of the acquisition of money itself.

This 'qualitative' point is now developed by addressing the 'quantitative' aspects characteristic of money as a fund, namely that as an end of exchange it has no inherent limit; for it may simply accumulate as a fund of means of payment indefinitely. However, I wish to advance the stronger claim: that value, as an end, must aim beyond any present limit. (This is of course true *only* of money as an end, not of money as measure or medium.) For money to set itself as its own end it must become different from itself while remaining itself, through expanding. Since the only quality of value is quantity, the sole possible aim is that of increase. In its process, money returns to itself but with an increment.

The key point is conceptual. If value is to become its own end it must realise itself *as Concept*. It will be recalled that value-as-Concept is present only through its incarnation, money, which must determine itself to an amount. It is as 'an amount' that it is present to circulation; but the Concept is distinct from any instance for it is their negative unity. The contradiction of infinity and finitude is that *if* a Concept is set as its own aim it has to unite each putative amount with different amounts. But the resolution is that in *movement* the contradiction is given room to subsist as two determinations in unity, when money increases from one transient amount to another. In this way the value Concept presents itself. The static opposition of amounts, and their universal concept, is resolved only as money *practically* unites these amounts in changing from one amount to another. This is the realisation of the self-determination of value as Concept.

I deal here with *the Concept*, and *its* determination as amount. Ideally the aim of increase in amount is endless; for there is no *other* determination in play that might introduce a limit, such as there may well be when someone is saving 'for a rainy day'. Such a target is certainly indeterminate but it would be neurotic to make saving unlimited. Moreover, the fact that empirically all sorts of limits to accumulation may obtain is irrelevant when we consider the *pure* concept.

The Concept cannot stand aloof from finitude because it exists only in some finite determination, i.e. negation, of the pure infinity which is the Concept. The Concept sums things up only in their negative unity, that which they are not. (Hegel's favourite example is that men, as finite beings, die, but the concept 'Man' does not.) So here money takes finite form as 'an amount' but this negates the infinity of the value Concept.

If someone accumulates lengths of wood, they are not thereby accumulating length as such, not even if these lengths of wood are rulers functioning as a standard of length. Some hoarder who claimed to have accumulated length would be thought mad. Likewise if one collects weighty things one can measure how much they weigh together in terms of a numeraire. But one cannot collect 'weight' as such because 'weight' has no weight itself, albeit it provides the dimension in which some things have weight. 'Weight' is existent only as weighty things. To say that 'I have put on weight' is simply a metonymic figure expressing the fact of getting heavier.

Just so, it seems, one collects valuable things, but one cannot collect 'value' as such because value has no value. But one *can*! All of us accept the saving of money as normal. The predicate 'of value' becomes, through money, the substance 'value' of which commodities are merely the shell, as we showed earlier. To be actual, value must be objectively autonomised in money, the incarnation of value-as-concept, and it can be acquired.

This absurdity is obscured by the use of a money commodity which makes it look as if it is merely a numeraire such that each piece of gold *has* value, whereas the monetary function presupposes that gold *is* value-as-concept regardless of its materiality. However, even with non-commodity money, the fundamental problem remains insofar as the monetary unit, a dollar say, presents value in *finite* form, in order to be the equivalent of the value of commodities of varying value. But this quantitative existence of value in numerically distinct dollars contradicts its qualitative character as abstract wealth, as simply value-as-concept to be applied *to* commodities, but not to itself so to speak, albeit one dollar is equal to itself, as we argued is required for money to be the real measure of value.

What happens then if money is set as an end-in-itself? Money as money can be stored for a future means of payment for commodities, an external end. But now we consider an end immanent to its deployment. This means any fixed amount, which measures itself only for the purpose of measuring commodity values, is not autonomous; but value-as-concept is measureless, only descending to finitude as money measure. For money to be its *own* aim is to retain value on the ground of the measureless infinite. But it really exists *only as* finite sums of money. This is the contradiction between its limitless quality and its limited quantity.

As we said, the concept is the whole of all possible instances, but it is at the same time their negative unity, just as they are all determinate negations of the concept. The Concept collects finite things together by 'eternally' positing and negating this content. How can money, value-as-concept, do this? – By positing finite sums only to negate them. How can it do that? – Only by setting every fixed sum aside in favour of another, as soon as it is posited.

The *static* relation of infinite concept and finite instance is dynamised. Capital *runs through in succession* its own instances, M, M', etc., not resting in any. This is how value-as-concept realises itself in finitude while at the same time asserting the hegemony of its infinity. It is always in the process of self-transcendence.

Money as money, value individuated, becomes money as capital, an individual that lives only as it overturns every fixed incarnation. Value achieves concrete universality, uniting its finite determinations in its movement through them. As absolute form capital dynamically unites its form with the content it gives itself.

Money is the actually existent *concept* of wealth, distinct from any stock of use-value, which might *fall under* the concept of wealth. As *material* wealth such a stock is always limited; but not, therefore, in *contradiction* with its concept. We argue that, as *abstract* wealth, it *is*, as a quantity, in contradiction with its concept.

The 'contradiction' between the quantitative limitation and the qualitative lack of limitation of money means there is no *inherent* stop to the aim of accumulation. No amount of money can be anything more than a finite amount. To try to realise the concept itself hence involves an infinite process, it seems realisable only in an infinite sum, beyond therefore all real endeavours. This contradiction remains fundamental to capital accumulation. To accumulate value as such seems impossible because it is only a notion but of course accumulating things *of* value is possible.

The contradiction is sublated when capital simply *defines itself in its movement* across transient quantities; hence it is never really fixed. (To say a particular sum contradicts the concept of (abstract) wealth does not mean money of itself tends to expand; but if money (as wealth) is set as the aim then a particular sum always falls short because money is conceptually infinite.)

Thus the significance of this contradiction remains latent until money is set as the aim of exchange. Because the Value Concept is not adequately realised in any finite sum, one absurdly imagines it could transcend such limitation in an infinitely large sum. But such a notion of measurelessness is the finite infinite, not the true terrain of infinity i.e. self-reference. To realise value as an end-in-itself the finite must go beyond itself.

Yet it is possible to realise value in its concept if its purely quantitative determination is raised to a higher power, so to speak, when the circular movement of money in process is abstracted from fixity in finitude. Now the aim is to realise the concept in the movement from one sum to a greater.

To be sure, at any given moment the sum is finite, but, as referred to another such sum as itself, it passes dynamically *through* its finite determinations without being tied down. Money as capital can never be at rest (thus collapsing to money as money).

For capital to aim at a fixed sum is contradictory to the capital concept; for capital to be capital must always transcend itself. Capital as money in motion is contradicted by 'an amount', because it is at the same time *not* that amount but a new one. It is not a question of realising an infinite amount but of being in the infinite process of becoming, negating every amount thus far realised.

Capital is always in the endless process of *becoming* what it has in it to be. Money as its own end must develop itself *to* its end *from* itself as origin. So, to *become* something other than what it already is, while remaining itself, money-as-capital must not merely be preserved but increased. Aiming always at 'more' is strange in human terms but is the logic proper (and peculiar) to capital. To be money as capital is to live through, while negating, its own shapes of existence, as it determines itself to these shapes *in succession*.

To preserve itself from shrinking away it aims at infinite increase, but the true infinity is its independence from fixity. For value to be its own end in money as capital it must do more than *preserve* itself as money as money but develop itself to be something more than it originally is; hence to aim at a monetary increment establishes money as capital, i.e. a *living* individual, not just an *entombed* store of value. This is an adequate transition within the systematic dialectic, giving sense to the notion that money must become an end-in-itself if the value concept is to be actual.

§ 33.22   *The Life Process of Capital: The General Formula for Capital*
Money as a 'living individual' is that which enters on its life process. If money is to preserve itself *as value*, not as an inert heap of gold, mere use-value, it must *act* as value. But in order to so act it must be capable of entering into exchange with commodities as a finite instantiation of value, just as they are presupposed to be, i.e. as a 'bit' of money in finite singular shape. It lives only in its movement from one amount to another. But it achieves this not by standing aloof from commodities, but by assimilating them to its ends. In its objective intercourse with commodities money sustains itself when set as the purpose of circulation. Although the bearer of value changes through the process of circulation, value in its concept preserves itself.

This contradiction in money (of the finite and the infinite) is effectively latent until money is set as the permanent end of exchange when the absurdity of such a motive (as the infinitising drive) becomes explicit. The transition to capital comes when the fund is set on a self-expanding mission. The original *opportunity* for this, logically speaking, lies in the possibility that prices are not everywhere, or at all times, the same; thus using a fund to buy cheap and sell dear is to use the fund as a capital. The classical miser may well view such chrematistic endeavours with suspicion: purchase of commodities is not problematic, but the re-conversion of the commodities to the favoured form of value, money, takes the risk that the 'death defying' leap in this part of the metamorphosis may not come off.

The category of money-as-money is prior to that of the life of capital in which this individual is considered as *sustaining itself*, precisely in its objective relations with commodities, as assimilating them to its life process and generating a monetary increment through that process of circulation. But it is an individual sum of money that embarks on this life process, opposing and composing itself with its world and even generating an offspring.

Now we consider money brought into motion and *assimilating* commodities to its process through them. In the circuit M–C–M′, the original M is a capital value that becomes a commodity only for the purpose of becoming capital once more. The individual capital in this process is intended to generate a monetary increment, 'm'. So M′ is (M + m).

Remark: A concretisation of the 'life of capital' is found in the circuit of industrial capital. Here in M–C–M′ money assimilates a commodity only to spit it out again; but there in the circuit of capital proper the purchased means of production are *materially* assimilated and an entirely new commodity is thrown on the market.[5]

§ 33.23   'Generation' of New Value

Thus the life process of capital is required to issue in the *generation* of new value. This is summed up by Marx in his 'general formula' for capital, M–C–(M + m).[6]

The distinction between a 'formula' and a 'form' is that the former has an overly general reference capable of accommodating a wide range of profitable transactions; but only when it takes responsibility for developing its content is it right to speak of a 'form'. This we will see when we come to capitalist industry.

---

5 This second context of 'assimilation' is deployed by Rebecca Carson in a discussion of the life process of capital in a draft doctoral dissertation.

6 It is interesting that Marx's German term for this is *'Die Allgemeine Formel des Kapitals'*. German distinguishes *'Formel'* from *'Formal'*; the former does not carry the sense of a form with an adequate content, as does the latter. One could say in English it is purely formular.

In M–C–M' value is referred to itself, particularising itself from money to a single commodity and then recovering its universal form through realising the particular value of that commodity. The self-reference of money in the circuit constitutes a new form of value, namely capital, which realises itself through the metamorphoses of money and commodities. Ideally, in this circuit the value realised at the end, M', is larger than M, because an increment, m, has appeared.

Remark: At this stage in the dialectic of concepts I simply presuppose that 'm' is formally possible. Here we simply characterise the logic of M–C–M' as such. We do *not explain* how, if there is exchange of equivalents, a monetary increment arises; we shall turn to the capital relation to illuminate that. So this is a form of value as yet entirely ungrounded.

The superiority of the capitalist over the miser is that he accumulates by throwing his money again and again into circulation. This iteration is absolutely necessary if the movement of M–C–M' is to realise capital, the truly infinite as against the finitude of the world of commodities. Posited as the totality of its determinations, capital takes commodities and money as its *own*. Commodities and money continue to act *as* commodities and money, but are further determined as capital, money in search of money. In fine, Capital has become 'Idea'.

§ 33.3   Capital as Idea

The Idea is *the* culminating value form of capital. It has three moments. The first (§ 33.31) is accumulation, i.e. the transformation of the monetary increment into capital, and the drive of accumulation for the sake of accumulation. The second (§ 33.32) is formal determination by capital of the reality it shapes. Finally (§ 33.33) the idea of capital, as self-valorising, is realisable as yet only in contradiction with its own presupposition, namely exchange at value.

I take capital as substance but now also as subject. What is the difference? Substance is capable of taking many shapes but is not *self-determined*. Thus one may say that value is substance insofar as it appears in the shape of various commodities, formed as values through their recognition by money. Capital passes *through* the shapes of money and commodities, but exists only as their negative unity when the reference back of the circuit to its origin is achieved: on the one hand, capital is money, capital is commodities, yet on the other hand capital is *not* money, *not* commodities, but it is what persists through them in its movement and makes the circuit an individual whole. If value is one substance incarnated in money, this applies just as much to capital and its 'product', an increment of money. As this increment is of the same substance as the principal it is easily brought back to the universal, brought into capital as an expanded capital.

However, neither commodities nor money are *subject*. It is only with the general formula for capital, M–C–M' that the bare bones of subjectivity are present insofar as the formula is self-reflexive, whereby capital measures itself against itself, and incorporates the aim of an increment of money to give it sense. What makes M–C–M' self-determining is not exactly that money as value lays itself out on specific commodities but that this is done with a view to bringing the particular increment of money arising in the circuit up into the universal again. The concept of capital is therefore posited by itself in its real movement. It is Subject.

I treated value first as a *relation* between commodities; then as a *substance* in money, which in price predicates value of commodities; finally value becomes *subject* as money in process, as capital. This internal relation of capital is one of *subject and substance*. As substance, it is money sustaining the commodity manifold. As subject, it is money in motion commensurating itself in the circuit of money capital. Capital-as-subject sinks into its substance in the money and commodities in which it trades; but it asserts itself as subject over against every such moment by sublating them in its process of self-valorisation. Although my presentation developed the subject (capital) out of the substance (money), the grounding relation is the reverse, that subject produces substance out of itself. It is the dynamic of Capital-as-subject that accumulates wealth measured in money. Yet the subject must descend to its substance in order to know itself when taking its measure of itself. Thus absolute 'reason' (rooted in 'the *fluidity* of the Concept') has to descend to the categories of 'understanding' (which deals in *fixed* definitions) when fixing equivalent exchange ratios or when drawing up annual accounts *as if* capitalism were like a natural system.

§ 33.31 *Accumulation*

When capital incorporates an increment, it gathers itself up for a new cycle, thus resulting in *both* the renewal of its elements, money and commodities, *and* renewing capital bent on accumulation. Accumulation has three moments:

§ 33.31/1 Transformation of the Monetary Increment into Capital;
§ 33.31/2 Rate of Accumulation Is the *Measure* of Capital by Itself for Itself;
§ 33.31/3 The Infinity of Capital.

§ 33.31/1   The Transformation of the Monetary Increment into Capital

Consider 'M–C–(M + m)'. If a capital, 'M', throws off a monetary increment, 'm', and simply *repeats* this process, it is not yet fully functioning *as* capital. The removal of m is an irrational external parasitism on the value concept. The requirement that capital be 'for itself' requires the transformation of that newly arisen 'm' into capital by merging it with the original capital such that it is simply an incremental addition to 'M'. In this manner, we have a larger capital, M'. In a formula: 'M' = (M + m)'. But this is *qualitatively* the same sort of thing as 'M', albeit larger. Thus (other things being equal) a good reason to valorise the original capital, is an equally good reason to valorise the newly accumulated capital. So a spiral of accumulation is set in train.

What is important about all this from the point of view of identifying the logical complexity of this category is that there is concrete reflexivity in the cycle 'M–C–M″', where 'M″' comes from the merging of 'M' and 'm'; since both poles of the cycle are qualitatively identical. In this way, capital makes itself present to itself as valorised value, rather than simply a sum of money saved from other sources. Now it is, as it were, virtually the result of always already accumulated capital. So capital ('K') at the start is not just an 'M' but 'K' because it is presupposed to be itself valorised value in the process of further valorisation.

Capital is here the negative unity of the cycle M–C–M', because both Ms, and the C, are united as the movement of capital, each of them becomes capital in turn, so to speak; yet they are present immediately as M and as C with the corresponding functions. To make them capital requires their determinate negation in their transformation into each other. Capital achieves its identity only as this process. It is qualitatively the same capital behind its transient shapes. The quantitative increase is sublated in the restoration of the qualitative identity of capital: K–K'.

§ 33.31/2   The Rate of Accumulation

Because capital is in continuous movement it seems to lack *measure*. Any attempt to *fix* its amount contradicts its concept. It is always in the absolute process of becoming, one might say. So at any given point it seems one simply has a measure of a *stock* of monetised value, a measure therefore of money as money, not money as capital which aims at the infinite, a sort of practical 'measurelessness'. Because the circle of self-referring shapes of capital is in the service of the endlessness of capital accumulation, within the framework of the form of capital there is no reason to say a limit is now reached. It is unable to reach closure. Certainly, money as capital cannot be measured in money as money. But is its concept then quantitatively indeterminate? What is the *measure* of capital?

There is in truth a proper measure of capital. Capital measures itself *against itself* in its rate of accumulation, 'm/M'. Once the money measure, already present in the spiral of accumulation, is taken reflexively as a *rate*, we have the proper measure of capital. The rate of accumulation is capital's true measure of itself in which its qualitative identity and its quantitative difference are united in 'm/M', this is how the performance of capitals is assessed. This measure will be concretised when Time is brought forward as an intrinsic dimension of value. Here is employed an abstract *logical* sense of time, namely that one quantity is present *after* another in an order of *succession*. So the measure as simple rate certainly presupposes 'M" is after 'M'; but the *quantitative dimension* of time is treated when we return to accumulation in the next chapter.

§ 33.31/3   The Infinity of Capital

The form of capital accumulation is powered by the *absolute negativity* of capital. Never content to remain what it is, it negates itself to become other than itself in its increment, but then returns to itself ever anew by adding the increment to the principal endlessly. As a process of absolute negativity, it is impossible to pin down. If this is attempted, a double definition necessarily arises. Consider 'M". Analytically, in its arising, this comprises 'M + m', it is *valorised* value; but that is only half the story; synthetically developed as the universal that it is, in its own movement it unfolds itself to M' + m, through *valorising* itself.

In order to be true to itself, capital must become ever larger. Yet this accumulation is conceptually open ended. No accumulated capital achieves the final realisation of the concept of capital but has to be thrown once again into circulation. Thus, capital is engaged in an endless treadmill of accumulation; 'more' is never 'enough'. However, the capital concept just *is* the *drive to accumulate*, refusing to be defined by what it is *now*; thus a *definite* amount of money-as-capital contradicts its concept, albeit accumulation exists in successive amounts.

If we recall the categories of 'infinity' here, a paradoxical result emerges. Earlier we distinguished between the spurious infinity and the genuine infinity. The first has a paradigm in the straight line; at any point it is a finite length but in principle can always be further extended. The process is endless in a bad way because it is never complete. The genuine infinity has its paradigm in the circle; to go around in a circle is also infinitely repeated but the circle is complete in itself, and at every point returns to itself. In concrete examples, Hegel takes this process to result also in a deepening of the content as it is endlessly restored.

The paradigm relevant to capital is that of the spiral of accumulation, which combines the two axes of incremental advance in accumulation and self-reference in the circuits of capital. At first sight therefore, capital seems to combine the genuine and spurious infinity. Capital returns always to itself ever larger, in its *cycle* of accumulation; but this expansion is in itself *endless*, in the sense of a false infinity. Nonetheless capital *does* achieve being-for-itself in its circuit. In a nutshell, *it has made the falsely infinite its very truth*, setting as its *own* goal the infinite task of realising absolute 'wealth'. Looking more closely at the matter, the circuit of capital, although borne by qualitatively different avatars is in reality purely a matter of a quantitative sum of capital in a process which returns to itself enriched only in the most mundane sense, as larger in amount. With capital, the deepening of the content is the absolute poverty of mere increase.

In a sense capital is the genuinely infinite in that the end of one circuit constitutes the beginning of another. Yet this means the truth of the genuine infinite (self-reference) turns out to be in the service of the false infinite (endless repetition of the same movement of accumulation). Capital has the reflexivity characteristic of Being-for-Self but the Self therein realised is the most poverty-stricken imaginable, mere empty increase, increase in emptiness. Capital is a falsely true Infinite.

Remark: When I say that capital accumulation is increase in emptiness, this is so formally. In reality capital has a double existence, because, as well as its self-referring form, it can accumulate only through securing for itself an adequate 'content' in the economic metabolism. Hence the spiral of accumulation generates a wealth of new material content, e.g. new productive forces, more extensive commodification, and so forth.

Capital must always be in the process of infinite *becoming*, of making itself *present*, but always equally vanishing in a new determinate negation, as an increment of money is no sooner thrown off, than added to capital, and sent again into a new revolution of the circuit. The Idea of capital is '$K' - K'' - K'''$ ...'. Its movement is that of capital's presentation of itself through its negativity, but the content resultant is not separable from the process of its generation.

Commodities have a finite life circulating as values, but, in contrast, money, value incarnate, circulates endlessly and eventually becomes its own end in capital's self-reflexivity. In capital's spiral of accumulation, each fixed amount is superseded by a greater. Moreover, as a system, capital is the negative unity of its instances; each and every capital might go under while capital itself marches ahead.

Through its drive to accumulate, capital achieves the unity of its form and content. As content, it is the *series* of capital amounts ($K' - K'' - K'''$ ...), but it is precisely as *infinite form* that, in its very concept, capital must ensure the continual process of adding new capital to the old. In the Absolute Idea form finally actually determines itself as content. '$K'-K''-K'''$ ...' is a *movement of pure form* in which the content is only itself as it is treated notionally as distinct from the process of negativity which it is.

We have now reached the point at which capital is posited as subject. Since the presentation is restricted to the logical form of capital, its presentation as subject draws primarily on the logic of the concept. Thus I do not treat such themes as consciousness and personality, only the fundamental *logic* of subjectivity. There are three levels of the Concept to be considered: Notion; Teleology; and Life.

Logically the category of subject can hardly be distinguished from that of the 'self-acting Concept', which determines itself from universality to singularity. We see such a dialectic incarnate in the 'I'. I choose from an indeterminately large number of options when considering what I want to become. Even if my particular choice is 'philosopher', for example, in order to avoid 'bad faith' I must not take this as foreclosed, but be aware I could change course at any time. This level of the concept is that of the 'subjective' or 'formal Notion'.

Next comes the consideration that in order to actively assert itself the subject must engage with the realm of objectivity. Here it selects and manipulates materials that may serve as means towards realising its projects. It engages in 'teleological positing'.

Finally, the form of 'life' unites these first two moments when the subject takes *itself* as its own project. The subject is self-developing.

All this applies to capital as we have seen. The universality of a fund is capable of being determined to many different investments. The only point is to aim at an increment of itself. The infinity of accumulation registers its immanent self-development.

§ 33.32   *Formal Determination by Capital of Its Real-World Existence*

Despite the formal definition of capital as self-created, there remains over against it the given realm of commodities. The capital form must determine these as *its own* in a material sense which goes deeper than merely inscribing them within its movement of form. The unification of the form with that which is formed I term 'formal determination', meaning the manner in which that reality is formed as value.

Formal determination comprises practical Idea, and theoretical Idea. In the first place, the immanent purpose of capital must bring under itself the material metabolism. So the practical Idea is 'subsumption' (§ 33.32/1). In the second place, commodities reaching the market have to *be valued*, so the theoretical Idea is 'valuation' (§ 33.32/2). Their unity is the 'realised Idea' (§ 33.33).

§ 33.32/1 Subsumption

In the formal determination of economic processes, the moment of subsumption registers how the purposes of capital are imposed on the reality confronting it. As a result of such subsumption, the material metabolism becomes informed with the purposes of capital. In order for there to be commodities to *be* valued, products, or whatever, must first be subsumed under the value-form ('commodification').

§ 33.32/2 Valuation

'Valuation' pertains to the cognition of the real world under its adequate logical description. Every commodity, formally determined as a value, simply to qualify as such, must, potentially at least, be *valued*. It must be determined what its value amounts to. This occurs in the real world of the market, here taken very abstractly as a process of fixing its price through practical commensuration. The valuation of commodities presented to exchange is a form-determination, but as pure form it is not evident what determines the magnitude at which any commodity is valued. A full theory of value is required to explain that. However, it is important that this form is presupposed to economic activity and regulates the expectation of agents. For example, a new entrant to a field will be conscious of the need to meet, or beat, the established price. In this sense, we can speak of *formal determination* of what is within the value form.

One crucial aspect of this is that, other things being equal, arbitrage will tend to ensure consistent valuation. The commodity exists in finitude as a co-present set of putatively identical commodities seeking sale under competitive conditions within a single market. Customers comparing prices soon effect their convergence on value. But a capitalist may intervene between seller and final purchaser to make profit on arbitrage. (Here this is *pure* arbitrage rooted simply in the contingencies of trade. Only when we come to merchant capital is it relevant to discuss the linking up of spatially distant markets.)

§ 33.33 *Capital Realised in Contradiction*

The complementary unity of subsumption and valuation asserts that there eventuates the positing of value as a reality in the world. Capital is the *realised Idea*. Notice that the previous section, that on formal determination, contained only the two moments of practical Idea and theoretical Idea. There appears no unifying triadic complement to them. However, this unity we term the realised Idea. But it is raised to the status of its own paragraph because, in addition to unifying the sides of formal determination, it unifies also the larger triad of the Idea that presented capital in its 'subjective' aspect (the pure form of accumulation) and capital in its 'objective' aspect (the trading of commodities 'at value').

But at the level of its immediacy this Idea turns out to be realisable only in contradiction with itself. (So it is not, after all 'Absolute.')

There are two problems with capital in its concept trying to make itself absolute *Idea of Capital* through the formal determination of reality.

1. *Subsumption* insofar as commodities are just given to the concept this is fuel to the fire that isn't really subsumed by capital, as it is when it produces the commodities; for example, 'found objects' do not count as values we shall argue. How does it happen that commodities imputed with the determinants of value appear on the market in the first place? Moreover, if commodities are presupposed to bear value then the ground of the latter remains unresolved.

2. *Valuation* Thus far, valuation seems only possible as an unintended result of *arbitrage*. But the eventual result of such activity, carried through systematically, is that every commodity appears on the market *at* its value, in accordance with the theoretical principle of valuation, namely that all examples of a commodity have the same price. There follows the contradiction that the realisation of the principle of valuation, exchange of commodities *at* value, leaves no room for the valorisation of capital, which does not seem possible on the basis of equivalent exchange.

The transition from the logic of the value form to its appropriation of the real economy is required in order to discover a ground for the monetary increment definitional of capital. For the tightly structured unity of the value forms means that capital is identical with itself *as form*; yet there is articulated also its difference from itself (in its increment). It is a *contradiction* in form therefore. The needed *ground* for this increment can only be found in its difference from itself, as *materially* embodied. This difference is real in two ways. First the successive moments M and M' must be different temporally so that the increment may really emerge. Second this new value must be created in the material sphere, albeit idealised.

It becomes necessary then to look outside the pure logic of value to solve the contradiction between the principle of identity and non-identity; the real content regulated by the form must provide the solution to the contradiction. Thus far the material content of the commodity has been treated as a mere bearer of the form; and the latter has thus far been developed in indifference to the specificity of its material support (albeit that the material of every commodity has a specific usefulness, and that commodity selected as money must have the material properties required for this use e.g. imperishability). The logic of the value form, developed from the commodity form to the money form to the capital form, was premised on the absolute negativity of the movement of exchange insofar as all *difference* of use-value that gave sense to this was neglected, i.e. 'negated', in the interests of following through the logic of *identity* arising from the common character of commodities as exchangeables. Now we reach a crucial turning point which requires the exposition to take notice of the sphere of use-values, for all exchange in its logic yet rests on a use-value sphere.

The culmination of the logic of the value form is that, so far from its achievement of logical perfection, it collapses into outright contradiction. When commodities are valued, they are to be found standing in relations of equivalence according to their law, yet they must contain non-equivalence to realise capital in its concept. The problem of how commodity circulation can result in both identity and non-identity is to be resolved in turning to what is itself both identical and non-identical with it, namely commodity production by capital. Turning to production, in order to ground a monetary increment, is to appeal to an important *condition of existence of capital*, which capital subsumes in its circuit but which always retains an irreducible material basis.

In this, the formal determination of *production* itself, by the demands of valorisation, results in the subsumption of it to capital. However, in truth, at this stage, this still has to be shown as accomplished.

Capital seeks self-valorisation against the opposition of nature and labour. Only if it can be shown capital controls all the conditions of existence of the production of commodities does it know its own ground and hence becomes absolute. It knows *itself* when the commodities are the result of its own production process.

But the mere *concept* of capital is clearly not absolute until it appropriates the material world and finds a source of a monetary increment therein. For capital to become real, not merely a logical formula, it must embody itself in the economic material. Even then, it is not absolute if this material is simply its condition of existence. An Absolute is unconditioned. So capital must appropriate (in the first place) and reproduce (as result of its movement) all of its conditions of existence.

Remark: The culmination of Hegel's logic is claimed to be Absolute Idea. There seems, then, to be a disanalogy in our programme of seeking homologies between the value form and the logic. For a discussion of this see the *Commentary on Hegel* in the Appendices below.

In the following chapters two more important moments are addressed.

First, to be active in the world the capital subject must take it into its possession, and shape it into its *own* world. This it does when producing itself on the basis of the labour, and production, processes. (Division II)

Second, the capital subject becomes fully rounded only through 'intersubjectivity', not only as capitals competing with each other, but also acting complementarily to create a self-reproducing *system* (Division III).

Summary

In this chapter value as 'the Concept' is first discussed formally, in its 'Notion', as I term it. The moments of the concept are Universality, Particularity, and Singularity. Money makes these moments present, first as a general form, then as amount, and finally as *an* amount. It is precisely this articulation of the Value Concept in amounts of money that enables commodities to be valued, the particular value of a commmodity being measured by a particular amount of money. This relation expresses a 'judgement of worth', once a standard of price is made available, such as a dollar. Two commodities both worth a dollar are, by the principle of abstraction, equal in worth. This relation of equality makes price transitive.

When two parties agree on a judgement of worth, a bargain may be concluded; with this we move to value as it appears in 'objectivity' (whereas price itself is a feature of its 'subjectivity'). An important form now developed is that of *teleology*. The sequence C–M–C′ is an instance of 'finite teleology'; the exchange M–C is undertaken for the purpose of exchanging M–C′. This is finite in the sense that means and ends are clearly distinguishable. However, every sale is at the same time a purchase from the perspective of the other party to the transaction. It is easy to see diagramatically (§ 32.33) that a sequence of such exchanges shows commodities arriving and leaving circulation while money remains in it as an emergent result. This presistent movement of money is characterised as 'infinite teleology'.

In the metamorphoses of money, M–C–M′, we see an immanent teleology; for the only purpose of it is to sustain and expand the moment of money. But for money to be its own aim, it must first take form as *individuated*. It is *money as money*; as such it is negatively related to commodites in that it takes itself as it object, not them; taken apart from commodities money exists as a store of value, as a fund available for many different uses, a general means of payment. This function is different from those of measure or medium.

It is notable that with gold money there is a contradiction in that money, as value in autonomous form, stands opposed to commodities. Yet gold *is* a commodity. But, because it is money, it cannot be sold, as commodities are destined to be. This contradiction is sublated with *ex nihilo* credit money. But we cannot treat that until later.

For money to be its own end it must be capable of becoming larger while remaining itself. In this process of self-transcendence it is the form of capital, a potentially infinite process of accumulation. It is important that money as capital can never be at rest, for then it collapses to a fixed sum, namely money as money. In the general formula for capital, M–C–M′, capital particularises itself to commodities and money, only to move on; it is their *negative unity*, living through them but transcending them. Capital as Idea unites the monetary increment, arising from its circuit, with the original capital, thus making of itself a (logical) subject. Substance (money as money) becomes subject (money as capital). Accumulation of capital combines the genuinely infinite (self-reference) with the spurious infinite (endlessness). What we have here is a unique form in which capital posits its end precisely in ever becoming larger.

The last section of the chapter introduces the hinge of the presentation between the logic of pure form and the informing of the real world with it. This is its formal determination of its world, first in *subsuming* commodites, then in *valuing* them on the market. However, the realisation of the abstract Idea falls into contradiction because, if all commodity exchange is that of equivalent values, there seems no ground for the emergence of a monetary increment. The conditions of existence of such an increase we turn to in the next Division.

The truth of the formal Notion of capital is posited only under its objective determination in exchange and circulation. It is better *grounded* in M–C–M' than it is in C–M–C'. Nonetheless the appearance of a monetary increment is not only here presupposed without argument, it is formally speaking even excluded by the rule of equivalent exchange. Hence the presentation has next to give an account of the *production* of new value.

DIVISION II

Capital Relation

∴

CHAPTER 9

Circulation

Introduction

In Division I ('Capital in Its Notion') I showed that the movement of capital is a spiral of accumulation. Its reflexivity means that it aims to ground value on value. However, the fundamental presupposition is that there is available a *source* of commodities and of a monetary increment. Now this is to be posited when I explore below the capital relation proper, in Division II. I consider how capital formally determines the material metabolism as carrier of its life cycle, and takes it into its possession. Given this analysis, Division III treats the capital *system* as a whole.

These later Divisions of my systematic-dialectical presentation flow from the *application* of the logic of capital, outlined in Division I; but this is not simply *my* procedure; it shows how the logical form of capital *applies itself* to the problem of production and embodies itself therein. I distinguish between *form-determinations* (such as those in Division I) and *formal determination*. The latter refers to the *activity* of the said forms. At the end of the dialectic of the value form narrowly conceived, that is as *pure* form, I introduced two such activities infusing the material with form, but at that level themselves purely *formal*.

The first is (formal) *subsumption*; even before determining their value the goods have to be granted commodity form; more and more of the life-world is becoming subsumed under the commodity form. The second is *valuation*, the activity of applying the money form of value to the commodities brought to market.

Below, where I treat the production of commodities for the market, formal determination takes on more significance in that the *real* subsumption of the product under capital changes the very material process of its production. This formal determination is distinct from causal determination; but it makes certain material processes of determination possible. Indeed, the Idea of capital, in order to become really effective, must regulate the material metabolism by its concept.

I use 'Notion' in the title of Division I to refer to the value form as a whole, in the same way that I consider the purely formal first section of Hegel's Doctrine of the Concept to be notional with respect to the rest of that Doctrine. Despite its highly internally mediated character, Division I on the Notion of capital appears as a one-dimensional *immediacy* with respect to the material inscribed within it, which latter makes of it something 'two-dimensional' so to speak. Thus the value form has immense inner complexity but ends up with the mere *formula* of capital accumulation. In this respect therefore, it is somewhat parallel to the sphere of Being *within* the logic. So the transition to Division II is a little like a transition to Essence, a sphere of relatedness, for example the relation of circulation and production, finally united in the form of reproduction. This then seems to reduce the value form to a presupposition posited by the real material development. Even so, however, the value form *formally determines* the purpose and direction of material production.

Division I and Division II together make up the structure of capital 'as such', roughly the same as taking a capital as singular, with merely external relations as when it buys and sells. But Division III greatly expands the horizon of the systematic dialectic of capital by addressing capital as a *system*. Capital unfolds itself into a world of many capitals and their relations. Following the parallel mentioned above, the third part is analogous to the logic of the Concept.

While the categories of Division I are purely logical, those of Divisions II and III are what I call 'mixed categories' in the sense that formal determination is supplemented by the economic determinacy of what is formed. So, while the triadic exposition is retained in these Divisions, it lacks the rigorous logic of the first Division. This is because, although the material is organised in a logical scheme, the forms concerned are given sense only because they simultaneously take up specific aspects of the material metabolism of the economy.

The transition here to circulation and production is justified by the possibility of retrogressively vindicating the general formula for capital in this context. In this respect Space and Time are taken broadly as given conditions of existence of the developed form of capital. But this is not merely in the mundane sense that, like anything real, capital exists in these dimensions, but that its Idea is conceptually bound up with its movement in space/time. Time and Space become *constitutive* of the Idea of capital, I shall show.

Division II, on the capital relation, divides into §4 Circulation, §5 Production, and §6 Reproduction.

§4 Capital in Circulation

The presentation now moves from the pure forms of value discussed in the first Division to its finite reality. So this part deals with the *reality* of circulation, whereas in the first Division it is taken purely formally, as a given. The logic of the value form culminates in the idea that capital must make itself a reality in what is *other* than it, yet is essentially related to it. Centrally this is of course labour, but I do not begin with that immediately. First I further explore circulation. Only then shall I begin to uncover the secret of valorisation, which in the first Division was left unexplained. In the development of the categories of the value form earlier, the relation between these forms and what is to be inscribed within them was undeveloped. The methodological legitimacy of this procedure is that the surface sphere of exchange and circulation itself is, in practice, founded on such abstraction from matter.

From the perspective of this relation to the material metabolism, the ideality of the value form as a whole appears as a simple immediacy. Correspondingly, the materiality of commodities served merely as the *bearer* of the form-determinations of value. However, throughout this Division, we shall see how the Value Concept succeeds in formally subsuming the material referents, and then really makes this matter adequate to capital's determinations.

The triad of *Capital in Circulation* is: § 41 Temporality of Capital Accumulation; § 42 Ideality and Reality of Circulation; § 43 Capital Posited in Otherness.

§ 41   *Temporality of Capital Accumulation*

The logic of relations between commodities becomes real only if we consider them as practically separate and co-existent. For this Space makes room, so to speak. Even more important is that Time makes real the notional sequence of M–C–M′. In considering the movement of capital, time is important because it gives the Concept the real possibility to *become* different from itself; in this way it becomes *existent* Concept, and, as such, *Idea*. Capital is *present* to itself only in real time. In time it reflects on itself objectively.

Whereas in Division I this reflexivity is merely a logical potential requiring retrogressive grounding in real time, here it is concretely present to itself only in its *motion* across its determinacies. It is not that capital develops *in time*; rather the temporality of capital is *constitutive of its Idea*. For it exists only as a *project*. What capital *is* becomes so, as it determines itself negatively against what it *was*. Capital is the movement of absolute negativity; it is absolute becoming. In the spiral of accumulation (see § 33.31/3 above) the linear movement is K′–K″–K‴ ..., which immediately is a movement of successive presentations of itself, but here (at the level of real time) this is achieved concretely by reference to the interval between nodal points, I shall argue. (In this section on circulation, time is treated formally; only later do I address 'periods of production'.)

Time is a central category of value theory. Formally it here takes shape in a fashion analogous to the elementary logical categories of Quality, Quantity, and Measure. The qualitative notion of time is that of simple *succession*; one event precedes or succeeds another. The quantitative notion of time is that of the pure *continuum*, infinitely divisible and infinite in extent. The synthesis of these two is that of the *interval*, the time elapsed between two successive moments. This allows a measure of time.

Succession was already accepted in our categorial system, when I analysed the metamorphoses of money, and the logic of accumulation. This is mere change in the qualitative sense, when various commodities pass through one's hands as a result of sequential exchange. It is further exemplified when the transformation of commodities into money is taken to be for the purpose of then transforming money into new commodities. So the C–M phase is logically precedent to the M–C phase in simple circulation. (Where we consider simply monetary circulation, implicit in it is *inertial motion*; the very same value circulates indefinitely. But with accumulation the movement of money springs from an intrinsic *drive*.)

However, for the qualitative category of temporal *order* to be quantifiable means we pass to the next category, that of *The Time Continuum*. This time is infinite, time passing but with no closure in principle. Moreover, when integrated, all concrete times are sublated in a common abstract time; this time is continuous, homogenous, and never ending. Nonetheless there are certain *nodes*, between which there is an *interval*, at which time is taken as halted, whether really or ideally, for the purpose of taking its measure across the interval. This is a qualitative measure of a quantitative dimension pertaining to the movement between two of these successive phases.

Although every material process with which capital is caught up has its own time, e.g. the time for beer to ferment, these are all subsumed into time in the abstract, *the pure time of capital*, mere clock time, or calendar time. An obvious example of this, which I discuss later, is the total time it takes to produce and market a commodity. This we shall see becomes important when we consider that every capital has a turnover time distancing its laying out from its recovering of itself, the period subtending a measure of growth from one time to another. The rhythm of capital's time frames its period of turnover. However, when disassociated from this rhythm of renewal, every capital casts itself as a metronomic beat across purely notional intervals. The rate of accumulation *per annum* constitutes a measure of capital in real time.

Capital is endless change that is not a change *in* anything substantial, but simply capital positing and re-positing itself in its movement of becoming ever larger. So capital exists only as the temporalisation of this passage between nodes. Capital is constituted through a backwards 'casting', and forward 'casting' as endless becoming-greater. As time, the infinite becoming of the concept has three dimensions: present, future, past. But this temporality does not apply to mere empirical finitude as such with its infinite sequence of 'nows'. Capital makes itself present to itself only through a casting of this complex sort, a time *past* made *present* as a moment of self-recognition informed with an orientation to becoming *future*.

The dialectic of capital is that of absolute negativity. Time is the *existent* Concept of capital because the logic of negativity needs time to accomplish its movement through its phases. Capital exists only as the *process* of negating its current form in favour of an expanded one. It is a continual surpassing of itself that must never collapse to a *fixed presence*; it is a continual 'presencing'. It continually denies what it was only in order to project itself as what it will be. It is not that capital – like all existent beings – exists *in* time; rather the movement of its time is its reality because it is actual only in its reflection on itself at intervals. It collapses to money merely, if fixed; so any such fixing has to be a notional vanishing moment.

It is important that this is *pure* negativity. It is said that the plant 'negates' the seed, but this is a metaphorical *abstraction*; in reality the plant merely replaces the seed. But, in our case, the logical abstraction of such examples really does *exist*. Capital accumulation is founded on an empty presence. Its presenting of itself is infinite becoming. But this also requires the moment of finitude in order to know the *rate* of accumulation. The time continuum takes a finite turn in the interval between *two* times, across which a rate of accumulation is computable. To know itself capital reflects on itself as a movement between virtual nodes in the continuum of abstract time (for example, a yearly accounting). Ideally the rate should tend to infinity. But this unrealisable outcome is sublated in the concrete notion of a *drive* to increase it. This Idea is logically prior to its enforcement through competition.

However, in the case of capital, it is the featureless real time that itself supports the reflexivity of capital's *ideal existence*, because capital's ontological poverty permits no more organic rhythm. But, through its 'casting', capital takes its own measures; it casts itself back to a previous time and projects its aims to a future time. The 'casting' by capital of its being in time allows it to take its *measure*.

The motion of capital in its immediacy is given abstractly in terms of capital's relation to itself as it is articulated in its rate of accumulation. But this movement *takes time*; thus the measure of capital *in motion* is not simply a continuing increase in its mass, but its *rate* of accumulation, taken over an interval. Moreover, it is this that enables a comparison of one capital with another; that which conforms most closely with its concept is that with the highest rate of accumulation.

Whatever the original masses of capital deployed, the one with the highest rate per annum will eventually overtake all others even on that measure, namely mass. It turns over faster and soon has more accumulated capital than the less 'energetic' one. Even a smaller capital with a higher rate of accumulation than another eventually becomes the larger one. The pure time of capital, centred on itself, comprises its immanent measure of itself once articulated as a rate of accumulation over time.

We have seen that in order to give its rate of return in real time capital must compare itself at one time with itself at another time, while yet positing itself as still the same capital, albeit grown larger. The time between two times is, as it were, the differential of the movement of time, reducing to a fixed quantity the continual passing of time; it becomes time passed as if time itself were accumulated.

Furthermore, the actuality of the magnitude of value requires a reflex *within* time such that it condenses to a real (sale of products) or notional (valuation of assets) *point* in time allowing synchronic comparison with other values. (For the purpose of annual accounts such values must be fixed notionally only.) To take its measure capital must reflect into itself at specified intervals in order to create two nodes in its continuous process of accumulation. Thus capital is both infinite (endless growth) and momentarily finite (measured in actuality as a rate). At all events, time is central to capital's measure of itself as a rate of accumulation.

The difference of levels of concretion means that the earlier qualitative notion of accumulation is now conceived as occurring across time, thus allowing comparison of two capitals in this respect.

Remark: At first it seems that every industrial capital has its immediate reality in a peculiar *period of production*. But these materially based differences between capitals in their time of production are entirely abstracted from insofar as capital as a pure form is concerned. So the measure of the rate of accumulation is taken as the rate of return *per annum*. The concrete times of circulation and production are subsumed by the *pure* time of capital in the abstract. When I deal with production later in our exposition (§ 50) time gains another significance. Capital in production has to engage with real time in a more intimate way, as 'duration', so that it makes sense to take as the relevant nodes the beginning and end of a production period when there is a real or notional sale.

§ 42 Ideality and Materiality of Circulation

Given that social production is located in dissociated enterprises, commodity exchange is the fundamental mediation that secures association. Commodities are doubly constituted as use-values and values, and the process of their exchange realises both determinations at the same time. However, the procedure I adopt here is to treat the issues separately. In the first Division the problems of exchange are bracketed; it is assumed all commodities are exchangeable as such. This is in order to focus on the *formal* conditions of existence of *value relations*. Now I concretise value by looking at its *existent* reality. So here the problem of the *realisation* of value in exchange is addressed. Even if commodities are *formed* as values the problem of their *exchange* as values in reality arises, because there is no point in exchanging equivalents. Exchange of equivalent values is mediated in exchange of different use-values wanted by different agents. This condition of existence of value transactions impedes the free movement of commodities.

Throughout the pure logic of value form (treated in Division 1) use-value issues were bracketed. The materiality of the commodity appeared merely as the shell of value. (However, the specific material requirements of the monetary medium had to allow money to be *used* as the phenomenal body of value. But later I show that money drops its material shell.) In this Division, use-value is now considered as having economic determinacy. First the issue is taken in its simplest, and most immediate, aspect.

Even if all parties agree to trade at perceived value things may stall because moneyless circulation of commodities requires the possible realisation of use-value as a condition of the previous realisation of value. For a real exchange to occur, there must be agents in search of specific use-values. Moreover, bodily differences in commodities support the variety of use-values that motivate exchange. Yet these very differences may block the realisation of value. In the case of direct exchange of goods there is only limited exchangeableness because the fit with individual need may not be present.

An exchanger requiring a certain use-value may endeavour to take their existing use-value to be means of purchase so as to buy others. But it may not be acceptable, because of its *limited* character as use-value. The problem of actualising exchange is solved if there is something incarnating what commodities have in common, a 'universal commodity' everyone will accept in any amount.

Looking back to the first Division, it is the universal equivalent form derived there, *excluded* from those in relative form. Given that special commodity, use-values can circulate through sale as values. This money commodity stands to regular commodities as their negative unity, something they are *not* but to which they have a common relation. Something that imposes commonality on heterogeneity is not any empirically given use-value, differing from others only in its popularity, but something designated as of 'pure exchangeability', unlimited by specific need, and this *abstraction* from the heterogeneous existence of commodities is why money plays the role of 'universal commodity' because it is wanted *as value*. So money has immediate exchangeability, meaning anyone selling will accept it, only because it represents, not its *material* use-value, but the *formal* use-value of constituted value, and it has that in direct proportion to its amount.

In the context of the process of exchange the most important use-value of money is that of monopoly of purchasing power. Presupposed as the bearer of *exchangeability as such* it acquires a 'formal' use-value, purchasing power; it enables its possessor to turn a value into a use-value, paradoxically just because it is not limited in its action by use-value constraints on its exchangeableness. Money is universally exchangeable because it is autonomous form of exchangeability; it has a power of exchange without its use-value *bearer* being wanted as such. Money as the actuality of value mediates the process of exchange. The opposition between use-value and value is inherent in the commodity. Money allows their realisation in sequence. Money as 'the universal commodity' interposes itself between commodities to allow the transmutation of use-value in simple circulation.

Materially the commodity is a use-value; its existence as a value appears only ideally, in its price, through which it is related to the real shape of its value, the gold which confronts it as its opposite. Inversely, in its reality gold counts only as the materialisation of value, as money. Its use-value appears only ideally in the series of commodities on which it may be laid out, here it confronts all the other commodities as the totality of real shapes of its use. These antithetical forms of commodities are the real forms of motion of the process of exchange.

This problem (that of the order of realisation of value and use-value) is resolved when money is present in its function of medium of circulation. It plays such a role because, unlike commodities in general, it is immediately exchangeable as value existent in autonomous form. To put the point paradoxically, money has the use-value of *being* value.

Commodity exchange implies two conditions: on the one hand, it presupposes that the identical values find a moment of difference, if only 'ideally', so that one commodity can be value in autonomous shape; on the other hand, exchangeableness of materially different use-values requires as a universal mediator a non-specific use-value ideally identically related to all commodities. Money is the solution to both. Posited as actuality of value money can serve as the universal commodity, which is immediately transformable into all others.

(The argument in this section for the necessity of money to lubricate exchange is purely logical. In no way is it to be understood as a historical account of the original emergence of money.)

Remark on Moneyless Circulation

This discussion is not part of the systematic presentation; it is included because of the historical prevalence of the topic in the literature on money.

It is worth exploring the problem of circulation of use-values in some detail through a thought experiment. I start from a situation without money, and I assume that commodities exchange at perceived value. However, the focus is now on the individual owners whose need for use-value is necessarily the motive for exchange (at this level of analysis). It is of great interest to the theory of value to see if this motive can succeed without money.

In the first Division we saw the logical requirement of a value *universal* had to be particularised in a money commodity to be actual. In this second Division the need to realise the *particularity* of use-value raises the issue of a universal use-value, a universal commodity, ensuring that the particular commodities are commutable within the same space of exchange.

So let us attend to the process of exchange. We assume all owners of commodities are alien to each other and meet in the marketplace as such. 'Selling' is the act of realising value. 'Buying' is the act of converting value into use-value. A, B, C, etc. are owners; *commodity* (a), *commodity* (b), *commodity* (c) etc. are their commodities.

Without money it seems impossible to say whether an offer to exchange is a proposal to *sell* a commodity or to *purchase* one. However, I argue it is an offer to buy for the following reasons. In simple circulation A sells *in order to buy*; i.e. they essay C–M–C. If money drops out, the moment of sale drops out, and A is trying to buy *commodity* (b) *directly* in the hope B will accept *commodity* (a) as a valid equivalent. A has no need for *commodity* (a) and therefore hopes to use it as a means to acquire something they do need. But key to my argument is that A wants *commodity* (b) in a *definite quantity*, one coat not two. A possesses bales of linen which are of absolutely no use to them, and they want to employ these to secure what they do want. However, while A is not worried about quantifying the amount of linen they are prepared to part with, they do have quantitative worries about the use-values to be acquired. A does not offer 240 yards of linen in exchange for 12 coats, because these are no use to them; they want one coat – no more no less – and they hope to get it for 20 yards of linen. The same happens when A goes round the market trying to secure definite quantities of tea, sugar, potatoes etc., and when they haggle they vary the amount of linen offered, not the quantity of the stuff they are buying.

This is because the quantity demanded is required by A as a use-value and therefore in definite limited amounts, whereas the quantity offered has no constraints arising from use-value. *A* is using it to acquire a use-value as if linen were *money*, i.e. means of payment.

Notice that because *commodity* (*b*) is wanted in a definite limited quantity this means that its value equivalent in *commodity* (*a*) must also be determined as a definite limited quantity. If *A* were a seller interested in realising the *value* of *commodity* (*a*) they would offer *any amount* (or a unit amount) of *commodity* (*a*) for its value *equivalent* in *commodity* (*b*), *commodity* (*c*), etc. But the notion of 'sale' is senseless here because *commodity* (*b*), or *commodity* (*c*), etc., is no better form of realisation of value than is *commodity* (*a*); value is still imprisoned in use-value.

To realise the *value* of *commodity* (*a*) requires that there exists value in autonomous form, namely money. As values all commodities are indiscernible even if their bearers are differentiable. There is no point here in realising the value of *commodity* (*a*) in *commodity* (*b*). This would have point only if *commodity* (*b*) had a special quality, namely immediate exchangeability.

A has no idea if *commodity* (*a*) is wanted by others, still less whether the terms of any offer are acceptable. *B*, by contrast, becomes aware that *commodity* (*b*) objectively possesses a social use-value (at least *A* wants it), and they have the chance of exchanging it if *B* agrees with A's estimation of *commodity* (*b*)'s worth. So there is an asymmetry in that *commodity* (*b*), but not *commodity* (*a*), is initially posited as a genuine commodity. Only *if B* accepts the offer is *commodity* (*a*) *posited* as a genuine commodity, and the objective existence of a value relation established. What is it? *A* wants *commodity* (*b*) as a use-value; but as a condition of obtaining it he must offer at least what it is worth. Thus *A* attempts to assure *B* that *commodity* (*a*) is the equivalent of *commodity* (*b*). Notice that *A* is saying '*commodity* (*a*) *is* the value of *commodity* (*b*)', not '*commodity* (*a*) *has* the value *commodity* (*b*)'.

However, there is a major problem about *A*'s offer to *B* as we have understood it so far. *B* is not *interested* in thereby realising the value of *commodity* (*b*). Just like *A*, *B* is wanting to use *this* commodity as a means to acquire definite quantities of *other* commodities. Even if *B* is into linen, they may not want 20 yards, but 10, or 40. So the contradiction of simple exchange is much worse than the issue of differing qualities of the commodities. *A* really does want a coat and *B* really wants linen; but this does not allow *A* to buy because in reply to their offer *B* may say: 'I'll only exchange with you if you give me 40 yards for 2 coats'. *A* will reply: 'but an extra coat is worthless to me!' The problem is both parties want to determine the *absolute amounts* for themselves even where they agree on the value *ratio*.

It follows from this that no solution to the contradictions of exchange is yet found; even if there is a commodity that is generally wanted, it has to be wanted in *any amount* if it is to be acceptable means of exchange. Even if everyone wants linen, *A* still does not have a general means of exchange, because linen is wanted as a use-value, hence in a specific quantity, so *A* cannot get people to accept an offer to buy at the amounts offered (and if *B* only wants 10 yards *A* can hardly buy half a coat). As we know, it is buyers who are interested in absolute amounts whereas sellers will sell any amount at the 'right price'.

The simple exchange system, without money, is dominated by the need to acquire use-value, and that is the only reason driving anyone to market; their own commodity is merely a means to satisfy their needs indirectly through a swap. It is not produced with a view to realising its value by sale. Value here is a constraint on ratios of exchange, not the motive of exchange activity. Hence the logically fundamental relation is buying, because its object is to acquire definite use-values.

The contradiction in the elementary process of exchange is that everyone wants to be a buyer, but no one can be, because no one has generally accepted means of purchase. If *B* does not want *commodity (a)* it is no use *A* protesting it is a value equivalent of *commodity (b)*; *B* is not interested in value but in use-value, just like *A*. Exchange stalls because no one wants to be a seller.

How might a solution arise? It *might* happen if *commodity (b)* became empirically the 'universal commodity', one that everybody wanted. Suppose winter is coming and everyone decides they need a new coat and makes offers to *B*. Inundated with such offers to buy, *B* is now in a sufficiently strong position to appear as a *buyer*, and to force the others to turn into *sellers*. For example, *B* says to *A*: 2 coats buys 40 yards of linen. When *A* protests that (even though this proposal is a fair exchange) they only want one coat, *B* says: I have here a list of people who came to me for a coat but whose commodities I did not want; you can easily trade that extra coat (i.e. employ it to buy something of use to you).

If *A* accepts B's offer *A* has become a seller because they have accepted a coat that is of no use to them *as a coat*, but which *B* has convinced *A* has a new use-value, that of power of purchase. Coats have now become empirically *the universal commodity* because possession of them allows the owner to turn one into any other commodity. Now all will accept the role of sellers and give *B any* quantity he demands indifferent to how much use-value is in the value equivalent *B* offers.

But coats are not money. They are currently the 'most marketable' commodity; but final demand is still for the use-value of the coat. They gradually leave circulation, and *B* must then wait until they wear out. The coats then are finally all realised *as use-values*, even if transitorily *A* accepted one as a non-use-value.

The story above is a roundabout barter. But money is never bought, it only buys, it is never sold so it never leaves circulation.

Money is *opposed* to commodities in being wanted for quite different reasons, as the instantiation of exchangeability as such, opposed to any *specific* want that might lead to a purchase oriented to consumption; money must never be consumed.

So there is a conceptual difference between the empirical universal commodity (above the coats) and the value universal borne by commodities but *opposed* to them as use-values, and becoming autonomous in money. Only this explains why world money took shape not as corn, or linen, or knives, but as a luxury item (gold)! There is no empirically universal commodity (bread with gluten is rejected by those allergic to it, gold by those who think ornamentation vulgar). But to then take the 'most marketable' is in any case to miss the point of the conceptual difference between an empirically universally saleable commodity, and money as autonomous value never sold.

§ 43   Capital Posited in and through Otherness

This section on the three different shapes of capital is a concretisation of the general formula for capital: M–C–M′. Capital in its general formula must engage with commodity markets. There are three elementary shapes of capital: merchant capital; money-lending capital; industrial capital. (This order is not intended to be historical of course.) In all cases the problem is not so much to show a monetary increment is possible, as to assess how well grounded it is. Moreover, a key issue is the conquest of otherness, namely use-value. The present discussion determines which shape of capital is constituted as a form proper, rather than an abstract formula, by its ability to regulate its own content.

§ 43.1   Merchant Capital

To begin with, trade in commodities does not take place in some dimensionless universe; every exchange is a certain distance from another, especially with the growth of a world market. Merchants deal in commodities, uniting spatially separated markets. (A similar possibility arises through connecting times also, buying cheap now to sell dear later.)

Capital tendentially unifies the spaces of exchange, originally through the efforts of merchant capital. Even in the same place different producers may offer the same commodity at different prices so the merchant can make money on their alienation; but differences due to spatial distantiation of exchange offer capital its best opportunity for arbitrage. However, such arbitrage rapidly squeezes out such variety in price; arbitrage across a distance likewise tendentially disappears such that the higher price of sale simply reflects transport costs. Spaces of exchange allow arbitrage *contingently* but when it is squeezed out only transport time enters into capital's calculus.

The merchant may specialise in transport; but at the most basic level merchant capital is not grounded on itself because the commodities in which it trades arise outside its circuit. There must be 'fuel to the fire', for trade to continue and expand.

§ 43.2   Money-Lending Capital

Money-lending capital short-circuits the circuit M–C–M' to M–M'. Someone may borrow for various purposes; the simplest is to fund consumption (in the case of basic usury), next to fund trade. It funds purchase of consumption goods, or producer goods, 'ahead of time', because the borrower is not yet in possession of means of payment. In the first case, someone wishes to engage in M–C before C–M', that is to say, buying commodities before having sold one of their own. Secondly, someone may embark on an M–C–M' circuit, without having in their own hands the originating capital. In all cases the money lender makes a monetary increment through the truncated circuit M–M'. However, despite its antiquity, and despite recent financial innovations, this circuit cannot be grounded on itself. It is parasitic on some real source of surplus.

Remark: My presentation deals with the more primitive categories before the developed ones. It follows that the two forms of capital just treated are not to be identified with commercial capital, and the modern banking system, in their modern sense, which I come to later. At this level of abstraction, only the most elementary version of these possibilities of monetary increment is intended.

§ 43.3   Industrial Capital

Industry concretises the general formula for capital in such a manner as to allow it to produce its own ground. (This I shall underline when I treat the immediate results of the production process.) Industrial capital is a synthesis of its abstract identity with the real difference introduced by commodity production insofar as capital not merely form-determines goods as commodities but takes charge of their production. Through taking charge of production, industrial capital solves the fuel to the fire problem; and insofar as it produces the monetary increment which it reinvests, it has become self-grounded, unlike the previous two forms. However, the source of its growth is still not yet explained. For that I must discuss the inner life of production.

These three real shapes of capital exhibit a dialectic of the sublating of use-value. Merchants circulate commodities but in reality they are at their mercy – the production of these commodities has to be taken as given. Money-lending capital 'conquers' use-value only by abstracting from commodities themselves. Industry combines both: it subsumes the use-value sphere by *producing* the commodities it markets.

Let us go deeper into the systematic justification for concentrating on industrial capital in the further development of the presentation. Formal logic, faced with the variety of ways in which the general formula of capital (advance of money so as to make money) may be instantiated, would simply treat them as species of the generic form. Dialectical logic, however, asks, what is the *proper content* of the form? What gives the form its self-subsistence? Roughly, capital may be shown to sink into the sphere of use-value in three stages; these are merchant capital (the immediate concretisation of the general identity of capital with itself), the formal subsumption of production by capital (the moment of capital's difference from itself in relation to itself) and the real subsumption of production by capital (the unity of capital with itself informing both production and circulation).

Merchant capital embodies in the real world of exchange the general formula of capital insofar as value transforms itself through its different instantiations to emerge as greater than it began; thus it *appears* as a self-reproducing substance; but it only subsumes the different commodities it buys and sells *within* its own determinations, it is not bringing them forth from itself *as* its determinations. It cannot legitimately declare the commodities it trades in are nothing but its own forms of development because its content is not brought forth from itself.

Only with industrial capital does the commodity brought to market originate from capital's own circuit when it buys means of production and labour power, and sets them to work to produce a new commodity which it hopes to market profitably. It is the difference introduced at the material level (surplus product) that ensures the process of production is simultaneously a valorisation process, thereby resolving the contradiction in the general formula. Thus, if capital as self-valorising value is to realise itself, the movement of value must take a more complex form than it does in pure circulation; it must be the movement which simultaneously produces value as its own premise. The phenomenon of circulation may now be viewed as the necessary form of appearance of capitalist relations of production. Industrial capital is hence a more authentic realisation of the Idea of capital just insofar as it has reason so to claim genuine unity of form and content in its production and circulation processes.

Capital gains actuality only as industrial capital, not as merchant or moneylending capital. The latter lack a proper content whereas industrial capital determines its own proper content in the individuality of its product which requires industrial capital to invest itself in a *particular* field of production. A merchant can set up as a 'general dealer'; his stock is an unmediated unity of substance (its value) and accident (the 'list'); but there is no such thing as a 'general producer'; production is necessarily the production of individual products by individual enterprises. Industrial capital thereby unites infinite form and the realm of finitude.

To be self-grounded, value must be produced by value. This means that only capitalistically produced commodities have adequacy in both form and content to value in and for itself. Thus to gain control of its conditions of existence, to 'posit' its presuppositions, capital must take charge of the production of commodities.

Industry has two conditions of existence worthy of note: the presence of a workforce, and the presence of households requiring commodities. 'Doubly-free' labour is present if the labourers are free from subjection to slave-owners, or feudal lords, and thus able to sell their services freely on the labour market; and at the same time they are 'free' from possession of means of production of their own, hence they are 'forced' to seek employment by capital. However, the systematic presentation need not look to the history of the creation of 'doubly free' labour; for I shall argue below that capital posits this presupposition in its own movement. Complementing wage-work are the households looking to spend wage revenues on commodities, to maintain themselves. Such demand is an essential presupposition of the reproduction of capital. (I do *not* assume the real wage is unchanging; it must increase if capital is to sell an increasing mass of commodities; but for the following sections of the exposition I take it as fixed.)

Summary

This chapter comprises the first in Division II of the presentation. This Division deals with the way the logic of value informs such material spheres as production and reproduction. This chapter, however, confines itself to the dimensions of circulation: Time, Space, and Body (meaning here the treatment of circulation as allowing that of specific use-values). The first section takes the formal notion of accumulation as requiring successive moments, discussed in Division I, and concretises its measure as a rate *per annum*. In this discussion I showed that *time* is intrinsic to the very concept of capital as *existent*. Capital casts itself back to measure its increase over an interval, and casts itself forward in the project of accumulation; only thus is it actual. Any fixity is to be sublated in its movement of absolute negativity.

The second section shows in detail that the circulation of specific use-values is possible only through the mediation of money, as the 'universal commodity', so to speak.

The final section argues that of all the possible shapes of capital only the form of industrial capital actually *produces* the commodities in which it deals. Hence capital in this form *grounds* itself on itself as it sinks into production and subsumes this under its imperatives.

CHAPTER 10

Production

§5 Capital in Production

In the previous section of this Division, I discussed capital in circulation (§4). Now, in this second section I address the very heart of the process of valorisation, capital in the production process, producing above all itself (as a capital *relation* we shall see) (§5). The third section will treat reproduction, namely the unity of circulation and production (§6).

In Division I, valorisation, and accumulation, I treated in terms of the completely simple and abstract notion of a 'monetary increment'. This chapter demonstrates how it is 'produced', and therewith makes possible 'surplus value'.

'Capital in production' is the category that traces how industrial capital, complete with its unfolding in time, appropriates the material metabolism of the economy. This it assimilates to its own life. In particular it is central to the *constitution* of capital that it subsume the labour process.

The category 'capital in production' divides into the following moments. §51 Industrial Capital in Its Notion: Genesis of Value in 'Time' (Production) and 'Space' (Exchange); §52 The Capital Relation Proper: the constitution of capital is grounded in a dialectic of negativity; here then production is studied in its moment of 'difference', in which capital constitutes itself only as it is mediated in otherness (especially in living labour); §53 Self-Valorisation of Capital: the genesis of surplus value lies in value-formed surplus labour; here we take the concept of capital as *already constituted* through the above movements of time and negativity. Taking capital as winning the struggle at the point of production, we show how a surplus value emerges.

§51 *Industrial Capital in Its Notion: Genesis of Value in Time (of Production) and Space (of Exchange)*

I developed the Idea of capital so far by starting from the claim that value is rooted in the negativity of its relation to use-value, that it is *not-use-value*. It posits itself as an ideal sphere *against* its material bearers in commodities. But this presupposes there *are* commodities to support it. Thus it is not self-grounded. For capital to be its own ground, then, requires that it *produce* those commodities it originally distanced itself from. But, if we retain the idea that there is not an atom of matter in value, it is unclear what commodity production can *produce* other than the very materiality of these commodities.

How could *value* be produced? It certainly cannot be in the same sense as the use-values are produced. However, if capital is positing itself as the originator of the values it rests upon, then the only way of giving this notion determinacy is if commodity production is taken in opposition to itself, as the mere *carrier* of the ideal movement of capital. Thus I take this movement as the simple *activity* of positing value; and its determinate being is found in the *time* of that very movement as its necessary basis.

It is important that, in line with my method of exposition, I began with the synchronic value relations of commodity equivalents; yet to ground the diachronic actualisation of value we turn now to the time of capital, specifically as it is found to take a definite time to produce commodities. The value of these commodities then gains actuality on the market as the various times of capital are commensurated synchronously with each other in the 'space' of exchange and circulation.

Remark: Here *logical* 'space', i.e. the notion that a set of values are synchronous, thus relatable in this mode, is distinguished from the *geographical* space articulated by distance. (Note that throughout this book I set aside *rent*, which is logically tied to space, and to economies of space, since I hold that it is parasitic on capitalist industry.)

The immanent dimension of value is *time existent* in the process of 'positing' new 'value added'. Value added *defines* itself through a necessary relation to *how it came to be*, with reference to time that has passed. This introduces a deeper dimension of time than we saw in circulation; for its coming to be exemplifies that of *duration*. (Here capitalist production is taken as a process within the pure *time of capital*, reference to labour time being held over to the section on the constitution of capital through the capital relation proper. There I discuss the consequences for the labour process of its subsumption under the valorisation process (§ 52).)

So in this section production is treated 'in its Notion', i.e. as a purely *formal* matter. First we trace that inversion whereby, when capital produces a material product, it generates value only as the *production* time is absented in favour of its logical equivalent, namely that of the *positing* of value.

At this level of concretion (that of Division II) the figure of 'positing' is itself more concrete than it is in Division I. There the relation of positing is merely formal. Now it occurs in the world of space and time; new value is objectively presented as a result of the *movement* of valorisation. This requires that its carrier, namely the material process of production, generates a surplus product, which is then imputed with new value. Hence capital accumulates in real time, whereas in Division I we have merely the level of its logical potential. There is here a 'concrete positing', as opposed to a simply formal one.

Immediately time is a simple dimension within which circulation takes place. Even with accumulation, as a process of ontological casting measured across a time interval, this is still a fold of 'real' time, time within which it occurs. Capital moves from time to time as a pure becoming, reflected into itself as a rate of accumulation. Now, however, the time of production makes of capital a peculiar *ontological being* in that in its very essence it is constituted by a transformation of time into 'space' of exchange, I shall explain. There is a metaphysical transition in the genesis of value from the time of value positing to the space of co-determinant posited values.

I said earlier that value as an *immanence* has no metric until the latter is brought into existence by money. Here I stress that the process of *positing* value is again mere immanence. Albeit known to be a process taking time, it lacks the determinacy of magnitude until this immanent time is retroactively imputed, when the synchronic determination of values on the market is achieved. It is only the setting of an equivalence relation between putative values that gives reality to such a comparison.

The *act* of positing value results in its own fixity in the resulting value. This result must have a material product to inhabit, but what counts is its social *form* as value, hence absenting its determinate *material* features and reducing it to nothing more than the *result* of activity. Thus the value 'substance' is nothing other than the *condensation of the activity* that posited the commodity as a value. If the relevant time dimension of value positing is pure duration, value is the crystal of the time that elapsed during the process of positing value. This elapsed time is not immediately value. The immanent *diachronic* dimension is *transformed* into value with determinate magnitude only through its *commensuration* with other such times in the space of exchange. 'Time' turns to 'Space' in the *synchronic* relation of commodities.

When the *becoming* of value *comes to rest* in a result, namely a marketable commodity, value is posited. The resulting value is simply *what has become* from the *unrest* of its becoming, its conclusion in finite determination, abstracted from its contingent use-value support.

However, this raises the question of how exactly to connect categorially the value endorsed in exchange with the positing of value as result of production. There is an inflexion of this category to be noted; originally when discussing the 'becoming' of value in the space of exchange, its *inner* moments were identified as 'Being' and 'Nothing'. Now, as already something, value is grappling with the sphere of its *non-being*, the domain of production as a real process of determinate transformation of use-values. 'Being' faces *its* non-being and must internalise it. This more concrete level of 'becoming' is an unstable unity of 'being' and 'non-being'. (On non-being see Chapter 5. Here it refers to the sphere in which capital *is not*.)

The only possible *result* of the passing *of* time (distinct from production *in* time) is the time that passed, totalised at the 'Schrödinger' point of intersection with another process of passing time, registered synchronically as the value relation. Dialectically, the '*being*' of value becomes determinate only in its '*being-for-another*', only in the *encounter* of one commodity with others that recognise it as valid. The *shock* of the encounter transforms the indeterminacy of time immanent to a determinate magnitude of value. So the truth of value requires both dimensions, diachronic and synchronic.

The elapsed time is not the *immediate* time of production, as this process occurs *in* time. For the material production process is determined ideally as the trace time-passing leaves in the world. This socio-historically specific shape of time is 'empty time', unqualified by any natural rhythms, because the force of abstraction is a practical reality. The time the process takes becomes fixed as the time taken.

Nothing is in truth produced (other than the materiality of use-value) when value positing takes the shape of the *pure form* of activity. But how can there be 'plenty of nothing'? This raises the issue of determining the *magnitude* of value. What is the immanent determinant of the magnitude measured in money terms? The answer is that this 'nothing' is a determinate nothingness resulting from the passing into fixity of the restless process of its becoming, a cessation that sublates its origin. It preserves the process in the product as a definite magnitude. The only measure of such activity is the time it goes on for.

However, if we have as the result of time passing only a *spectral* 'body of work', it can be measured only through the peculiar immaterial dimensionality of money. The dimensionality of the source (time) is simply given a different categorial status in the produced commodity as finite result of so much time that *has* passed. A crystal of precipitated time, the fixing of time passed, is the magnitude measured in money.

So value is not made out of something other than itself, but it comes from itself in motion to itself then taken in fixity. *Qua* process, its magnitude is time but, posited in a determinate relation to other such times, through the mediation of money, elapsed time appears as the immanent determinant of the value measured in money.

The reason for this is that in this commensuration the concrete heterogeneity of the processes of production, as capital moves in matter, are sublated; only abstract time is considered. Concrete time is measurable *extended* time as it is determined by concrete processes, such as the time it takes to produce a commodity. However, all such concrete times sink into *abstract* time, the pure time of capital. Thus the space of synchronicity *concretises* time because only when the specific times are brought into relation systemically are they socially actualised as values.

Remark: Production time is subject to relativisation in which labour time measured by the clock is only one parameter influencing capital's time, which imposes a set of times *relative* to the mass of capital that turns over. (This I argue later: § 82.3.) So-called 'turnover time' abstractly considered is clock time similar to circulation time narrowly considered, and it is relevant to the *rate* of profit.

The importance of my account is that it avoids both the simple identity of value and time, which might involve absurdities such as 'the measure of value is time', or 'the measure of time is money', on the one hand, and, on the other hand, an external quasi-causal determination of value *by* time.

Because it is capital that brings commodities into relation, and capital that commensurates them, it is *capital's* time that counts. Capital having sunk into production, the time of production is the *time of capital*. Capital is not primarily interested in the particularities of the determinate transformation of material, only in the reproduction of value. In this commensuration the concrete heterogeneity of the processes of production, as capital moves in matter, is sublated; only abstract time is considered.

The difficult problem is to understand production as at once a material process and the bearer of value in motion. At the level of the production of real being, use-value undergoes a determinate transformation from raw material to goods, mediated by concrete labour. When we examine a product, we may judge that 'a lot of work has gone into it'; but such work is generalised concrete labour evident in the carving, polishing, etc.

Now the absolute negativity of capital takes this within its grasp such that all productive activity is reduced to the bearer of the abstract activity of transformation, namely negating of use-value. While capital produces a material product, it generates value only if its *production* time is absented in favour of its logical equivalent, namely that of the *positing* of value.

Remark: The logic of capital generally treats the forms generated in accordance with their purely logical status. Here the activity of capitalist production is the carrier of value in process. So complementary to the material production is the value posited along with it. The process of production carries that of the positing of value.

The time of capital in its fluid form is pure immanence, a process which fixes itself in its result, retrospectively making itself present in this dialectic of fluidity and fixity.

But, if value is time condensed to a spectral objectivity, then from the perspective of this result, time passing is the activity of a spectral 'subjectivity'. The time that passed in the production process, the time it *takes*, is now posited retrospectively by the spectre of capital as the time it *took*. The former is folded into the latter. Value then exists in two states, when the fluid form is posited retrospectively by capital as the subjective source of what is then present as a phantom objectivity.

This makes it seem that mere time passing *is* 'production of value', and thus to think 'waiting' is the source of profit. But, interpreted as the time capital is necessarily tied up in production, we see the objective validity of the fetish-character of such a movement of time. Time is not what value is 'made of' because this suggests a relatively external relation of form and matter (e.g. 'the statue is made of marble'). Rather value *is* time in a transformed shape, crystallised rather than fluid.

It is not quite correct to say that value has 'two measures', the immanent, time, and the external, money.[1] Time is certainly an immanent *determinant* of value; but this determinacy is merely notional because, *as immanence*, value lacks determinate magnitude *until* the money measure forms it, and posits the time taken in the context of systemically determined value measures.

Time itself cannot 'produce' anything of course; but it counts as the value 'substance', once the produced commodity is granted the form-determination of value. In this context, value is grasped as the reification of time. The time that passed in the production process, the time it takes, is now posited in value retrospectively as the time it took. Time takes frozen shape, a phantom like substance, invisible except in its avatar, money.

Time disassociated from all concrete processes of valorisation appears as a 'flat' mundane dimension *within which* these processes go on and serves to commensurate them, subject to the requirement that the time be validated as socially necessary. Valorised value makes itself present as summing the time that passed in accordance with its own protocols (i.e. the clock times are recalibrated when validated to a greater or lesser extent). Time lies immanent in value but *appears* in sublated form. What *is* an external quasi-causal determinant of value is the specific times of production conditioned by the mix of labour and means of production that every product embodies. However, these times have to be transformed into times that capital *counts* as 'necessary'.

The intersection then of time of production and space of exchange results in the creation of a special immaterial entity posited by its pure becoming. This spectral 'substance' is a presencing of time passed.

Remark: Marx made a mistake when he said somewhere that all economy is 'economy of time'. This is so only from our modern perspective. In pre-capitalist society time was not an issue, precisely because it cost nothing (and in any case

---

1 For a criticism of Marx's *Capital* on this score see Reuten 2005.

it was dictated by natural cycles). As for post-capitalist economy: it is clear now that economising on scarce resources will be prioritised over economy of time, even were that to be time for the free development of the individual.

§ 52 The Capital Relation Proper

Now we consider how capital is itself produced through the mediation of the labour process. Here it is important that living labour is an input that is not produced by capital; so I now come to the second great turning point in my presentation. At first labour was set aside on the ground that the value form abstracted from use-value consideration, in particular from the *origin* of the traded commodities. Now we bring labour into the presentation, for capitalist industry relies upon it. The reason it marks a turning point is that living labour comes from 'outside' capital; yet it is an essential condition of existence of capital. However, capital posits this condition of existence *as* its presupposition when it reproduces the capital relation in its movement. Moreover, when employed by capital, living labour is unable to function outside it; for the production process itself is now dominated by its service to capital; it is now a *capitalist* production process.

This raises the vexed question of the application of the categories 'form' and 'content' here (see Glossary for the three senses of 'form' used in this book). In what sense is there a 'fit' between the ideal and material sides of the economic order? It seems that to begin with all use-value considerations are mere 'matter' in the abstract to be idealised: the value form cannot know the things themselves. (Here it must rely on its character mask: the capitalist.) Because the *material* reality of production is *given* to capital rather than created by it, capital has to transform this material into a suitable shape more or less adequate to it; this I call the 'formal determination' of production as capitalist.

Within the value form there is a puzzling antinomy. On the one hand, it is clear that without money there is no value; commodities as such face each other as use-values merely. On the other hand, given that a basic function of money is that of measure of value, there must be an immanent value magnitude to be measured, which seems to presuppose that value exists prior to money. The first alternative opens the door to purely market determinations. The second alternative leads straight to a naturalism of value with money as a mere veil of the essential relations. My solution to this antithesis is first to derive money as pure form, presupposing but not positing a determinate content, and then to show how the dialectic of the ideal form itself demands a certain material basis in labour time. The separation of the treatment of form from that of its appropriate 'content' might seem strange or even misguided. However, not only is it possible, it is itself a reflection of reality. In the case of value, ideal form and real content are actual only in an unhappy combination. This is because the ideality of the value form is *alien* to the material inscribed within it. Although they are interpenetrating opposites, and mutually condition each other, they are never harmoniously unified but are always in tension. Moreover, it would be impossible to start with labour and show that exchange and circulation are forms of labour. But it *is* possible to develop the value form to the point at which one can see capital must appropriate productive labour.

In my preliminary considerations (i.e. in Part 1), I show that the peculiar form of social synthesis of dissociated production founds a dialectic of pure form estranged from social labour. This must first be treated in its own terms, while bracketing for a while the separation of ideality and materiality.

So now I continue the systematic development of the Idea of capital by addressing the dependence of capital on labour. Indeed, I shall argue that capital's very constitution lies in this relation and its contradictory form. Throughout this section I assume the immediate identity of capital's time with production time, and of the latter with labour time. (Later the relevant distinctions will be drawn.)

To begin with, the famous category of 'abstract labour' will be problematised. Insofar as labour time is reduced to pure time (of capital) all its materiality is *absented*, labour therewith being counted as an abstraction of itself. Then, in order for capital to move freely in the production process, it must secure the real subsumption of living labour. Here living labour is posited as the use-value of capital. Then the 'labour theory of value' will be reinterpreted as a case of capital realising itself through otherness, because living labour is potentially recalcitrant to its exploitation for capital's purposes. Through the *negating* of living labour the *constitution* of capital is actualised only through the negation of this its negation. Capital, apparently *self*-valorising, is grounded on a dialectic of negativity, wage labour being *in and against* capital. Thus living labour realises itself only as its opposite, the 'non-being' of labour, that is to say, the 'being' of capital. It is alienated labour. Hence the capital relation is the contradictory *unity in otherness* of capital and labour.

In review, I treat now the following:

§ 52.1 'Abstract' Labour
§ 52.2 Formal and Real Subsumption of Labour
§ 52.3 Constitution of Capital in a Dialectic of Negativity

§ 52.1   'Abstract' Labour

New value cannot be generated all at once, but takes time, because living labour takes time to produce what *has* value, as distinct from value itself. I argue that capital abstracts from living labour so as to leave only the pure activity of value-positing. The form of 'abstract labour' arises through the reflection on the labour process of the unity of production established by capital on the ground of pure time.

As it is inseparable from the movement of capital itself, living labour is therefore determined as the *carrier* of the time of value-positing. Just as the useful character of the commodity is abstracted from in the resulting value, so must the labour that produced it be abstracted from. Labour enters into value not *as* abstract labour, but rather as its concrete reality is abstracted *from*. The value form is *imposed* on living labours as an alien universal, identifying them *against* their reality as concrete, rather than elucidating a generality they already have.

Earlier I theorised the *infinitely negative judgement* on the exchangeable commodity that resulted in a pure singularity awaiting social determination as the bearer of value. When value totalises all *commodities* in the form of an abstract identity, even though they differ materially, use-value is *sublated*, that is, both preserved and negated. Now I show that the infinitely negative judgement on their *production* results in the movement of empty time borne by its carrier, labour.

There is a clear parallel here between the timeless positing of the spectral body of the commodity, as the *bearer* of value, and the positing of the spectral movement of value positing, taking the labour process as its *carrier*. All the material characteristics of concrete labour (including expenditure of energy) are absented so as to leave the pure *act of positing* (the ideal equivalent of producing). The result of this Becoming is the pure Being of value, incarnate in the commodity; but this is more concretely posited as what *has become* in the reality of space and time. The production process counts as pure activity, hence a movement in pure time, which, through an ideal inversion, shapes every real time in ways yet to be determined.

In the production process, labour is not regarded under its specific useful forms, but it is posited as an abstract activity. Thus, even though all real labour is particular in its action, here indifference towards the specific content of labour is not merely an abstraction made by theory, it is effectively made by capital. What really moves is always a concrete material process, yet this is determined as the carrier of the ideal logical movement of *capital*.

All the material differences of labour are absorbed in the homogeneity of the valorisation process, and this posits the labour process virtually as a *universal* production process carried out by *undifferentiated* human labour. The *absenting* of the concrete determinacy of labour leaves an abstract residue, namely time passing. It is not at all obvious that labour as such should be measured by its duration; but it *is* necessary that pure activity exists solely in the dimension of pure time. It is not that in exchange *labours* are commensurated under *their* common property of taking time. It is *capital* that commensurates *its* time. Nonetheless, because *labour* time is inseparable from the genesis of commodities, capital in its time of passage rests upon that of labour.

It is a mistake to think that abstract labour can be effective only if it is identified with a material universal such as physiological work. Rather, the *abstract* 'concept' of labour is precisely what is posited as actual by capital ideally. The practical abstraction absents all labour qualities *including* expenditure of effort, to leave pure activity. Since it is internal to the value form, *abstract labour* cannot be its *given presupposition*; rather it is capital that form-determines *living labour* only as an abstraction of itself. This objective hypostatisation is made real when capital presents abstract labour as if it were the *basis* of the universality of value; but it is the *result* of abstraction *by* the value form. Nonetheless capital's universal interest in economising on its time requires its representative, the manager, to engage with concrete labour because only the latter may be minimised in various ways. So time counts doubly; as concrete in the real labour of the production process; and abstract as a carrier of the ideal movement of capital's self-valorisation.

Yet, if we consider the collective labourer, the sum of labours making up the collectivity seems a false aggregate because it really exists only as a material combination of detailed labours, not just as one type of labour defined by the product. While such labours cannot be aggregated *concretely* in any meaningful way, capital *makes* this senseless aggregation *ideally*; and it does so under the aspect of time only, because it needs to get the commodities to market as quickly as possible. Capital must time labour, because that is central to its competition with other capitals. Capital not only posits the *qualitative* reduction of 'labour' to its abstract identity, but its *quantitative* reduction to simple time of production as determinant of magnitude of value. The given inputs of concrete labours are the raw data aggregated by capital to serve in the determination of value magnitudes.

It is capital that selects out time-passed as of the essence. But, *immediately*, it seems that development is on the side of the content in that changes in labour time feed through in a linear way to the magnitude of value. Yet, *mediatedly*, labour time is a determined determinant in that it is capital that continually seeks to increase the productivity of labour.

Nonetheless, the materiality of production is economically determinant. For, materially, only *concrete* labour is subject to reshaping. Capital cannot 'economise' on labour in the *abstract*. Only labour as concrete can be measured and minimised, and each industry has its specific way of pumping out such labour, even if ideal demands are presented to it abstractly and require concrete interpretation by managers. (The structure is tailor-made for institutional blindness:

'Don't tell me how you do it, just meet that order in time'.) However, ideally, the living labour capital exploits is determined as the carrier of its own predicate: the time it takes. Through this objective hypostatisation, the workers are predicated of their own predicate. Living labour provides the necessary bodily counterpart to the pure activity of value-positing under the rule of capital. But it does not 'produce' anything over and above the commodities that *have* value. The abstract act of value-positing, *in production*, issues in the commodity valued, *in exchange*, in proportion to the time of this movement. Materially the worker moves in time, but ideally time moves in them. In the valorisation process it is not that *the worker takes time* to produce something; rather *time takes the worker* as its carrier. The labour process is determined as the trace time leaves in the world. This socio-historically specific shape of time is 'empty time', unqualified by any natural rhythms, because the force of abstraction is a practical reality.

The spectre of capital posits itself through negating *dialectically* (i.e. *preserving* the material side within it) the realm of the real labour of production. So far from labour embodying itself in commodities and thereby constituting them as values, capital embodies itself in production, subordinates its purposes to value creation, and realises itself in the product, posited as nothing but its own result. When production is formed as production *for exchange*, the new product is potentially formed as *value*.

It seems there is nothing wrong with abstracting *from* the concrete character of the various material production processes *as long as* the abstraction is not hypostatised and said to be the real basis of the concrete, such that the concrete is then simply a body for the logic. But this mystical inversion is a *reality*. For there is indeed an autonomous existence of the ideal insofar as the concrete labour processes carry a distinct set of abstract determinations that posit value. Here the abstract formula of production, namely 'positing', is *in its very abstraction* a reality. A real inversion has occurred; value positing is the 'truth' of the labour process, and it determines the latter as the effective carrier of the valorisation process. Living labour becomes a *phantom* 'labour', and its result, value, is a *phantom* 'objectivity' borne by commodities.

If new value arises in production under the impulse of capital to valorise itself, the capitalist production process is from the start form-determined. When inputs entering production, including labour power, are commodities purchased with money capital, they are not 'devalorised' when they become active as material factors.

It is usual in value-form theory to say money is the measure of abstract labour. However, this requires careful explanation. After all, money is the measure of *value*, not of such a supposed determinant. Moreover, it is not a matter of making do with an external measure because we cannot measure directly, it is that the magnitude that is to be measured is itself *indeterminate* until money makes value actual and therewith determines how far the time of production counts socially. Nonetheless it seems clear that the dimension of time is the *immanent* determinant of value magnitudes, although the time of value positing only becomes a money magnitude in its phenomenal *existence*. Capital cannot compare the various times of production directly (nor labourers their 'toil and trouble') because the only given form of commensuration of products is in money *price*. The point is that the elapsed time of the production of each commodity underlies the synchronic relation. It is this transformation of process into product that gives rise to the dimensional discrepancy mentioned above. Hence there is a substantive relation between the parameters time and price. (This does not mean there is a simple linear determination of prices by labour time: see Chapter 13.)

I have introduced a peculiar refinement when reducing form-determined labour to a pure activity sublating material labour *altogether*. This is based on two arguments, firstly, that value is not 'produced' but posited by capital over the dead body of the worker's labour; secondly, that, if the real connection of labours is solely through their inscription in the form of value, living labour is present only as *negated* when reduced to the mere carrier of the movement of capital, just as use-value bears value as its other. What is abstracted from is not merely the particular shapes which make labours *different* from each other but also the characteristics of labour that are *common*, such as the fact that labour is expenditure of energy; this is because the abstract act of value *positing* does not involve expenditure of energy, although of course *producing* commodities does so.

Capital in its material incarnation, e.g. the factory, confronts living labour, and it subordinates it to the aim of generating value, through appropriating the powers of labour. Labour takes a particular shape to correspond to the particular substance of which a particular capital consists materially; but since capital *as such* is indifferent to every particularity of its material substance; the labour capital confronts is presupposed to have this same indifference to its particularity. In sum, while *only capital's time* (once transformed) is the 'substance' of value, as its *material carrier* labour time is the hypostatised truth of the aggregate of concrete labours.

I now distinguish two kinds of universal; it is important to distinguish the abstract universal, which ignores specific difference, and the concrete universal, which includes within itself its particularisations. Concrete universality expresses itself in *different* particularisations of the universal and they are held within it as part of its sense. Abstract universality negates particularity and covers a set of singulars taken to be *identical* with each other in some common respect.

Labour is certainly a concrete universal because the workers deploy the same labour power when they move fluidly from one task to another, or change occupation from tailoring to bricklaying. Moreover, the whole labour force is such a universal in which all the different workers are assigned their specific tasks, with fluidity of labour allowing their reassignments as requirements change. To be sure, retraining may be necessary, but there are no insurmountable social, or natural, barriers to the potential universality of labour. If the labour theory of value is to be operational this fluidity must be assumed. However, this has nothing to do with the notion that may be abstracted from this, that of labour as such, *opposed* to its concrete specificity.

In this light let us now review the determinations assumed by labour in capitalism. a) to begin with living labour takes concrete specific shapes, which differ according to the specific form of production; it is undoubtedly the case that living labour is concretely universal in being able to move fluidly between different tasks, here the universal collates the concrete not in opposition to the particular but as *self*-specifying in its particularisations; b) by contrast, the concrete shapes may be mentally disregarded so as to generate an abstraction, 'labour in general', but this is an empty universal, although within capitalism it has practical relevance for someone 'looking for work', *any* work; c) practically abstract labour differs from this last; like (b) it is opposed to specificity, but it also establishes a real connection – if only an abstract one – between labours through the mediation of the value form.

The concrete labour that produces a commodity is in fact that of the *collective* worker. The concrete universality of labour allows the labour force to be assigned to any array of jobs required by capital, a material multiplicity which forms the labourers as a collective worker. (This whole picture of capital and labour as an articulated whole is distinct from the expropriation of surplus labour from individual workers taken in this respect as abstractly identical for the purpose of commensurating their products.)

There is an interesting dialectic here if we attend to how this is made up of individual labours, which, when abstracted from this whole, have no meaning. It is not a social whole made up of whole individuals; rather the singulars of which it is composed are themselves merely abstract moments of it because they have no subsistence outside it. The worker is reduced to a fraction of the concrete wholeness of the labour producing the commodity when the bearer of this universality. The collective worker is like a giant machine in which each motion is parcelled out to individually detailed labours. (Conversely, a welder for example does much the same work whether in a car factory or a shipyard.)

Such work is not necessarily unskilled, but its character is determined by capital, and it is unable to act outside the collectivity of labour. So here the whole is what is concrete and unifies its abstract moments. But the singulars do not in return constitute the collective as their *own*; rather they see it as an alien totality to which they are 'indifferent'.

When really subsumed by capital the workers become like bees, with no necessity to understand the ultimate purpose of their activity. The only purpose of work for the labourer separated from the objectives of production is the wage; hence if this is all that counts the workers may well be indifferent to the content of their labour. However, indifference is not the definition of abstract labour; it is the consequence of the double abstraction imposed by the value form on the product and on labour power.

The determination of labours as abstract flows from the fact that their unity is objectively constituted only when so 'conceptualised' by capital. The reason for this is that it is capital that organises the collectivity such that, although really specifications of the concrete universal, the labours are alienated from their own sociality. As alienated from their human bearers the labours' own universality is supplanted by capital's universal presence.

The concrete labour producing a commodity is, then, in one sense nothing but the 'labour' *of capital*; because its production is here subordinated to the purpose of valorisation. But in a further twist this 'concrete labour of capital' is itself rendered abstract through the *social* division of labour. What is striking about the value form is that the wealth of productive power generating an enormous range of commodities is collapsed to a single result, value, imputed to a single source, abstractly identical 'labour'.

Yet the social integration of private producers through exchange involves different determinations than those characteristic of the collective worker in the factory. The latter is organised by capital as a concrete whole of labours; but the former is predicated on an asocial sociality in which the ideal totality sublates the array of private 'labours' organised by capital as a system. The different capitalist production processes supporting value positing are structurally ignored for the sake of commensurating the values to be realised. While all industrial capitals are value creating, the specific forms of the pumping out of labour from the immediate producers is ignored in this abstract universality which registers them all as homogenous with one another.

However, social labour is the suppressed precondition of the abstract whole because capital requires this concrete universal if it is to allocate and regulate labour as required, not only in the factory, but across the economy. Indeed, the social division of labour, and the possibility of its redrawing, is a precondition of capitalist production. It depends on a concretely universal form of labour able to transfer easily between different occupations and tasks, unconstrained by natural scarcity of talent, or social barriers to mobility. It may well be that the concrete universality of social labour is a necessary precondition for the positing of abstract labour but it is not to be identified with it. (But this social totality of labour never exists immediately, because the totalisation is effected by capital, which reduces concrete labours to moments of *its* totalising drive.)

So it is important that labour can *really transform its expression* from one concrete labour to another, and that such supplies of labour power are readily available to capital. Here the stress is not on the *reduction* of the concrete to the same featureless abstraction, but, to the contrary, on the wealth of different forms taken by labour as a universal activity. This brings out that here labour is a *concrete universal*. But this has to do with its productive power in relation to use-value. However, it is a separate point that, when concrete labours realise themselves as use-value, simultaneously capital posits their product as value. *They* do not do this themselves; they simply carry out this alien intention.

This *social abstraction* has actuality only on the assumption that the products concerned are products of capital. As a *result* of the social equivalence of commodities established in capitalist competition, the labours are socially related only through the value form of the product, which results in the absenting of *all* characteristics of living labour. The labour process, in the absence of such concrete determinations as *make* it labour, is simply a *spectral* movement, once capital has formed it as a valorisation process, expressed as such only in objective form. But this is a spectral objectivity. Value is a spectral substance which inhabits commodities and money, but absents their materiality so as to give the ideal substance a 'body', but a spectral body since it is dematerialised.

Value-in-process is carried by the labour process; but, when the unity established in capital's time is reflected onto the labour process as if that were its ground, it appears as if the material labour underpinning value positing is labour in the abstract i.e. hypostatised as such. But this is an ideal imputation; and because value can only be generated along with the commodity that bears this social imputation it is easy to conflate the ideal social process with the material production process.

Thus the process of production of capital might not be distinguished from the material process of production in general. The determinateness of its form is then extinguished. The upshot is that the material process of production in its immediacy *appears* as 'the self-moving *content* of capital'. Capital, as absolute form of value, determines everything inscribed within it as its own; but having taken possession of labour it can absent itself and make its avatar do all the work.

Because labour *serves* as carrier of value-positing it seems as if work as such is immediately 'productive' of value, and as if then value were a 'product' of labour like use-value. Since practically abstract labour has only a spectral existence it is easily confused with more real generalities such as expenditure of energy. The result is that such a general form of labour is fetishised as if it produced value.

An *abstract concept of* labour ignores as irrelevant to value theory the kinds of labour and the person whose labour it is (however relevant this is to – say – works of art). This is *not* the same as a *concept of abstract* labour, which presupposes that the predicate has an ontological bearing on the labour itself, not just how it counts for *thought*. Since *all* labour is necessarily concrete (one cannot just 'work' without doing something specific) to operate this imputation of abstract, as opposed to concrete, labour, it must be socially produced as an objectively valid determination.

However, to treat the abstract concept as *substantial* is to commit the fallacy of hypostatisation because it seems that labour is necessarily always concrete. The answer to this puzzle is that labour-in-general is *practically* hypostatised through the equivalence established between its products in the value form. Hence *it* is posited as the genuine substance of the concrete specific labours. If such a hypostatisation of the abstract concept of labour is objectively present, it appears as valid to say that its bearers, the real labours, actively 'produce' value along with use-value. It is this conflation that causes confusion.

Remark: Riccardo Bellofiore has underlined in many places that labour is the victim of a triple hypostatisation. He argues that: in the *final* commodity market objectified labour as a real hypostasis is predicated on the exchange abstraction; in the *initial* labour market labour power is subject to a real hypostatisation process through which the worker becomes the predicate of their own capacity to work; and in the *centre* of the valorisation process living labour is 'other-directed' work where the real hypostatisation is that the worker becomes the predicate of the time of their own labour.[2]

A common version of the labour theory of value relates value to 'abstract labour', with 'concrete labour' assigned to that required by the specificity of use-value. In order to avoid the charge that this abstraction is as empty as 'utility', it is said that it is not a mental fiction because it actually exists in the physical expenditure of energy *common* to all work. This physiological identity of labours underpins the notion of 'embodied labour' evidently. But this is a naturalistic metaphysics lacking the socio-historical determinacy of capitalism. The

---

2 See, for example, Bellofiore 1999, p. 56.

naturalistic view that each hour of 'embodied labour' *is* value fails to see that value is a social form and that it is this social determination that reduces labour to an abstraction of itself, to elapsed time.

It might be thought that if 'abstract labour' is a shape generated by capital, then it is unreal, merely a 'shadow' cast by capital. 'Utility' is just such a shadow-form cast by the value form.[3] Because two baskets of groceries have the same price it is fallaciously assumed that they must contain something identical reflected in the equal prices. It is termed 'utility'; yet this is a metaphysical construct with no effective reality. But is the 'abstract labour' embodied in the groceries equally a shadow-form of heterogeneous concrete labours, in the same way that 'utility' is abstracted from the ineliminable specificities of use-values?

However, the *abstract* 'concept' of labour is *not* just a shadow-form thrown onto the labour process by capital. For, in the case of labour, its abstractly universal determination is really *posited* by capital as a form of *existence* of labour; so it is not just a shadow-form but has effective reality as the bearer of capital's movement, determining in this way the magnitude of value. This is possible because *wage* labour is not 'outside' capital. Once, on this basis, living labour has been *internalised* it appears as capital's *own* use-value, although one must never lose sight of labour's tendential resistance to exploitation. This allows us to finesse the problem that 'abstract labour' might be a mere 'shadow-form' cast by the capitalist production process.

Remark: Notice the conceptual difference between our earlier discussion of abstraction in exchange and this more concrete notion of 'abstract' labour. 'Utility' is an empty abstraction; it cannot therefore support the attribution of exchange-value to commodities. So I argued that this is not a result of an abstraction of some feature of the commodity *from* it. Rather we argued that the form of value is a transcendental form imposed *on* it. 'Labour' is not an empty abstraction but a concrete universal form of activity capable of determining itself to specific shapes of labouring. However, in opposition to that, here we say that labour as such, abstracted from concrete labours, is *posited* by capital as the proximate determination to value.

Let us sum up this section on 'abstract labour'. It has no meaningful existence (any more than 'utility') unless it is conceptualised as abstract *by capital*. It is capital, in virtue of *its* form as temporalised, that form-determines labour, such that it is counted simply as the carrier of time passing. In effect, everything

---

3 I take the term 'shadow-form' from Patrick Murray. There is an extensive discussion of it in Murray 2017, Chapter 5.

about labour is abstracted *from*, leaving merely its putative measure, time, left standing as the time of value positing by capital. It is as if the collective labours are the complicated shell of a hypostatised universal substance. But this immanent time of capital becomes determinate only with the shock of the product's encounter with other products in the socially systemic value relations.

The operational determinacy of the concept of 'abstract labour' requires that it be fluid enough to respond to the demands of capital. This is possible because labour itself has the character of concrete universality. However, this is *not* the same notion as 'abstract labour'. which is figured as *opposed* to everything concrete about labour.

§ 52.2   Formal and Real Subsumption of Labour

The category of subsumption is central to value-form theory. On the one hand, there is the commodity manifold, which is in itself incoherent; on the other hand, there is the universal value form within which commodities become inscribed in orderly fashion, the latter are subsumed by the former.

With respect to the value form, I do not think use-values, or for that matter objectified labour, are a genuine 'content'. In a dialectical relation of form and content not only does the form posit itself in the content but the content gains its proper existence in the form. However, when a product is inscribed within the value form this is by no means a form appropriate to it, but an alien form imposed upon it. So here 'form' impresses itself on what it presupposes to be a lifeless substrate; but the capitalist has to mediate this by knowing how to shape matter according to capital's demands. This requires the *real subsumption* of production, not just the 'idealising' of matter by inscribing it in the form. This is still more the case when living labour objectifies itself in the commodity only to find itself estranged from it. Thus capital 'takes possession' of labour so as to subordinate it to the purpose of valorisation. Rather than a proper 'content', labour is the real *condition* of value creation.

Once really subsumed labour appears as the use-value of capital itself. Capital in its practice must concretely engage in the 'labour of the negative' and struggle to really subsume labour. But when it presents the commodity to exchange it represses this knowledge of its origin in blood and sweat, as if its ideality infuses its material ground with the form of pure activity. In commensurating labour, time is what capital selects as its relevant parameter; other determinations of labour (effort, fluidity, fragmentation, indifference) are cognate to this key attribute but not to be identified with it.

With the real subsumption of labour under capital there takes place a complete revolution in the relation between capitalist and worker. The social forms of their own labour are constituted quite independently of the individual workers; the workers subsumed under capital become elements of these social constructions. This is the more real the more their labour capacity is modified by these forms, so that it becomes powerless when it stands alone. *Outside* this context of capitalist relations its capacity for independent production is much diminished. Generally it can be exercised now only in capitalist factories.

The *capitalist* mode of production changes the shape of material production. The machinery too is subsumed under capital. For the means of labour end up as an *automatic system of machinery*, and the shape in which the immediate means of labour was included into the production process of capital is superseded by a form posited by capital itself and corresponding to it. It now has a shape *adequate to capital*. Whatever changes fixed capital undergoes it must accord with this requirement. Moreover, the material recalcitrance of labour is minimised through the very design of the factory.

With the real subsumption of the human and material elements of the production process, capital takes them into its *possession* in a more than legal sense; having them within its power its spirit is present there. The productive power of labour and machinery is now capital's own power.

A capitalist firm is specified formally as a mass of value. But capital must always be materially instantiated if it is to have determinacy. In order to produce efficiently capital must combine definite complementary factors of production in the relevant proportions. The category of 'subsumption' is required in order to construe this relation between value and use-value, more specifically between the general form of capital and the material it subsumes. If the factory is 'the body of capital', its 'soul' is the living labour process as it is appropriated by capital as a valorisation process.

In short capital is a relation of production. Yet capital presents itself as the prime mover in the economy. Since the labour process is subsumed under the valorisation process, productive labour *belongs* to capital. Capital is productive insofar as it 'produces' the *compulsion to do surplus labour* on the part of the workers. Given this, it seems *capital creates capital*.

There is here a double subsumption.

First, capital as self-valorising appropriates the productive labour of *isolated* workers. Because capital employs legally each worker *individually*, surplus labour is likewise expropriated from each singly. This has to do with the social positing of labour as belonging to capital, through the wage contract.

Second, capital is the personification, the reified shape, of the productive powers of social labour. As a productive power capital is incarnate in the *collective labourer*. Despite the use made of their individual skills this collectivity is plausibly represented, not as that of the associated individuals, but as capital's own productive power insofar as its principle of organisation flows from capital, which subsumes the individuals under the hierarchical division of labour imposed on them. (Here the labour of superintendence, the design and management of the production process, occurs as if the representative of capital were like the conductor of an orchestra.)

Capital as 'subject' is *incarnate* in the factory regime. Capital embodied in means of production (its inorganic body) employs every worker as a labour-power machine (its organic body); they are its 'hands', subjugated to the discipline of the factory regime. Materially the factory embodies an intention alien to the workers and brings them into connection externally so as to constitute a collective labourer they do not comprehend. It is *collectively* that concrete labours are *really* subsumed under capital when it imposes material shapes of co-operation, division of labour, and machinery.

In addition to serving as exploited source of surplus labour, the immediate producers are alienated from their *own universality* as *socially* productive, since the labour process is not that of freely associated producers but subsumed under the despotism of the capitalist factory. Once *internalised* by the ideal totality of capital labour becomes posited as capital's internal other. Thus when it realises itself in its social manifestation it appears in value only as reified. *Remark*: When these two inversions are *conflated*, the result of the first, which posits capital as creator of profit, may be seen as the act of capital *qua* thing (the factory system); conversely the power of produced means of production may be seen as that of capital *qua* monetary form.

§ 52.3   The Constitution of Capital through a Dialectic of Negativity

I come now to an important point. To say that value is crystallised time is to put the point formally. In reality this time is predicated on capital's relation to living labour, because that is its required carrier, not merely passively, but only as labour is pumped out of recalcitrant workers. In the previous section, we treated capitalist production in its immediacy, considering production only as capital's production time. But in this section we see a radical difference there because capital relies upon living labour, which is fundamentally *other* than it. Thus the justification for this focus on labour here is to examine capital's appropriation of it, and its positing as capital's 'internal other' (as I term it, in contrast to the 'external other', Nature).

I argue that value *is* nothing but a crystallisation of the time of production. An ontological transformation, from a motion to a fixity, is posited in the value form of the produced commodity. However, this 'time of capital' is identical to labour time insofar as labour is negatively related to capital as the other it must control.

In the first place the production process is a material metabolism. Looked at in its immediacy, disregarding its social form, production is a material transformation of given material into products (whether 'final' or 'intermediate') with specific use-value. In order to accomplish production, the worker employs instruments, whether simple tools, or machinery which implies cooperation and a peculiar division of labour. It is important to distinguish between the production process in general and the labour process narrowly defined. In the next section it will be argued that value should be taken as a function only of labour time not of production time in general. But for the moment we speak as if production time were labour time.

As a consequence of its real subsumption, waged labour engages in its own objectification process as a *mode of existence* of capital. The power of *preserving value* and creating *new value* is therefore capital's power; so, formally, the process is one of capital's *self*-valorisation, while the workers who produce what *has* value – value *alien to them* – are, in contrast, impoverished. Thus living labour realises itself in the mode of denial, when reified in value.

Even if the individual is reduced to a cog in a machine, social production, including the production of knowledge, becomes more powerful albeit in alienated form. Nevertheless, the motor of the dialectic of the capital relation is self-constituting capital, while labour reproduces the wage-labour relation because it is forced to do so, as capital confines it to propertylessness. In the capital relation, there is an interpenetration of opposites such that there is a dialectic of determining of the determinant, whether capital or labour, each is struggling for supremacy. The *principal* aspect of the capital relation (hence properly so-called) is capital.

In the factory the collective worker embedded in the configuration of machinery appears as a sort of concrete universality but this labour is alienated, because as waged labour it functions as capital so that capital, originally ideal, is concretised in moving matter. But living labour is always, even under real subsumption, *other* than, and external to, capital, continually *recalcitrant* to the ideal totality in principle. With waged labour, capital appropriates it in *form*, but labour power is ever in excess of this conceptualisation of it as mere human capital (hence its potential liberation in socialist relations of production).

Pure time is the immanence phenomenally present only 'as' time of value positing hidden in that of labour; economy of this time is then a matter of addressing labour times. When I said time is value-as-immanence, I *now* say this time is grounded in the time of 'pumping out' living labour. If this appropriation is taken as already accomplished, we may then proceed with capital's development of further forms.

Recall that in the first chapter I discussed the triad: sociation, dissociation, association. The association of productive enterprises, through the exchange and money system, does not abolish dissociation but achieves the resocialisation of these dissociated enterprises under a very peculiar form, the value form. What are the consequences of this dialectic for the labour of the immediate producer? Dissociated labours, presented in the commodities exchanged, become labours recognised in the social form of money only in their abstract identity, because, just as use-value is not represented in the value of commodities, neither are concrete labours in their variety recognised. In all societies labour has a social form but only in capitalist society is production socially mediated in this abstract universal form. In other societies, whether feudal or communist, labour is immediately social. This is true even where, in a five-year plan, labour is socially equated, and treated as a concrete whole to be divided and assigned as required. In such a case labour is a concrete universal, but in commodity production labour becomes social only as the abstraction of itself.

What then is the relation of living labour to value and its magnitude? It is the *carrier* of capital's productive activity. Once appropriated through waged labour, living labour becomes in effect capital's agent in its self-valorisation, capital itself being the prime mover in the process. Albeit living labour is essential to material production it is recognised in value only through one isolated determination, the time it takes. Not only is concrete labour not recognised in value, labour itself, just insofar as it is always concrete, is absented.

What about the immediate producer, the worker, who supplies living labour without which nothing at all would get produced? I argued that this material basis of production is *abstracted from* in the time crystallised in the value of a commodity. Now I examine more closely the capital relation that structures production. In this I consider, not now the formal negation of living labour in its absenting in value, but its real negation, in that labour under capital is always, in principle, *forced* labour.

As potentially recalcitrant to its exploitation by capital, living labour is negated in a more complex way than simply its positing as carrier of capital's valorisation process. Although capital posits the commodity as its own product, it requires living labour to undertake the transformation of matter. Capital achieves this more or less efficiently when subordinating it to capital's own aims. Here living labour is *negatively posited* as the sublated condition of existence of value. Living labour takes a positive determination when it is acknowledged as the creator of use-values: it is negatively determined as what it 'costs' capital to overcome its recalcitrance to exploitation. Capital constitutes itself only through a dialectic of negativity, waged labour being *in and against* capital.

In the capital relation proper, we see that, on the one hand, this seems to be characterised by a confrontation between capital and labour, on the other it is rightly characterised as the *capital* relation because labour here is already formed by capital as waged labour. Workers have no option but to sell their labour power to capital.

It is in this context that the difficult issue of the labour theory of value is raised. As I have argued it will not do simply to identify labour and value; for a start, it is clear they have different states; one is a movement, the other is its result. Labour is the negatively posited sublated ground of capital value, so its time is the carrier of capital's time. This is the time capital is tied up when it is obliged to undergo the trouble of pumping out labour from the workers.

Now the original phenomenal definition of value as a power of exchange is supplemented by the immanent determinant of value as (labour) time appropriated, each having a measure peculiar to it. The relation between the two is not causal in the sense of an external relation of correlation. It is the becoming of value from a state of unrest to that of rest.

It is not quite correct to say that living labour is the 'source' of value because that suggests a positive effect. In truth, capital posits value only through appropriating, while 'negating', living labour, forcing recalcitrant labour to produce and positing the resulting commodity as a value. The product *as a value* marks the success of capital at pumping out labour from the immediate producer.

Capital creates value, but it does so only through its appropriation of the labour that creates the bearer of value. On the ground of the separation of the worker from the object of productive activity there results the *subordination* of the workers to capital, and therewith the expropriation of their productive powers by capital which exploits them for its own ends; but the essentially contested nature of this exploitation requires a new understanding of the labour theory of value as a dialectic of negativity.

Adam Smith thought the labourers need recompense for their 'toil and trouble'; this was the basis of his value theory; but there is no process through which the individual labourers commensurate their toil and trouble with that of others. The products have a unitary form as products *of capital*. Thus capitals commensurate *their* toil and trouble, namely the time they are tied up in the production process, the time taken to pump out labour from recalcitrant workers.

While it is common to speak about the 'production' of value, such a notion is problematic. There is no doubt that the workers produce the commodity, and that the commodity has value. But these moments should not be telescoped such that labour is taken to *produce that value*. Value is clearly a social determination acquired by the commodity when capital commensurates commodities in the market. It seems odd to treat it as a product over and above the bodily form of the commodity. The issue is even more paradoxical; for the labour supposedly 'producing' value is said to be abstract in character. However, I believe these paradoxes obtain because of the peculiarity of the value form, insofar as it constitutes a realm of ideality overlying the material reality. If an abstract activity cannot produce an object in the usual sense, it may yet produce an ideal objectivity, especially if we logicise the term production and treat it as a 'positing'. Thus the activity of valorisation posits its result as value.

Very well. But this ideal objectivity is surely not a product in any substantive sense, merely the activity taken as resulting in an ideal predicate of the commodity. Nonetheless, I claim this positing does result in the creation of an *ideal social substance*. This category I developed earlier in the dialectic of the value form. In its dialectical self-presentation, value passes from a relation to a property to a substance to a subject. The substance of capital is accumulated value, endlessly valorised anew. If capital is accumulated it must be a substance. Certainly this substance cannot be hefted in the hand, but it *is* an ideal substance whose weight is felt on the economic scales.

If the valorisation process is subtended by the labour process, value is produced at the very same time as labour produces the commodity that has value attributed to it. Just as the commodity is interpellated formally as 'a value' (note the real metonymy here) so the labour that produced it is interpellated formally as that which supports the process of positing value, an abstract logical process to be sure. But, insofar as capital takes possession of material production, its agent, labour, carries the abstract activity of generating new value (not just new use-value), as if the labour *itself* were abstract. Because of the hidden inversion of material and ideal, it appears as if labour *as such* 'produces value'. This is not a fault of consciousness but a 'fault' in reality. If the root of this hypostatisation is not recognised then material labour is fetishised. This has important consequences for the fetish-character of commodity production. The social positing of commodities as values leads to the fetish-character of commodities because the commodity as product *per se* appears as a value. If the commodity is fetishised it is reasonable to surmise that the activity producing it may be fetishised.

This is true of those who claim to have seen through the vulgar form of commodity fetishism on the market to the *production* of commodities. So productive labour is taken as value positing in classical political economy (and especially by Ricardian socialists), yet its apparent power of creating value really registers the effectivity of the *social form* within which production is carried on. How does this happen? Just as value inhabits the natural body of the commodity so we find value positing is carried by living labour. This makes it look as if it is *living labour itself* that 'produces' value as well as use-value. This is nonsense if taken as a natural property of labour, but this attribution of a power of producing value has a certain 'objective validity' just as in the parallel case of the commodity itself.

This double character of the labour process (positing value at the same time as use-value) is objectively determined. The positing of labour ideally as pure activity gives material labour a fetish-character because the pure movement of value is introjected into its carrier. (Just as the value form is internalised by the commodity.) If this abstract labour is identified with the material labour *given* to the value form then we have full-blown fetishism. If the social valorisation process is conceptually collapsed to the labour process that bears it then productive labour in some material definition is taken to produce value. Labour – understood as a material activity – is fetishised as inherently productive of value. If the attribution of value to the commodity has a fetish-character so the claim labour produces value has a fetish-character. But, no matter that we show how this fetish-character occurs, it is not merely an illusion. Just as the commodity provides a 'body' for value, so the appearance that 'labour produces value' has objective validity when the labours are determined as carriers of the positing of new value.

The imposition of the value form on the product of labour is complemented by the material reality of exploitation which must go beyond the technical economising of time to the 'pumping out' of labour, so it is determined as forced labour as well as abstract labour. Value is the result of forced labour, and its magnitude is determined by the time of such exploitation.

While value is not *produced*, it is *created*. How do I make this distinction? Clearly in both cases something new results; however, value is created when a new *form* is acquired by *what is produced*. Productive activity transforms one configuration of matter to another. Thus 'a product' is 'made out of' such material. But, if value is essentially a social form, and contains 'not an atom of matter', it is not 'made out of' anything at all; rather, it gives social form to what production has made. It is an unobjectionable metaphor to speak of the product as the objectification of living labour; but this fact should not be translated into a claim about the value character of the commodity.

Labour, considered positively as essential to production, is that concrete labour objectified in the specific use-value of the product. Labour, considered negatively, is forced labour exploited by capital for whatever time is socially necessary to produce a commodity.

Capital *wants* its production process to be frictionless, but, as forced labour, production retains the moment of negativity. The determination of labour as immanently bound up with value is preserved in that negation of the negation wherewith capital negates that which opposes it (the recalcitrant worker), and presents value as a positive result. So this negation of its negation allows capital to posit itself as the author of value and surplus value.[4]

In sublating the living labour that is the material ground of valorisation, capital sublates therewith the specificity of its shapes of dominance and the character of any recalcitrance overcome. This is why in exchange-value labour does not appear at all because capital represses its origin in this negativity and presents the commodity to exchange as its own product. However, this is a *determinate* negation such that its origin in labour is preserved in sublated form. The term 'sublation' indicates that something is denied, here that the valorisation process is a labour process, and something preserved, here that waged labour is a precondition of value positing. In short, capital is the subject of production, producing above all itself, while labour is negatively posited as its sublated ground. In this Alice-in-Wonderland sense waged labour may be considered the 'source' of value.

Labour is abstracted *from* because there is no genus such as 'labour' as an abstract universal, e.g. as physiologically similar, that is effective, any more than 'utility' is effective. But just as the bodily product supports the *spectral body* of an ideal value substance, so pure time is carried by living labour. But the relation is inverted in that labour is predicated of time, as time's material carrier. The value form absents the various concrete times of production when the ideal time of self-moving value takes possession of them and homogenises them.

In the absence of resistance, workers are no less 'personifications' of capital than the employers, reduced to 'human capital', labour machines, a resource to be managed. If labour were perfectly reified this is all that would need to be said. However, it is not; and this introduces a new dynamic to our consideration of living labour, we shall argue next.

Living labour does not appear as value, because value-in-process, capital, both absents it formally, and negates it materially, such that living labour is presented in value not as realised but as *de-realised*. (Yet it remains, albeit sublated, as the material basis with its effectivity as the root of *time taken*.) It follows that violence is done to living labour in a more radical sense than its treatment as an abstraction of itself. Living labour is *realised* only in the mode of *unreality*. The abstract objectivity of value mediates itself in the abstract activity of value positing. Conversely what abstract activity 'produces' can be only an abstract product such as value, whose magnitude is a function of the amount of derealised labour absorbed.

---

4 See Lebowitz 1992, p. 85.

Marx picks out the implications of this transition from labour into value when he writes that this process of the realisation of labour (in the product) is at the same time the process of its de-realisation (in the value of the commodity); it posits itself objectively, but it posits its objectivity as its own non-being, or as the being of its non-being, the being of capital.[5]

This is a stupendous insight from the point of view of this chapter. Capital is a subject; counter to it is living labour; but in the capital relation this labour is self-estranged.

The self-affirmation of capital and the self-negation of labour are identical, distinguished only as mutually presupposing moments. However, the 'capital relation' is properly so-called (i.e. capital is both part and whole) since it affirms itself therein, while labour is reproduced as the propertyless other of capital. While the logic of difference is suppressed it remains an immanent source of critique. This is not because 'really' labour is everything and capital is nothing, but because the re-forming of the *human* reality of the labour process by the *inhuman* form of capital generates an *inverted* reality. The 'true' and 'false' ontology of capital are coexistent.

Labour I call the 'internal other' of capital; its exploitation is central to capitalist production but it is always 'other' than capital even when thoroughly subsumed by it. The 'time of capital' which is a determinant of the magnitude of value, is 'carried' by the 'time of labour', but only in the context of the capital relation. Labour's objectification in value realises itself paradoxically as the being of its non-being, namely the being of capital. Conversely capital has labour as its subjectified non-being that it subordinates to its aims.

Alienation characterises the unity in contradiction of labour and capital, in which living labour generates capital as its non-being, but also capital has to pass through the otherness of material production alien to its ideality. To be sure, social labour realises itself as a concrete totality at the material level in a wealth of use-values. But this positive universality is simultaneously negative in the generation of the value totality, as capital, because it is the *alienation* of living labour, its realisation as something opposed to it.

However, given there is this relation between capital and labour, the contradictions of the capital relation may be examined from two sides, first, here, from the side of living labour; it is able to realise itself only when made into capital's own activity, acting as the use-value of capital; second, from the side of capital, which *constitutes* itself only through a dialectic of negativity; finally, I argue that capital, as the principal aspect of the contradiction, has to be con-

---

5 Marx 1994, p. 202.

sidered as successful in winning the struggle at the point of production, and reducing labour to a manageable 'resource', if we are to advance the presentation of capital's epochal dominance, and give an account of the determination of the magnitude of value.

To say that the movement of production is powered by the self-activity of the Concept sounds like the sheerest idealism, an inversion of the true relation of the material and the ideal. But in the case of capital this inversion in reality, brought about by a peculiar material practice, *exists* and it has profound consequences. There is an interpenetration of ideal and material determinants. In no way is the generation of value and surplus value a linear reflection of living labour in its movement. To be sure there is a sense in which labour inputs are ontologically more fundamental, but the peculiar constitution of capital, including its presence as many capitals, means that determinations proper to it shape the process (as we see later).[6]

However, despite the hegemony of capital over labour in the capital relation, the original separation between the material and ideal remains. The right term to characterise the rule of capital over its material presuppositions is 'subsumption'; yet, although labour is appropriated, internalised even, by capital, there is never a final harmony in which capital properly recognises in labour only itself in material shape. Although it seems the ideal totality inscribes within its forms labour and Nature, this is not finally true because all along there is the 'excess' that cannot be 'idealised' by the concept, namely the concrete richness of social labour. Moreover, this cannot be left aside as having no economic determinacy because the dialectic of form and content means that each is mediated in the other.

There are two moments. The development of the value *form* is naturally entirely on the side of the form, as value takes on more complicated shapes. But it requires at every point material grounding. The material appropriated, including labour, it formally treats as mere stuff, and materially makes into a shape adequate to its demands. Nonetheless, it is perfectly possible for determination from the side of the 'content' to be economically effective. For example, large-scale production impels the development of joint-stock companies. In the contradictory relationship of capital and labour, capital is the *principal aspect* in that it realises itself albeit on the basis of a dialectic of negativity. If we assume in the further presentation that capital continually wins the struggle at the point of production, we may present 'after the harvest' calculations of value and surplus value as if capital is in truth now *constituted*.

---

[6] Bellofiore 2014, p. 183, distinguishes between the circular movement of self-positing capital and the linear input of living labour to this process.

Capital faces material, means of production, and living labour. It has to realise its Idea through the 'labour of the negative' in subsuming these. But only in the case of labour may we properly speak of potential recalcitrance, in the sense of a *practical* contestation of capitalist exploitation, through strikes, sabotage, and so forth. It is true that empirically cases may be found in which workers enjoy their work, and are satisfied with its rewards. However, *potentially*, the working class is a *counter-subject* to capital. If labour power became totally reified, indistinguishable from a robot 'work force', then our argument would not hold. In such a case *all* the time of capital would count equally for it, whether labouring, machining, or 'naturing'. However, this possibility has little plausibility. Human beings have to deploy their knowledge and experience to keep the production process going. Even in the limiting case of forms of real subsumption so extreme that labour appears 'robotic', it is still the case the workers have to force themselves to act as robots, they still *act*. Likewise, although capital treats the social power of labour as its own, at bottom it remains the power of human beings, albeit appearing as a power alienated from them. Yet our dialectic must uncover the reality of capital's hegemony here.

We resume the dialectical development of the Idea of Capital in the next section on this basis, namely the understanding that capital is to *constitute itself* in and through the capital relation. In this it takes the labour it appropriates as its own use-value, valorising itself through this carrier of its movement.

§53   *The Self-Valorisation of Capital*

I distinguish between the labour process and the valorisation process that is borne by it.[7] The elements of the labour process are labour itself, the means of production and the material worked upon. The product is a commodity with some (real or imaginary) use. The valorisation process is that in which the value of the material and means of production (termed 'constant capital') is combined with the expenditure of labour power to create the value of the commodity. The reward for the workers' surrender of their labour power is the wage. The reward for capital is surplus value.

Given what I have explained earlier, I think it is the real, or potential, recalcitrance of the labourers to capital that justifies the theoretical attribution of value to labour, and the reduction of other determinants of price to a secondary status. But if one speaks of recalcitrance, it is clear that one means recalcitrance

---

[7] Confusion between these processes still pervades economics today, despite Marx's dissection of such errors in his chapter on the so-called 'Trinity Formula'.

to exploitation. But this insight means that in a peculiar way the category of exploitation is *prior* to the category of value itself.[8]

The usual reading of the labour theory of value suggests labour produces value and then capital steals some of it. We reject this view in favour of a reading in which capital produces value in the very process of exploiting workers. Value on this reading is the form in which competing capitals commensurate their degree of success in exploiting labour. Recalcitrance to this, assuredly takes concrete forms such as working slowly. Thus exploitation is a qualitative matter, involving such concrete measures as the division of labour, speed up of the line, and so forth. (The quantitative issue of the very possibility of the genesis of 'surplus value' we treat below: §53.2.) Labour is subject to a double determination. At the immediate level of valorisation, it is simply the carrier of capital in its movement of positing the commodity as a value with definite magnitude. At a deeper level, because it is recalcitrant to capital, this introduces a dialectic of negativity in which capital succeeds in valorising itself only through thoroughly subsuming labour to its purposes. On that basis labour time is peculiar and to be distinguished from other times for which capital is tied up.

I divide this discussion into §53.1 Value Added; §53.2 Genesis of Surplus Value; §53.3 The Wages of Labour.

§53.1   Value Added

The value of a commodity is the product of two factors: the value of the means and material 'embodied' in it (unchanged) is termed 'constant capital'; new value is added to this during the course of production. We have related the genesis of this new value indirectly to labour time. Now this must be determined more precisely. To begin with, my very definition of capital refers to the determination of time; it is not merely the generation of a monetary increment, but the rate at which this is accomplished that is the true measure of capital as self-valorising value. For exchange of capitalistically produced commodities, the natural basis for it is the different times during which capital is tied up in their production. It is commensurated across competing capitals. This means the value of a commodity must be related to that time *socially necessary* to produce it. This is the first form in which the magnitude of value is determined.

Here I treat production time as capital's time. One problem with this is that the coefficient that harmonises the concrete times of production departs from

---

8   Even some Marxists today see a break in the argument from simple circulation to capitalist production, as if market relations and capitalist production are conceptually opposed. See my reply to Jacques Bidet on this in Arthur 2005a.

them in a series of transformations beginning with the form of 'socially necessary labour time', and then further disturbed, we shall see, by the effect of organic compositions and so forth, which means some times count for more or less than others. The most difficult issue to analyse is the nature of this 'time', for capital's time is different from the empirically given time of the material process of production. In the real world every production process takes its own time; but it would be clearly absurd to have a lazy worker 'create' more value in the product than an energetic one in exactly the same sort of product. The market, when it assimilates these products to the same class with the same price, will discount these real times.

Commodities exchange at value, that is, in proportion to their socially necessary labour times, since dynamic competition within a sector causes capitals to approximate to such times. But what is the time socially necessary? One might think that it is the time taken by the firm employing best practice; for clearly the other firms wasted time relative to this one. The firm with best practice will make additional profit, because of its lower labour costs, until the other firms have caught up.

But I do not define 'necessary' as best practice but as the 'average' one. Why? Because this approximates to the time the market will *recognise* as necessary. But what is 'average'? Statistics recognises in a distribution three possibilities, the mode, the mean, and the median. Many take the mean as the relevant parameter. However, if the point is to explain that value at which the bulk of commodities easily exchange it seems better to take the mode. I take the modal time to be the right parameter. In static competition, this should be taken as the *mode* of the (weighted) distribution of times, rather than the *mean*. Price reflects the *modal* socially necessary labour time established by the spectrum of capitals competing in the same industry, because that is the value which is most likely to be present in the experience of capitalists.

Remark: Assuming that commodities exchange in accordance with modal socially necessary labour times has an interesting consequence for the notion of 'wasted labour', if it is the case that the distribution of times in different sectors is skewed differently. For a sector, A, with a large 'tail' of relatively inefficient capitals, such capitals will secure less than the social average rate of profit, while in a sector, B, with most firms at the cutting edge of innovation the same firms will have above average rates until the others catch up or drop out. Other things being equal the sector with the larger number of backward firms has *wasted* labour. Thus the sector as a whole is penalised. But there is *no* so-called 'transfer' of value to other sectors. Rather, this labour counts no more than does the extra time worked by a supposed 'lazy' worker within a single firm. Conversely the innovating sector will be rewarded with a 'technological rent' because labour uses more powerful machinery. The theoretical importance of this is again the same: there is no one-to-one correspondence of hours actually worked and the value arising.

At all events the unity established between competing firms in a common price means that hours in the less efficient firms count for less than in the more efficient. Such an abstraction from the real times already makes clear that abstract labour time is socially imputed. In the case of weight, an individual weight is given regardless of the weight of other objects; but the valuation of a product of labour depends on that of all others.

It is necessary to distinguish the labour in socially equalised 'abstract labour' from the labour commensurated in 'socially necessary labour time'. The former – a qualitative notion – is socially abstract labour pertaining to the comparability of all commodities as values. The latter reduces to pure time the concrete totality of labours that are materially necessary for production of each specific commodity (thus allowing for additive quantitative determination). In the production of a commodity the various concrete labours have to be homogenised so as to be *added*; and then averaged over firms to establish the time socially necessary.

To return to the main argument here, labour is the necessary bearer of capital's abstract activity of value positing in the process of production of commodities. Insofar as such labour is taken as completely reified, it appears as purely mechanical motion, as the mere passage of time from one state of the process to another, in such a case, value is the condensed form of pure time, of which the worker is the mere predicate. So the labour theory of value is indicated only when labour time is distinguished from other 'times' of capital through which it passes in its circuit. Labour counts doubly: it counts abstractly as pure time, like any other time, but concretely it is *distinguishable* from other times because it resists capital's attempt here to economise on time.

It is important that we put at the centre of our discussion the category of time; yet there are other production times than labour time, for example, crops ripening, steel cooling, wine fermenting, and the like; in short, Nature 'naturing' albeit under the direction of the producer. But why is not Nature exploited? For it plays a role, measurable in time spent, in many production processes. My view is that there is an ontological difference between 'naturing' and 'labouring'. The former simply takes time but the latter is recalcitrant to its exploitation by capital.

Capital creates new value (and transfers existing value) only if it wins the struggle at the point of production to *subordinate* (not merely formally subsume) living labour to the demands of capital. Of course, capital *does* 'count' the time spent on naturing; but from our point of view only the time of labour is *constitutive* of value in the first instance. This struggle to appropriate labour is characteristic of the social reality of capital even though labour is formally subsumed under the wage contract as if labour power is a resource like any other.

In the idea of capital, physical space always reduces to time; for example, transport from place to place creates new value in proportion to the time it takes. Here value recollects what passes, making it *internal* to what is now present to us in outer form. For my pure notion of value, all the use-value aspects of production which make the commodity are ignored, so value is now *nothing* but the very form of the 'timelessly passed', i.e. simply the time its making took, which of course leads to our further distinguishing of times. For naturing does not count, and nor does pure circulation; but the time of the retailer does count because it is prior to consumption and involves exploitation of shop assistants. Many service workers, including those working for firms of estate agents, are productive labourers because of this.

§ 53.2   The Genesis of Surplus Value

At the same time that capital accomplishes the production process it generates surplus value. Part of the value of the commodity repays constant capital, 'c'. From the value added capital must fund the wage bill. As it seems to be paid by capital Marx terms this 'variable capital', 'v'. (The point of calling it 'variable' is to tie it conceptually to the emergence of value added. Later I contest this term but for convenience I use v to refer to the wage-bill so as to maintain congruence with Marx's exposition.) Yet there is a surplus left over, 's'. So the value of the commodity may be further disaggregated into '$c + v + s$'. How do I explain the genesis of this surplus?

Historically, vulgar economy talked of 'profit on alienation'. But because value is always self-identical the origin of surplus value must lie on the use-value side. The problem lies in the fact that circulation is premised on exchange of equivalents, yet as a result of this process a surplus value emerges. Whence? The answer to this must lie in what is identical but different within capital and that is its production process. If the production process is carried on beyond a certain time the counter-value of the wage is exceeded and further value is added, which is available to capital. In a working day of sufficient length, labour power creates more products than it embodies as a result of the consumption of the real wage. This surplus product is appropriated by capital in the form of surplus value.

Even if we assume that surplus value comes from surplus labour there is still the question: why labour? Some say *disutility* of labour; some say *creativity* of labour; I say *recalcitrance* of labour to its appropriation by capital. It is *capital's* toil and trouble in subsuming labour that is the key socio-political dimension of 'economics'. Thus I hold a properly *political* economy.

Despite the equality supposedly present in the bargain through which the worker gets a 'fair wage' or a 'living wage', only some of the value added is returned to the worker, in accordance with the prevailing 'value' of labour power; thus a sufficiently long working day provides more value than that, namely a surplus appropriated by capital. On the one hand, capital is self-grounded in form; on the other, it feeds, vampire like, on labour.

Now let me examine a way of posing the issue that I regard as defective. It is argued by some that for valorisation to occur, a capitalist must sell a commodity above its value (or purchase from another capitalist a commodity below its value). Here, it is said, the total value cannot increase; it may only be redistributed; the clever trader's profit is effectively a theft from others. (This happens but it cannot explain the systematic generation of surplus value by capital on the basis of exchange of equivalents.) Equally deficient is the pre-Marxist theory of profit: that it is a theft from the worker. The objection to the 'theft' argument, that theory must assume all commodities, including labour, are sold at value, is finessed by the plausible reply that labour markets are different; the workers are price-takers, forced to work on capital's terms because of their powerlessness. Only when labour is scarce might wages approximate the real value of labour.

This position was forcefully rebutted by Marx who insisted that, even if the worker is paid the full 'value' of what he sells, even so, the surplus value mysteriously appears. Since it cannot be created in circulation it must first appear in production. Marx's brilliant solution in truth is only partially adequate. He correctly distinguishes between labour power and labour. Despite appearances, namely that often labour is priced by the hour, labour as the very 'source' of value cannot have a value itself. The wage, in any case, is not paid for labour but for labour power. Marx then explains that the value of labour power is determined like that of any other commodity by its conditions of production, not by its use.

But, as Marx himself acknowledged, it is different in that the real wage has historical and moral determinants. The very core of the capitalist system, the condition under which capital appropriates alien labour, is in fact radically indeterminate. Marx recognised this with respect to the length of the working day, stating that in a struggle of right against right force decides; but the same is true of wages especially after the formation of unions. Yet capital still has the upper hand.

Now, since labour power is not produced in capitalist factories it has no value. Although sold, it is not a commodity; but it has commodity form; hence it has a price corresponding to that of the real wage bundle necessary to ensure the reproduction of the worker and their family. 'Necessary' here is relative; it is not a physiological minimum, it has moral and historical determinants. By 'moral' I understand the class struggle and its current balance of forces; by historical I understand the level of productive forces that makes possible mass production of goods for workers. Clearly, if today wages were to be reduced to a level at which the workers could not buy TVs, then not only would the workers revolt but the economy would enter a terminal depression with wholesale destruction of capital, beginning with the TV manufactures.

It is only for methodological reasons that the real wage is taken as given here, when we see how capital pumps out surplus labour, assuming the balance of class forces is set.

In my account, exploitation is an ahistorical category in that there are relevant continuities across all class societies in which, in one way or another, a surplus product is appropriated by the ruling class. In one sense, the issue is to explain how this can happen in a market society governed by the rule of equivalent exchange.

Marx's solution, distinguishing what is sold, labour power, from what it yields, labour time, is ingenious, but not as exact as it might seem, for the reason that the price of labour power is indeterminate. It is not a commodity produced by capital, and its market determination is affected by its historical and moral component. Nonetheless, it is certainly true that workers labour longer than the time necessary to generate their wage and this surplus labour is the basis of surplus value, however mediated is the connection.

Living labour has no value whatsoever so there can be no question of whether 'all the labour time is paid', because this is a misleading appearance. What is paid for is labour power, whose use-value is labour. If the wage is set sufficiently low the possibility of a surplus value consequent on the exploitation of labour is present. So the working day may be notionally divided, the time necessary to produce the counter-value of the wage, and the surplus labour time that accounts for surplus value.

For simplicity we begin by taking the real wage as fixed (only when we discuss the tendency of the rate of profit to fall must this condition be relaxed we shall see). Marx thus equated the so-called value of labour power to the value of the means of subsistence. As for 'subsistence' this has historical and moral determinants. Here, for the purpose of pure theory, it is equated to the current real wage.

In all this, what is important conceptually is that, in its original constitution, capital is formed out of the exploitation of labour. Living labour creates its own wage, while, at the same time, in its circuit capital moves on its own basis, reproducing and extending itself. The dialectic of form runs up against its own limits when it cannot account fully for its own material content. That workers are able to produce more than they consume is not a logical point but a given *condition of existence* of the system. Nonetheless, through real subsumption capital has brought this fructiferous agent *within* its own form of existence.

I convey the complexity of the capital relation by drawing a distinction between the 'original' *constitution* of capital, through a struggle to pump out labour from the exploited class, and the movement of capital on its own basis, as *already constituted*, as if labour were reified, although of course the 'original' process of subsuming labour under capital is always ongoing in reality. Here we still do the former. Later the latter (§ 81.2).

§ 53.3   The Wages of Labour

In elucidating the magnitude of surplus value the distinction between living labour and labour power is important. The 'production' of labour power is investigated below. But insofar as this distinction between labour power and labour is itself form-determined neither is to be taken here in its simple materiality, i.e. as an ahistorical distinction between a capacity and its exercise. Here living labour is form-determined as a 'factor' of production, presupposed as such in *separation* from the other factors, as pure activity, until *capital* determines it as a specific concrete labour by uniting it with its means and its object in that peculiar configuration of the production process characteristic of capital's incarnation in the material basis of valorisation. Likewise, labour power is figured by capital as a featureless potential to labour, inseparable from the labourer, but separable, indeed separated, from the collectivity of social labour; every labour power exists in a 'dot-like isolation' from its social and physical content. It is an indeterminate potential as part of the capitalist labour force until assigned (and trained if necessary) to a specific job in the division of labour.

However, before something exists as form-determined it exists previously 'on its own account', so to speak. Labour power and land are capital's 'others', which it simply *encounters* in an external sphere but which it posits, in its logic, as its *own* others. This it does formally by finding a way to commodify them even though they are not commodities in the proper sense of products of capital.

Yet, under the wage form, labour power *is* presupposed to be a commodity, *as if* it were like any other commodity. The irrationality of this is suppressed by capital when it is always already presupposed. Historically it may be presented as the result of a process of expropriation of the object of labour leaving labour power 'doubly free' and hence unresistant to a tacit agreement with capital to treat the 'labour market' as like any other. But this surd in the logical totality of capital is sublated when capital develops its own law of population. Although capital cannot 'produce' labour power, it does reproduce its presence as a resource available to it in its own accumulation process. Reliant on wages, the labourers must return daily for further exploitation. But Marx's genius lay in his account of the continual reproduction of the reserve army of labour.[9] What appeared at the outset as a *historical presupposition*, namely that free labour is given to capital as a resource to be appropriated by it, becomes logically *posited* in capital's own rhythm of development. Almost like a process of breathing, capital sucks in labour, and then, when skill shortages present themselves, expels labour again through the introduction of labour-saving machinery.

Labour power is a paradoxical commodity. In a purely capitalist system all inputs must have been outputs, but it is an input which is *absent* as output. Yet it has to be *present* for capitalism to work at all. It must then be an output of a sphere which is not one of commodity production but which sells its output as if it were, the domestic sphere in fact. (Although there is much more to say about domestic labour, in no way is it immediately productive of new value, I shall argue in Chapter 16.)

If it is to be made present *by capital itself*, instead of being a non-logical condition of capital's existence, this presupposition must be posited in the logic itself. How? It seems this must be capital's limit condition, beyond the scope of its dialectical systematicity. However *subsumed* by capital, labour power is never a *product* of capital. Yet, when capital takes possession of its material presuppositions, it is able to reproduce them as its *own* material presuppositions. If it does this then the external conditions become assimilated to the interior of capital. The impossibility of the commodification of labour power is finessed by treating labour power's absolute exteriority as always already surpassed. Capital fills the empty place of this 'commodity' through a peculiar set of mediations that sublate the historicity of free labour and make it timelessly present to capital.

But the domestic sphere is internal to capital reproduction in that it is the centre of a sub-circuit of capital, namely the worker's circuit. Complementary to capital's circuit is a secondary circuit: that of the reproduction of labour power by the workers themselves. The worker takes the wage and expends it on the means of consumption required for the reproduction of labour power. Labour power is reproduced domestically, thus it is not a capitalist commodity despite appearances. From this point of view the domestic reproduction of labour power occurs in a 'black box' in the circulation of commodities, with

---

9 Marx 1976, pp. 783–4.

the value coming out equal to the values entering. Commodities enter and labour power leaves, requiring to be paid a wage to cover its 'subsistence' costs. Although the domestic sphere is thus formally subsumed by the capitalist system it is materially beyond its purview. This circuit is deeply paradoxical. On the one hand, it seems to take place in circulation only, the labourer sells labour power and buys means of subsistence. But the transformation of the means of subsistence into labour power is surely a form of production? Yet it is unknown to capital. However, insofar as capital exerts its hegemony on both sides of the domestic sphere it has *formally subsumed* it under its own rule.

In this way labour power becomes commodified, despite its otherness to capital. This peculiarity further underlines the centrality of the capital relation. Instead of 'digging into' the domestic sphere in order to give domestic labour a wage form, capital subsumes it within its own surface forms.

Having treated production in this chapter, in the next we take up reproduction.

Summary

This long chapter covers my account of some of the central terms of Marxian value theory, such as 'abstract labour', 'subsumption', 'alienation', 'surplus value', 'value of labour power', and 'socially necessary labour time'. The three sections develop from the more abstract treatment of capital in production to the more concrete, as in the presentation as a whole.

It begins (§ 51) with the exploration of the bare 'Notion' of capitalist production as occurring in time and space. The 'time of production' remains a pure immanence until it is concretised through the encounter of two produced commodities on the market. The activity of production absents its materiality when it is posited as the carrier of valorisation; for it now counts only as the pure activity of value positing; the act of positing value results in its fixity in the resultant value.

The next section (§ 52) begins with the elucidation of a crucial turning point in the presentation, namely the need for capital to engage with living labour, if it is to produce itself. It is argued that labour in the production process is determined as 'abstract' in a very radical way. Everything about concrete labour is absented; it becomes *pure activity*, once posited as the carrier of capital's valorisation process. Furthermore, as really subsumed by capital, labour is posited by capital as its own use-value. Thus, in the capital relation capital, affirms itself, while labour denies itself. Indeed, Marx says it posits itself 'as its own non-being, or as the being of its non-being, the being of capital'.

Thus labour is the 'source' of value only in the paradoxical sense that capital must overcome the resistance of labour in order to create value. Labour is negatively posited as its sublated ground. My 'labour theory' is founded in a 'dialectic of negativity'; waged labour is 'in and against' the capital relation.

The presentation then (§ 53) develops the central forms of capitalist exploitation. Of all the times in which capital is tied up in commodity production it is labour time that is constitutive of value and surplus value. This is because of the peculiar recalcitrance of living labour to capital's subordination of it. Capitals commensurate in value their relative success at appropriating living labour (and hence the surplus labour that underpins surplus value). This view is different from the usual theory of value, in that it is argued here that value has no reality except as it is grounded in capitalist exploitation.

The distinction between labour power and living labour is partially acceptable as germane to the explanation of the existence of the surplus labour capital expropriates from workers. But the conflation of labour power with capitalist commodities is rejected, because it is not produced by capital, even if a good case can be made that domestic labour is subsumed by the circuit of capital.

Because the real wage has moral and historical determinants its composition is somewhat indeterminate. For methodological reasons it is taken as constant in much of what follows here, in order that the presentation may further develop the parameters of capitalist reproduction and of competition, isolated from movements in the real wage. Now I have shown how capital is *constituted*, I henceforth consider *already-constituted* capital as given.

CHAPTER 11

Reproduction

§ 6   Reproduction

With the temporality of circulation, I showed how capital becomes different from itself while remaining the same (as opposed to the formal difference between M' and M). But *this* difference is no difference if it lacks all grounds. The grounding movement therefore identifies a real difference of capital from itself in the 'other' it expropriates, namely surplus labour. This then incarnates the movement of determinate reflection through which is comprehended the actual reproduction and accumulation of capital. The overall dialectic of our presentation of the capital relation begins with capital as formally presented, but then it is reflected into production, where it is understood that, underlying the surface form of capital, is the generation of surplus value in the production process. Finally, the unity of production with circulation grounds reproduction.

What is reproduced is the capital relation itself, together with the mass of capital in play. Production is mediated in circulation and yet circulation is mediated in production. Circulation *informs* the production process. Production shows its effects in the circulation of capital. So they are united in the actuality of *reproduction*, in which each side finds its effectivity vindicated. This has the M–C–M' circular form, but also the 'linear' appropriation of living labour, made available to capital under the wage form. Capital sets the goal, and regulates production accordingly, while production supplies the surplus product to be formed as valorised-value.

On the one hand, the presentation of the value form pivots on the turn to production required to ground the emergence of surplus value. The treatment of production therefore presupposes that it is always already structured by the imposition of this aim. On the other hand, since production is obviously something taken up in all societies, should not the value form categories be taken as the specific social form in which we find the age-old problem now met? I argue that the pure forms of capital, having autonomised themselves from their bearers, have sufficient efficacy to regulate production in the interest of accumulation. Capital returns from production with its hard-won surplus, having engaged in the strenuous process of subsuming its other, labour. On the other hand, there is no surplus unless labour, and its means and material, act effectively as a simple production process, albeit subsumed under capital.

In circulation categories, including that of 'accumulation', I treated capital notionally in its form of self-reflection, but then, with the turn to production I reach a sphere of otherness in which it is *really* reflected in its difference from itself. Most importantly, I treated the dialectic of negativity in which living labour is always potentially resistant to capital. But from here on I 'quiet' that constitutive struggle methodologically, for the sake of looking at how capital proceeds on the basis of the hegemony it has secured in the subsumption of labour to its aims.

Circulation and production subsist only in their relation; for each on its own lacks determinate form, and it is hence shapeless chaos; something must be given to circulation, production must be vindicated by sale. Hence each is a determined determinant. However, a true unity is secured in that they are moments of the circuit of capital, which realises itself in their negative unity. *Production*, as the sphere where difference emerges in opposition to the identities of logical form, allows a surplus value to arise in the sphere of *circulation*.

This section, that on reproduction, virtually organises itself: it covers § 61 Simple Reproduction, § 62 Extended Reproduction, and finally § 63 Results of the Immediate Process of Reproduction.

§ 61   *Simple Reproduction*

I deal here with the immediate production process undergone by a typical capital. It is assumed here that any surplus value produced is consumed by the capitalist. (In the following sections, I consider the extended process of reproduction in which the surplus is invested.)

It is here that Marx makes his important diagnosis of the inversion of the law of appropriation, even at the level of simple reproduction. Following Marx, I develop the argument by finessing the issue of an 'original' capital investment altogether. Since all value is sourced in labour, ideally all the funds expended by capital must have been at some point accumulated from the exploitation of labour. Certainly, once the system is up-and-running, this has to be so; the fund accumulated at the end of one period provides the initial outlay at the beginning of the next period. Nonetheless, we seem to be committed to the original existence of a capital fund to get the process going. Whence comes this original capital? Does it arise for example, in the hands of the immediate producer as the result of their own labour?

Some such *presupposition* seems necessary, since only commodity owners with equal rights confront each other, and the sole means of appropriating the commodities of others is the alienation of someone's own commodities, commodities which, however, could only be produced by labour. Now, however, property turns out to be the right to appropriate the unpaid labour of others or its product, and the impossibility on the part of the workers of appropriating their own product. The separation of property from labour thus becomes the necessary consequence of a law that *apparently* originated in their identity.

In the beginning, it appears that the capital employed must be advanced from funds accumulated in some way independently of the unpaid labour of others, and that likewise the fact that free labourers are available for hire in the labour market is a happy accident for capital. But the capital relation in its action transforms these conditions of its existence into its consequences. Although the capitalist believes that he lives off profits, and *retains* his original capital, in truth he *consumed* the original capital after a limited number of cycles of reproduction; the capital he throws afresh into each new cycle soon consists of nothing but the surplus value extracted from the labourers in previous cycles therefore. What at first was merely a starting point becomes, by means of nothing but the continuity of the process, by simple reproduction, the characteristic result.

So the exchange of equivalents is now turned round in such a way that the result is the continual appropriation by the capitalist of the surplus labour of others. The relation of exchange between capitalist and worker becomes a mere semblance belonging only to the process of circulation; it becomes a form alien to the reality of the transaction itself, and merely mystifies it.

The property laws of commodity production undergo an inversion, so that they become laws of capitalist appropriation. Notice that here these property laws are not pre-capitalist ones, but those 'derived' from commodity production itself. For nothing is formally changed when labour power itself becomes a commodity. The workers treat their own labour as a property alienable at will through a contract. The capitalist purchases this labour power along with the means of production. From a juridical point of view this is an equal relationship. Buyer and seller contract as free persons, who are equal before the law; each dispose only of what is their own, and they exchange equivalent for equivalent. So it is not necessary that such an 'inversion' in the material content of the relationship of private property be marked by any difference in the legal form of property. This continuity of legal form is extremely convenient for the bourgeoisie because it allows them to confuse two different kinds of private property, one of which relies on the labour of the producers themselves, and the other on the exploitation of the labour of others.

This interpretation of the inversion abandons the historical perspective, with its problematic of *causal* genesis, in favour of an account of 'genesis' in *logical* terms, that is, it articulates the ground of the system's *self*-production. We do not presuppose here a mode of simple commodity production giving rise out of its own development to capitalism. Such a history is a 'virtual' one.

It is history as it must be written from the vantage-point of capitalism as a *given* totality retrojecting its interior moments into the 'past', as if an imaginary simple commodity production were its foundation and justification.

It is the logic of *this* system that is investigated here in order to show the inversion of 'the law of property' involved. If we presuppose capital already exists, then we leave aside its historical genesis as a field of inquiry. What I do is to point out that it stands in a logical relation of inversion to its own logical preconditions. As capitalist commodity production, it logically presupposes simple commodity circulation, yet inverts 'the law of property' derivable from it, namely that the commodity must have been produced by its owner's labour. This change in the relation of labour to property is truly a 'dialectical inversion'. But this inversion should be understood as a 'virtual' rather than a 'real' process. What we have is a totality of capitalist commodity production which posits it as an interior moment forever already sublated. The virtual 'original capital' is a vanishing moment, since capital posits itself as its own condition.

§ 62   *Extended Reproduction*

Whereas in simple reproduction the surplus is assumed to be drained off, in *extended reproduction* it is taken to be re-invested. Extended reproduction exhibits the intentionality of capital in its pure form because the reinvestment of new value changes the apparent end (surplus value) into means (for further accumulation). There is here a moment of 'standing back', and gathering itself together (M + m), verifying that the motive for investing M still holds for M', in order to launch a new project.

§ 63   *Results of the Immediate Process of Reproduction*

Since, before workers enter the process, their own labour has already been estranged from them, appropriated by the capitalist, and incorporated with capital, it now, in the course of the process, constantly objectifies itself so that it becomes a product alien to them. Therefore, the workers constantly produce objective wealth, in the form of capital, an alien power that dominates them and exploits them, and the capitalist just as constantly produces labour power separated from its own means of realisation, in short the workers as waged labourers.

It is therefore not an accident that capitalist and worker continue to confront one another in the market as buyer and seller; for the process of capitalist production, seen as a process of reproduction, produces not only commodities, not only surplus value, but it also reproduces the capital relation itself, on the one hand the capitalist, on the other the waged labourer. It is clear from this that the question of the origin in time of the capitalist system is a separate question, once we demonstrate the ability of the system to constitute itself as a self-reproducing totality. Capital is *self*-subsistent.

If capitalist production presupposes a division between the product of labour and labour itself, between the objective conditions of labour and subjective labour power, then this foundation of the process reproduces itself through the transformation of labour into surplus value. The most important result of reproduction is that the capital relation is itself reproduced. However, this relation is properly termed the 'capital relation' because capital preserves itself, or even accumulates, while alienated labour remains impoverished and unable to escape the relation. This is true even though capital *depends* upon the appropriation of alien labour; for labour enters the relation on capital's terms

Methodologically, an important point of closure is here reached. At the outset of the systematic presentation, exchangeable commodities were presupposed as simply given; now commodities are presented as products of capital; so the beginning is itself the result of the form predicated on it.

What now follows from the fact that, to reproduce itself, capital *produces commodities*? It means that the value form has now been presented with a 'content'. All the forms discussed in Division I are those under which are expressed the value of the commodities for which production is responsible.

However, what about those things, taking the shape of commodities, but which are *not* produced by capital? We are now in a position to remark a real difference between these and capitalistically produced commodities. This is not possible at the level of simple commodity circulation. Now, however, we are able to distinguish those commodities that belong to the sphere of generalised commodity production from others, because *their* value is the outcome of capitalist production; they are *grounded* in it. Other commodities are *not so grounded*.

Why, however, is a stipulative definition of value as the expression of capital better than one immediately referring to the expression of labour? The answer is that only the dialectical development of the form of capitalist production *posits* value as both its presupposition and result; only in *this* context is labour, now conceptualised in the shape of waged labour, demonstrably a condition of it. Conversely, non-products must be excluded from counting as genuine values. albeit many are *priced*.

But is not this distinction somewhat factitious? For I insisted at the outset that the exchange relation comprehends heterogeneous material. It helps if I introduce here the notion of 'real definition'. It is common in science to address a chaotic manifold of phenomena discriminated by superficial features. Then order and law are introduced to it in such a way that the central category is given a firmed-up *real definition*, usually related to its attributed causal power.

Much that cannot be explained by this is now declared outside the scope of the new theoretical domain.

So, here, value, originally a surface phenomenon thrown up by exchange, is given a real definition as the outcome of capitalist production. Hence, I now say only those commodities expressing value thus defined 'count'. Capital, indeed, *defines itself* as their origin, we might say.

Remark: For an illustration, consider pneumonia, originally defined as a syndrome of symptoms. An excellent explanation of it was found in the presence of a certain bacterium. Yet not all cases were related to it. The other cases were then set aside, and given their own terms, for example 'Legionnaires' disease'.

In sum, commodities grounded in capitalist production are properly distinguished from putative others, as embodying value and surplus value.

Since it posits its own presuppositions, capital may claim to reproduce itself. However, thus far this result remains abstract. The individual capital depends on inputs from other capitals, and it must dispose of its outputs. So only capital as a system may be self-sufficient. In Division III the system of capital is articulated; there reproduction will be outlined on a social scale.

Summary

Reproduction is thematised in two stages: simple reproduction and extended reproduction. Any supposed 'original capital' is eliminated from the presentation when capital posits itself as its own condition in the circular movement of M–C–M'. From the point of view of the architectonic of the presentation, the most significant result of reproduction is the mass of commodities that at the outset had to be taken as given. However, the reproduction of a single capital is comprehensible only if we turn to thematise reproduction on a social scale.

DIVISION III

The System of Capital

∴

Introduction to Division III

In Division I, Capital in Its Notion, the dialectic of the value form is traced from the commodity, through money, to the general formula for capital. In Division II, the Capital Relation, the value form is shown to sink into production to ensure capital's reproduction on its own basis. Both these parts deal with capital as such, although relations of capitals are implicit in such notions as 'socially necessary labour time'. Now, in Division III, capital as a system is addressed, with a view to establishing that it is a unified self-reproducing totality of capitals.

The first Division dealt with the forms of generalised commodity exchange. In the second I grounded this on capitalist production in such a way that only commodities produced with waged labour count as proper 'values'. Thus from here on I narrow the focus of attention to a system of generalised commodity production. But within that we attend only to *capitalist* production. We presuppose that petty commodity production by the self-employed is sufficiently marginal that it does not impede the expansion of capital.

Generalised commodity production is partly a manifestation of capital's power but it is also a condition of existence required to make itself fully present, through providing a large enough arena of competition in order to develop itself. The hegemony of the capitalist mode of production in the economy is not simply a matter of it being more efficient than the modes it displaced, it is a matter of the perfection of this mode itself. Thus 'generalised commodity production', 'waged labour', and 'capital', are mutually implicative moments of the inner totality of capitalism.[1] Nonetheless, capital depends not only on a supply of waged labour but also the existence of households to absorb the commodified output. Thus the main non-commodity production (addressed later) is that provided through domestic labour in the household.

The first section (§7) of this Division deals with the notion of this system in purely *formal* terms. Here is explained the unity of universal capital with individual capitals at a formal level. But only the unfolding of the *material* structure of the system shows how the Idea of capital is realised in a self-reproducing system.

So the second section (§8) deals with the system of capital proper, and it becomes an extended treatment of the objective dialectic of the moments of the concept. In this the system of industrial capital is articulated on the lines

---

[1] See Saad-Filho 2002, p. 41.

of the logic of the Idea. Beginning from the core notion of capital, I develop the triad universality/particularity/singularity in two perspectives: capital's reflection *into* itself, and capital's reflection *against* itself. Every form-determination here unites with the material metabolism in specific modes. They are expressed therefore in *mixed categories*. I propose my own take on the famous 'transformation problem', and I add some novel observations on the status of the falling rate of profit.

Then, finally, in the third section (§ 9) I show how the logic implicit in industry externalises itself in finance capital. The last section deals with how the spirit of capital achieves apparently autonomous existence in finance; but this has conditions of existence in industry, on which it grounds itself. I treat finance as the 'spiritual' centre of capital and discuss its relation to industry and commerce. Taken together, as one totality, this is implicitly now capital as Absolute Idea.

CHAPTER 12

Capital as a System of Capitals

§7 Capital as Universal and Individual

Here I treat the formal Idea of the system of industrial capital, the system in its Notion so to speak.
Remark: Under the influence of Marx's *Grundrisse* the distinction between 'capital-in-general' and 'many capitals' has been much discussed.[1] In its most common variant it is assumed that this implies *two levels* of analysis. First capital is to be discussed without reference to competition between capitals, and only later is competition to be thematised. The approach to capital here has nothing to do with that; for the interplay between the Universal and the Individual is essential to the very idea of capital, and it is present at *all levels* of my exposition of the system.

Because I consider the system in this section in its pure Being, I can deploy effectively the logic of 'attraction and repulsion' paradigmatically employed when we developed earlier the logic of value-for-itself (§11.3).

The homogeneity of their value substance means the several capitals are *not fully individuated beings* and hence liable to coalesce again very easily. If we set aside their material integument and concentrate attention on their value substance, capitals differ only in amount. In their relation of 'attraction and repulsion', the moment of 'attraction' is present in that two capitals become one once brought together, just as two amounts of money put into a certain account become one amount of money; each such capital is indistinguishable from others except in size, thus attract in the sense that, if brought together, they become one single sum merging their previously separate amounts. To ensure their separation requires a moment of repulsion; this is secured materially if capitals are active in separate enterprises, but even accounting schemata may serve, as when my capital is distinct from that of others in a joint-stock company because I own numbered shares. The moment of repulsion, which maintains separation, is required to constitute them as singular; there has to be some determination that prevents them collapsing together, such as differentiated ownership.

---

[1] See Arthur 2010.

We presuppose in what follows that capital is Idea. This was presented formally in the first two Divisions and must now be developed in its *determinacy*, as a system of capitals, constitutive of the real world of capital.

In the logic of the presentation, this system, in its Notion, has three moments: every capital is an individual subject in that it unites concept and object in its spiral of accumulation; but its universal quality as capital is necessarily always *finitely* determined in particular ways, contrasted with others, a particular capital invested in a particular enterprise (§ 71); indeed a particular capital has as part of its determinacy its being-for-another, namely its competitive relations to the other capitals in the system, which requires it to *act* as capital (§ 72); but the whole system of individual capitals is subordinated to the overarching movement of capital as Universal, capital as One Idea, making up a *social* Individual, which posits its self-sufficiency against the transitory elements subject to the contingencies of competition (§ 73).

Throughout I shall endeavour to follow the terminological rule I set forth earlier in this book, namely a distinction between the 'Singular' and the 'Individual'. The former is used as an interior moment of a whole, complementing the 'Universal' and the 'Particular'; 'Individual' by contrast I deploy to characterise just such a whole of intermediation. This rule gives rise to a certain refinement because I consider each *individual* capital to be just that, namely characterised by individuality. But I consider the capital system as a whole attains the unity of the Individual. So *within* the system, then, individual capitals may well be taken as bearers of the moment of *its* singularity. (See in the next chapter the Table pertaining to *The System of Industrial Capital*.)

Capital is a concrete universal that realises itself through determining itself to particularity and singularity, instead of opposing itself to them. While the universal, in order to be itself a particular moment of the concept, *is* opposed to the other moments, this moment of division is fully sublated in the unity of the concept. Taken in its unity, as a whole of mediation in its moments, capital is a concrete *Individual*, as opposed to that abstract *singularity* that opposes itself to particularity and universality.

The moments of the capital system in its formal notion are:

§ 71 Capital as Subject; § 72 Individual Capitals; § 73 Capital as One Idea

§ 71   *Capital as Subject*

In this section, the determinations of the concept are considered purely logically, and are not given the material content they acquire later in the presentation. However, the twist is here that, since value is intrinsically a quantitative concept, values always have a particular magnitude. While a value is still a value whether it is large or small, magnitude is not external to its concept because the *only* specificity of values lies precisely in their amounts. Moreover, capitals *by definition* are bent on accumulating *greater amounts*. One might say that capital's only quality is precisely that its telos is quantity. The adequacy of any given capital to its concept is measured by its rate of expansion. At the same time, in its material existence capital particularises itself in the production of specific commodities.

For Hegel the paradigmatic incarnation of 'the Concept' is the 'I'. Every reasoning being knows itself as *universal*, as the possibility of abstracting from everything determinate about itself, and its situation; yet it is existent only with a *particular* determinate object, content, and end. But these moments are themselves only abstractions; for what is concrete is the universality which reflects its determinations *into* itself. This unity I term *individuality*; this individuality is in fact none other than the concrete concept itself. So the subject is the concept *posited* as totality.

Every capital has just this logical structure of subject. This has two moments. First, it is capable of treating itself as a self-determining universal, abstracted from its varying specific content and related to itself in its individuality. This is achieved insofar as, in M–C–M', capital as an all-embracing subject alternately assumes and loses the form of money and the form of commodities. Second, it has a built-in aim, namely accumulation. Capital determines itself to itself when integrated into a spiral of accumulation: K'–K''–K''' .... This free subjectivity remains active even if capital is determined on every side by the material potentials of its use-value integument.

However, capital is *indifferent* to the specificity of its investment so long as use-value is effectively subsumed by the valorisation process. Thus it is not so much notionally free from its determinacy, it is free *in this very abstraction*, being itself abstraction in motion. Its freedom cannot be the peculiar formalism of interest-bearing capital, because it gains a surplus only through conquering the use-value sphere sufficiently thoroughly to achieve regular returns. There is here a latent *material* limit. But in *form* every capital is free subjectivity.

§72 Individual Capitals

What has just been outlined applies both to a notional, single capital and to the system of capitals as a whole. The fundamental point is that the universality of the system is to be taken substantively. It is not to be taken as an abstraction opposed to individual capitals, but rather includes them as determinate parts of its being. So capital-as-universal particularises itself to *individual capitals* of differing amounts. Capitalist enterprises are specified formally as 'lumps' of capital. In such a light the material side appears rather as a predicate of such inner essence. But capital must always be materially instantiated; hence as tied to specific sites of enterprise it must appear as many different capitals. Capital is the unity of identity (capital-value) and non-identity (the material in which it is invested). The material basis introduces a ground for *qualitative* difference and relation, while as pure form the only difference that counts is in *amount*. It follows that in the constitution of individual capitals *two kinds of particularisation* are simultaneously realised: on the one side, the *formal* existence of capital as value must be *quantitatively* determined as an *amount* of capital; on the other side, the *material* existence of capital invested in commodities (notably means of production and labour power) must be *qualitatively* determined, and situated in specific *sites*.

Remark: While one has the same capital whether one puts it 'into' shoe factories or shipyards, the material *particularity* of branches of industry is the root of the notorious transformation problem, we shall see later. Use-value therefore plays a role as an economic category for its material particularity is determinant of the *form* of capital in particularising it.

I earlier argued that a particular capital must engage in a certain line of production, but now the complementarity of all particular capitals is to be considered, in that each has a specific embodiment which interchanges with others in the whole system. Every single capital is both formally particularised as a definite amount of capital, deployed by an enterprise, and materially particularised in the business of that enterprise.

If we set aside their material integument and concentrate attention on their ideal substance, as value capitals differ only in amount. In this way, capitals are not fully individuated beings. They subsist only in their relation rather than bumping up against one another, as it were, in purely external relations. Because of this, in turn, the particularity of value, as merely quantitative variation, has less determinacy than might be expected; but the necessary material integument of capitals in factories, and so forth, *does* provide concrete individuation. The result is that capital is marked by a duality between its infinite mobility in ideal form and its fixity in its material avatars.

At one level this unity of value with use-value is achieved for each and every capital singly, e.g. this particular factory is constituted as a capitalist enterprise like others. At another level, however, all these instantiations of capital are subsumed formally under their universal concept, just as money actualises the identity in essence of commodities. But requiring material bearers, and even more as requiring material sources of surplus value, they are determined materially as different, contrary to their identical shape as value. This is a central contradiction in the idea of capital.

We need to address and resolve two contradictory discourses. The one asserts that total capital is an effective power and individual capitals simply replicate its categories as aliquot parts of it, picking up their share of the total surplus value as if they were merely shareholders in a single enterprise. The other discourse insists that capital necessarily exists as individual capitals *confronting* one another in competitive struggle, that only thus are the determinations of capital as such enforced on each.

It is important that the many capitals are not merely complementary instantiations of their general notion. Capitals in the same line of business are engaged in the life and death struggle to win that market for themselves. Moreover, it is only such competition that ensures they recognise the demands of their concept; they are shaped thus as capital against capital, quite as much as they share a common form and aim, namely self-valorisation.

§ 73   *Capital as One Idea*

The *competition* of capitals means that the freedom of each is constrained by that of the others. But capital as a whole, indifferent to the fate of particular capitals, marches ahead to realise its Idea. The transition from the analysis of capital as such to capital as a system finesses the problem that any given capital may go under in the competitive struggle. For the capital system as a whole preserves itself and expands, albeit that many capitals may have only a relatively temporary existence. The system supports their rise and fall, and it survives them, enforcing through competition the norms of capital on them.

While capital is realised only through the competition of capitals, these are so subsumed systematically under the drive of the whole that the specific determinate capitals are merely interior moments of the system. These many capitals are 'subsumed' by the whole for two reasons: first, a single capital is not *fully* individuated, because as value it is a specific determination of capital-value as such, as it flows through the economy ideally, although it is *materially particular* (at a given time) hence different from the other capitals; second, the system has emergent laws unintended by any individual capital. To say capital is essentially *one* means that each individual capital is conceptually homogenous with capital-as-universal; the whole may rightly be considered then as a supra-individual Individual. As such it is implicitly present throughout the system.

This 'total social capital' is not a simple aggregate of self-subsistent capitals but the truly universal moment. It is a concrete universal and as such is Individual itself. In dealing with the 'spirit' of capitalism the formal side, having its own economic determinacy, may be treated purely theoretically without the theory attracting a charge of false abstraction. It is a mode of the system itself. However, the move to concretion is a necessity of the system as well as in its theoretical exposition. Moreover, at this level of concretion the reproduction of capital, as a unity of production and circulation, discussed previously, is also to be incorporated in the Idea of capital as a system.

It is necessary to avoid 'the fallacy of composition'; this lies in moving from the observation that each individual industrial capital traces a *circuit* in its action to the assumption that total social capital performs such a circuit. Such a conclusion is conceptually incoherent. That *a circuit* (rather than a *system* of circuits) of total social capital makes no sense is obvious as soon as we see that the very notion of a circuit, involving purchase of inputs and sales of outputs, logically presupposes the separateness of industrial capitals, each having their own circuit but necessarily interlocking with others. A good part of aggregate capital (viz. constant capital) never leaves the hand of universal capital; so it does not circulate (in the sense required) *as an aggregate,* but is only conceivable as circulating when capital is *disaggregated.*

Thus total social capital does not perform a circuit, it consists of a *system* of circuits: interlinked, they presuppose one another and condition one another, and it is precisely by being interlinked in this way that they constitute the movement of the total social capital. Certainly the different capitals here are not in the position of shareholders in a joint-stock company, in which the dividends are evenly distributed, according to the size of the investment they each of them has put into the common enterprise.[2] There is *no* 'enterprise' harmoniously carried on in common! Even if it is possible to calculate the general rate of profit, capitals do not tamely queue up for their appropriate share. They remain within the system as competitors always looking for a better return than average.

However, capital-as-a-whole confronts the labourers-as-a-whole. There is no fallacy of composition in considering all the interchanges between capital and labour at a global level. Indeed, there is every reason to believe that class relations fundamentally condition individual transactions. While it is true that the self-repulsive character of capital gives rise to intense competitive struggle between capitals, they are 'as one' in their concern to confront globally their 'other'. Fundamentally capital is *constituted as a social power* in this global relation to labour. It is therefore logically prior to the disputes among capitals over how to share out what has been won from exploiting labour. Moreover, if capital is the general economic basis of a capitalist class distinct from the working class, then it is *constituted* in its unity of many capitals by its negative relation to the working class.

---

2 But a purely *notional* such distribution is part of our discussion of the transformation problem: see § 82.3 below.

There is a relation where capital acts 'as one', as universal capital, this is against labour, but at the same time another relation where it acts as 'many', that is, upon itself through competition. Thus the definition of 'total social capital', specified in opposition to labour, is merely a *partial* one, because capital necessarily appears as many capitals imposing the inner determinations of capital on each other through competition. A *universal capital*, one without alien capitals confronting it, lacks the constitutive moment of determination in and through otherness, exemplified in competition.

I pass now from this formal characterisation of the *system* of industrial capital, notionally realising the Idea of capital, to the elaboration of this Idea in its structure of differentiated material determinations.

Summary

This first chapter of the thorough treatment of the system of industrial capital explores the formal relation of capitals to themselves and to the whole. So the key logical categories here are those of the moments of the Concept; but also we consider that of 'individuality'. To begin with every capital is deemed an individual subject; but its universal quality as capital is necessarily always *finitely* determined in particular ways, contrasted with others, a particular capital invested in a particular enterprise. In the constitution of individual capitals *two kinds of particularisation* are simultaneously realised: on the one side, the *formal* existence of capital as value must be *quantitatively* determined as an *amount* of capital; on the other side, the *material* existence of capital invested in commodities (notably means of production and labour power) must be *qualitatively* determined, and situated in specific *sites*. But the whole system of individual capitals is subordinated to the overarching movement of capital as One Idea, making up a *social* Individual, which posits its self-sufficiency against the transitory elements subject to the contingencies of competition. For the system supports their rise and fall, and it survives them, enforcing through competition the norms of capital on them.

CHAPTER 13

The System of Industrial Capital

§ 8 The System of Industrial Capital in Its Double Determination

I begin with an overview of the way the system of industrial capital is explored in the following presentation. The Table on *The System of Industrial Capital* below is key to their articulation. It shows how categories treated formally in the previous chapter are embodied in material differences, beginning with the fundamental relation of capital and labour. The categories of industrial capital arise from the double determination of 'particularity', both in logical form, and in the finite specificity of investment in definite lines of production.

The System of Industrial Capital
(The Box numbers give the order of exposition of paras in the text)

Reflection into self ⟶

Reflection into other ↓	Universality (self-identity)	Particularity (difference 'within' capital)	Singularity (self-relation)
Universality (§ 81 capital as such reflected into itself) Row 1	*Box* 1. (§81.1) The Rate of Surplus Value	*Box* 2. (§81.2) The metamorphoses of capital	*Box* 3. (§81.3) Simple price = Cost price plus profit. Rate of profit
Particularity (§ 82 difference between capitals) Row 2	*Box* 4. (§82.1) Many capitals in competition absolute & relative surplus value	*Box* 5. (§82.2) Organic composition of capital	*Box* 6. (§82.3) Production price = Cost price plus uniform rate of profit
Singularity (§ 83 systemic unity of social capital) Row 3	*Box* 7. (§83.1) General law of capital accumulation	*Box* 8. (§83.2) Reproduction of total social capital via Departments of Reproduction	*Box* 9. (§83.3) Reproduction price General Rate of Profit
	Col. 1	*Col.* 2	*Col.* 3

Here capital is objectively articulated in two essential determinations, those forms that pertain to capital reflected into itself, and those forms that reflect capitals into one another. While the structure here is demarcated logically, the categories concerned are 'mixed categories' because the logical forms are here borne by material relations that have their own economic effectivity. While formal determination is at work, there is at every point the interpenetration of logical form with material shapes having a material nature. Thus the system is determined both by the ideal and the material. Capital in its notion unfolds itself into a world of finitude, in which objective relations are established between capitals, and between them and the whole system of total social capital.

In the Table the three rows and three columns show this concept of capital distributed on two axes, capital's reflection *into itself* to articulate its interior moments, and capital's reflection *against itself* generating difference between capitals. The significant *conceptual* arrangement is characterised by the moments of the concept, namely Universality, Particularity and Singularity, as differently specified thus in the glosses attached to them in the Table.

The intersection of the rows and columns generates nine 'boxes' subject to determination *along* rows and *down* columns. The point of this nine-box table is not merely to display the logical relations in which these moments of capital stand to each other, but to assert that the logic determines on this basis their mutual interactions. (The *box numbers* in the Table are there simply to show the *order* in which the categories are discussed here.)

It follows from the way it is organised that each box presupposes what is to the left of it and what is above it. This is because the order of determination is from Universality to Singularity in both rows and columns. The top-left box (presupposing what has already been achieved here) is the core idea of capital, as self-valorising, which then unfolds itself, finally to arrive at the concrete complex shown in the bottom-right box. The sections below (§ 81, § 82, § 83) follow the categories of this Table by going row by row. This sequence traces the *inter*-action of capitals reflected against one another, finally treating the laws of the whole. By contrast, the movement along columns, subsumed in the larger movement, traces the *inner*-action of capital reflected into itself to achieve its self-relation in its rate of profit. Both culminate systemically in the determination of the general rate of profit.

The rows are ordered by *conceptual* level; these go from the most abstract shape of the Idea, with relatively few determinations, to the most concrete, exhibiting systemic determinations.

The first row goes through what capital is in its notion, the forms that make it what it is. Notice that this has itself three subdivisions according to a dialectic of reflection-into-self, exhibited in the Boxes numbered 1 to 3. To begin with there is the simple self-identity of capital as productive of surplus value, which then is determined *within itself* in its metamorphoses, and finally capital measures itself against itself in the form of the rate of profit.

The second row treats the reflection of capital against its others as these many differ relevantly; here are marked, in Boxes 4 to 6, the forms that shape differences between capitals, as they immediately pertain to surplus value and profit. Thus, the identity of capital is realised in its determinacy only as it is determined 'for another', that is, in competition to maximise the rate of surplus value. This is achieved in two ways, the generation of *absolute* surplus value and *relative* surplus value.

When the terms v and c were introduced earlier they were the cost associated with the purchase of labour power and means of production. Now they are to be considered as variable capital and constant capital. This inner *difference* in the *composition of capital* is also the source of important differences *between* capitals. Moreover, not only may capitals differ in their organic composition, but such a difference between them has significant consequences when the many capitals relate to each other.

The final box of this row asserts the requirement that capitals *ideally* share a uniform rate of profit. Thus the 'simple price' of the previous row is replaced by a system of *production prices*.

The third row treats the systemic unity of total social capital, through Boxes 7 to 9, and especially the way the capital relation leads us to group these material determinations at a 'macro' level in the distinction between wage goods and capital goods. Finally we elaborate the forms of the 'general rate of profit' and of 'reproduction price'.

Price and profit issues are ordered in the right-hand column, namely capital in its conceptual development as self-related, through the phases in which it measures itself against itself in its rate of profit. In § 81 capital as such is treated, and in § 81.3 we define formally the rate of profit; but in § 82 the competition between the many capital is introduced, and especially the fact that these different capitals have different organic compositions, so in § 82.3 their unity is concretised in 'production price' on the rule that a uniform rate of profit is imposed; then, finally, in § 83, total social capital as the interweaving of complementary circuits is introduced, and I take up especially Marx's genial suggestion that the whole is best disaggregated in 'Departments' of industry, and in § 83.3 is treated total social capital in its existence as the unity of its interior determinations, yielding reproduction price and the general rate of profit. These are three levels of form-determination of price and profit, each having a specific effectivity, carried forward in the whole development.

It is important to the presentation that the movement from 'simple price', to 'production price', to 'reproduction price', is not *temporal* but *conceptual*. So at every level at which price and profit are addressed certain *physical givens* are taken as constant, notably the real wage, but also the mix of means of production and labours. The question is: how and where are prices to be determined?

It is a feature of my presentation of the Idea of capital that the movement of thought from abstract to concrete does not register merely an initial deficiency in our *knowledge* of the system; the deficiency is 'out there'; it is an ontological one in that the more abstract level fails to achieve actuality *even as a model*. Certainly, initially the magnitudes of c and v are to be taken merely as 'given', because the relevant variables are not yet conceptually *determinate* in the presentation; so *how* their magnitudes are determined is unknown here.

I shall present the system row by row; but within each row the columnar determinations have their effect. Thus we move from the elementary identification of the meaning of the row through *inner* difference to the way in which the form concerned relates to itself in and through the movement across it. In the first row, the surplus aimed at by capital is secured through the reiteration of the circuit that recreates every moment of valorisation through their mutual mediation, finally to measure itself as the relation of a monetary increment to the original investment in a *rate of profit*. In this the entire capital, $(c + v)$, is considered as what is reproduced and accumulated, not just its fructiferous part. This is not merely how capital registers the surplus it generates in its books, it is actually effective in the drive for accumulation (note the importance in this respect of reducing the cost 'c'). Again, in the second row, the elementary dialectic of competition, outlined in Box 4, moves through relevant differences in the composition of the capitals concerned to the resultant prices of production predicated on a uniform rate of profit. This is how the system of capital imposes itself on commodities, the notional simple prices are now seen as unactual, when systemic determination is considered. Finally, in the third row, the reproduction of the capital relation, at the level of the system as a whole, mediated through exchanges between departments of reproduction, allows the actuality of systemic reproduction as it is registered in reproduction prices of c and v. So the third row is the unfolding of the systemic unity of capital, while the third column yields the final registration of the relation to itself of capital. Both culminate in the general rate of profit.

All the above determinations are required before it is meaningful to speak of capital as self-grounded. For only the *whole* is actual because that is where there is a structure of capital capable of sustaining itself. The importance of distinguishing levels of abstraction in the presentation is pertinent to this. If we consider an exposition moving down the rows this is a process of concretisation in that row one abstracts from row two, and row two from row three. Thus the Row 1 is formal in its elucidation of capital as such; thence I move to the specific differences between capitals (Row 2) and finally I take them in the unity of the social whole, the most concrete level of the system (Row 3). If the third column only is considered in this context then we see it outlines how capital takes the measure of its output, first in general (simple price), then as many capitals in competition (production price), finally as a single system (reproduction price).

In this chapter I treat the dialectical development of *form*, from elementary and abstract to complex and concrete. It follows that it is not possible to show, even abstractly, how the *magnitudes* of price and profit are determined until the very end (§ 83.3). Earlier forms are too partial to provide any such determination. The system becomes determinate in this sense only with the forms of 'reproduction price' and 'general rate of profit'. In accordance with this systematic arrangement, there follow these sections:

§ 81 Capital as such Reflected into Itself (as shown in Row 1);
§ 82 The Difference of Capitals (as shown in Row 2);
§ 83 Systemic Unity of Total Social Capital (as shown in Row 3).

Remark: There is a difference between this exposition and Marx's; for I treat the material in a very different order from that of *Capital*. While my columns roughly correspond to Marx's volumes, my presentation is orthogonal to his, such that, instead of following the columns as he does, it follows the rows. I believe my order is superior to his because it first exhibits capital *in its notion* in which its reflection into itself, achieved in its rate of profit, is its own measure of itself. The rate of profit *completes*, as much as it *disguises*, the concept of capital accumulation. Moreover, Marx's order is more complicated than mine, for mine conforms better to the principle of moving from the abstract to the concrete, from the mere notion of capital to its system wide concreteness. Marx continually moves, volume by volume, to the concrete whole and back again to another elementary form. I think my expositional order is especially perspicuous in that I exhibit the transformation procedure, as it copes with the inadequacy of simple price and profit, *before* the more concrete level of reproduction, as the outcome of the interplay of its departments. Because he treats production prices later than departments of production, Marx is forced to abstract violently from organic composition when showing, in his Volume Two, how departments reproduce; this comes at the cost of arbitrarily setting the compositions as equal in his arithmetical examples. The fact of multiple compositions has no effect on the transformation procedure we shall see, *but* it is crucial to the principle of equating input/output prices of departments.

§81 *Capital as such Reflected into Itself*

The presentation of the system of industrial capital begins with the core notion of capital as such, identical to itself. This core notion resumes the upshot of my earlier investigations, especially that of the genesis of surplus value (§81.1). This is accomplished in reality within the circuit of capital, wherein the metamorphoses of capital expand the simple self-identity of capital to its process of production of itself through particular phases, as it achieves valorisation (§81.2). From this results the rate of profit, in which a capital measures itself against itself, and it registers its success in its own rate of profit (§81.3). These elementary forms are presented in the following sections: §81.1 Rate of Surplus Value; §81.2 Metamorphoses of Capital; §81.3 Simple Price and the Rate of Profit.

§81.1 The Rate of Surplus Value

As showed earlier, capital is self-valorising value, but it depends upon the exploitation of living labour that new value arises; this is divided, and distributed, to the worker in the form of a wage and to capital in the form of surplus value. Thus, in order to illuminate how capital is constituted, I emphasise its dependence on labour. Right at the start, I say the value of a commodity is 'c + new value', and this expands to '$c + (v + s)$', where 'c' is the value of the means of production used up plus that of the raw material used up, and the added value is '$(v + s)$', where 'v' is given as a revenue for labour, which covers the cost of the commodity component of the existing real wage, and 's' is the surplus value arisen. This takes its proper measure in the *rate* of surplus-value: s/v. (This may be expressed in percentage terms, for example as 80%.)

Now this is also a measure of the rate of exploitation of labour. Thus, the working day, albeit it seems homogenous, may be divided into the time of necessary labour and the time of surplus labour. 'Necessary labour' is defined here as the labour time *yielded* in return for the wage with which to purchase so-called 'subsistence goods', however priced. (It is very important to notice that this time has no necessary relation to the time *required to produce* the said goods: I return to this issue later.) There remains the surplus labour time appropriated by capital in the form of surplus value.

If the composition of commodity value is '$c + v + s$', how is this to be properly conceptualised? Is it to be resolved into '$c + (v + s)$', or into '$(c + v) + s$'? In the first case 'v' is conceived as arising with 's', both being divisions within new value-added. In the second case 'v' is conceived as an *input* to commodity value along with 'c'.

I distinguish between the *constitution* of capital, to which the first formula applies, and the movement of *constituted* capital, within which the second composition interests the capitalist. Since the organic composition of capital (c/v) is not explained until the next section, on difference, and yet the symbols 'c' and 'v' are used now, these cannot stand for 'constant' and 'variable capital' initially. But this is all to the good because I do not accept that the term 'variable capital' makes sense when discussing the original constitution of capital as yielding a 'value added'. Once that is understood, then we may give it a different meaning later when we deal with *already constituted capital*. Then, taking it as a part of 'cost price', for simplicity I shall treat both c and v as *capital* advanced, when I take capital as already constituted valorised-value in the process of its circuit.

I shall follow, then, Marx's rather clumsy terminology in speaking of 'constant and variable capital'. What is important is that new value is traced to the exploitation of labour; it is really a residual once c is deducted from the returns gained from the sale of commodities. For c is not really a value 'carried forward', as it is said, because it disappears with the consumption of its material bearer. (Below we say more on the importance of this point: see § 82.3.)

What is wrong with '$(c + v) + s$'? This formulation obscures the origin of new value in living labour; it makes it seem as if s arises from capital, since capital paid for both c and v, and this investment is surely the source of it. But the other formula, '$c + (v + s)$', makes explicit that labour produces its own wages as well as profit. So, at this level of analysis, there is no question of assembling from somewhere a 'wage fund'. (The figure of the circuit, below, will show funds for both c and v arise from previously valorised value in principle.)

However, *both* resolutions of commodity value have their place. For capital, working with already constituted capital, both c and v count as costs whenever they are paid for, and wherever the funds come from. Yet it is fundamental to our theory of capital constitution that workers produce their own wages (the political relevance of this is obvious), as well as capital's profit. (In fact, the workers give the capitalists credit, insofar as they are paid after, not before, contributing their labour.) The capitalists are under the illusion that they provide wages out of their capital, whereas it is a *conceptual* truth that they disburse it from new value added, *regardless* of the relative length of the production period and the wage period.

Although 'v' may be taken as determined by the so-called 'value of labour power', that last expression itself makes no sense since labour power is not a capitalistically produced commodity to be productively consumed. Labour has a price but no value.

I use the letters 'v' and 'c' in the presentation simply to stay in line with Marx's familiar notation, in which 'v' stands for so-called 'variable capital', contrasted with so-called constant capital, 'c'. In truth 'v' is simply a revenue derived from added value; it is not merely *equal* to wages, it is here *identical*. Moreover 'variable capital' is a bogus notion. The category makes no sense because there is nothing that varies. Even if v were to be advanced before production begins, *it does not swell*; rather when labour power is employed, the new value it yields has no necessary relation to its cost. (That depends, for example, on the length of the working day beyond the necessary part, while new value arises in proportion to the length of that day.) At all events, although I use 'v' in my notation, here it means a revenue distributed *by* capital *to* workers *from* the new value arising.

Thus a *simple price* is the sum of c and new value. This new value is then distributed to the workers (equal to 'v') and capital (equal to 's').

The elements of constant capital must be in place materially before production begins, and its material consumption notionally results in the 'transfer' of this cost to the value of the product. The difference between constant capital and the wages of labour is that constant capital is a *product of* capital to be paid for and then consumed by capital; yet labour power, while its consumption is necessary to generate new value, is *not produced* by capital, but comes from the domestic sphere, as wages are spent on 'subsistence goods'. Thus constant capital is internal to exchanges within capital as a whole but capital faces labour power as something other than itself. It is not part of capital to be reproduced as a commodity in a similar way to means of production.

In sum the unexplained m treated in Division I is combined with the secret of valorisation shown in Division II. This is presented in the circuit of capital.

§ 81.2   The Metamorphoses of Capital

I consider next differences *within* capital as it moves in its circuit. What is dealt with in the following discussion is no longer *simple commodity circulation*, but *the circulation process of capital*. This is because I now have to deal with the circulation, not of commodities as uncomprehended givens, but of *products of capital*, and therefore shapes of capital's own life cycle, necessarily appearing as its results as well as its premises, hence as essentially reproduced within the self-determining capitalist totality. Now I do not treat capital in the process of becoming, but begin with capital which has become. There follow three sections: §81.21 Fluidity and Fixity of Capital; § 81.22 The Three Circuits of Capital; § 81.23 The Circuit in Its Conceptual Unity.

§ 81.21   *Fluidity and Fixity of Capital*

The basic principle of capital's circulation process is that all those presuppositions which originally appear as prerequisites of its becoming – and therefore could not arise from its action *as capital* – now appear as results of its presence.

Capital, setting out from itself, creates the presuppositions for its maintenance and growth, it maintains itself through maintaining them.

In the metamorphoses of capital and its circuits I consider the particularity of capital as it concerns specific shapes the *same* capital takes on as it is reflected *into* itself. (I do not yet consider the difference arising *between* capitals, which is reached in Row 2.) Even with capital in its self-relation (§ 81.1), there are found many inner differences, e.g. the division of the working day and the division within value added. However, these are not particular forms *of capital*. Such forms emerge when we show that valorisation is a process in which the same capital changes in shape, from money capital, to capital in the production process, to valorised value in the output, a process of metamorphosis. These different functional forms of industrial capital are money capital, productive capital and commodity capital. Moreover capital *functions* as capital only insofar as it remains qualitatively identical with itself in the different phases of its circuit, which occur in succession. These three functional forms are particularisation of capital. Industrial capital is present only in the *unity* of its particular moments, its functional forms, as well as determining itself *to them*. These forms are held together only by their connection in the movement aimed at accumulation. It is repeated to make a circuit proper.

As a result of this totalisation, in the circuit the separate existence of circulation in the narrow sense, and of production, are sublated. Money capital, productive capital, and commodity capital, do not denote independent varieties of capital, whose functions constitute the content of branches of business that are independent and separate from one another. They are simply particular forms of industrial capital, which takes on all three shapes in turn. However, a delicate dialectic is played out here, for in the circuit the guarantee of valorisation depends on capital assuming a certain fixity in appropriate forms, namely money, means of production, product, and so forth. Thus capital as *circulating capital*, requires the transition from one phase to another. But it is, in each phase, also posited in a specific determination, which negates it as the subject of the movement as a whole. Capital is the negative unity of these its negations.

In the dialectic of fluidity and fixity, capital maintains its identity with itself through its flow; we are not faced with a Heraclitean flux, nor a set of things disconnected from each other, but a truly dialectical concept: identity and difference unified *in motion*. It its process of determination capital is *fixed* in a certain substance, for however long it takes to gather itself for the next transition. But all fixity is relativised in the fluidity of circulation as a total process.

§ 81.22 The Three Circuits of Capital

When discussing the generation of a monetary increment I showed this in the context of the circuit of money capital, in which an initial 'M' expands to 'M +

m'. However, it is not only important that money returns to itself in its circuit but that *every moment* of the circuit reproduces itself through the mediation of the others. Because the system of determination takes the form of a circuit, the point of departure is posited as the point of return and the point of return as the point of departure. However, *as* a circuit, any point may be taken as such a departure and return. Thus I distinguish three such views of the circuit of capital in its metamorphoses.

These are: the circuit of money capital; the circuit of productive capital; and the circuit of commodity capital.

§ 81.22/1   The Circuit of Money Capital

The general formula for capital, which I treated earlier, was M–C–M'. If I now concretise this by including the process of production, we have a circuit we shall explore below: M–C (mp & lp) ... P ... C'–M'. Superficially this seems to show that capital makes money *advances* in order to purchase means of production (mp) and labour power (lp). ('P' refers to capital in the phase of the production process.) However, it is essential to this formula that it is circular; the 'M' at the start is nothing but that coming out of the previous circuit. (I abstract, at this elementary level, from any bank loans taken out to accelerate the accumulation process.) Moreover, in real life, wages, and other costs, may be paid out at any time during a period of production. Nonetheless the notion of 'cost price', which merges very different things, has to be accepted as we follow capital's form of appearance. (See its importance for profit below: § 81.3.)

It is merely for expositional clarity that the formula begins with the phase of purchases and ends with that of sales. Thus, with respect to the purchase of the elements of production and of labour power, these purchases are placed in our formula at the start of the monetary circuit regardless of when, during a period of production, a capital in practice expends the relevant funds. (We stick with this even if some capitals pay no wages until funds are made available from sales.)

As I have said, 'in its concept' so-called variable capital is not capital at all but a revenue distributed to the workers who 'created' it. Nevertheless as a *necessary* disbursement, it is counted *by capital* as a *cost*. Insofar as I have moved from discussing the *constitution* of capital to the movement on its own basis of already *constituted* capital, the exposition of the metamorphoses of capital treats so called variable capital along with constant capital as an expenditure required to ensure production is maintained. Although wages are always paid *ex post*, the labour contract is *ex ante*, so capital generally knows what will have to be 'advanced' for wages at some point, so for simplicity we consider this disbursement at the opening of the monetary circuit alongside the cost of means of production.

Here I therefore start from the already constituted concept of a capital, and I treat wages as a virtual 'input' along with the constant capital. So the money capital circuit begins with money depicted as expended on both '*c*' and '*v*' in order that capital may be valorised in production. Only now is there a certain sense in which we can speak of 'variable capital' (and thus later of the 'composition of capital'). Nonetheless, despite my doubts about the term, I shall use it henceforth.

The conceptual character of capital is such that it cannot be immediately identified with *any* of the forms M, P, C. It is rather their unity, a process going on through their connection in a circuit of *transformation* of capital. Money, for example, is not *in itself* capital; it is so only in relation to the other elements of the circuit, a whole within which the moments are internally related. However, it is equally important that capital assumes the money form, because money is required to pay for labour power and means of production. Yet capital value in its monetary shape can perform only monetary functions, and no others. What makes these into functions of capital is their specific role in the movement of capital, hence also the relationship between the stage in which they appear and the other stages of the capital circuit. Isolated from this determination 'M–C' would be expenditure of a revenue whose object would be consumption of diverse use-values, including services.

I am dealing here with the money circuit of capital, which has expositional priority over the other circuits, because only in the shape of money does value possess an independent form by means of which its identity with itself may be asserted. Only here do both start and finish of the circuit come to capital as a homogeneous entity; it measures itself against itself as pure quantity and hence determines whether or not its current employment generates acceptable 'wealth' (given this social form of measure of wealth of course).

Taken in this context, the money pictured as opening the circuit is nothing but that brought forward from from the end of the previous circuit. It is therefore not a simple sum but conceals within it the complex form of valorised value, namely capital in its identity with itself, as money *capital*, which I symbolise as 'K'. Therefore the form of the monetary circuit is pictured as follows:

K–C (mp & lp) ... P ... C'–K'

Having started with money capital, the next stage in its circuit is the transformation of money capital into 'productive capital'. Money capital functions both to bring together the factors of production, and therewith to form them *as the use-value of* capital.

Capital as value in motion invests itself, in its phase as productive, in means of production *and* labour power. This is only possible because capital finds labour power can be constituted as *a value form* insofar as the wages system is evolved. Capitalist production presupposes the appropriation of all the 'objective' and 'subjective' preconditions of production in value form and hence their constitution as elements of capital. With regard to those inputs that are not products, some – notably labour power and land – nonetheless are priced. So, again, money payments are required. At the same time it is important to note about this circulation phase that this form of capital is only possible on the basis of a certain social relation whereby labour is excluded from its object. This presupposition is a function of the universality of the capitalist production process. Money can purchase labour power and thus transform itself into productive capital only because of this. Thus the circuit of capital is not possible unless a class of wage labourers exists. This presupposition is reproduced through the system's own effectivity.

Next I consider the final transformation: that of productive capital into 'commodity capital' in the shape of the product. If, at the end of the whole circuit, the value of the output is realised in money form, then the capital value and surplus value exist again in the same form of value as that which was advanced. However, there is an internal relation involved in the merely quantitative measure of this sum, it no longer appears as mere money, but is expressly posited as money capital, expressed as value that has valorised itself. Thus it appears as a sum of values that is conceptually internally differentiated. But this is expressed simply as a result, without the mediation of the process whose result it is. This circuit therefore occludes the importance of the phase of production, in which it may be taken as 'devalorised'. From its point of view the surplus seems to arise simply from a 'mark up' over costs.

Money as the independent existence of value thereby expresses the 'drive' of capital for valorisation, within which aim productive activity appears simply as a middle term between sums of money capital. As such an aim, the new money capital must reopen a new circuit.

Given this repetition of the circuit, we can separate off other points with which to start and finish it, namely P ... P and C–C'.[1] Now I turn to examine the circuit again from these angles.

§ 82.22/2   The Circuit of Productive Capital P ... C'–K'–C ... P
Here circulation narrowly considered appears only as the mediator of production, and hence money only as an evanescent form. As Marx says, this circuit 'constitutes a critique' of the first insofar as it demonstrates money has no inde-

---

1   In his manuscripts Marx raises the possibility of a 'fourth circuit', see Arthur 1998, pp. 119–24.

pendence as locus of valorisation. More generally, neither in the form C′ nor in the form M′ is the valorisation that has taken place a *function* of the money capital or the commodity capital; whereas it is the case with productive capital.

But, conversely, it is a mistake to derive the properties of productive capital from its mode of existence as the means of production etc. At this material level P ... P cannot be distinguished from non-capitalist labour processes. Indeed, on this account money may be taken as a mere 'veil' of the 'real' economy. Once again, it is form that makes a difference, and, once again, the form of the matter is given in the totality of the relations and processes established in and through the circuit of capital.

§ 81.22/3   The Circuit of Commodity Capital C′–K′–C ... P ... C′

Turning now to the circuit of commodity capital, this capital is, for example, neither 10,000 lbs of yarn, nor its value of £500, if it is to be grasped *as capital*. It is only an internal relation that makes the yarn into commodity capital, namely the relation comprised in the magnitude of its value compared with the value of the productive capital contained in it before it was transformed into commodities. Insofar as commodity capital is necessarily a result of valorisation (whereas money capital and productive capital could be taken merely in their simplicity as advanced capital), commodity capital has the inner complexity of being valorised value. Even though 'M ... M′' sets the aim of capital and 'P ... P' reproduces it, what *is* reproduced above all through the movement of circulation and production is the material wealth of the social whole.

I differentiate this form from the others on the ground that it starts from already valorised value. Taken in isolation, a bushel of corn in a warehouse is simply a product not a value and, even if considered as having value, any putative surplus value is simply not visible. However, it must be taken within the totality of determinations that constitute it not just as a commodity but as valorised value.

§ 81.23   *The Circuit in Its Conceptual Unity*

These circuits are purely internally related figures of a given whole of self-positing capital which unifies its own phases and exists in their unity. In their distinction they are characterised as follows: the circuit of money capital expresses the drive of valorisation in its *form*; the circuit of productive capital starts with the valorisation *process* itself; the circuit of commodity capital begins and ends with *valorised value*. But industrial capital exists in, and reproduces, all phases simultaneously, so the entire circuit is the *real unity* of its three forms. The forms are therefore fluid forms, and their simultaneity is mediated by their succession. It is necessary to grasp the phases of its motion, as *internally related* to each other; for in isolation its moments lose this determinate economic meaning, being reduced to determinations characteristic of simple circulation or production in general. Hence capital can be conceived *only as motion, not as a thing at rest*.

The technical name appropriate for characterising the manner in which capital and its specific functioning emerges in the relationships of the three moments of its circuit all of which have their own functional specificity – all as such *less* than capital – is 'sublation'. This is a special case of the phenomenon of 'emergent properties' in which the emergent property does not merely passively reflect the epiphenomenal effects of the functioning of the 'original' or 'basic' elements, but itself has an active principle or law which turns its determinants into determined determinants, and hence it shapes the functioning of the base elements in accordance with the requirements of the emergent function. In this case the emergent function of valorisation dictates the terms on which M–C, C ... P ... C, and C–M are undertaken, i.e. circulation and production become dominated not by the use-value considerations 'originally' to the fore, but valorisation. The original functions become 'sublated'.

So capital does not appear in its *complete* determinacy in any of its phases but only in the whole circuit. The shapes can stand alone and operate as money, commodity etc., but not thereby *as capital*; only in the circuit does this function emerge for them. Thus the three shapes of capital, M, C, P, are not species of a genus but internal self-differentiations of a single whole, and acquire their potency as shapes *of* capital only within this whole.

Remark: The implicit functional differences here become the possibility of a real opposition when these moments are externalised, as finance, commerce, industry. (See Chapter 15.)

Capital itself is an emergent form that cannot be reduced to a particular inner moment or phase of its cycle of activity; but only through these stages is capital *constituted* as capital, and these forms of its movement are constituted as *its* forms only by virtue of the real unity of the circuit. If the circuit is analytically broken down into its parts, into *disconnected* stages, there is no longer any trace of capital; all that is left is simple circulation and the immediate process of production.

Furthermore, it is precisely the circuit of money capital that makes this explicit. The other versions of the circuit yield interesting insights but they are subordinate to M–M', for P ... P, and C–C', give no clue in their end points that there is a *drive* to expand and accumulate capital in monetary form. Only M–M' embodies this drive for *m*. For example, in isolation P ... P may be understood as production for the sake of production, whereas it is for the sake of *m*, i.e. for valorisation. This is the all-embracing moment of the circuit. But M–M' must not be taken in isolation, forgetting the moment of valorisation is required through the mediator P.

As earlier noted with respect to the M–M' circuit, in positing the circuit so, the material process of production – wherein valorisation actually originates – is occluded. In order to focus on that it is necessary to reduce money merely to its function of purchasing under their commodity form those particular factors of production that allow a labour process to be simultaneously a valorisation process. The circuit 'P ... P' therefore brings this into prominence by positing circulation merely as a means of renewing, and expanding, valorisation, which requires its passage through the universal again.

Yet something special happens in this form; it is the *material* character of the process that becomes important; for the particular commodities bought are productive capital only because as factors of production they can be consumed in such a manner as to yield their potential for producing specific commodities. The values are consumed for the sake of the use-value of transforming their material properties and functions into a new value. This is especially true of labour power of course; for it is only the fixing of the labour it yields in a particular product that grounds the valorisation process. But these material forms are predicated on the material particularisation of capital (not immediately as particularisation of value) on which they depend for their effectivity. Capital as money capital must transform itself into them when particular productive activities are undertaken and commodities are sold as valorised value so as to realise the profit generated during production. It is precisely this material particularity of productive capital that gives rise to all sorts of technical problems in its movement. Thus, the proportions in which a production process can be expanded are prescribed by technical factors.

The material determinations of productive capital, which in a general way feature in all industry, may come in varying proportions according to how labour intensive (or not) is a particular industry. (This therefore is a potential *difference* between capitals that is effective in the corresponding form of the value composition when taken down column 2 to Box 5.)

It is a basic fact of the distribution of resources in capitalist society that all commodities are privately owned and thus only available through purchase. Because of the social division of labour, inputs to one industrial capital are generally products of other capitals. We see here then that not only does a single capital have its essential form as a circuit but that this circuit necessarily intertwines with others. The problem of realisation of the output, together with the need to find inputs in the same form, point to the *system* of wealth, and relates the comodity capital circuit to the revolution of the entire 'social capital'. It is primarily, therefore, the form in which to consider the confrontation and interchange *between* individual capitals, and between capital and households, to grasp the overarching individuality of total social capital as a circuit of circuits. Thus it forms a transition from this part to such matters as reproduction schemes.

Capital is essentially *motion*, albeit its determinateness is secured only in the moments of its circuit. However, for capital there is always the danger of dissolution should it not be able to move freely in its substance; for capital must *invest itself in matter*, something that may in fact be resistant to it. While everything is inscribed in the value form this matter is always 'in excess' of this conceptual determination. So the material basis of the capital circuit introduces an element of contingency.

In virtue of its form, capital aims to appropriate and reproduce all its conditions of existence. Even if this is judged unproblematic in the case of produced means of production, it seems questionable where land and labour are concerned; for land is not produced at all and labour power is reproduced outside the capitalist factory, namely in the 'domestic' sphere. However, while *materially* this is true, *socially* land and labour are subject to the capitalist system, which reproduces their value form. Labour power requires value inputs for its reproduction, as well as domestic labour, and it can gain these only through marketing itself as a value. The dull compulsion of economic necessity forces the labourers to make themselves available to the capital circuit, and the reproduction of the capital relation perpetuates this necessity. Thus the domestic economy is thoroughly subsumed under capital, albeit it has something of the character of a 'black box' in the reproduction of the capitalist social formation insofar as this is conceptualised *from capital's point of view*. Ideally all its inputs and outputs are value formed because it is inscribed within the hegemonic commodity capitalist system. (For more on domestic labour see §101.1.) Nonetheless there is no doubt that in depending on land and labour at the material level, capital falls short of the ideality of its concept of self-reproduction.

Conceptually, capital exists as a circuit of successive forms; it is the identity in difference of all its functional forms; each such form is less than capital because it has only the functions appropriate to it as a differentiated form, while at the same time, as integrated in the total form, these very same functions acquire the significance of stages in the process of valorisation; hence each form of capital is determined in its ideal significance by its relations to the others and to the whole; for all premises of the process appear as its results.

§ 81.3   Simple Price, Profit, and the Rate of Profit

In order to set up the category of 'profit' I must transform the definition of commodity value as '$c + (v + s)$' to '$(c + v) + s$' (in money magnitudes), in which '$(c + v)$' is termed the cost price. This cost price, whatever its money magnitude, is compared with the surplus value, whatever its money magnitude, to give the rate of profit. So the 's' when now compared with the cost price is transformed into 'profit', and instead of the rate of surplus value 's/v', we now consider the rate of profit: '$s/(c + v)$'.

Here, wages, treated as deductions from value-added in § 81.1, appear as a 'virtual cost', such that they count as part of the cost price, '$c + v$'. (Note that other revenues industrial capital is forced to disburse, such as rent and interest, need not be treated here as virtual costs, because only the wage bill is the 'cost' that absolutely must be paid, because capital needs to exploit labour if surplus value is to arise.)

The concept of valorisation involves the comparison of *successive* quantities. Indeed, it is only this that establishes the category of value with any substantial content. Time is a feature of all economies, but of *capital above all*. For the whole idea of valorisation rests conceptually on just such a comparison of capital value across time. It is between these times that capital accomplishes its circuit of transformations. Its rate of profit is existent therefore only as a rate *over time*, for example *per annum*. This notion of the rate of profit *per annum* is an important turn in the presentation because this is the shape in which capitals compare themselves immediately (see § 82.3).

Even though labour produces its own wages the simple result of the circuit takes into account that, if the original constant capital is used to generate new value out of living labour, the wage must be deducted, as a virtual cost, before concretising the form of surplus value in profit. The *form* 'simple price' is thus analysed as 'cost price plus profit'. With regard to the generation of profit, an ideal activity of valorisation cannot *produce* the surplus product but the material reality of this product is *imputed* as the bearer of its value because the latter is the concrete fixing of the *abstract* act of positing value, including the surplus value.

What then of the *magnitude* of 'simple prices'? Notionally, commodities exchange in exact alignment with the only determination of value thus far presented, namely socially necessary labour time. However, this is a radical simplification of capitalist reality; we shall see that further determinations of value, such as the organic composition of capital, replace simple prices with production prices. This means that simple price magnitudes are purely notional; they are impossible in reality because the structure of production and circulation so far outlined is so abstract it has no self-sufficiency *even as a model*. For the capitalist system to be seen to be self-sufficient requires a discussion of how it reproduces itself through competition; we are as yet far from having determined its conditions of reproduction.

Remark: For simplicity I accept throughout that all living labour is materially exploited alike as the consequence of system-wide class forces; similarly I treat the real wage as uniform and as constant (until we treat the falling rate of profit).

Thus what are sometimes called 'labour values' have *no actuality*. They are virtual prices at best, the result of *abstracting* the class relation from the whole order, and then registering in a price form the material fact of exploitation. This last is an ahistorical notion, and as such may well involve other factors than sheer time; but here, time is to be considered as a virtual determinant *within* capitalism's terms of reference.

Why then even speak of simple prices? Why is it useful first to elucidate the form of simple price, especially since its supposed magnitude is merely virtual, given it is unactual? Even in the further presentation it remains the case that price is defined in form as 'cost price plus profit'; the issue yet to be explored is how these magnitudes are determined. The magnitude is a money price, and it arises in my scheme simply to reflect *immediately* the fundamental capital relation through which each and every capital exploits living labour. It is important that this determination is registered separately from the further determinations bound up in actual prices, because without this one there is no consistent profit-making, as we argued earlier. Simple price, however, is *too* simple to claim actuality, so we undertake a further conceptual development of the systemic determination of price to a form that *does* have a coherent claim to actuality. The conceptual gain won in 'simple price' is the idea that labour time appears qualitatively as value, here taken over abstractly, hence the determination of price *magnitude* is to be further analysed.

It is important that the system of industrial capital becomes determinate only as a whole. In this the effect of competition is crucial, and I shall develop this notion in §82. If we take on board what has just been said then values are indeterminate at this level of abstraction; so I take discussion of a single capital to refer to capital only in its elementary notion; in this way differences between capitals are blended away. The problem remains that this level of analysis is very abstract and requires further concretisation. I shall argue later that the *finished form of value* is that of what I shall call 'reproduction price'.

At the level of the *constitution* of the idea of capital as a relation of capital and labour, the only consideration relevant is the maximisation of the exploitation of labour. This, however, is concealed when organic compositions are taken into account later. Notwithstanding the paucity of determinations so far elucidated we have enough to explain the form of profit even though we have abstracted from differences between capitals.

Moreover, when I turn next to discuss the effects of competition it must be borne in mind that, if simple prices are superseded, the formula 'c + v + s' becomes true at the level of the whole by comprehending it in terms of some total social capital exploiting the working class. However, if *total* new value has ontological priority, then the inability to determine so-called 'individual values' at this level, because simple price is inadequate, is immaterial. From my standpoint, the notion of an 'individual value' *prior* to its placement in the whole makes no sense. Value is always *socially* determined; even the notion of 'socially necessary' is conditioned by the relation of commodities to each other.

§ 82   *Capital in Its Difference from Itself*

The following sections treat differences *between* capitals on the basis of which they are in competition with each other; initially this is sheer difference (§ 82.1), which means that the self-relation of capital is achieved only through the competition of many capitals. Here we treat the concretisation of surplus value. Then we consider how particular differences in capital 'composition' (§ 82.2) result through competition in 'production prices', rooted in a uniform rate of profit (§ 82.3). The divisions are as follows:

§ 82.1 Competition: Absolute and Relative Surplus Value
§ 82.2 Organic Composition of Capital
§ 82.3 Uniform Rate of Profit and Production Price.

§ 82.1   Competition: Absolute and Relative Surplus Value

At the start, I treat the difference of capital as merely numerical (but with implicit differences in size), and the relation of these differing capitals as that of (formal) competition. This form is simultaneously structured by its presence in the form of 'self-identity' because what makes capital what it is depends minimally on the interaction of the determinate elements of the capital relation. While further differences *between* capitals are addressed later, capital in its simple self-identity is the search for a surplus. In what sense then can the category of particularity be cashed out here? The answer is that, if the more specific differences are left to the next section, all I need discuss here is that the Idea of capital is concretised finitely in the context of competition.

Earlier we argued that the complementary action of capital on capital is required to realise the concept of capital as inherently bent on accumulation. In this sense competition is intrinsic to the concept. Now, at this more concrete level of discussion of competition, there are two differences to be considered when competition takes place. There is that between capitals in the same line of business, termed 'dynamic competition'; here this struggle tends to reduce socially necessary labour time. Then there is that competition between capitals in different lines of business, termed static competition; here the commodities exchange in accordance with current socially necessary labour time; but there is still competition in that other imbalances bringing about unequal profit rates will be rectified by the entry of new capital into the most profitable sectors.

Remark: The concept of socially necessary labour time used in this book refers strictly to the immediate production process. No account is taken of the idea of a socially necessary pattern of production to meet the current pattern of *demand*. I believe it is wrong to entertain such an equivocation in reference, and I dissent from variants of value-form theory that run with this second, very different, sense of socially necessary at this level. (It is indeed true that there is a relationship between effective demand and socially necessary labour time as far as economies of scale are concerned; but that issue must be addressed at a more concrete level of analysis.) Why do I insist on distinguishing between these two senses of socially necessary? It is because they are pertinent to different level of abstraction. When considering the idea of capital as such, supply and demand are bracketed. Only when a more concrete discussion of competition is reached should factors affecting *market value* be introduced to the theory.

Remark: It is intrinsic to capital that differences in supply and demand mediate competition such that the notion of a 'balance' is purely virtual. It is merely for convenience in the presentation that at this high level of abstraction it is taken as obtaining.

The pure movement of capital's difference from itself is that of many capitals in competition with each trying to maximise their rate of surplus value. There are two ways of increasing surplus value: absolute, and relative. These flow directly from the elementary terms of the capital relation in which capital pumps out surplus labour from the workers.

In §81.1 I developed the rate of exploitation s/v. Here, I unfold the difference of the two factors of this rate, both from itself, as their ratio changes, but, more particularly as each component changes relative to the other. Thus, s may change if the working day expands while v remains the same, such that more surplus value is expropriated; this is termed an increase in 'absolute surplus value'. On the other hand, v may itself fall while the length of the working day remains constant, thus also increasing s; this is termed an increase in 'relative surplus value'.

Not only is it logically possible to extend the working day so as to appropriate more surplus labour, more surplus labour may be appropriated if necessary labour is reduced for whatever reason. Should the price of labour power fall, because improvements in productivity directly or indirectly change values in wage goods industries, necessary labour naturally falls, and surplus labour increases to the same extent within a set working day; thus 'relative surplus value' increases.

It is here that a fuller account of relative surplus value is needed on the basis of the way that competition inflects the notion of the exploitative capital relation. Every individual capital in a certain branch of production has an interest in increasing the productivity of labour; in this way if it succeeds in selling all the output at the prevailing price then necessary labour time is reduced and more surplus value appropriated. However, dynamic competition in this branch soon brings about a generalisation of the new method, socially necessary labour time falls, the value of the commodity concerned falls, prices fall, the advantage of the innovator disappears, and (other things being equal) we are back to square one with the original rate of surplus value restored. The advantage of this process now redounds to the consumers who have cheaper commodities at their disposal. Here comes the twist. What if the branch of production concerned supplies means of subsistence for workers? If the real wage is kept constant its value now falls. Now, for all capitals 'v' may be reduced, and relative surplus value increased. Historically capital soon exhausted the material possibilities of increasing absolute surplus value. Thus the search for increasing exploitation has been largely directed at increasing relative surplus value.

Remark on the Intensity of Labour

It remains to consider another way it which it is claimed absolute surplus value is increased: namely increasing the *intensity* of labour. It is claimed that a speed-up of the labour process has the same effect as lengthening labour time, namely generating more value in a day. Besides time, does intensity determine the magnitude of value created? Is it the case that changes in the intensity of labour are generalised across the economy through competition between labourers? I doubt this latter point, but in any case, since time is the only relevant determinant of value, I regard intensity as irrelevant to the determination of value magnitudes.

More precisely, it is relevant only to intra-industry competition when it is translated into a lower time to produce a commodity. An increase in intensity simply means more *use-values* are produced in a given time, which means the unit value falls, just as if the machinery became more efficient. The illusion that intensity increases value is due to *dynamic* competition, where the most vicious exploiter has an advantage over the others by getting products out in a shorter time, just as with the innovator in machinery. But *inter*-branch commensuration is immediately independent of relative intensities; it takes into account only socially necessary labour time. It is not even to the point to argue that the intensities of labours in different industries are incommensurable (as I would), because only times count.

Remember *workers* do not commensurate their labours. It is *capitals* that commensurate, and the only thing they care about is the *time* it takes to produce and market a commodity. Intensity is not relevant as an *additional* factor of which account must be taken. It is relevant *only* insofar as it reduces the time embodied in each item because more are produced per hour. In sum, there is no way of assessing the degree of intensity in a given sector except by reference to its effect on the time taken per unit of output; no 'intensive magnitudes of labour' are in reality compared across sectors; only time is compared. (This is true even though the *physical experience* of exploitation may vary.)

Within the *same* sector, intensities may well be comparable. Every capital tries to reduce the time taken per unit of output, and one way of doing this is by increasing the intensity of labour, but when the others in the sector catch up the effect cancels out, price per unit drops, and the rate of surplus-value in money terms remains the same. There is no need to worry about whether or not intensity can be generalised *across* sectors, because capital takes no account of it, it being already 'taken care of' in its effects on time. (Moreover, I find the whole notion incomprehensible. How can the intensity of working on a factory line be compared with the intensity of computer programming? Concrete difference overwhelms any abstraction here.)

The issue here is conceptual, not practical. Even if relative intensity could be measured through charting the calorific intake required by every kind of labour, capital would not be interested in such a comparison; capital cares only about the time for which it is required to be tied up in different branches of production. So the intensity of labour helps to determine the socially necessary labour time to produce a specific commodity. But values of *different* commodities depend comparatively only on such socially necessary labour times. (Of course, if intensity increases in wage-goods industries then this may result in an increase in *relative* surplus value.)

§82.2 Organic Composition of Capital

Now I reach the intersection of two kinds of *particularity*; every capital has difference *within* itself, most notably registered in its organic composition, 'c/v' (the ratio of the value of constant capital to that of variable capital), but also the turnover times of its different fractions. However, these very same differences also form the basis of differences *between* capitals, for example, different capitals may have different organic compositions, and different turnover times.

This is the first relevant place to thematise the inner difference of the organic composition of capital. As a result of the drive to increase relative surplus value a greater mass of means of production, materially speaking, tend to be employed by labour. This is termed the 'technical composition of capital'. Any change in this tends to be reflected in the relation of c to v. This is termed the 'value composition of capital'. Insofar as this is determined by the technical composition it is termed the 'organic composition of capital', namely 'c/v'. Note that the form of organic composition is not purely logical; because the value composition is predicated on the technical composition it is thus a 'mixed' category.

Remark: The value composition may also change for reasons other than those relating to the technical composition.

Moreover, the organic composition of capital has no reason to be uniform; it must be assumed to vary between capitals. This variation has problematic effects (theorised in the next section), namely the formation of production prices on the basis of a uniform rate of profit.

Remark: Turnover time likewise varies between capitals. I do not deal with it here. It raises problems similar to those of differences in organic composition, and is to be dealt with in a similar way.

Through the interaction of many capitals the inner differences in capital's composition, held only implicitly in the categories of the universal, are made explicit, as competition brings them out. Moreover 'c/v' is both an inner and an outer difference which determines competition more concretely than in the previous section, as we shall see.

Remark: As well as this ratio characterising all industrial capitals, it may also be taken on general scale, such that we may discuss the change in the composition of total social capital, we shall see (in § 83).

Note that, when I come shortly to give a mathematical treatment of the transformation procedure, this is a static analysis (§ 82.31). The organic composition is thus given and constant. No account is taken of the dynamic consequences of changes in productivity. (Such changes are very important when considering the tendency for the rate of profit to fall; see § 83.3 Addendum.)

§ 82.3   The Uniform Rate of Profit and Prices of Production

This section, on the development of 'prices of production', is rather complex. It is situated as a concretisation of the account of price and profit given above (in § 81.3). But now this is considered in the context of the difference between capitals that structure competition. It follows that the rates of profit, which register the result of competition, must all be measured in the same way, namely as a rate of profit *per annum*. It will be recalled that we derived this notion proleptically earlier (§ 41). The argument there rested on the distinction between capital accumulation, incorporating what we there termed abstractly 'a monetary increment', as a movement across time intervals, and the changing bearers of its movement. As a purely ideal movement it is measured in the form of a rate of profit *per annum*, regardless of such material measures as the length of a production period. Thus in order to treat the *systemic* determination of the rate of profit we henceforth take it as a rate *per annum*.

A long-running debate on the derivation of 'prices of production' has been termed 'the transformation problem'. I believe there is no genuine 'problem'; so I prefer the term 'transformation procedure' (TP).

Remark: I do not attempt here an interpretation of Marx. Rather I take Fred Moseley's magisterial 2016 book, *Money and Totality*, as the 'state of the art' with respect to the so-called 'transformation problem'. I accept its superiority to what he calls the 'standard' (mis)interpretation of the transformation procedure, which claims to find in it a 'problem' about the status of the 'inputs'. It is important to my treatment that (following Moseley) I take the magnitudes of v, and of c, as given, although we do not initially know *how* they are determined. Nonetheless they are what they are and there is no occasion to enter upon a bogus 'transformation' of them. If I have learnt much on 'transformation' from Moseley, I qualify his view by drawing on Riccardo Bellofiore's criticism of it.[2] I regard Moseley's treatment as somewhat 'idealist', and to be corrected therefore by the 'materialist' account of value relations promoted against him by Bellofiore. This tension I resolve below in the chapter on *The Dual Ontology of Capital*. My own position lies between them. For I believe both views may fruitfully be integrated.

It is useful to preface a more detailed discussion of the substantive issue with some reflections on *method*. There is a difference between conceptualising something in the empiricist one-to-one way, and the method of conceptual development. I do not move from concept to concept so much, as present the process of the concept realising itself. Thus the process of concretisation of price and profit is a matter of developing the concept from an overly abstract one to that of a self-mediating actuality. It moves from the more abstract, hence less true, to the more concrete and complex, characterisable as a system of self-supporting truth. A form such as value is only truly known when what it has in it to become (self-valorising value in the first place) is exhibited.

So, here, the less adequate notion of value, namely 'simple price' (SP), is supplanted by the derivation of 'production price' (PP). But production price is a

---

2 See Bellofiore 2004.

transformed form of value. This *new* form of value is in truth a more *concrete* form of value because it is the outcome of systemic determinants abstracted from earlier. It is still true that value is sourced from living labour, whatever the price rule. Yet it apparently denies its origin in this transformed shape because there is no linear relationship between these moments.

In my view, since value gains magnitude only as price, the transformation from one price to another should be considered as a development of value, from an overly abstract form to a more concrete one. It is not simply a matter of additional complexity, as when the law of motion is modified by friction, etc. Rather, the original positing of the form of value is less true than its developed shape embedded in the system of capitalist competition. So I claim that production price is not a distorted form of value, but a stage on the way to the *finished form of value*, since value is fully determined only when the movement of capital has brought into play all its necessary moments, at the level of concretion achieved when the system of social capital is presented (§ 83.3).

It is not merely a matter of expositional strategy in moving from abstract to concrete, by adding further determinants to a simple model adequate in itself (if not to reality), a process motivated externally by the theorist's wish to exhibit the matter perspicuously, through first abstracting the general law from contingent perturbations. Rather, a dialectical system moves immanently, through sublating the initial starting point as overly abstract in itself, and in need of grounding at a more concrete level. (For example, if the theorist abstracts commodity value from the object before us, capital, and presents the relation between two commodities in these terms, promising to bring in later money, and capital, then the result is that there is no reason whatsoever to assume that two commodities exchange at value; this claim is too abstract to stand; it requires grounding precisely through its further determination in the movement of money and capital.)

The Idea of capital is not an abstract universal covering-concept for freestanding capitals; it is actual in uniting and regulating them. But in the exposition, in order to exhibit the basic categories of capital, I first took capital as such as the focus. What is occluded therewith in the presentation is that ontologically capital as a whole is divided against itself as *many* capitals. However, an 'individual' value, prior to its placement in the whole is senseless because value is always *socially* determined in the systemic relationship of commodities and labours. (There is no question of reading off a so-called 'individual value' from the simple material facts.)

It is important when discussing 'transformation' to pay attention to relevant ambiguities in the word '*determine*'. There are four different notions to which the term may refer:

a) to 'find out' e.g. to consult a price list;
b) to 'measure' as when a judgement of worth determines value, e.g. when a bargain is concluded, ideally the price is determined to the satisfaction of both parties;
c) to 'causally generate' as when surplus value arises from the exploitation of living labour;
d) to 'determine *conceptually*' by being *theoretically* produced, as when water is discovered to be H2O, or when value is said to be labour objectified.

For the resolution of disputes over the transformation procedure I shall argue that *finding out* the magnitude of price and profit is very different from ascertaining how these magnitudes are *generated* through a real process of exploitation and competition.

At the start, certain magnitudes have to be presupposed as 'given'; but then later some of them will be *posited* as results of systemic determination. Throughout the discussion of transformation, the real wage is taken as given; it is the result of the level of development of capitalism, and of the ongoing class struggle; but we are considering how to price products 'after the harvest' so to speak.

Simple price is a notional form that has no actuality; only when price and profit are actualised in a system of reproduction are they *comprehended* by the Idea of capital as 'long run equilibrium prices', so to speak. The transformation from simple price to reproduction price (RP) is a purely conceptual movement; it does not mirror any real process, nor require any *objective* new development of form. Rather, the existent form, namely price in its actuality, is discovered to be 'reproduction price' through sublating other abstract possibilities, which are shown to be unactual relative to the truth of price. Nonetheless something is won at each level of the exposition about the price of capitalistically produced commodities, albeit still incomplete as an account of it. Even the abstract level of simple price registers the need for commodities to be the outcome of a valorisation process rooted in exploitation.

Since the development is conceptual, any numbers *given* in the presentation at the initial levels of the treatment are merely illustrative. It is not simply that some variables, e.g. 'v' are unknown, they lack conceptual *determination* because the set of relevant determinants have not yet been theoretically produced in the exposition. Moreover, what is ontologically prior at the level of the whole is initially an *indeterminate mass* of products, with a measure in value *socially* formed in ways yet to be explained.

Let me lay out the basic categories formulaically.

Price $= c + N$ (new value added) $= c + mL$. Here 'm' is derived from a stipulated accounting identity of new value (at prevailing prices) in aggregate and abstract labour in aggregate, giving 'new value produced per hour of abstract labour', and, conversely, the 'money equivalent of labour time' (MELT).

Surplus value = $mL - v$ (it will be shown later how 'v' is to be determined).

If it is accepted that exploited labour is the source of all new value then the MELT is consistent with any set of specific prices, and even in aggregate it is correlating variables in different dimensions. Total surplus value is a residual magnitude given by deducting total v from total N (N = new value produced).

As such, the MELT is *not explanatory*, but relies on the labour theory of value (LTV); it is merely a stipulated accounting identity asserted as a corollary of the LTV; but the LTV itself needs its own argument. As such the MELT is *not* a *theory* of determination of value by labour. That theory we developed earlier in this book as a 'negative' labour theory of value (§ 52). However, it is to be noticed that this theory claimed merely a *qualitative* dependence of value on exploited labour; it does not provide a theory of determination of individual prices.

Although I propose to ascertain aggregate new value empirically through 'adding up' the individual cases *however determined*, in truth these 'individual values' are systemically determined in a way yet to be explained. Until the conceptual development is complete we do not yet *comprehend* aggregate surplus value because the notion is not yet theoretically produced. Yet it is real enough and it is the purpose of theory to explain its source.

The magnitudes c and v are unchanged through the transformation procedure, albeit there is a development of form in the presentation. Their magnitude is conceptually undetermined at this level. They *become* fully determined only when the system is shown in its actuality as a whole capable logically of reproducing itself in its form (see § 83.3).

The givens, c and v, are not theoretically produced prior to their analysis at the level of the system as a whole. However, it is unnecessary to know how c and v are determined when treating the issue of how capital generates surplus value with these 'inputs'. Eventually it will be explained *why* we determine them as 'reproduction prices', and how these magnitudes are derived. The problem arises when we consider that all the different capitals have different organic compositions of capital. But at this level it is legitimate to abstract from that and to consider a typical capital as if it were an aliquot part of the total social capital in play.

This section is divided as follows:

§ 82.31 The Derivation of Production Prices Mathematically;
§ 82.32 The Rationality of the Rate of Profit;
§ 82.33 Transformation Dynamically Considered.

§ 82.31 *The Derivation of Production Prices Mathematically*

It is intrinsic to its concept that *ideally* the rate of profit is *uniform*. This requirement of uniformity is supported by the demands of the concept, because as self-valorising value every capital is identical to every other and hence ideally will gain the same proportionate reward. Thus here I *impose* the category of 'uniform rate of profit' (URP) in order to see what would then happen to capitals in competition. The category of URP is the notional correlate of the actuality of social capital as a homogeneous mass yielding at any time a profit distribution to the many capitals pro-rata, for there is nothing that *conceptually* differentiates capitals as value bodies in motion. (This is true despite the inner difference in organic composition.) This URP is virtual because it pertains to the most elementary notion of capital abstracted from the systemic developments that generate the General Rate of Profit (GRP), to be treated in § 83.3.

(Note that I reserve the term GRP for the systemically determined rate. With the URP the stress is on the *identity* of many capitals *as* capitals. With the GRP the stress is on how the *whole* social capital measures itself as a general rate of profit even if there is a certain amount of contingent variation individually.)

Here competition is assumed to be carried on always within the context of capital in its ideality over-riding all difference through its determination at the level of the whole as imposing a URP. As a result simple price is set aside as unactual, and the form of 'production price' is elucidated through a *transformation procedure* in which value is more concretely determined as cost price ($c + v$) plus a pro-rata reward of surplus value, allocated, in accordance with the 'Concept', uniformly to each capital in proportion to this investment. For this is at the level of the relative inter-connectedness of many capitals, not that of capital as such in which fundamental determinants such as the state of the class struggle prevail.

Production prices, with a uniform rate of profit, make up a consistent and coherent result of competition. In this Transformation Procedure are taken as given the physical facts about the production process, and the division of the product between the real wage and the surplus product. *However*, the mass of wage goods and surplus goods, as heterogeneous use-values, lack measure as such; they become socially recognised only under their value magnitudes. It is this mass of goods that cannot be 'redistributed' across the derivation of their prices; but their socially recognised values are not given *prior* to our development of the finished form of value (namely RP); and in our presentation this concept is developed through a number of levels of abstraction.

The issue to be addressed is that of rightly determining production prices 'after the harvest' so to speak. This problem is distinct from that of discerning the *causal* process determining the values to be measured, such as capital's drive to appropriate living labour. (Recall what I said above about the meanings of 'determine'.) That question is 'upstream', so to speak, of the present problem, namely the derivation of production prices, displacing simple prices in the presentation.

A numerical illustration is provided in the table headed *The Transformation Procedure*.

The Transformation Procedure
This Table compares variables (1) before, and (2) after, the transform

	(c + v)	c/v	s/v 1	p1	Simple price	Rate of profit 1	p 2	Rate of profit 2	Price of production	s/v 2
Capital a	40c + 60v	40/60	100%	60	160	60%	50	50%	150	50/60
Capital b	60c + 40v	60/40	100%	40	140	40%	50	50%	150	50/40
Total Capital	200	100/100	100%	100	300	50%	100	50%	300	100%

(1) *Simple Price and Profit*   (2) *Price of Production and Profit*

(c + v) = cost price, c = constant capital, v = variable capital, c/v = organic composition of capital, s/v = rate of exploitation, p = profit, r = rate of profit. Equal sizes of the capitals, a and b, is artificial, it is simply to make clear the comparison of organic composition. All capital turns over together. Total Simple Price and Total Price of Production are set equal. Total profit 1 & 2 are set equal.
NB: s/v (1a) = s/v (1b); r (1a) ≠ r (1b); r (2a) = r (2b); s/v (2a) ≠ s/v (2b) for *capital a* now has a rate of s/v less than 100% and *capital b* more than 100%, even though the average remains as originally assumed, namely 100%.

In the table on 'The Transformation Procedure' there is a left-hand (LH) side representing a purely hypothetical 'original position', and a right-hand (RH) side in which prices of production are formed.

Taking columns from the left we have first the cost price of each capital, and their aggregate. It is very important to observe two things. First, the numbers (always money magnitudes) are purely illustrative. If the cost of *c* is '40' this must have been arrived at by knowing the value of *c*; *but*, at this level of the presentation that value is not yet even given a conceptual determination. (In truth it is determined as a 'reproduction price', but that has not yet been elucidated.) The same goes for *v*. Second, this very same cost price underwrites the numbers on *both sides* of the Table. It cannot change, for it is what it is, even though it is not known how its magnitude is determined. It is important that *v* and *c* are constants throughout the presentation of the TP, simply given at the start. Their magnitudes are effectively determined only at the level of the system; in our presentation they are shown as RP, but at the start are not conceptually determined as such.

This means the v and c are in '*ex post* prices', so to speak; thus the TP is merely a very restricted part of their explanation, just as is the account of exploitation explaining that the prices includes a surplus value.

The next column gives the resultant organic compositions. Once the rate of surplus value, s/v, is set arbitrarily at 100%, then the surplus, or profit, p, is derived in the following column. Adding it to the cost price yields what is termed here 'simple price'. The final LH column shows that capitals a and b have different rates of profit. The bottom row shows the total profit is '100' and the average rate of profit is 50%.

On the RH side the first column shows the total profit split pro rata to the relevant capitals, which ensures that they both have the *same* profit rate of 50%. Their prices of production in the penultimate column vary from the equivalent simple prices. The last column shows that their rates of surplus value also vary from the common rate of 100% on the LH side.

The Table gives a highly simplified illustration of the trouble that variant organic compositions cause to the integration of the many capitals into a single system. For there is no reason to suppose a tendency towards the equalisation of their organic compositions. The LH side shows that for the two capitals (or industries) of different organic composition very different profit rates ensue.

This is contrary to the concept of capital as ideally homogeneous, merely notionally distinct in *constant*, and *variable*, capital. The concept of capital *in its purity* requires a uniform rate of profit. Thus my presentation of the TP is not simply predicated for simplicity on a URP. (But it does not presuppose that there is any URP in reality, still less that individual capitals aim to secure it; they are assumed here to be maximisers, and a sector normally has a stratified distribution of profit rates.)

A comparison of capitals with differing organic compositions selling at simple prices, quickly shows that such a situation conflicts with this principle of uniformity. Allocating the putative aggregate surplus value to capitals in proportion to their cost prices, yielding production prices, results in the uniform rate. This TP is simply a comparative exercise relating an incoherent set of prices to a coherent one. This latter situation is shown on the RH side of the Table, in which the surplus value distribution between capitals a and b, secures they have the same rate of profit. This generates 'prices of production' distinct from simple prices. (In § 83.3 I go on to introduce what I call 'reproduction prices'.)

Because the TP is simply a conceptual development, the magnitudes on the LH side of the TP chart (all in money quantities) are either algebraic variables yet to be determined, namely 'c' and 'v', or *notional* numbers to be replaced, namely price and profit rate. It may be asked: what is the point of the TP, as given here, if the left-hand numbers are unactual? The answer is that it is exhibited in this way *why* such an array is necessarily unactual, and how a consistent set of prices and profits are obtainable. Moreover, the aggregate new value produced is also treated as a given – perhaps one could say 'empirically' given by summing the observed added value over the economy. It is important again to notice that these are *ex post* prices. So in no way is the TP giving a linear derivation of prices because the aggregate SV is derived from comparing two *ex post* magnitudes, added value and given 'v'. Thus it makes little sense to say that this aggregate is 'prior' to the derivation of production prices except in a simple expositional sense. The aggregate profit is conserved from LH to RH sides only because it is in *ex post* prices already (not simple prices).

It is not relevant to consider how over time the first state would turn into the second. Rather, the first state is there simply to present, and refute, a stumbling block to the 'labour theory of value'. The intention in the transformation procedure is to show that, if there is a tendency to realise the uniform rate of profit, this is consistent with the 'labour theory of value' taken at the aggregate level.

At the start I consider a hypothetical situation in which commodities are produced with the same money rate of exploitation and with values in simple prices; clearly, owing to differences in organic composition (and turnover), the rates of profit will differ. It might be thought this is contrary to their 'concept'. Then I consider a situation in which profit rates have been equalised by a distribution of surplus value in proportion to the invested capitals; this determines prices differently and generates production prices; then there are no differences in *profit rates*.

Here, the formation of production prices makes it appear that value is realised only in its denial, because commodities do not exchange at simple prices; but I argue that value's determination pertains to the whole system in its complexity, not to each and every capital's supposed generation of a determinate value and surplus value. The immediate relation of competition among capitals as such establishes capital not just as *conceptually* reliant on the form of many capitals, but now concretely brings back the difference between them to more complex categories than those of § 81.3. Since § 82.3 registers again the rate of profit here, it must be that which takes into account the difference in organic composition. It would seem that each capital has its own rate of profit, but the point here is that all such forms are located within the reflection of capitals against one another; so, given this, it has meaning to speak of a notional uniform rate, mathematically identical to the general rate of profit, albeit in reality systemically arising revolutions in value endlessly defer any tendency to uniformity.

The relation *between classes* at the level of total social capital underpins the general rate of profit, which is distinct from the way the distribution of capitals across industries determines the average rate of profit *between them*. The general rate of profit and the average rate of profit are *semantically* distinguishable even if they are *numerically* the same. The 'general' rate of profit has an ontological reality that the term 'average' does not connote.

It is important to sort out what magnitudes are to be taken as given from the outset, and – more importantly – in what sense are they given. In the case of 'c' and 'v', these are constants in the TP, but at the start they have not yet been theoretically produced, and here appear algebraically, so to speak. But the total net output, as value added, is given empirically, and then 'accounted for' by total labour time, regardless of the way prices are in fact determined. Hence aggregate surplus value is not *adequately* known, because the v to be deducted from value added is here simply presented prior to any account of its determination. It follows that the magnitude concerned is not yet theoretically produced; it remains *undetermined* until a full explanation of the systemic determination of the relevant variables is given later.

However, in considering the distribution of the aggregate surplus value to individual capitals this total may be properly taken as logically prior to that, *if* we assume that the conditions of class exploitation are uniform in principle because of the formal determination of the whole on its parts. Moreover, the social surplus product *is* ontologically prior to its value measure, however that measure is construed.

The Table here has a final column demonstrating that an ineluctable consequence of equalising the rate of profit of a and b is that their rates of exploitation are now correspondingly different, in money terms, which balances their different organic compositions. Should this worry us? Not at all. The only cause for alarm would be if this money rate of exploitation were to be confused with – what I call – 'the material rate of exploitation', which – simplifying – we assume is set socially by class struggle. In every case we assume that (in this context) the ratio of necessary and surplus labour is equal and constant for all capitals. So the *experience* of exploitation by all workers is the same, so long as the money wage allows the purchase of the real wage in prices of production. Notice that in this Table the *aggregate* rate of exploitation remains the same. The money measures of prices are capital's concern so to speak.

Simple price is too abstract a form to have any actuality; as soon as competition between capitals is brought into the picture further determinations take effect. Nonetheless the fundamental determination of price by socially necessary labour time is always present however 'transformed' in its effect. At this point in the argument the oft-repeated quibble that 'inputs should also be transformed' may raise itself. But this is irrelevant here: v and c are what they are (although as yet not determined conceptually); it is only the subsequent prices of production that are in question.

It follows that there is only one 'distribution' of value, that which is derived simultaneously with the general rate of profit. Moreover, it makes little sense to treat this 'standing distribution' as a process of allocation from a given pot, even though it is determined by system-wide determinants such as class struggle. The aggregate and the distribution evolve together. The possibility of this in actuality must be developed in a dynamic consideration of how competition works (see 82.33). Certainly in the TP presented here there is *no* 'redistribution' of an 'original' distribution as a real process. There is merely a *comparison* of two logically incompatible distributions. There is no real movement from one to the other, just the discarding of the inadequate one.

This means that in the Table the LH side is not temporally prior to the RH one. Rather, it is merely expositionally 'prior'. Starting from the same givens (e.g. cost price), they are alternative outcomes. The overly simple distribution on the LH is found wanting and it is *replaced* by the RH distribution. The LH does not generate the RH in any meaningful sense. All that the LH side says is that price must include a surplus value on top of cost price, but the cost price here is taken as given in reproduction prices.

So what is achieved here is very limited, for we take the *ex post* measure of c and v to derive the rate of exploitation and profit when calculating so-called SP. However, once we say v and c are given in ways yet to be determined conceptually then we already implicitly appeal to a more concrete level of development of the value concept than that of simple price. They are always already transformed values, so to speak. The elementary level is not capable of yielding fully determinate magnitudes if key variables have to be taken as given without conceptual determination.

In the transformation procedure, the distribution of surplus value to the many capitals is unaffected by their *internal* composition. For at this level of *abstraction* the 'production prices' here hold regardless of the different organic compositions of a and b, for all that counts is the cost price of each capital, which is taken as known. This derivation of production price holds regardless of unequal compositions; for that is finessed through taking the *total* cost price as the relevant basis for the derivation. So c and v stay as givens yet to be determined; they are shown later to be 'reproduction prices'. All I do now is to replace an incoherent profit system with a feasible (if ideal) one. Moreover, when I later derive RPs from the interchange of departments of reproduction this does not have an unpleasant retrospective effect on the transform; it merely concretises it by determining just what magnitude c and v have.

Because the problem is entirely mathematical, in my view it makes no sense to interpret the transformation as occurring across production periods. Thus the physical conditions of production, and the real wage, are given; they cannot be supposed to have changed during such a period. (Of course, when real periods of production are addressed then capital goods and wage goods as inputs must have been also outputs. This issue we take up in § 83.3.)

Later I come to what I term 'reproduction prices' (a *full* discussion of the notorious 'transformation problem' I reserve for that). It is perfectly consistent to separate these discussions because this abstract level of the presentation is concerned, not with the concrete unity of the system, but with the way in which differences between capitals are recognised, compared, and adjusted, in accordance with the demands of the immediate capital concept. But, when we come to the reproduction of total social capital, reproduction prices will be *inputs* to the Departments, as well as *outputs*, and this raises certain problems.

However, the usual discussion of this issue has been vitiated by the treatment at once of these two different questions. One is the stipulation of a uniform rate of profit and the transformation of prices consequent on that. The other flows from the requirement to balance departments. I separate these discussions. In the present scheme 'production prices' come before the Departments of Production and their 'reproduction prices'. My exposition clarifies the issues at stake in this respect by first discussing how a uniform rate of profit could be secured by varying prices; then the further complication caused by the systemic requirement to balance Departments is addressed later, because this is at the level of capital as a whole system of reproduction. So the concretisation of price is divided into two; here I treat *production* prices, later I treat *reproduction* prices (in which the 'input' and 'output' prices are identical) as a consequence of the introduction of the departments. In this order of presentation there is a two-step argument; first to show that the uniform rate of profit is achievable through further determining prices; and then later to show how balanced reproduction is achieved through further price adjustments.

It is important that just as simple prices (§ 81.3) are hypothetically derived from a given cost price, so production prices are also predicated on the very same given cost price. In neither case do they characterise the *actuality* of the idea of capital, and the resultant reproduction prices. The minimum condition of capital's actuality is that it produces not only itself in its abstract immediacy, but a *system of reproduction* of itself as many capitals in the interplay of the moments of the concept, universal-particular-singular, in both the dimensions articulated earlier (see the Table on the *System of Industrial Capital*).

The presumption of a uniform rate of profit to accommodate differences in organic composition requires the establishment of a production price for every commodity. The point of it is to show that a uniform rate of profit is consistent with the theory that all surplus value is sourced from the labour process. But this is merely a stage in our development towards the concrete whole of capital. It is still simply unifying many capitals merely *abstractly*. The production prices derived here merely demonstrate that capital exploits labour not so much one-to-one but as a whole, and in principle a uniform rate of profit registers this, albeit with transformed values. The rate of profit here is therefore still a virtual notion of profit rate, located within the capital relation. Moreover, the magnitude of the URP is not fully determinate, for as yet the elements of cost price are still taken merely as givens without explanation of their magnitude. The discussion therefore remains somewhat abstract. However, the apparent contradiction between simple prices immediately reflecting exploitation, and production prices congruent with it only at the aggregate level, is resolved.

Thus differences between capitals, such as organic composition, are integrated. In a sense *we* are comparing capitals, and unifying them, in principle. It is only later that we see capitals *compare themselves* in a totality of interrelatedness in which outputs become inputs as well as inputs become outputs. So the implicit reference of the circuits of commodity capital to the interrelatedness of capitalist circulation is then concretised as the reproduction of departments, which in turn gives rise to reproduction prices and a systemic rate of profit.

As a whole of reproduction this idea of capital may be properly termed concrete. Here, I still abstract from other relevant factors, for example, market fluctuations, but this is a legitimate simplification, not a vicious abstraction, if production prices have actuality in a logical sense. The set of simple prices is hypothetical, because absurd; the set of production prices is hypothetical because over-elegant, but it is *coherent*.

The form of total surplus value is not just a way of avoiding discussion of a so-called 'individual value'; it reflects system-wide determinations such as the balance of class forces and the ontological priority of the universal over its individuated parts.

The transformation procedure keeps the *material* rate of exploitation conserved, but value, as the social form within which it is (mis)recognised, displaces this simplicity with a *money* rate of exploitation that cannot be reduced to the former rate in magnitude, albeit the former has an underlying effectivity on it. Certainly, if it took the whole working-day to produce the subsistence wage there would be no surplus labour; hence no surplus value; in that sense the material level is basic.

The great advantage of the form of aggregate surplus value is that the individual case is finessed because the aggregate is blind to these cases until we explain the individual case as resulting from the pro rata *distribution* of surplus value, achieved through competition.

The traditional reading of TP assumes there is an 'original' *standing* distribution (based on exploitation of a firm's own workers) then subject to a *re-distribution*. In my case there is no need for the term 're-distribution'; because there is only the one distribution pro rata according to size. (There *is* a redistribution from industrial profit to that of other capitals in the shape of rent and interest; but here I treat the *production* of surplus value only.)

To end, I underline again that the magnitude of production price adduced here is unexplained. This is for two reasons. First, the magnitude of cost price in unexplained. Its elements are determined as reproduction prices; but we have yet to develop this form. Second, the uniform rate of profit notionally applied here is derived from the aggregate surplus value, itself derived from aggregate new value. But the last aggregate can only be *known* in *ex post* prices. So what is achieved by deriving production price is somewhat limited, however necessary to the levels of determination in the system of forms.

§ 82.32   *The Rationality of the Rate of Profit*

The price of production is a form of value, appearing in competition, and hence present in the consciousness of the ordinary capitalist. But it is wrong to disparage such appearances to vindicate the inner reality of value. The 'external' price is not a veil to be discarded as it is lacking the truth of the Concept. It is *necessary* that essence appear and that the actuality of the concept concretise itself at the phenomenal level. So far from being misleading, the price of production is a fully rational manifestation of the Concept and essential to its fully articulated meaning. Prices of production should not be counterposed to 'value' but understood as a more finished form of value. This is because value exists in determinate shape only as the result of capitalist competition; therefore, the concrete concept takes determinations springing from competition into account when arriving at its finished form. While this results in the displacement of so-called 'individual value', it is equally true this is bound up with the proper actuality of the value concept. To be blunt, the category of 'individual value' has no sense in this context.

At this level of analysis, in which differences of organic composition are taken as essential determinants, resulting in production prices, it is clear that some capitals are more efficient than others in resurrecting these original values in new form. More constant capital is transferred per hour by one production process than by another. This is properly recognised if capital-intensive industries gain more value (in the shape of production prices) in their self-valorising process than labour-intensive industries do. As capital moves through its self-valorisation process, it transfers to the result the input values (to which it has added new value) at a definite *rate*. Its measure of success is properly '$s/(c + v)$'. We may speak of a socially average power of resurrecting value consequent on the organic composition of capital. Here the average is socially imputed and supplants the 'concrete' rate of transfer, just as, at a higher level of abstraction, socially necessary labour time supplants concrete labour time.

So-called 'constant' capital is treated far too casually, when deriving the value of a commodity, if it is said the value of the constant capital is simply carried forward to reappear in the value of a commodity. But it is not. It is totally destroyed during the production process. The capitalist has undertaken an enormous risk in sacrificing all their capital in this way. The constant capital is all productively consumed. They can only pray that, if the commodity is sold at the right price, their capital is *resurrected* in new material shape. When I look at capitalist production I find that *two* important things go on during the valorisation process: as we know, new value is *created*, but as importantly, and as a condition of that, the original capital value is *recreated*; it must be resurrected in a reflux from its destruction.

Production is not pure activity but work *on* materials *by* labour *with* instruments of production, all getting used up. It both generates new value, and, *also*, resurrects in a new material shape the value of constant capital. (That ability to transform inputs into outputs, such that their value is resurrected, really *is* an intensive dimension of productive power, one might say.) If a firm turns over more social capital per hour than average, it must be rewarded accordingly, even if this changes its rate of surplus value. It turns over with greater *momentum*, so to speak. I conclude that the new rate is in accordance with the concept of capital.

Production may be organised *within* a branch of production efficiently, yet in this one respect differ *between* branches, namely in the mass of constant capital set in motion in the production process, and its effectiveness at resurrecting such constant capital. This underpins the formation of prices of production, co-determined by the uniform rate of profit. The resultant surplus value is predicated on the fact that each fraction has recreated capital anew in its own sphere, and it requires a reward in proportion to that success. Those branches that have higher labour costs have 'wasted' social labour, so to speak, because they effectively use social capital less productively than others.

In truth, the category of uniform rate of profit is a rational one. To be sure, it incorporates the falsity of the way in which all capital appears productive, not just the fructiferous part. Yet there is a real sense in which the *whole* of capital reproduces, and accumulates, itself. The standard treatment of constant capital, as simply carried forward into the value of the product, neglects the fact that there is a need to *resurrect it* materially as a constituent part of the product. Thus profit *should* be proportional to the whole capital in motion.

§ 82.33 Transformation Dynamically Considered

The Table on *Transformation* shows an exercise in comparative statics. The transformation procedure outlined there may appear as an artificial 'fix' to the possibility of very different rates of profit if sales are at simple prices. But it is intrinsic to the Idea of capital that production prices arise naturally in the development of competition, we shall show.

On a point of terminology, I speak of 'productive power' (singular) of capital (e.g. of items per day), reserving 'productive forces' (plural) for the labour, cooperation, skill, intensity, and especially machinery, etc. that contribute to this power.[3]

I have shown purely formally how the distribution of the total surplus value in accordance with the rule of a uniform rate of profit generates production prices differing systematically from immediate simple prices. I have underpinned this with an ontological reading of the total mass based on the notion that capital as a whole confronts the working class as a whole in the capital relation. In considering the social character of class exploitation underpinning the notion of a general rate of profit, I abstract from the greater or lesser efficiency of industrial capitals at pumping out surplus labour. If, for simplicity, we assume every capital has the same rate of surplus value, then the relevant rates of profit differ markedly. This is the problem solved by the transformation procedure.

But now there emerges a complementary problem: once a uniform rate of profit obtains then assuredly the associated rates of surplus value now differ from each other. (See the last column in the Table above.) In one sense this is of no importance; capitals aim at the rate of profit and their rate of surplus value is only one, if fundamental, determinant of that. But it may well be asked: how in reality could such different rates of surplus value emerge if the original position were assumed to be a rough equality? The answer is that, if competition within a branch leads to the introduction of new productive forces by a firm, that firm will realise extra surplus value at prevailing prices.

---

3 The rest of this section owes much to Reuten 2017 (but he speaks of productive power of labour).

As other firms enter, or catch up, such that the new productive forces of that sector become generalised, then prices fall. *But* not to the extent that the original rate of surplus value is restored; this is because the new means of production imply extra constant capital. Thus maintaining the original rate of profit means *maintaining a higher rate of surplus value*. So entry to the sector dries up once the rate of profit approaches the general rate of profit, which mobile capital is always in the process of establishing.

The point of this way of thinking about it is that the higher rate of surplus value is *prior* to competitive adjustments across the economy (rather than its *result* as seen in the Table). In this dynamic treatment discrepancies between rates of surplus value arise *immediately*, although in the static treatment we have shown unequal rates of surplus value are a corollary resulting from transformation. In the ideal case the new price would be exactly that dictated by the virtual transformation, namely the production price reflecting the more mediated value magnitude. In effect the usual way of establishing production prices takes a static set of capitals, and harmonises the inter-sector difference in the rate of profit, at the cost of introducing different rates of surplus value. It could be argued that such a transformation procedure does not develop *immanently* from so-called 'simple price' to so-called 'production price', but adds externally to 'the law of value', in its immediate form, the requirement of a uniform rate of profit in the face of different capital compositions. A counterfactual array of prices is manipulated abstractly to generate a coherent (if ideal) set of production prices.[4]

However, in reality, the competition of capital works within the system to develop production prices. One might say that the theoretical need for a transformation procedure is finessed because the problem is already solved in the very moment of its arising, as production prices, and capital compositions, develop together. Difference and unity are co-determinate. Thus a sector with a higher productive power generates value at a higher rate than would be the case if value simply reflected the time of production as if value is created at the same rate. It follows that in such advanced sectors the rate of surplus value is higher, even if, because of a concomitant increase in organic composition, the rate of profit is not. However, the dynamic process just outlined shows how the higher rate of surplus value in practice arises through intra-sector competition with *no generalisation* of the new productive power across sectors.

---

4 Reuten 2017, on the basis of his dynamic treatment of the matter in which the higher rate of surplus value is prior to competitive adjustments across the economy, argues that prices of production are redundant (and hence are all dual account systems).

Nothing 'corrects' this variance; for there is no obvious mechanism whereby new productive powers in one industry are necessarily generalisable across the economy.

At a material level, an increase in the productive power of capital is registered in an increase in the output of use-values per day. The point at issue here is, whether this simply means that the same value is spread over this greater mass of use-value, or whether, in some fashion, a permanent increase in value arises from production of a higher power than before. Although the innovating capitalist loses much of his advantage as competitors in the *same* sector imitate the new productive force, there can be no such process of imitation that is necessarily effective *across* sectors. Rather, what happens is that, in the case where the increased productive power of capital is not costless, but is linked to a higher capital composition, then a new general rate of profit ensues, which retains within its generality a higher rate of surplus value in the innovative sector.

Even if the average rate of surplus value increases, through the generation of relative surplus value, the traditional sectors are penalised through a lower than average rate. But, since the innovative sector generates more value than average during a constant working day, necessary labour time is thus *compressed*. This is not because the value of labour power falls; so the extra surplus value is a form of *absolute* surplus-value. (However, this is a matter of semantics; if relative surplus value is defined as a shift in the division of the working day *for whatever reason* then here it is then a case of relative surplus value.)

I argued above that just such inequalities in the rate of surplus value emerge even in the mathematical presentation of the transformation procedure. In the first situation, there are equal rates of surplus value, and consequently unequal rates of profit. In the second situation, applying the rule of a uniform rate of profit to generate production prices yields the result that there are now *unequal* rates of surplus value, in money terms. So labour-intensive industries end up with a low rate of surplus value, and labour-saving sectors a high rate of surplus value. This inequality in rates of surplus value is derived, not as a consequence of the existence of differing capital compositions, but as their very premise. Thus we reach dynamically the same result as the transformation procedure above exhibits statically.

If we take the rate of surplus value to rest on the rate of exploitation, it is true that this monetary revaluation of the rate of surplus value leaves untouched what may be called the *physical rate* of exploitation, namely the labour time 'embodied' in the surplus product compared with that required to produce the real wage. It might seem that, since it is a premise of the problem that the same physical configuration is maintained across the transformation, the rate of exploitation cannot change. Yet, in money terms, it has!

This is not merely an analytical problem but a conceptual one, for it touches on the very nature of value and surplus-value. (This will be explored further in Chapter 14.)

§ 83   Systemic Unity of Total Social Capital

The system grasped a whole, in its unity, and the relation of capitals within it, generates systemic tendencies (§ 83.1). (See *Glossary* on 'tendency'.) However, the system has numerous inner differences. The most notable is that the total social capital is concretised as the interweaving of many circuits; but this abstract point may be complemented by their sorting into 'departments of reproduction', here the production of wage goods and of capital goods. So below are considered those inner differences of social capital namely these departments and their exchanges (§ 83.2). When I discuss the importance of departments, and the theoretical need for them to balance both in physical terms and in value terms, I do not consider *how* prices are systemically determined. This issue is taken up in the final section (§ 83.3), in which the general rate of profit, also systemically determined, sums up the resultant of all the determinations considered; as such it is determined as a magnitude along with the distribution of surplus value through the formation of reproduction prices. Once I have theoretically conceptualised reproduction prices below, I have determined the c and the v inputs given in the mathematical determination of production price. But this is consistent with the ontological priority of the whole. (In addition, I treat at the end of this chapter a theorem on the tendency for the general rate of profit to fall.)

The Divisions of this section are:

§ 83.1 General Law of Accumulation: Concentration; Centralisation; Reserve Army;

§ 83.2 Reproduction of Total Capital via Departments of Reproduction;

§ 83.3 Reproduction Prices; General Rate of Profit;

Addendum A Note on the Neo-Sraffian System;

Addendum A Note on the Tendential Fall in the General Rate of Profit.

§ 83.1   General Law of Accumulation

The following sections are concerned neither with the way a capital relates to itself, nor to others, but with how the *system* of capitals relates to *itself*. Here the general effects of competition are present, notably the general law of capital accumulation. I draw attention to the importance in this of the dialectic of 'attraction and repulsion' (already treated formally in § 82.1). So I reconsider the fundamental capital relation, but now on a social scale. It is systemically reproduced both across the competing capitals but also as a feature of the unity of social capital.

Thus the organic composition of capital is not only as a mark of *difference* between capitals but also as an *overall* structure of the capital system, which *develops* over time. (It tends to increase, as a result of the drive by individual capitals to maximise surplus value through the introduction of machinery.)

In this context, competition gives rise to the dialectic of repulsion and attraction of capitals, to and from each other. (This is of a piece with the homogeneity of capital *as a form*.) Capitalist competition results in both the concentration and centralisation of capital. Concentration means an increase in the command over labour of the individual capital as it grows, while centralisation means the takeover of many capitals by one.

Increase in the accumulation of capital on a social scale implies, generally, an increase in capital's organic composition, because the productive power of labour increases therewith; this helps to avoid the problem posed by a limited supply of workers, and a consequent upward pressure on wages. In general, the capital relation is reproduced on an expanded scale, with more, and bigger, capitals at one pole, and more wage workers at the other. The rhythm of accumulation brings about the attraction and repulsion of workers to and from the system, with the resulting creation of the 'reserve army of labour' a permanent feature of this development, independently of population growth.

§ 83.2　Reproduction of Total Social Capital via Departments of Reproduction

I deal now with social reproduction of total social capital. The reproduction of an individual capital is simply impossible to understand without examining how it interweaves with the totality of capitals. However, *social* reproduction clearly entails much more complex forms than are treated when considering an individual capital.

In the framework of the attempt to exhibit the actuality of value through a movement of the presentation from abstract to concrete I have now reached a level of concretion in which it is demonstrable that ideally value and capital may be reproduced systematically in a coherent fashion. More specifically this consideration is located in the Table of *The System of Industrial Capital* at the intersection of the Row in which I treat the forms of social unity of capital, and of the Column designating the realm in which differences *within* capital are presented.

Formally there are an indefinitely large number of individual enterprises, but these are unified within total social capital through exchanges between them. The circuits of individual capitals interweave with each other through commodity capital circuits. However, the category of *particularity* comes to the fore when I consider the most important difference between them from the point of view of establishing the reproduction of the whole, namely some firms produce means of production, or capital goods (collectively termed 'Department I'), and other firms produce means of (final) consumption (collectively termed 'Department II') whether bought by workers or capitalists.

So the following reproduction schemes consider just two departments of production, namely that producing means of production and that producing means of consumption. In order to present the relation between the two in the simplest way I absent the difference marked earlier, namely differential organic composition. We assume that each department has the *same* organic composition of capital.

Remark: The reason for it is the elegance of isolating the problem of balance without bringing in at once other determinations. Only in the following section do we then take unequal organic composition into account. Just as potential varying organic compositions have been finessed in our earlier discussion of production prices, so then such variation must be taken account of in the final determination of reproduction prices. However, then the self-realisation of price and profit requires that the input/output scheme addressed here be taken into account.

For simplicity I consider here only *simple* social reproduction (disregarding accumulation of capital) with the surplus, s, being spent by capitalists on their means of consumption.

Reproduction occurs through complementary interchanges between the departments, in which physical and monetary flows are balanced. For reproduction to be achieved there must be a certain material proportion of good produced by the different departments, and not merely are the different goods to be allocated to where they are needed, but for this to happen they must first appear as exchanged commodities. Hence I must explain how the monetary flows are also capable of balance.

For simplicity I assume that the total constant capital is used up in the same period of production across the economy.

Department I

Let us first consider Department I, which produces means of production. These are differentiated precisely by their destination: some are bought by firms located in Department I itself, these are collectively termed 'c_I'; while others are bought by firms in Department II, these are collectively termed 'c_{II}'. The total sales of the department are thus '$c_I + c_{II}$'. This income is spent as follows. The capitals in this department must each newly purchase replacements for their own means of production, which we already know (assuming simple reproduction) is collectively 'c_I'. Then the aggregate wage bill for the department will

THE SYSTEM OF INDUSTRIAL CAPITAL   317

need to be met; let us term this 'v_I'. Finally there is the appropriated departmental surplus, termed 's_I'. Capitalists will spend all this on means of consumption, under conditions of simple reproduction. In sum the following equality obtains: $c_I + c_{II} = c_I + v_I + s_I$.

Department II
Now let us consider the complementary sphere, that supplying means of consumption, namely Department II. The firms in this sphere supply means of consumption to their own aggregate work force, but also to the workers in the first department. In total this amounts to '$v_I + v_{II}$'. They also supply commodities to soak up the revenues of the capitalist class in both departments, in total '$s_I + s_{II}$'. On the demand side they buy '$c_{II} + v_{II} + s_{II}$', assuming capitalists spend all their revenues. The equality here is therefore: $v_I + v_{II} + s_I + s_{II} = c_{II} + v_{II} + s_{II}$.

The balance condition
If internal transfers are netted out we have for the first department '$c_{II} = v_I + s_I$', and for the second '$v_I + s_I = c_{II}$'. So Department I sells means of production to Department II, and it receives in return means of consumption for its workforce. With Department II the converse relation applies. This identity secures the balance condition.
In summary form:

Scheme of simple reproduction (no growth; all surplus is consumed)[a]

	Means production		Wages		Surplus		Output	Sales equivalent	Balance condition
dept.1[†]	c_1	+	v_1	+	s_1	=	x_1	$c_1 + c_2$	$c_2 = v_1 + s_1$
dept.2[‡]	c_2	+	v_2	+	s_2	=	x_2	$(v_1 + v_2) + (s_1 + s_2)$	$v_1 + s_1 = c_2$

a Thanks are due to Geert Reuten for providing this table.
† Producing means of production: both for internal use (c_1) and for department 2 (c_2).
‡ Producing means of consumption: both for workers (v_1 and v_2) and for capitalists (s_1 and s_2).

The logical possibility of balance considered here should in no way be confused with a metaphysical supposition about a tendency to equilibrium, or of the likelihood of balanced growth, for tendencies to balance are always upset by 'revolutions in value'. In truth the supposition of 'balance' is grossly counterfactual. What is the point of discussing a counter-factual situation? In this case it is because its very counter-factuality indicates a possible source of systemic crisis: a 'crisis of disproportionality'. So the heuristic virtue of the schemes is obvious as a benchmark to assess real situations.[5]

§ 83.3   The General Rate of Profit and Reproduction Price

In this account of total social capital we have shown formally how the two departments may balance each other (§ 83.2). (For conceptual reasons we present the system in uniformity and balance in § 82.3 and § 83.3.) However, if the *reproduction* of the system in its complexity is considered, all the earlier determinations must be considered when determining reproduction prices and the rate of profit. It is *these* reproduction prices that determine the magnitudes of c and v we have taken as given throughout, for example in the transformation procedure. As themselves values, all the determinations of value adduced earlier have a bearing on them; but their *concrete* determination requires as a minimum condition that they be *systemically determined*. Such prices depend in the first place on their ideal determination in the context of the reproduction scheme as long-run equilibrium prices (however idealised and abstract the notion of the equilibration of departments may be).

While this section looks at the consequences of the systemic determinations adduced in the third row of the Table on *The system of industrial capital*, these are registered under the head of the third column, namely categories of singularity. Here we find the *concretisation* of the rate of profit. To begin with (§ 81.3) there is the elementary notion that capital measures its success in its *rate of profit* (*per annum*). Then we introduce the figure of the *uniform rate of profit* in order to correlate conceptually the relations of *different* capitals (§ 82.3). That discussion abstracts from the problem of harmonising departments of production, and their input/output prices were not considered. Now we introduce the notion of a *general rate of profit* determined as that of total social capital. This may be identical in magnitude to that of the earlier deployed uniform rate of profit (underdetermined at its introduction), but it is conceptually richer because it pertains to the system *taken as a whole*, which reproduces itself, among other things by reproducing relations between departments.

The same *concretisation* applies to value. That value itself only exists concretely in money form was shown in Chapter 7. When the presentation subsequently speaks of 'price' it is generally the case that a price expressing value is meant. To begin with I show the immediate influence of the capital relation

---

5 It is possible, not only that simple social reproduction may be balanced, but that balanced *growth* is possible. I shall not address the latter. However, Marx introduces simple reproduction only for didactic reasons. He argues it is inconsistent with capitalist production (Marx 1978, p. 586). For a treatment of Marx on expanded reproduction see Reuten 1998.

on prices (§ 81.3). Then I show these are mediated by the assumption of a uniform rate of profit, generating production prices (§ 82.3). Now here I take into account the differing organic composition of whole departments of production, such that I adduce the category of reproduction price (§ 83.3). It is these prices that in principle are those at which v and c are traded.

Only at this level of development of the concept of industrial capital is it shown as *actual*. Nonetheless these earlier determinants (especially exploitation) are *preserved* as part of the whole story. Since value is always at bottom socially determined, this means that in its finished form it is identical with reproduction price. For, taking account of the transformation of values requires the category of reproduction price to concretise it further, as a system grounded on its own inner determinations in accordance with which it reproduces itself.

Note that the category of 'actuality' does not refer to contingent empirical facts. Rather, a developed actuality achieves *its own effectivity*, which may be retained in the face of contingent disturbances of its action. Mere 'existences' lacking any essential reason for being, or failing to live up to it, are not properly actualities. Here total social capital is developed in its actuality, in this sense (see *Glossary*). It follows that the 'finished form' of value is 'reproduction price', because, if price is subject to further influences (e.g. those consequent on supply and demand), it is not thereby registering a *development* of value.

In § 82.3 I was concerned with the identity of all capitals abstractly, taking into account only their various organic compositions. Now, at a more concrete level, it is the identity of total social capital as a unified system of reproduction of itself that is to be assessed. Here the difference in organic composition of the departments is taken into account as it affects reproduction price and the general rate of profit.

I consider only two departments because my interest is in how their bringing into balance yields the resulting reproduction of industry. In developing these categories, I make no empirical claim about equilibrium; the test of equilibrium here is a logical corollary of the perfection of competition at this level of the theoretical presentation of the capital system in its minimum articulation. Indeed, RPs are still relatively remote from the fluctuations characteristic of empirical reality. But they are *logically* actual in the sense that they are *conceptually* conformable with the minimum structural dimensions required for the reproduction of the system.

All three levels of determination of price and profit we treated are required to fully comprehend the determination of value. But the more abstract levels yield only illustrative magnitudes while in § 83 we take the capital concept as a self-reproducing one. Thus individual prices and profits are not finally determined until comprehended as the result of capital's self-determination as a *concrete* whole. The minimum requirement for dialectical truth here is that the Idea of capital achieves actuality as the result of its own activity.

To be avoided is a false concreteness of the abstract level of form. It is important methodologically to treat each form in the hierarchy of determination at its appropriate level of analysis. Thus our account of production price later than simple price does not cancel, but conserves at its level, the fundamental facts of exploitation. Likewise the adoption below of a neo-Sraffian derivation of reproduction price does not overthrow the earlier analysed determinations.

At the start c and v are simply given magnitudes. Now they are to be theoretically produced as *reproduction prices*. They are situated in terms of the systemic reproduction of capital as a unified whole. It is important to notice that the earlier development of the category of production price is abstracted from this. In effect it is a purely *mathematical* exercise replacing an obviously absurd array of relative prices with a coherent one. But the study of departments is about real *periods* of production. This is somewhat obscured because it is presupposed that input prices and output prices are to be identified; for the system is taken to be in equilibrium; so it looks like a static exercise.

Remark: I underline again that, while the ratio of the organic composition of capital is a central determinant of reproduction prices, this leaves untouched the validity of the transformation procedure because there such difference is abstracted from, in using *cost price* as the relevant magnitude in the distribution of total surplus value. At its origin I consider v not as capital but as a revenue generated by capital; but when the system is turning over the disbursement of wages appears to capital as a cost provided from it. Since we are here concerned with such surface forms I define cost price as '$c + v$'.

Since I am interested in the philosophical significance of the value form categories rather than strictly economic analysis, I assume here that the system of simultaneous equations deployed by Piero Sraffa yields the RP.[6] He constructs an input/output matrix in terms of physical quantities, labour inputs, the wage share of 'income', and a system of simultaneous equations based on these physical quantities. From this is derived a system of relative prices. (What is missing is the relevance of the circuit of capital in money terms.)

These RPs are then the magnitudes of the c and v that I have all through the discussion of the transformation procedure taken as given. The question of how these magnitudes came about through a conflictual process of production is a separate question.

---

6 Sraffa 1960.

Two issues arise of theoretical importance. Moseley raises the issue that in the Sraffa system reproduction prices and the general rate of profit are determined *simultaneously* in contrast to the derivation of production prices on the basis of a prior profit rate. Furthermore, neo-Sraffians claim their system of determination of these variables makes the labour theory of value redundant. My view is that the Sraffa system is perfectly consistent with the transformation procedure set out here, because they address different issues we shall see; furthermore, the Sraffa system does not make the labour theory of value redundant because it is required in order to develop the concept of capital as one structured by *levels* of determination. (This second issue I take up later in an Addendum to this chapter.)

Remark: It is interesting that Moseley says he agrees that 'Sraffian theory can derive prices of [re]production and a rate of profit from physical quantities without reference to values [simple prices]'.[7] Moreover, he once thought this simultaneous determination of these variables consistent with his own account of the determination of production price in the context of capital's drive for a monetary surplus.[8] I think it *is* indeed consistent; and I assume the relative validity of both approaches.

Two different senses of 'determine' are pertinent here, because there are two different problems to be addressed. The *simultaneous* equations *discover* what prices and profits *are* ideally; but the *sequential* determination of prices and profits *explains* how they come about. There is no need to choose between these forms, because they are *complementary* determinations. (Moreover, borrowing this bit of economic analysis from Sraffa does not commit us to a generalised metaphysics of equilibrium which neglects capital's incessant revolutionising of value magnitudes.) Thus, firstly, there is the *discovery* of a consistent array of prices; for this some 'simultaneous' arithmetical operation is adequate. Secondly, there is a diachronic story to tell about how these value magnitudes are brought into existence through capital's drive to accumulate at a maximum rate of profit. It takes *time* to produce commodities, and this is a time of *contestation* over the exploitation of living labour. Both these enquiries coexist because they address different problems.

For simplicity 'reproduction' prices may be considered as long run equilibrium prices, and calculated on that basis by a system of simultaneous equations, in which inputs are identical with outputs across the complementary departments. If the simultaneous equations discover what the 'reproduction'

---

7   Moseley 2016, p. 231.
8   Moseley 2016, p. 25.

prices *are*, they do not explain the process of their *formation* ('upstream' as it were). For this their determination through the capital circuit, and through the contested terrain of exploitation is required, but vanishes in the result. The capitalist production process is always latently conflictual because the exploitation of labour power leaves its imprint on the *bodies* of the workers because they are inseparable from their labour; similarly, their *spirit* must be appropriated by capital so that their activity may be directed by others.[9]

So, behind the mathematical determination of 'reproduction' prices, lies the central problem of capital's drive to accumulate on the basis of revolutionising the process of production. Yet, if we abstract from their process of formation and take the resulting values 'after the harvest' so to speak, then the Sraffian theory is helpful *within these limits* to mechanically generate the prices and profits.

So 'reproduction' prices are those which would hold if the system were in equilibrium with a general rate of profit. Reproduction prices are needed so that departments *reproduce* each other in a coherent fashion, ideally with a uniform rate of profit.

Let us turn to the category 'rate of profit' and *the General Rate of Profit*. The rate of profit runs like a red thread through the system of capital. In our Table it runs down the third column according to the developing levels of concretion of the Idea. In § 81.3 the form is derived for a typical capital simply through refiguring the surplus on the cost price to generate a rate of profit distinct from the rate of exploitation predicated solely on the so-called 'variable capital'. But here, along with the category of reproduction price, a concretisation of the rate of profit is developed. At this level I take the systemic unity of the whole into consideration, including the consequences of a reproduction of total social capital through the interchanges of the departments of reproduction. *Now* I arrive at the general rate of profit on the basis of movements in the reproduction and development of total social capital. This yields what I also call the 'systemic rate of profit.' In sum, tracking down the third column shows the development of the rate of profit from a simple form to the measure of the system taken in its self-relation as a single whole.[10]

My own presentation *first* derives production prices, with its two aggregate conservations in place. The point of it is merely to demonstrate that a uniform rate of profit may hold if suitable valuations of commodities take place.

---

9   See Bellofiore 2004, p. 185 and p. 187.
10 Reproduction Prices may be calculated *either* by iterating outputs into inputs in the procedure of generating production prices *or* by calculating the set of simultaneous equations balancing departments. But it may be shown that the first method approaches asymptotically the results of the second.

In the *second* step of my presentation of the problem I consider the reproduction process required to harmonise the input/output matrix of the departments. I consider these reproduction prices to be the finished form of value; for simple prices, and production prices, have merely a virtual character because they arise at too abstract a level. Only with departments do we have a system which achieves the bare logical minimum for it to be self-sustaining (although of course many other conditions of existence must be satisfied).

Remark: I distance 'market price' from 'reproduction price' by taking into account the prevailing pattern of demand. In this way, I maintain the distinction between value as an inner determination and contingent market-driven phenomena, albeit it in my own terms.

Addendum: A Note on the Neo-Sraffian System

This discussion is a diversion from the systematic presentation, but it is required in order to underline the difference between Marxism and its most trenchant critique; a counter-critique, then, serves a useful purpose.

We begin with a special case: a thought experiment in which total automation of production is envisaged. This is used as a refutation of the labour theory of value.[11] The point is that even with no labour input it is argued that there are still positive profits. I agree that there may well be such 'profit' proportional to the time capitals are tied up in production. However, in truth this argument is a *reductio ad absurdum* of neo-Sraffian theory, because it shows that it cannot distinguish capitalism from other social forms of production. The so-called 'profit' is a hopeless abstraction from the reality of capitalist exploitation. In a totally automated economy those in possession of its fruits are not drawing profits from it but *rents*; for here production takes the form of a complexified natural force like a waterfall, albeit investment is required to maintain it. This error is an example of a general failure in neo-Sraffianism. Their physicalist ontology omits the central place of *social forms* in production. The mode of production is treated as a technical, not a social, process. Capital has a *specific* mode of pumping out surplus labour; it is through this that the 'surplus' is *created* in the first place; but neo-Sraffianism considers only the physical output 'after the harvest' so to speak. So the neo-Sraffian system is too narrowly focussed, and its latent physicalist metaphysics is wrong-headed. My work, by contrast, takes capitalism in terms of its *social ontology*. But the neo-Sraffians go

---

11   See Steedman 1985, pp 125–8.

from physics to prices such that any social concept of value is therewith made redundant. As Moseley says,[12] in their system labour power is no different from any other cost; 'exploitation' emerges merely in the distribution of the product.

However, I think it is possible to make use of their derivation of reproduction prices *on this narrow front*, while rejecting their metaphysics. For me too, the general rate of profit, the aggregates, and the specific reproduction prices, become determinate simultaneously. Neo-Sraffian critics of Marx say that this means that the labour theory is an unnecessary, and in any case faulty, detour on the way to such determinate prices; this in turn leads them to reject the labour theory of value. I do not draw this conclusion. In other parts of my presentation class struggle at the point of production is brought to the fore in the genesis of surplus value.

This is the nub of the issue. Neo-Sraffianism treats the entire production process as a purely physical one, takes it as given, and then uses a set of equations to derive reproduction prices. What is missing here is the social reality that production is the site of struggle, and that is the basis of the labour theory of value. The labour theory is not a detour, it is a foundation of value theory. Production is not a function of physical inputs alone; it is a contested social terrain in which there is a historically specific mode of pumping out labour from the immediate producers.

I abstract from different organic compositions at the start, not so much for expositional simplicity, but rather to focus on the central relation of capital, namely its relation to labour. Relations among capitals themselves raise different issues, and it is here that differences between capitals (rather than their common relation to labour) are relevant, and they are important in the formation of a general rate of profit. There is a *hierarchy* of determinations to be explored.

Thus labour exploitation is of great importance in exhibiting the very *constitution* of the capital relation. Only through overcoming labour's potential recalcitrance does capital *constitute* itself. This is surely the most fundamental fact about it, and it has to be developed prior to relations between capitals. Once it is seen how capital is constituted, one may leave aside any mention of class struggle through subsequent discussion of capitalist competition.

The issue may also be addressed as one of social standpoint. What is of interest to capital is the rate of profit as it is finally determined by competition between capitals. What is of interest to workers is the rate of exploitation determined by class forces on the basis of historically determined conditions of

---

12   Moseley 2016, p. 31.

production. What is conserved throughout the transformation of values is the division between wage goods and surplus goods; but these are socially measured differently; or rather, since I attach no concrete significance to so-called simple prices, these heaps of commodities cannot have determinate measure until capital sets, and reproduces, prices through competition. The existence of a surplus is ontologically prior to its measure, but its magnitude may be measured at different levels of determination.

Addendum: A Note on the Tendential Fall in the General Rate of Profit

The entire system of categorial form, treated in this book, is largely static in the sense that movement pertains to the self-reproduction of capital. But an important corollary of this is the dynamism giving rise to a direction of growth. We saw this already in the tendency to concentration and centralisation. But now we *add* to our discussion of the system-wide rate of profit a theorem deriving a tendential fall in the General Rate of Profit over time (TFRP). Rather than a value form, this is a tendency inherent to the capital system.

While this is a moment of capitalist economic *development*, not a structural *form*, I wish to say something brief about it, partly because of its importance in the literature. In my account, 'the falling rate of profit' is a *theorem* about systemic change, which should in no way be considered a *prediction*. As a theorem it is predicated on axioms. It would be a prediction only if these axioms were to be interpreted as unalterable empirical facts.

The context of the discussion is clearly that of the competition of capitals. In order to study this in its pure form the relation of capital to labour is abstracted from (just as that relation itself must first be studied in abstraction from differences between capitals).

When studying how capital exploits workers it is relevant to take as given the real wage. The methodological reason it is taken as given, and constant, in discussing the origin of surplus value is to rule out any explanation of profit based on its reduction. This assumption of a fixed real wage is maintained throughout the presentation of production price and reproduction price.

Only now is this assumption out of place; for the falling rate of profit theorem takes as axiomatic not a fixed real wage but a fixed rate of surplus value. The latter is inconsistent with the former. If the productive power of capital increases with a constant rate of surplus value then an increase in the output of use-values necessarily results; so *the real wage must rise*, even if its value remains the same, as also the surplus product. In truth the benefit of the increasing productive power of the economy might be given all to the workers, or all to capital; but our axiom assumes they benefit in proportion to the given *constant* rate of surplus value. The other possibilities are irrelevant to the TFRP *theorem*.

Why, here, is it methodologically pertinent to take as constant the *rate of surplus value*? For one thing, the tendency of the general rate of profit to fall is very definitely not to be explained by any tendency for the rate of surplus value to fall. However, more important is the need to take each level of determination of the system separately, and for this purpose holding others constant. The relevant parameter to take as given is the rate of surplus value because we now abstract from the study of the generation of surplus value, and we assume that capital has assigned to the workers what their share of the total value output is to be. This rate of *surplus value* determines the two shares of the pie, so to speak, but now we consider how capitals, as 'hostile brothers', compete to get the largest slice of *their* portion, and what the unintended consequences of that might be. (But of course there is no *empirical* necessity for the assumption of a fixed rate of surplus value. If we were to consider it empirically then an increase in it may generate a crisis of realisation.)

The mathematics of the TFRP theorem may be simply set out. Axiom 1: a constant rate of surplus value; axiom 2: all capitals try to improve the productivity of labour in their own firm by mechanisation, therewith, *ceteris paribus*, increasing the organic composition of capital; axiom 3: surplus value arises only from 'variable capital'. Conclusion: the rate of profit falls because s moves in line with v, yet c increases relative to v as more powerful machines are put at the disposal of the workers; hence the profit ratio '$s/(v + c)$' falls.

(However, prices register not merely the presence of new value consequent on the exploitation of labour but also the *resurrection* of the value embodied in the constant capital productively consumed, as I explain above.)

Once it is understood we have here a theorem, then the so-called 'counter-tendencies' to the TFRP fall on very different logical levels. First, take an increase in the rate of *surplus value*; this is ruled out by the axioms and thus fails, as an objection to the theorem. Second, consider shortening of turnover time; this certainly increases the rate of profit, but it is ruled out by the usual *ceteris paribus* conditions accompanying all theorems. Finally, we reach a genuine counter-tendency in that it takes us to the heart of the claim here being made. This is that there is a problem with the axioms themselves; they assume that the only relevant effect of an increase in productive power is to increase the proportion of 'c' to 'v'; this is because these new machines are supposed to be more expensive. But the very point of their introduction is to cheapen unit costs. Such cheapening surely applies also to these machines themselves, as their supply generalises. So, although it is likely they are more expensive than those which they replace, there is a genuine counter-tendency to consider.

The tendency is thus combined in reality with many others that I take to be outside the framework of this treatise. Moreover, in reality the 'counter-tendencies' may prevail over the so-called 'tendency'. The latter, then, cannot be identified with a predictable '*trend*'. (For the distinction between an intrinsic *tendency* and an empirical *trend* see *Glossary*.)

It remains to refute a foolish objection: that capitalists would never do anything to reduce their rate of profit. The point here is that, under competitive conditions, every capital in a given field tries to get ahead of the others by seeking to be the first to use new technology therewith gaining a 'technological rent'. But when everyone catches up, they are all worse off. The objection rests on a fallacy of composition: it takes all capitals to act as one does, but in reality these capitals do not act in the aggregate, but singly. Normally there are several competing firms which may be considered as forming a *stratified* system, with those using the best technology at the top and those still employing old technology at the bottom (the latter may still make an operating profit so are not driven out immediately). Firms seeking to improve their position in the stratification inadvertently undermine the profitability of the sector itself.[13]

What is the conclusion at which I arrive? The TFRP theorem is valid. *However*, if it is given an empirical interpretation, the axioms have to be checked against the facts, and its effects must be considered as subject to the influence of other tendencies.

Summary

This long chapter on the system of industrial capital is structured according to the moments of the Concept in two axes which intersect. There is capital's reflection *within* itself, and there is the reflection of capitals *against* one another. The system is doubly determined throughout by the ideal value forms, such as price and profit, on the one hand, and, on the other, the material conditions of these, such as exploited labour and departments of reproduction.

The presentation begins at the most abstract level by developing the elementary notion of valorisation as a circuit of capital, showing how capital transforms itself from a monetary investment into the required factors of pro-

---

13 Stratification is exhaustively discussed in Reuten 2019. For a thorough discussion of the TFRP, considered dynamically and cyclically, see Reuten and Williams 1989, pp. 116–38.

duction; then as productive capital it valorises itself in the shape of the produced commodity, which is then transformed to money again. The most important philosophical point here is that capital cannot be identified with any of these functional forms, but is constituted in its *movement* through them. Only because the three forms are taken up by the encompassing circuit do they function *as capital*. The final term at this relatively abstract level of the presentation is that of the profit rate in which the surplus is related to the cost price. Here the term 'simple price' is introduced but it is important to take note of the fact that, just because of its overly simple determination, its magnitude is unexplained; any such magnitude here is to be deemed *unactual*. The next phase of the exposition takes a step closer to actuality by taking into consideration the effects of competition. First of all, the distinction between absolute and relative surplus value is explained. Then, having distinguished in the cost price the components constant capital and variable capital, the important notion of the organic composition of capital, namely their ratio, is introduced. This eventuates in the necessity for a transformation procedure through which the form of production price replaces simple price. Production prices are generated by adding to cost prices a surplus value on the assumption that a uniform rate of profit obtains. This is a purely conceptual argument. No claim is made about the empirical status of uniformity; nor is the actual general rate of profit explained until we address the most concrete level of the system, namely that which takes as its theme the forms characterising total social capital. This begins with the notion of a 'law of accumulation' (taken from Marx), which foregrounds the concentration and centralisation of capital, together with the role of a reserve army of labour. Then (following Marx again) two departments of reproduction, complementing each other, are described, one producing capital goods, and the other consumer goods. The balance condition between them is outlined but this makes no claim to empirical necessity, for revolutions in value continually disturb any such tendency. What is important now is that these departments may well differ in their organic composition. So the problem of assigning a *production* price, as was done earlier, is complemented by the more complex issue of finding the determinations of *reproduction* price on the assumption that in equilibrium input prices and output prices of the departments are consistent with each other. No claim about the empirical reality of such equilibrium is asserted. Nonetheless this is the ideal basis on which the forms of reproduction price, and the general rate of profit, are developed. Whatever further determinants of price remain to be addressed, the presentation has now reached an important result; for I concretise our investigation of valorisation within the framework of competition, and present the system in terms of its fundamental conditions of reproduction.

CHAPTER 14

The Dual Ontology of Capital

This chapter is not part of the systematic presentation itself (hence its lack of section numbers denoting the introduction of a new form). Rather, it continues the reflections of Part 1, in that I stand back, as it were, to situate what was presented in the previous chapter in the context of a 'bigger picture' of my diagnosis of the inverted world of capital.

The transformation problem (of supposed 'values' into supposed 'prices') is usually thought to require a mathematical fix; if such a fix is ruled invalid then the Marxian theory is to be abandoned. In truth, the supposed problem is due to a fundamental confusion between the realm of material processes and the ideal movement of capital; these combine only uncertainly. Right at the start value is to be taken here as distinct from, indeed opposed to, use-value. Later, however, once the value system is shown to take possession of the material process of production, use-value must be granted as having its economic determinacy. But – and this is crucial – to collapse the value system into material determinants (for example, concrete labour times) is to reduce value theory to a naturalism. This neglects the specific determinacy of capitalist *social* relations. Such a neglect is encouraged by the way capital occludes social relations and makes it look as if material production is the be-all and end-all.

In truth the transformation problem has an *ontological basis*. Once one locates the transformation procedure in the context of the interpenetration of two opposed systems of determination, two things follow. First, one understands why there is a problem for the naturalistic approach; second, one understands there is really no problem at all. The problem arises only if it is assumed that c and v are measured first in simple prices (SP); but there is no reason to make such an absurd assumption and every reason not to do so, for the magnitude of these prices is systemically achieved only through 'reproduction price' (RP).

In the reproduction of capital as a system, the relation of competition *between* capitals distorts, or even subverts, the capital relation in the narrow sense. However, this is of no moment since simple prices derived from the latter are in truth merely virtual, just numerical illustrations of the abstract shape of the capitalist relations.[1]

---

1 This has not been generally recognised; for F. Engels (in his *Supplement* to Marx's *Capital* III) persuasively advanced the view that a regime of 'simple commodity production' would yield

This is because the life of capital is concretely determined only as competition between many capitals. Once competition is taken seriously the difference between capitals makes a lot of difference to the constitution of the whole. Because capital reproduces itself only through interchanges between departments at prices of reproduction, these categories are central to the capital concept. I argued above that prices of reproduction are the *finished form* of value because they are intrinsic to capital's reflection on itself in its total interconnectedness. What causes the emergence of a problem is the requirement that departments balance which means that so-called input prices and so-called output prices must be the same. However, the reproduction prices ensure there is a uniform rate of profit and departments are integrated.

While I have questioned the meaningfulness of simple prices, I accept the great importance of what underlies them, namely the labour times required to produce the wage bundle and the surplus product. The rate of 'exploitation' given in the ratio of the labour 'embodied' in surplus goods (whether luxuries or capital goods) to the labour 'embodied' in wage goods is *prior* to, and independent of, the determination of prices. Moreover, it gives something of a parallel to exploitation in pre-capitalist systems such as the direct appropriation of slave labour.

Even if it were allowable to give sense to simple prices of wage goods and surplus product, it still does not follow that any conservation of their aggregates should obtain. We are dealing with quite different states of the same thing; the initial state is determined by the one-dimensional structure of exploitation; the second, two-dimensional state, re-determines the first by the impact of relations between capitals.

If v and c are calculated at SP their magnitudes will normally differ from those calculated in terms of transformed values, of RP. If it is stipulated that total SP is unchanged when transformed to total RP, the *balance* of v and c within all cost prices, and their aggregates, change. This means that the total profit (added value minus v) in SP terms will differ from that in RP terms, and the relevant rates of profit also.

This can of worms is avoided if v and c are given as RP in the first place, hence not in need of any transformation. What remains true at the level of the aggregate is that, with all measures in RP, the total M invested yields the total M', with the added value, total m, given, and the total sv easily derivable, together with the GRP. The MELT links the total added value with the

---

determinate values, and that such determinacy would carry over to what he called the 'modified' prices of capitalist production. I have elsewhere demolished Engels's view; see Arthur 2005b.

total socially necessary labour time, as we have seen. This fundamental theorem, so to speak, lies at the basis of the determination, in the sense of precondition, of prices and profit, albeit that it leaves RPs yet to be explained in full.

Incommensurability of different states of the same thing is well known in physics: ice is bigger than the same amount of liquid water, indeed here even the normal unit of measure differs, litres and cubic centimetres. In our case, we are dealing with socially determined ideal magnitudes. How much less, then, should we expect conservation across situations in which additional social relations come into play? It helps when dealing with the transformation of value into more finished forms to recall that value is an ideally constituted substance. Thus it is 'soft', so to speak, and re-formed according to the forces to which it is subjected.

The general rate of profit in money terms, and reproduction prices, are mathematically co-determined (whether simultaneous equations, or an iterative procedure, are utilised). But ontologically prior is the physical mass of waged goods and surplus product. This mass cannot be changed by how it is priced, and how value is distributed in such terms. If the distribution of the product cannot be changed in physical terms, the social *measure* of its fractions is not theoretically determinate until the level of reproduction prices. However, one can always retrospectively impute such 'finished' values to the inputs of immediate production, and then the 'conservations' hold tautologically, because the inputs are now given in *ex post* prices, 'already transformed' so to speak.

The material process, namely the regulation and exploitation of labour, other things being equal, would express itself at a level of phenomenal prices in linear fashion. However, capital, as a peculiar form of production, exerts formal determination on the supposed content. There is a 'problem' if we recall (§ 52) that materially living labour is subsumed, appropriated, and exploited, by capital, but it is in itself *other* than capital. So we need now to show how this plays out within the ideal system of pricing. It is capital, according to *its* self-determining movement, that locates living labour as the other that must be appropriated. It is capital, with its own measure of itself as a rate of accumulation, that determines labour is to be measured in time, not in intensity or whatever, and that a relevant issue is not merely the rate at which new value is added but the rate at which the constant capital is resurrected.

The *dual ontology* of capital refers to the original separation between material and ideal levels of reality. The latter is the *value* system and, as such, is itself a *single* system; there is no question of counterposing value and price because value is actual only as price, and the transformation procedure moves from an overly abstract account of value to a more concrete, because systemically determined, one.

The importance of the material level is underlined by Riccardo Bellofiore.[2] He stresses the salience of the category 'real wage' (which is taken as given by Marx through most of his argument). He draws attention to the crucial role played by the division of the product between the real wage and the surplus product. Indeed, if the labour time to produce the real wage took the whole day there would be no surplus for capital to appropriate. This ratio is a real measure of exploitation and our theory must explain how it is reproduced. In order to do this, it is convenient to keep the real wage constant through the analysis (until the tendency to the falling rate of profit is addressed).

It is perfectly consistent with this presupposition to assume at the value level that so-called variable capital is likewise fixed. There is no need to favour one constant over the other. The value of the real wage bundle must be ultimately explained; but at the start it may be taken as given, and not requiring any transformation. (See § 83.3.)

It follows that the duality gives rise to *two different definitions* of 'necessary' (and hence 'surplus') labour: one refers to the labour *required* to produce the real wage bundle; the other refers to the labour *yielded* to get the money wage to purchase it, at prevailing prices. These are two different magnitudes if, for instance, we take the real wage bundle at production prices.

One problem with capital is the way the underlying material reality is obscured by the value system through which capital cognises it. If the source of surplus value is surplus labour this *qualitative* point is obscured by the highly mediated determination of its *magnitude*, and the apparent ratio of exploitation in value terms. That is why it is essential to begin with the elementary capital relation in order to show how the surplus is produced in the struggle of class against class before addressing the more complicated relationships consequent on capital competition. Nonetheless the systemic determination of value is also crucial.

The ontological duality reaches right back to the absenting of use-value at the start of the value form dialectic, because ideality, although a fold in materiality, has its own effectivity; the two realms interpenetrate, such that each movement conditions the other. There is no 'third' to these two; so the capital system is intrinsically unstable, albeit it may find temporary 'fixes' to its problems.

---

[2] Bellofiore 2004, p. 208.

When we accept some such equilibrium derivation of RP and GRP as Sraffian theory proposes, this does not dispose of the *deeper ontological reality* intrinsic to the capital relation. Moreover, even within the value system, the magnitudes of c and v theoretically *discovered* by simultaneous equations cannot displace the *explanation* of their actual *production* through the exploitation of living labour in the capital circuit.

The TP derives PP timelessly in making a mathematical calculation of how surplus value is distributed to each capital. However, the *origin* of total surplus value depends upon class struggle at the point of production over capital's effort to pump out labour from the recalcitrant labour force. It is not necessary to know what determines c and v in order to explain the production of surplus value as the outcome of exploitation.

Albeit the traditional transformation 'problem' is a false one, the material organisation of living labour must be taken as the reality presupposed to the price and profit questions. Certainly, I think it *is* a problem that the price determinations occlude the fundamental material relation between capital and labour, in which the real wage allocated to labour is a key parameter reproduced by the system. (Notice that any transformation from simple prices to production prices will change the general rate of surplus value, because at production prices aggregate surplus-value and aggregate wages, sufficient to cover the real wage, will normally differ from the same magnitudes as they were expressed in simple immediate prices.)

Capital's regime of truth confuses the ideal and material realms; so we must deconstruct this double-sidedness of capital. In the capital system there is an identity-in-difference; for the same 'stuff' is differently form-determined when considered in the context of a class relation, and when considered as 'valued' in its ideal actualisation through capitalist competition. Explaining the division of net material output is as important as explaining the monetary increment appropriated by capital.

Certainly, because this system is exclusively in monetary terms, it makes no sense to refer prices back to some sort of 'labour values' measured in time.[3] However, such monetary realisation of value, and surplus value, does not mean that the physical rate of exploitation, expressed in virtual labour hours, is irrelevant. The *physical* rate compares the labour required to produce the real wage with the expropriated labour required to produce surplus goods. Moreover, this

---

[3] 'Labour value' is not a term used by Marx. Both Fred Moseley and Geert Reuten espouse a 'single system' of value relations, but each for different reasons. See Moseley 2016 and Reuten 2019, pp. 69–71 and 74–6. Moseley 2016 claims to be an interpretation of Marx, but Reuten 2017 has a different take on Marx's exposition.

rate is of great interest to both classes, and determined in the struggle at the point of production. Whatever the price rule actually in operation this physical rate remains a crucial underlying parameter.

It is not just a question of abstracting out an important variable for study, for this abstraction is rooted in the ontological duality characteristic of the capital system. On the one hand, we have the material side of the economic metabolism, of prime interest to workers; on the other we have the ideal side, predicated on the self-movement of capital, wherein it re-conceptualises the material variables under its alien measures. Thus the working of the system must be appreciated from two class standpoints.

If the concretisation of the abstract notions, through which capital *comprehends* itself, fails to preserve the material register of exploitation this is no reason to neglect this fundamental material form. There is here a deeper truth, obscured by the measures capital takes to be real, namely the truth of exploitation in all its rawness.

In all this the real wage is of basic importance to the working class. C–M–C′ is the workers' circuit which allows labour power to be made available for purchase by capital, but which is reproduced domestically insofar as money wages purchase the real wage bundle. The workers are interested in how long it is necessary to labour in order to fund the real wage; anything above this is surplus labour for capital. This is a key ratio regardless of how the real wage is *priced*. It is the same as the rate of exploitation *in money terms*. In value analysis it is this time that counts as necessary labour; surplus labour time above that is appropriated by capital.

This ratio of necessary and surplus labour is not necessarily identical with that between the labour required to *produce* the real wage bundle itself and the labour required to *produce* the surplus product. As we see in the table of TP, if *capital a* is a representative fraction of the means of production department, and *capital b* is a representative fraction of the real wage department, it follows that the rate of exploitation registered in the simple price of each output is changed if the rate is recalculated in *production prices*. But the final determination of the rate of surplus value in money terms is of no importance for the workers, and their own competition. It is of concern to capital as the outcome of capital's competition.

Which system do the workers care about? Trapped as they are in the duality, they are doubly determined; immediately they want a money wage to cover the cost of the real wage, however priced, so that leads to one definition of 'necessary labour time'; but the underlying reality of the labour time required to produce the real wage is another way of looking at their exploitation. The second has the (dis)advantage of continuity with other historical forms of expropriating labour that were less disguised than here; for here the intuitively obvious material measures are overturned by money measures. Given capitalist mystification, uncovering this layer of reality is an achievement quite as much as insight into how the ideality of profit works.

In considering this ontological duality, there is felt a tension between two methodological principles. We are surely concerned to identify, and analyse, the basic law of motion of a system, disregarding superficial perturbations. This might lead us to prioritise 'labour values' measured in simple prices. Yet, at the same time, since it is a basic principle of dialectic that truth pertains only to system, then such labour values, if wrongly taken as substantively valid, are nothing but a false concretisation, because the true concrete is the totality, of which every part is subject to systemic determination. From this second point of view, simple prices are, at best, purely virtual, illustrating a fundamental relation to be sure, but a relation (the capital relation) that is co-determinant with others (the relation between capitals, for instance) that constitute the totality. To insist that *physical* exploitation (the ratio of labour time embodied in the surplus product to that embodied in the real wage) must be conserved in its *socially measured* shape is an abstract materialism that does not grasp the ideality of social form.

This last consideration is very powerful from the point of view of systematic dialectic. Yet it surely puts in question the fundamental Marxian theorem: that all value arises from the exploitation of labour. In my opinion this last can be supported only on ontological grounds, not on the claim that labour inputs are the best predictor of empirical prices, for instance. The exploitation of living labour is the *explanation* of the genesis of new value. This ontological truth remains fundamental, *whatever* the prices socially assigned.

So far from value being an ahistorical form distorted by capitalist relations it is only within capitalism that value becomes a truth. The peculiarity of capital is that the source of value in *labour* is so hidden, that it looks as if value is the reward for *capital's* toil and trouble. (How could it be otherwise if there is a pro rata reward for the whole of capital?) Nevertheless, once it is recognised that capital is a social form with ontological depth, categories holding at one level may be redefined, or even inverted, at another. Because there is interpenetration of opposites, ideality and materiality, each side is reproduced by its other; but neither system reduces otherness to its *own* other.

First capital *encounters* labour power in exteriority, then internalises it through the wage-form, and then subsumes living labour under the capital relation that reproduces it in its position as capital's own other. The determination of magnitude looks as if it flows from labour time, but this is a determined determinant for it is capital that pumps out living labour in the most efficient way available to it. In this way, the linear determination of value by labour is at the same time intrinsic to the spiral movement of capital accumulation.

Value is *real* only as a highly mediated result, because it is embodied in a totality of relations, not a single commodity. I myself simplify value when I identify it with reproduction prices in abstraction from market contingencies such as supply and demand. Many would say this is wrong because socially necessary labour time is a function of demand, e.g. an oversupply and a fall in value is consequent on 'wasted labour'. For me it is legitimate to distinguish value from market prices if the former is a function of the *minimum* set of determinations that yield a concept of self-mediated reproduction no matter how abstractly this is taken. Hence the finished form of value is the reproduction price and then more concrete determinations further modify prices on the market.

However, if one gives magnitudes at too abstract a level, these merely *illustrate* the simple determinations concerned, but must not be considered as being *real* values, merely taken apart from secondary influences. They are the result of a violent abstraction from the real process of value determination. But they reflect something that *is* real, namely the *material* process of exploitation which in one sense is the very nature of the economic metabolism, despite the impossibility of going smoothly from so-called 'labour values' to prices of production. This impossibility is founded on the *ontological inversion* that transforms in a very deep sense the magnitudes concerned. Contrary to neo-Sraffians, the labour ratios are not transformed out of existence; they remain as a discrepant surd in the ideal value system, reflecting the *material* reality of capitalism.

Although distribution cannot change the total mass produced, it is necessary to consider carefully *what* this mass is. It is the physical mass of workers' real wages and the corresponding surplus goods. But how these are *socially expressed as value* can be changed. Under the (virtual) price rule of 'simple prices' we get one aggregate value, under the price rule of 'reproduction prices' we get another. The former makes explicit the underlying class relation, the latter is the form under which capitals fight for their shares. Because these measures are rooted in different ways of conceptualising production, there is no possibility of 'deriving' one from the other. Yet both measures show us something *real* about the economy; it is not a matter of choosing one as more adequate. This becomes clear if we attend to the basic fact of expropriated labour. At the material level, there obtains a ratio between the labour times required to produce the real wage and that required to produce surplus product. At the ideal level, there is a different measure: the labour required to gain the money wage and the surplus labour that underpins surplus value. Both material and ideal measures co-exist.

Summary

This chapter looks at the ontological basis of the transformation 'problem' in the dual ontology of capital, as it contains within itself ideal and material relations. Over-prioritising the material side leads to a naturalism of the value form, neglecting its *socially specific* character. Over-prioritising the ideal side leads to the occlusion of the economic effectivity of material determinants. The real wage and the surplus product are certainly material presuppositions of the TP. What is problematic is their reading as conditions of social forms, and especially of the systemically determined value measures. In this broad context are situated the forms addressed in the previous chapter, namely simple rice, production price, and reproduction price.

CHAPTER 15

Absolute Capital

§ 9   Absolute Capital

I refused the category of 'Absolute Idea' in Division I above, for the latter culminates in a contradiction intrinsic to the pure logic of the capital concept. But, when the unity of the value form dialectic, and material production, is established, the Idea of capital articulates the system of industrial capital: the culmination of this is the form of capital as *Absolute Idea*. In this the 'spirit of capital' is embodied in the financial system because it is there that the Idea of capital achieves systematic reflexivity, and all particularity is subsumed in a universal measure of itself, the prevailing rate of interest on capital.

Absolute capital unites the formal notion of capital with the finite objectivity of departments of industry. The general rate of profit is a measure of the fruitfulness of industry, but with financial capital we find capital reflecting on itself, and making the aim of accumulation explicit in the capital markets. It is the form of capital in its purity in which 'the spirit of capitalism' is present in its notional shape. In the capital market the system seems formally closed. However, the *source* of surplus lies ultimately in industry so capital must sink into this material substance, submit itself to the rigours of 'the labour of the negative' to actualise itself. But production is ever open to otherness, hence to contingency.

This section is divided as follows. § 91 Absolute Capital in Its Notion: The Banking System, Credit, *ex nihilo* Money; § 92 Externalisation of the Moments of the Circuit of Capital: § 92.1 Finance; § 92.2 Commerce; § 92.3 Industrial Production Proper; § 93 Capital as Absolute Idea Unites the above Differences in a Whole of Intermediation.

§ 91   *Absolute Capital in Its Notion*

Let us consider first the contrast between money as a *commodity* and money *proper*. At the level of 'Essence', the value of commodity A is supposed to be commodity B; but the value of B is A. This immanence cannot be sustained. We simply have the barter of the associated use-values. Money, as value in autonomous form, allows each commodity to register its value in money, and thus they may then stand as equal to each other *as values*.

Now, initially in the presentation, a certain commodity, gold, figures as the bearer of money. Although a commodity, it is posited as *counting* as money. But this means barter is still not transcended. All commodities enter circulation by sale, *except gold*. It enters as a produced commodity *with* a potential value, which remains unexpressed in price, hence it could be said to enter through barter. In order for money to oppose itself to commodities *as money*, not as any sort of commodity, this defect has to be overcome. Money must be as immaterial as value itself.

This does not mean that the presentation was in error in first showing how a commodity counted as money. The supersession of commodity money now certainly takes shape as a criticism of it; *but* this 'self-criticism' is *immanent* to the presentation itself. The systematic dialectic develops precisely through positing and negating every form presented. The original form of money is now sublated: what is preserved is the positing of the presupposition that value must achieve autonomy; what is discarded is the makeshift wherewith a commodity, excluded from others, is designated as the bearer of value in autonomous form.

Since it cannot be present as a peculiar commodity, but purely *as* money, it must first be created from *outside* the realm of commodities, and then be presented to them. The logic of the value form does not allow that there is anything outside the realm of commodities, so money must be created *from nothing*. Thus banks create credit money *ex nihilo*. Such money is value in genuinely autonomous form, because not created first as use-value that happens to be valuable. So this nothingness inhabiting money repeats the earlier dialectic in being *pure form*, in this case the form of the credit/debit relation. However, only if the money created *as money* blossoms into money *as capital* does it achieve actual presence, when the banker, and the industrialist, show a profit on their books.

Bank-issued money is denominated in a historically given standard; but that is now a meaningless reference, with inconvertible notes issued by the Central Bank. What counts now is the trustworthiness of banks, and of the state in the case of Central Bank money. The Central Bank issuing legal tender is the Absolute Idea of capital existent *logically* before the appearance of industry and commerce. However, even if the state grants a monopoly to the Central Bank to issue 'legal tender money notes', there is no such monopoly to *create* money, for every bank can issue lines of credit, albeit denominated in 'legal tender'.[1] *Ex nihilo* credit money, issued by the banking system, enters circulation without being the counterpart of previously produced commodities.

---

1 See Reuten 2019, p. 113.

For value to be properly self-valorising, industrial capital need not be funded from its own limited resources, perhaps from sales, but have available to it funds advanced by banks.[2] The final apotheosis of the value system appears in the shape of bank credit. In a perfected capitalist system 'saving' is unnecessary to capital investment.[3] In principle, the entire outlay may be covered by a line of credit created *ex nihilo* by a bank. This is the only money immanent to capital. The importance of bank money is that this is the money which capital itself creates, since banks are a particular form of capital. Such money is not an external given. (Moreover, it is a limitation of a commodity money system that the funds required to accelerate economic growth can only come from newly produced gold. Non-monetary uses of gold compete with its monetary, of course. So this creates a further complication.)

Let us consider a pure case of credit, in which money is money of account, and the firm has its account at the bank issuing the loan. (All accounts are denominated in the socially accepted monetary medium.) When the firm borrows a sum of money from the bank this appears as a credit in the firm's account, and at the same time as an entry on the asset side of the bank's ledger, because the firm has an obligation to pay; and this is balanced by booking the same sum as a liability on the other side of the bank's ledger, because the bank guarantees to service cheques issued by the firm.

It is striking that this is a real case of '*creation out of nothing*'. Once again we find at the conclusion of the value form presentation the very form with which I began: nothingness.

It will be recalled that, when I began with 'Nothing', I said this gains presence as 'nothingness', if it were possible to sustain the dialectic of negativity wherewith Being is posited as not not-Nothing. This falls in on itself unless concretised in a determinate relation with another, equally Nothing, such that the not-Nothing is, in the second Nothing, *something other*. Then, given two commodities, the commodity defines itself as other than its other, albeit that neither has any determinacy except that constituted in their relation of exchangeableness. The commodity becomes determinate in its Being-for-another, that is to say, when it realises its exchangeableness in another commodity. But this relation is not self-grounded for it exists only on the condition that two commodities are present.

However, the extraordinary feature of *ex nihilo* money is that the difference is brought to birth purely *formally*. Now something *is there* solely in virtue of

---

2 For Marx on the credit system see Campbell 2002a, pp. 212–27.
3 See Reuten 2019, p. 147, p. 172.

its *inner* difference, which allows the determinacy of the relation to obtain as *pure form*, without the need for bearers such as commodities to sustain the difference. Here, then, value arises out of its own movement. It is *self-grounded*. Nothingness makes itself present in *ex nihilo* credit money as pure form in the credit-debit relation.

Originally value emerged as the possible result of the relation established between two commodities. Yet since as material beings these are completely heterogeneous it seems value is merely the contrary of use-value; in itself it is *nothing*. Yet nothingness achieves its own *determinacy* in the development of the value form; it becomes autonomous as money. Earlier we took it that there must be a commodity *bearer* of money, such as gold. Now, with the creation of money *ex nihilo*, value finally *liberates* itself from commodities. It is present without being the value *of* something. In general it makes possible the domination of the money form of value over the commodity form and it is the basis of capital's ability to determine the direction of production.

Just as at the start I took commodities to be essentially related as values, so now value is present in a relation. A relation of what exactly? An *absolute relation* of value to value, as such. When creating a line of credit for a firm, the bank's ledger lists assets and liabilities created by striking a balance between form-determinations of nothingness. It is present only in the determinate relation of positive and negative sums of money in the ledger, which sums sum to ... *nothing*. Both are clearly present. Yet these determinacies are effective in economic circuits because of the *determinate reflection* of its two complements.

The money created is *neither* the credit, *nor* the liability; it is the third that is *identical in their opposition*. Yet the third is made present *only* as the difference (it is neither the positive *nor* the negative) of the difference (the positive *and* the negative). It is nothing in itself, but it *exists* in its circulation. There it is actually effective. When a loan is redeemed it might seem that the sum is once again simply zero; but there is something new, the interest paid (or continuing to be paid if the loan is unredeemed). This is indeed the creation of something out of nothing. Yet this new value *does* correspond to a material result, it is diverted from the sale of the newly produced commodities containing social surplus value.

If all goes well the capital and interest will be covered by final sales. But notice that here there is a *temporal inversion*; value existed as credit *before* value was produced by the firms concerned. Value has been produced by value. Having thoroughly subsumed its material bearer, capital appears grounded on itself. All other spheres it subsumes in various ways to its ends. When new money is advanced to firms, this may be characterised as 'ideal capital'. It *becomes* real only as active capital in industry when it generates returns to the originating bank: value creates value; capital creates capital. This is capital as Absolute Idea.

§ 92 Externalisation of Inner Moments of the Circuit of Capital

Implicitly, the existence of banks means that the form of money capital has been differentiated from capital in production as a particular moment. In general we find the externalisation of the moments of the circuit of capital present on a social scale. Earlier we saw that the circuits of money-capital/production-capital/commodity-capital are in unity with each other implicitly, in that each moment can be mediator or mediated according to the point of view taken on it. This notional difference implicit in the metamorphoses of capital becomes determinately posited when they are externalised differentially in autonomous shape, and then again united in absolute capital, or *capital as absolute reality*. Thus these functional moments also take shape explicitly, 'for themselves' so to speak, as three distinct particularisations of capital, financial capital, commercial capital, and industrial capital in the strict sense, distinguished from the other two.

Remark: Earlier (§ 43) I treated money-lending capital, and merchant capital, before industrial capital, because they have fewer logical presuppositions than it. It is important that, although these forms of capital pre-existed industrial capital, they have been transformed by industrial capital itself into its own moments in the shape of finance and commerce. As moments of the entire system of capital they are thoroughly determined in their action by their specific function within it.

§ 92.1 Finance

The financial system gives the universal form of capital an autonomous existence, alongside that of the 'real' individual capitals. In the capital markets, in which financial firms compete, there is a prevailing rate of interest. Capital markets spring naturally from the identity in form of all capitals. Here capital posited in a *totality* has ontological priority over the individual elements, just insofar as the system is totally permeable, i.e. capital can move. Finance capital can move directly; industrial capital can liquidate in one branch and invest in another. Every capital can be shown to be ahead or behind the game through the concrete existence of a general rate of profit established in the average rate of interest, even though the latter is not a simple expression of the former. Capital here exists as *universal capital*, under the control of the bankers as representatives of social capital. It is distributed through the banking system in accordance with the specific requirements of production.

Here all capital's determinations are dissolved and its material elements are occluded. Money is in truth the very shape in which the distinctions between commodities as different use-values are obliterated, and hence also the corresponding distinctions between industrial capitals, which consist of these commodities and the conditions of their production. In the reproduction process of industrial capital, the money form is an evanescent moment. But on the capital market, by contrast, capital always exists in this form. The financial institutions of capital provide both a rough measure of the general rate of profit and the facilities whereby financial capital can be mobilised from one sphere of production to another accordingly.

The 'personification' of capital in the shape of 'the industrialist' is complemented by that of 'the banker'. Bankers' judgements align reality with the demands of the capital concept. This secures a form of *ante-validation* of productive labour.[4] Ante-validation is not merely a one-to-one relation of a bank to a firm, but the regulation by the financial system of total social capital and its creation and distribution. When bank finance to industry ante-validates valorisation it at the same time posits the living labours as carriers of a homogenous social substance. Thus the whole circuit of industrial capital is form-determined.[5]

Bank advances to firms institute a 'meta-circuit' in that there is a reflux of interest to the bank from the circuit of industrial capital. However, its formal character means the financial sector is more than a provider of a service to industry. It has its own determinations, which give rise to such phenomena as the process of 'financialisation', 'derivative trading' and so forth.

Thus the form 'money as money', here a fund, remains as a distinct moment in the reproduction of capital. Although distinct, this moment, as bank finance, is a necessary complement to the reproduction of industrial capital. Moreover, it has broader functions, such as the increasing importance of the provision of consumer credit, especially to the working class. The workers' circuit is C–M–C', but they may be forced to borrow means of payment. The money, serving as an intermediary for the worker, functions for capital as a moment of capital. This leads to the compulsion on labourers to become subordinate to capital in a way complementary to that which forces them to seek employment.[6]

---

4 For penetrating discussion of the category of 'ante-validation' see the work of Riccardo Bellofiore: Bellofiore 2004, pp. 188–9; Bellofiore 2019, p. 531. Also see on 'pre-validation' Reuten and Williams 1989, pp. 83–4, and Reuten 2019, p. 686.
5 This is an important point in Bellofiore's reconstruction of Marx's monetary theory; it allows him to finesse problems that are supposed to arise if theory abandons the assumption that money is a commodity. See Bellofiore 2004, p. 200; 2018, pp. 353–88.
6 Reuten 2019, pp. 187–8.

Finance is the all-embracing constellation of the capitalist economy. Abstractly, all types of credit fall under the form of a M–M′ circuit necessary to it.[7]

§92.2   Commerce

Commercial firms specialise in distributing and marketing particular commodities to other firms and to households. In this sphere, contingency runs riot in ever more absurd product lines. (This is the place for a discussion of how need and demand are manipulated by capital.)

§92.3   Industrial Production Proper

Industrial production, narrowly considered, shows all capitals bent on accumulation are in a similar relation to their other, namely the working class. The capitalist, already acting under the purview of the banks, now attempts to 'pre-commensurate' the values they work with, and produce, to suit the ordinary demand on the market. They anticipate the realisation of expected value on the market by engaging in this ideal *pre-commensuration*.[8]

While the production process goes on, capital is in 'otherness' but nonetheless exercises hegemony over it. The subsumption of material production by the ideal valorisation process is achieved because it is value-formed from start to finish: bank finance at the start, and realisation of anticipated added value at the end, of the circuit. This results in the formal determination of the material process, thus re-determined according to capital's requirements. The specifically capitalist production process cannot be understood without this. (It is certainly not an ahistorical production merely represented in a commodity output in circulation.)

§93   *The Absolute Idea of Capital*

The spheres of finance, commerce, and industry are systematically unified to form the capital system. The *Absolute Idea of Capital* unites these differences in a whole of intermediation. Each may be considered to mediate itself through the others. The whole is their negative unity as One Idea. Together they constitute capital as Individual (§ 93.1). Important here is the question whether there is a single unifying centre to the system. I argue to the contrary; there are two (possibly three) centres of determination such that the movement of the system is *elliptical*, for it is objectively equivocal if the centre is ruled by finance

---

[7] Suzanne de Brunhoff speaks of a 'special monetary circuit': de Brunhoff 2015, p. 20.
[8] See Reuten and Williams 1989, p. 67, Reuten 2019, pp. 56–7.

(ideal unity), or industrial capital as a living individual appropriating otherness (§ 93.2). Nonetheless Capital is *Idea* (§ 93.3).

§ 93.1   The Absolute as Individual

Now the Absolute itself may be considered as constituted by the intermediation of finance, commerce, and industry. In the sphere of finance, capital is the *permanent* Subject, which swallows up the fleeting individual capitals, in competition, through centring its aim in the capital markets such that its *systemic logic* prevails. However, each sphere mediates the others and mediates itself in them. Only the whole is the Absolute Idea of Capital. In form finance is self-knowing capital, but it cannot really know need and productive activity, still less take them to be merely its own manifestation. No matter that capital subsumes them; it has to come to terms with their material potential.

The universal as the common basis of all the many capitals is not a mental abstraction for the theorist to classify the real capitals, it exists as a real structure binding them in practice. This is given implicitly in their identity with each other as merely amounts of the same substance, namely value incarnate in money. But this universal moment has to be made explicit and dominant in the capital markets predicated on the separation of finance capital from industrial capital.

In order to realise its concept, capital must posit itself doubly: as fluidly universal, on the one hand, and in determinate shapes of existence, on the other. If capital is to act in accordance with its Idea there has to be a place where it is fixed (in industry) and a place where it is in solution (in the money market).

In sum the universality of capital as self-specifying is exemplified in the capital markets where amounts are lent to individual firms for their own purposes, yet controlled by the general interest of capital in profit. Thus these 'many capitals' are considered not just as instances of the class of 'capitals', but they are subsumed by universal capital as *its* determinations through a real process such as we find in the relationship of the financial system to the singular individual capitals that are constituted *as* capitals by the loans they take out from this pool of aggregate social capital. This is in truth a concrete universal uniting all capitals in a single system.

What makes a totality an Individual rather than a mere collection? Obviously a *relative* totality in which everything affects everything else is clearly not an individual; for that to obtain, the whole must be *centred* such that a moment of decision is located, which determines the particulars to which the universal is to determine itself.

Formally the moment of individuality is given when bringing together the moment of the universal as the financial system and particularity as the circuits of total social capital, so as to constitute the capitalist *system* as a unitary whole. The system is *centred*: the financial system is not only as such the universal moment distinct from the characteristic particularity of industrial capitals, but it is also the centre of the system, where bankers assess the viability of specific applications for loans, albeit it is displaced from the real source of growth.

When 'Capital' as such takes shape as such a unitary *system*, it is Individual. In its universality, as well as the folding out of particularity into singulars, the latter fold back in, to constitute, not the simple immediate universal they descend from, but a *concrete concept*, totalising particularity and singularity. We see this moment existing independently in the capital markets. Here capital is distributed and redistributed. Logically, the many single capitals are particular *internal* divisions of one total social capital, albeit that this divides itself into many single capitals, each concerned with generating its own particular profit through its own particular circuit.

Just as the self-determination of each incarnation of the capital concept is secured through the moment of self-reference in its circuit so does the capital system achieve its reflected unity as a totality of capitals in the financial system, taken as a unity centred in a capital market, with its prevailing rate of interest. *Remark*: Capitalism is essentially a monetary system, and as it has developed this has become more, not less, the case. The enormous impact of money, and its movements, on the totality of capitalist relations must be acknowledged. In particular, it is crucial to distinguish between theories of money in which it is figured as a passive mediator of other forces, and theories of 'active' money, in which, as finance, it initiates the hegemonic circuit of the capitalist economy, and, as 'abstract wealth', it sets itself as the aim of that circuit. The importance of money as active cannot be overstated. Money rules. It is the form in which capital, as self-valorising value, measures itself against itself. This prefigures the dominance of buying in order to sell in developed capitalist relations. In M–C–M', money cannot possibly be seen as passive because a monetary increment is set as the aim of the circuit. Money is the most active thing there is in the economy, and an important goal of any theory of money should be to explain this.

§ 93.2 The Elliptical Movement of Capital

I have argued that capital is *one. Logically* there is nothing to stop all the many capitals merging into one giant firm, because they differ formally only in magnitude, an 'external' determination easily sublated in their aggregation.

However, capital is particularised in two different ways: while *ideally* each capital exists as 'an amount' (what a firm is 'valued at') of a homogenous substance, *materially* each capital is invested in some special business that sets it apart from others.

It is because of the essential unity of capital that theory claims to have achieved a concrete account of it only once it is shown, however abstractly, to reproduce itself through systemic determinations. But this requires the *material* differentiation of departments of capitalist reproduction. However, the double nature of capital as both ideal and material, creates a systemic absurdity. The point of production is the ultimate origin of economic growth; but the self-reference of capital is displaced to the sphere of finance. This *derangement* puts the financial system at the centre of affairs. (At present it is centred on Wall Street and the unity achieved in the capital markets.)

So the difficult issue that arises in this last part of the dialectic of capital is the relation between finance capital, ruling the capital markets, and industrial capital, the site of the ultimate production of capital. In one sense the matter seems simple; if all profit originates in production then the tribute exacted from industry by other fractions of capital in virtue of their specific functions must surely be a secondary issue, no matter how they legitimate their share. But it is not so simple, because the moment of *decision* lies with the capital markets where industry seeks funds for expansion. An individual capital measures itself against itself in its monetary increment, and more especially the rate at which it is generated. But it is the whole system that judges the adequacy of that rate, whether it is above or below the general rate. Ultimately the performance of all capital is assessed in the sphere of finance, in monetary terms. This is the explicit existence of the universality of capital, in a specific moment of the whole.

There is little doubt that, if capital is 'Spirit' in some sense, the financial sphere is its centre. But the ideal determinations overlap the material ones only in their displacement. The *material* interface is at the point of production where capital has the task of appropriating otherness. This double-centredness of capital naturally creates considerable grinding in its gearing because the requirements of each are not necessarily in harmony. The problem lies deeper than a mere quarrel over a redistribution of the surplus; it is an ontological issue; the political representatives of each fraction of capital are subjectively convinced that their position is central to the success of the system, and each has reason.

As the conscious centre of decision in the system, in the money market, finance capital is the embodiment of the spirit of capitalism. Accordingly, here capital as the Absolute Idea realises itself as a conscious appropriation of a real content.

A centred totality seems the perfect figure of the totalisation by capital of all productive activity. But it might appear that industry has lost its central place once finance capital comes to the fore, and makes money from all kinds of circuits, not just the meta-circuit incorporating the industrial circuit. This is indeed true, as far as *pure form* is concerned. The financial sector passes judgement on the performance of industry. But the financial sphere is still entangled with (rather than fully penetrating) industry and commerce.

However, *materially*, the source of all surplus ultimately derives from exploited labour. So the claim of industry is surely vindicated. But in truth these two centres struggle for dominance. Indeed, we may speak of rival centres of the spiral of capital accumulation. In this sense, the movement of capital is not circular but *elliptical*.

The constellation of industry, finance, and commerce is the nearest thing we have to an Absolute, but it is not quite as self-transparent, and free, as that. It is true that with finance capital the system achieves a version of self-determination in that the capital markets give shape to the moment of decision. But the original fracture between ideality and materiality remains. It is expressed now in that the movement of the system has two centres (possibly three because of need and demand), namely finance and industry, each exerting their own specific demands, with an obscure, conflictual, and shifting, relation between these two poles. Self-knowing capital in the financial sector lacks real knowledge of the problems addressed by industry exploiting workers. In the capital markets the 'spirit of capitalism' knows itself only ideally, blind to its ultimate conditions of existence in the labour process. Only the objective system of the circuit of industrial capital ensures the reproduction of the system as a whole by ensuring accumulation. From this point of view finance is a moment separated off so that capital can get a measure of its success. But finance looks at industry as just one avenue for investment because its abstract form loses sight of the material conditions of existence.

It is notable that in the capital market, capital takes itself as its own content, when it is treated as a quasi-commodity to be traded and hoarded. Hence this return into its own logical interior looks like the closure of the system. But in another sense the system is open. For the centre of the capital system is subject to refraction; ideally capital is immediate interest-bearing capital, but this is parasitic on the surplus value arising in the industrial sphere; so the financial system and the industrial system are in uneasy combination. The system has competing centres; hence its movement is that of an ellipse. This ellipse is the consequence of the dual ontology of capital, formally *self*-centred but materially *other*-centred.

What, then, is the *centre* of the capital system? On one reading it is the financial system, which mobilises and distributes capital. On another reading it is industry, as the site of the ultimate origin of surplus value and of revolutions in the mode of production. These act in concert clearly, but often conflict; thus the two circles cannot map one another congruently. Rather the effectivity of each is registered separately as *two* poles around which capital moves in elliptical fashion.

But how is the whole system to be characterised, namely that of capital as an *Individual*, if both finance and industry could be seen as the all-embracing moment, reducing the other moments to complementary moments within which it is mediated? But it seems that if both effectively strive to rule there is no unitary individual and we see the logical basis for fractions of the capitalist class jostling for dominance. (Moreover, these face the working class as implicitly a countervailing subject.)

The issue may be posed neatly as follows: do we have a genuine *unity-in-separation* (in which the differences find their place as substantially one with the whole) or do we have a *separation-in-unity* (in which the different spheres are in unity with each other but retain irreducibly *other* determinations)?

§ 93.3   Capital as Absolute Idea

Once industry is situated in the meta-circuit initiated by bank finance, the original notion of the circuit of capital must be reconsidered. The three versions of the circuit, of which the monetary circuit was only one, were taken as complementary readings of figure of the circuit. But now, with the externalisation of the moments of the circuit into their own shapes of existence, we may rightly prioritise the money-capital circuit. This has priority because finance for firms is created *ex nihilo* and is required for the real possibility of industrial growth. At the same time it must be allowed that the totality is decentred because it is productive capital that generates the surplus through applying the knowledge, and cooperation, of social labour. (Moreover, the standpoint of commodity capital must not be forgotten because it links all the circuits together in a social whole of material reproduction.)

Capital is a self-moving system of form, which takes possession of the material economy and determines its logic of development. For the power of formal determination of the material world by the ideal form normally overcomes its recalcitrance to capital's purpose. The form of capital shapes matter into a content *adequate* to its aim. Capitalists and workers are merely the bearers of the economic relation prescribed for them by capital. However, in no way is it the destiny of labour to achieve its perfection in wage labour. Rather this determination is forced upon it because of the 'doubly free' status of the labourer, itself reproduced in the capital relation. The material world is posited by the capital Idea as its inorganic body. Insofar as the material world has its own laws, capital employs 'the cunning of reason' to adapt these potentials to alien purposes.

While the Idea of capital seems Absolute, in the sense of grounded on itself *in form, as such* it is merely an abstract Absolute, because it forms itself separately from its material substrate. However, while it is not the *form of* that matter, the Idea *forms it* into an adequate basis. This process of *formal determination* of the economic metabolism constitutes the concretisation of capital. The all-embracing moment is that of *form*. Even if the system is materially dependent on surplus labour, it is the formal determinations that subsume and regulate living labour.

Earlier (in § 71) I showed that an individual capital may rightly be characterised as an *individual subject*. However, I speak here of capital as 'subject' without consciousness or personality. I start from the minimal definition: that a subject is capable of comprehending things under the universal. Then it has an immanent end implicit in its being. The posited unity of the concept is the logical skeleton of subjectivity, although of course the moment of 'will' is required to *effect* the self-determination of such a subject. (The required consciousness and will are attributes of the *capitalist*.)

Remark: In one sense this is 'a process without a subject'; but I claim that there is indeed a good sense in which capital is a subject, albeit that it takes shape as a *spectre*. Just as money is posited as the actuality of value in autonomous form, so capital is the spectral existence of self-valorising value.

Now I further claim that total social capital may *itself* be considered as 'Individual'; and here I wish to speak (without considering it merely a *figure of speech*) of it as a unitary 'social subject'. This is the appropriate designation for the whole system that faces us. For what faces us is not a *class* of capitals but a single *whole* determining itself to ever-changing specific shapes. Capital is 'the enemy' in a different sense from that in which Disease is an enemy. The latter is a personified class name for empirically distinct diseases that have enough in common to group and personify. But 'Capital' (with a big 'C', so to speak) has a reality as an individual whole. It is not just a *class* term for Ford, Shell, Apple, etc. These are not so much members of a set as they are capital's own concretisations in numerically separable shapes which nonetheless are constituted as organic parts of the totality and move within it. The Idea of Capital is not a collation of these many capitals; it is a concrete unity, a totality, that persists in and through its effectivity upon them.

Summary

This chapter treats the culmination of the capital Concept as formally Absolute. To begin with (§ 91) it is shown that the nothingness, which the presentation up to now has implicitly sought to ground, appears explicitly in the shape of *ex nihilo* money, created by the banking system. It is liberated from any attachment to a commodity; it exists as pure form. It appears only in the dialectic of the *absolute relation* of value to value, that is to say, of credit to debit. In principle these collapse to zero; but capital sustains them in their difference, albeit they are the same thing given positively and negatively. Present *as* different, their relation has economic effectivity. Finance supplied to industry becomes active in its circuit and generates a surplus. Here there is a temporal inversion in that value exists prior to its becoming the value *of* anything, for example a produced commodity. Value is now truly grounded on itself.

In the following section (§ 92) the inner moments of the circuit of capital are shown to gain autonomous existence in finance, commerce, and industry. Here the form-determination of industry requires the presence of certain 'ideal' forms, namely 'ante-validation' of production by banks, and 'pre-commensuration' of valorised value by capital.

In the final section (§ 93) the Absolute Idea of capital comprehends the whole as itself Individual. But is its movement a spiral of accumulation which presupposes a definite centre? Here the dual ontology of capital asserts itself again. The financial system, as the centre of decision (as 'Absolute Spirit', so to speak) appears to itself as the be-all and end-all. But it is only industry, as it appropriates the material metabolism of the economy, that creates a surplus product. Without this there could be no profits. As such, capital is characterised by an objective aporia: is it to be seen as a unity-in-separation or a separation-in-unity? In truth, then, capital is double-centred; hence its movement is *elliptical*.

Finally it is claimed that the system of capital is a unitary social subject. 'Capital' is not merely a class term for the many capitals; it is itself the totality facing us as such.

CHAPTER 16

Capital and Its Others: Labour and Land

§10   Capital and Its Others

After a brief discussion of the capitalist corporation I treat capital's internal 'other', labour, and its external 'other', land, first as they give rise to revenues capital must disburse, and then their more general status as its conditions of existence. The sections are §101 Capital; §102 Internalisation of Capital's 'Others'; §103 General Conditions of Existence of Capital.

§101   *Capital*

In the presentation thus far the personification of capital has been taken as the figure of 'the capitalist'. This is now concretised in that we leave behind possible human bearers of this designation, with all their vagaries, and consider capital in its pure form. The institution of the capitalist corporation, with limited liability, establishes a legal subject, as real a legal person as any human. The corporation is owner of the capital it employs, albeit the shareholders have claims to revenue. But this means a corporation is simply capital personified, and more thoroughly so than the old-style entrepreneur. The latter may well fail to embody completely personified capital because of other human interests they possess. The corporation, however, is legally obliged to consider only the interests of capital. Its executives are obliged to adhere to this principle. As the subject-object of the economic order the capitalist corporation is indifferent to all other considerations. The corporation has property in its disposable capital, but as subject is nothing but the latter's personification.

While capital is substance-become-subject, the worker, while a legal subject, is deprived of all property in means of production. They have only their own bodily substance to alienate, and to make the object of a contract.[1]

§102   *Internalisation of Capital's 'Others'*

It is important that the capitalist totality primarily consists of relations that are internal in the sense that each side of the relation requires the other in its very definition. Thus money is related in this way to commodities as what

---

[1] 'The irony of capitalist society is that the worker is in full possession of himself only when he is unemployed' (Kay and Mott 1982, p. 11).

it purchases, and to capital as what it becomes when reflected against itself. The method of exposition relies on this to generate through such conceptual necessities transitions from notions incomplete in themselves to more self-grounded ones. External relations obtain in systems wherein contingent causal effects hold things together, for example the solar system can easily be reduced to massy bodies in motion then linked up by reciprocal gravitational forces.

In the investigation there are problems to be addressed when that which in principle is external to capital, notably labour and land, are necessary to it as conditions of its existence, having been appropriated by it through some peculiar form of value, here wages and rent. This means they are *internalised* by capital yet, in themselves, remain alien to it. I term living labour 'capital's internal other', and land 'capital's external other'. While capital mediates itself in them, their peculiar material effectivity on capital is equally important, whether this is enabling or frustrating.

The concept of capital is *existent* only as Idea, which is the Concept in unity with its material conditions of existence. Even the Absolute Idea of capital, in the big triad finance/commerce/industry, is not yet beyond capital in its mere concept, because it moves freely in otherness only if that is its *own* other. But in truth capital as pure *form* cannot shape that otherness, namely labour and land, without addressing the task of their subsumption, the internalisation of moments that are in principle 'outside' capital.

These are internalised through disbursing two revenues, namely wages of labour and rent of land. Labour and land are not internal to the capital concept in the way that capitalistically produced means of production are. Yet owners of these factors, entering as quasi-commodities, draw a revenue. These pose problems for any attempt to show that capital is grounded on itself. For capital to unite concept and object requires the subsumption of labour – a contested business – and also the subsumption of Nature. Here then I must complete our presentation of the Idea by treating the 'others' of capital and their subsumption under it. Here I show how far capital subsumes its others under its forms; and I deal with how these are, as always at root not-capital, in excess of its Idea, and potentially destabilising of it.

§102.1   Capital's 'Internal' Other: Labour
The most important other is labour power. The internal other comes from outside, from the domestic sphere, even though it is internalised by capital, for it is absolutely necessary to capital accumulation as the carrier of valorisation.

The question of the articulation of the modern domestic sphere with the capitalist factory, in which the wage-worker is employed, is a subtle one. Insofar as the worker receives wages it seems that labour power is a commodity. But, although sold, it is not a true commodity, for the reason that it is not produced by capital; hence there is no possibility of determining it as a value, still less of determining the magnitude of that value by the time of its production.

There are two common mistakes that a proper view of the matter must avoid. One is that labour power has a value representing the productive labour of the domestic worker, usually a woman. The other is that, since this domestic labourer works without wages, capital appropriates their labour for free. The first mistake I have just refuted; labour power has a price but no value. Is it then, as a use-value appropriated by capital from unpaid domestic labour, given to the capitalist for free? By no means! The wage of the employed worker is supposedly sufficient to cover the subsistence costs of the entire family, *including* the subsistence of the domestic labourer.

Thus far so clear. The issue, however, needs further analysis. Naturally a shape of labour from which it does not immediately profit is offensive to capital. It reduces its prevalence in two ways. First capital commodifies it through such measures as fast food preparation, laundries, and other domestic *services*. Second it offers labour-saving *commodities* such as washing machines, vacuum cleaners, and so forth.

In the case of the purchase of means of production, capital buys them at a price that includes the surplus value appropriated by the firms selling them. What happens, then, if all domestic labour is 'out-sourced'? All meals are take-aways, purchased from capitalist firms, all cleaning is provided by service-sector firms, even child-care is provided by nurseries run for profit. In a perfected capitalist system, this would be the case, although in reality there are limits to such out-sourcing of domestic services. The charges of these service-sector firms would have to include surplus value. Hence this is more expensive than the services of unpaid housework. Other things being equal, factory wages would have to increase. The upshot would be that industrial capital must share its surplus value with the new service-sector firms. But, of course, other things would not be equal; for the erstwhile domestic labourer is now free to seek paid employment, thus providing for their own subsistence. This is, indeed, the existing tendency, further impelled by the production, and use, of labour-saving domestic appliances.

Certainly, there can be no question of treating domestic labour as value generating; it is *not employed by capital*; it is as simple as that. Capital requires initially the commodification in form of labour power in order to make productive labour available to it. But capital becomes a self-constituted power only insofar as this other is posited as capital's *internal* other, which is reproduced *within* capital's circuit as an exploitable resource. However, if, *within* the capital relation labour may be considered capital's *internal* other, it has yet its own actuality and remains recalcitrant to its subsumption. Ontologically, then, the reproduction of labour power is a flaw in the sphere of capitalist production and circulation, in that capital cannot produce labour power immediately but relies on a non-capitalist mediation. (This domestic sphere *may* provide a point of resistance to capital; but this claim needs argument.)

§ 102.2   Capital's 'External' Other: Land

Properly speaking the external other is Nature, which includes wind and water; but I will simplify by speaking only of land (which also covers buildings and so forth here neglected).

What of land? It is leased from its owner for a specific rent, which is an income for the owner. This is a factor of production unproduced by capital. Hence unworked land has no value. But it is naturally scarce, hence rent arises from considerations such as the fertility of the soil and the richness of the mine, outside the core concept of capital. Strictly speaking modern landed property is outside the Capital Concept but not outside its Idea. Land has become a form of capital. There is no longer a landlord class. Today it is a financial asset, which means partly that it derives its price from its rent and partly that it is a vehicle for speculation (because it is not a product).

Thus rent is a share of surplus value capital pays to itself in its appearance as landed property, which allows for the possibility of opposing fractions of the capitalist class. So the real existence of capital as Idea has rent of land as a necessary condition which is not just an unwanted contingency but is inevitable, just as much as wages have to be disbursed.

As it is a *secondary* disbursement, I do not pay a lot of attention to it because it is not part of the Concept, although it *is* part of the Idea rooted in an external condition of existence, whereas the very possibility of the surplus value to be distributed is rooted internally in the identity of capitals' time and labour's time. The disbursement of surplus value in the form of rent is not based on capital proper but on a parasitic monopoly of a use-value.[2]

Labour power and landed property are peculiar in that they have a value form (wages and rent) and thus *formally* are subsumed under capital, but they are not *in themselves* determinations of capital in the way that produced means of production are *internal* to capital's own circuit. They were not produced by

---

2 Because rent is not central to the concept of capital I largely abstract from it in this book. Indeed, I have nothing to add to Marx's splendid analysis of it in *Capital* III. According to Geert Reuten 'rent' is a feudal category. Nowadays the more general category is 'lease'. For this see Reuten 2019, pp. 195–6.

capital, albeit subordinated to it; they are prosthetic limbs of capital, but not bone of the bone, so to speak. Capital can subsume them to its purposes and block alternative uses. But both presuppositions of capital have an existence only partially determined by capital and require recognition as complementary to, but distinct from, capital. However, in order to posit them as moments of the totality of its relations, capital must yield two revenues from the new value created.

What all this means is that these two 'others' are in excess of the Capital Concept. Instead of capital recollecting that it is identical with its otherness, here there are given outside it land and labour, which it successfully internalises formally but only partially subsumes materially.

§103   *General Conditions of Existence of Capital*

In the previous section I showed how capital creates special value forms, wages, and rent, to secure the subsumption of its 'others'. Here I broaden the analysis of their relation.

Throughout the presentation, the 'fit' between ideal and material determinants is problematic. That required me to devote a chapter to the issue of the 'dual ontology of capital'. (This has specific reference to the so-called 'transformation problem' but has wider import.) Capital in its movement of formal determination of the economy faces a 'not-capital' which requires subsumption under its forms. In virtue of capital's logical form, it claims to be the truth of the reality it in-forms with its Concept, realised more or less adequately. The recalcitrance of this material (notably living labour) means that capital has the endless task of realising itself in this other.

Although the task of accumulating is likewise endless this does not mean capital never realises its aim, for its truth is attained precisely in the accumulation *process*, an absolute negativity wherein it continually surpasses itself while remaining itself. Its truth is not found in some determinate accumulation of wealth; rather accumulation for the sake of accumulation is its mode of being. Capital accumulation has an immanent teleology progressing without end, but yet takes its self-expansion precisely *as its end*. Although the not-capital has its own determinants (some of which are manipulated through the 'cunning of reason' of capital) which have an impact on the rate of capital accumulation, capital is sufficiently powerful as a *sui generis* subject to maintain itself as epochally dominant.

Although its struggle to prevail is a 'labour of the negative', it is generally successful at subsuming the economic process to itself. Capital, as 'subject', then 'subjects' living labour to itself, and for its own reasons attends to such empirical facts as 'socially necessary labour time'. But value is not, on that account, reducible to physical parameters. Capital is *grounded on itself*, and takes possession of the material metabolism, not as its origin, but as its support. Labour time is always a *determined determinant* responsive to capital's demands, insofar as that is feasible. Nonetheless, while capital posits the not-capital as its *own* other to be possessed and exploited, ultimately there are limits. While capital *claims* to create 'wealth', I argue that it merely *subsumes* the material content of the economy under the forms of value. The *logical* form of capital is by no means absolute but insufficient to maintain itself; it requires a transition to a domain of reality regulated by the form but by no means inessential to it; capital is not free to develop in its concept alone, but must confront the problem of its lack of self-subsistence as mere *concept* of self-valorisation.

The dialectic of capitalist production is one in which the form seeks to secure and stabilise itself through subsuming material production and turning it into a bearer of self-valorisation. But the logic of capital accumulation would run down pretty quickly were it not for the *material* fact that workers produce more than they themselves consume. Capital did not create its world afresh, but found its others already in existence before it subsumed them under its own process. Once in motion, setting out from itself, it continuously presupposes itself in its different forms as consumable product, raw material, instruments of labour, and labour power, in order to continually reproduce itself in these forms. They appear first as conditions presupposed by capital, and then as its result. In reproducing itself it reproduces its own conditions. However, in truth capital subsumes, but does not create, its internal other, the worker, and its external other, Nature.

A unity of the ideal and the material is projected in the Idea of capital. If it succeeds then it is the result of its own movement, the production of capital by means of capital. Capital produces capital through *subsuming* human and natural powers, formally but also 'really' to a great extent. However, despite the thoroughgoing transformation of the production process once subsumed by capital, it remains the case that capital cannot properly claim to produce all its conditions of existence. It may be said that what is at issue here is merely contingent concrete diversity, easily contained within the logic of the system. But living labour is *recalcitrant* to such subsumption under the logic of capital. The appropriation of labour is problematic because the labourers potentially have ends of their own to realise. They cannot be considered as 'human resources' no different in principle from other 'natural resources' exploited by capital. Moreover, capital cannot grasp the reality of the importance of scarce natural resources.

Capital sinks into its material metabolism so as to shape it into an adequate basis for its growth, but labour and Nature remain in reality always in excess of capital's conceptual determinacy. So, at the end of the day, value and use-value do not stand in a relation of dialectical unity, but merely become configured as a combinatory. This relation is open to contingency in that either side may support or frustrate the other.

It is true that I began with a dialectical derivation of value as not-use-value. But the contrary does not obtain: use-value is never not-value but is posited by the value form as the non-being of value. (See Chapter 5, and especially the Table: 'Being-in-exchange and its other'.) This is a relation of contrariety to be sure but not a contradiction capable of resolution in a higher actuality. As a fully subsistent actuality (albeit deformed by capital) use-value has *no need* for the value complement. Of course, it is possible abstractly to begin from either side (value or use-value), taken in its immediacy, and trace its mediation in and through its other; but since this works both ways there is always a tension between the sides, each having the capacity to realise itself as the dominant one.

So here capital is the constitutive subject that builds a world for itself, but on material foundations, including human labour, that are in excess of its concept of itself, and potentially destabilising of it. (The counter-subject, labour, is trapped in the capital relation whereby the relation is played out in a counterpoint such that it is the very same movement that comprises both the self-constitution of capital and the self-negation of labour.)

With *ex nihilo* money, value is grounded in the movement of absolute negativity. But it is only in *form* that capital can claim to be Absolute; it cannot create the material it subsumes. Living labour returns from its repression by the capital relation to undercut the reign of capital. In this respect, the spirit of capital has a false consciousness because it claims to be Absolute but in reality it cannot do more than subsume and re-orientate *our powers*, which potentially we may recover for ourselves. *Epochally*, however, capital rules. The spirit of capitalism is not in origin a *subjective* orientation. It is a socially constituted *objectivity* imposing its logic on its human bearers.

Capital tries to subordinate its material conditions of existence to its own aims; but there is always present something irredeemably 'other'. The proletariat, produced by capital itself as its negation, capital must not merely appropriate but actively negate this its negation continually, because the proletariat is potentially a force in its own right. Thus the capital relation exists only through a dialectic of negativity, continually generating a proletariat but continually imprisoning it within capital's own forms, reifying its activity, expropriating its product, and colonising its consciousness so that it is interpellated as agent of capital.

My strategy has been to explore the supposed closed totality of the Idea of capital in its own terms, finally to reveal the material presuppositions that may obstruct it. Next I reconsider capital's two most immediate conditions of existence: the immediate condition of existence of value: use-value, which both supports, and frustrates, the Idea; and the immediate condition of existence of capital, labour, which is 'in and against' it.

Remark: The presentation traces the way in which the economic forms support each other in systemic fashion. However, it is clear that the system requires support from other dimensions of social life. In particular, the state and law are necessary conditions of it. However, I here abstract from any presentation of the capitalist state.[3]

§103.1   The Immediate Condition of Existence of Value: Use-Value

The exact relation of value and use-value is very complex; bandying about the term 'contradiction' does not help; however, we are certainly faced with more than diversity or duality. Since the ideal is *constituted* in opposition to the material, this is *not* a case of so-called 'real extremes'. Yet the abstract contraposition of the ontological levels means each has its own specific effectivity in the economy as a whole. The interpenetration of value and use-value rests on the complicated intermediations in which the ideal (value) is effective as the *formal determination* of the real, while the material inputs (living labour) taken up, and transformed, by capital, are conditions of its existence which help to *materially determine* the magnitude of value. Whether form determines matter, or *vice versa*, is aporetic. Because these diverse determinations are *combined externally*, however intermediated, no harmony may be presupposed; yet the possibility of contingent 'fixes' to problems is always there, as these determinations of the commodity now assist, now fetter, one another.

Thus the 'big picture' is a complex interpenetration of value and use-value. However united in practice, this division remains. On the one hand, commodities are formally conceptualised as all values; on the other hand, they are exchanged because they are different goods; yet value as such does not exist *in* the commodity. Turn and twist it as we may, we shall only find material properties, not social ones. There seems to be an unbridgeable gap between the claim that the homogeneous ideality of value rules the commodities and their persisting material variety.

The commodity is determined both as a use-value and as an exchange-value. But this is not like saying something is red and round, because these determinations stand in a relation of opposition to each other. While it is a condi-

---

3   For a thorough attempt at a dialectical exposition of the economy and the state together see Kay and Mott 1982, and Reuten 2019. For economy and law, specifically, the old work by Evgeny Pashukanis is still valuable (Pashukanis 1978).

tion of exchange that a commodity be useful in some way, it acquires in the value-form the new determination of exchange-value, which negates all difference between commodities and declares them identical as values. From this point of view, the material commodity counts only as the bearer of its value.

The developing *priority* of the ideal over the material is key to understanding the development of the value form through money to capital, but with the circuit of industrial capital it all becomes more complicated; for now, to accomplish valorisation, capital must *embody* itself in certain specific use-values – above all labour power – capable of producing a surplus product. This means that the peculiar material properties of the bearers of so-called 'variable' capital, and 'constant' capital, are functionally decisive for valorisation. Now the specific difference of the use-value 'makes a difference'. Dialectically speaking the inversion (of ideal and material) is itself inverted. What counts now in the production process is the specificity of the means of production and the particular skills of the labour power employed. However, the inversion of the inversion remains *within* capital. (If someone goes to the antipodes they do not return to Greenwich by standing on their heads.) The production process is a capitalist one, not an asocial, ahistorical transformation of matter. The value form of the process has not disappeared but remains implicit; for it determines the shape of the process (e.g. real subsumption) in virtue of the positing of the material process as a valorisation process enforced by capital's personifications (e.g. managers, whose personal qualities also now become germane to their effectiveness).

In sum the interpenetration of use-value and value ensures both surplus product and surplus value emerge.

The experiential starting point of the theory of capital is that wealth today takes the shape of a heap of commodities: for the product of labour is a commodity. This beginning is abstracted from the 'chaotic whole' of our experience in general, but it has the advantage of universality of reference and historical determinacy (at least in its second aspect, that products for the most part are commodities). Unfortunately, this beginning is thoroughly dualistic. We experience the commodity precisely as a puzzling *combination* of diverse determinations, use-value and exchange-value. This dualism is not a philosophical error but a fault in reality, experienced by us at every turn.

But what *drives* the development is the movement of self-positing value, albeit supported by use-value determinations throughout. In the opposition, use-value versus value, it the latter that is the principal pole, however mediated in its other. If the material commodity is an immediacy in *experience*, the immediacy of *value* is not present on the surface of the commodity; rather 'value' is an immediacy gained by thought through *abstracting* from the network of exchange relationships. It is an exceedingly dubious presupposition which cries out for a grounding movement. It has been shown, I believe, to be self-grounded *in form*, albeit completely dependent on the material it subsumes for its realisation.

The pure categories (or value forms) are developed in the presentation first, and only then is taken up the way these categories in-form material reality (for example, how the value form regulates material production). The presentation of the value form is one in which value is developed as pure form up to the general formula for capital; only then must it be shown that use-value has an economic role. But how then are value and use-value related? The practical abstraction from use-value characteristic of exchange gives rise to the form of pure value. Because the dialectical development of categories, traceable from this origin, is not taking place in thought, it requires at every point support in the material forms of interchange between commodities. In this sense, right from the start the commodity must be considered as a combination of value and use-value. But, in the development of the value form up to the general formula for capital, value is borne by the material body of the commodity without the specificity of the commodity playing any economic role.

Once we pass from the general formula to the reality of material production value and use-value are seen to interpenetrate. What sort of relation is this? I dissent from the claim that value and use-value are dialectical opposites, such that each side can be shown to be nothing but the other once grasped from the standpoint of the perfectly unified whole. Dialectical totalisation normally requires that all opposition be sublated such that the two sides are understood as internal self-differentiations of the Absolute; alternatively, that one side is taken as effectively itself the whole such that the other is reduced to its own other, swallowed up in it.

Because value and use-value interpenetrate, in the last analysis use-value may disrupt the effort by capital to become a self-subsistent totality. Either the rebellion of living labour, or exhaustion of natural resources, will undermine it. However, capital as self-valorising value is epochally hegemonic, and in the two-sided whole of intermediation it has prevailed up to now, hence theory must recognise this. However, the relation of value and use-value is asymmetrical; use-value does not need value to complete its concept, while value completes itself only in negating and subsuming use-value.

The illusion that 'value' and 'use-value' are complementary forms arises because the latter is generated abstractly as a placeholder manufactured to stand for what is not value, namely 'use-value-for-others'. Clothes are useful to keep us warm; food for nutrition; but there is no such thing as 'useful in general'. Outside exchange theory, the term has little application; use-value is always *specific*. In reality, then, the commodity is a combination of a *universal* social form, namely value, and some *specific* use-value, for example a warm coat. I speak of such singular commodities being 'inscribed within', or 'subsumed by' the value form, because their specificity is not affirmed but negated in it. The form which affirms itself in its dialectical development is that of value; it first gains its autonomy from use-value as a result of the practical abstraction which generates the value form, then it subsumes the use-value sphere, and finally 'takes possession' of it. As we know, production is for profit, not for need; indeed, need is manipulated by capital.

Let us consider the opposition between the value form as a whole, i.e. capital as Idea, and the material metabolism of the economy. Capital wants to make the spirit of capitalism infuse the entire economic order, including the material metabolism, but the dependence of the 'spiritual' forms on their required material basis undercuts this excessive arrogance on the part of capital. The sides do not share a common substance; rather there is a bizarre consubstantiality of ideal and material dimensions. Thus the mode of production is doubly determined by both sides together, by the formal and material determinations. This unhappy marriage of convenience brings together incommensurable orders of being.

The value form strives to autonomise itself *from* use-value so as to articulate its specific determinacy and then impose these determinations *on* use-value. But at every point the use-value side has economic determinacy to which capital adapts and upon which it depends. The central case is that valorising itself rests on the pumping out of surplus labour. It is true that material production is inscribed within the value form and it is therewith formally determined by capital and its aims. However, there much going on in production that is outside capital's concept of it. On the one side, capital claims to be self-mediating in that it returns to itself in a circular flow having reduced the phases it runs through to shapes of itself. On the other side, there is something outside capital which it does not create, namely labour power. But this it successfully subsumes under the value form. Then the very effectivity of living labour, now posited by capital as *its own* use-value, is manifest only in alienated form, since capital expropriates labour's product and determines it as value. Value reflects labour time but only as in a distorting mirror because capital's own inner determinations are also active.

Yet this linear input is necessary for the supposed *self-expansion* of capital. The diagnosis I make here is that there are two intersecting ontologies; the ideality of the value form confronts the materiality of production. To be sure, determinants from the latter feed into the former, but only as *transformed*, so as to become the abstract content of an abstract form. Thus if labour time is determinant of value magnitudes, it is so only as abstract time, labour only as abstract labour; the concrete rhythms of the labour process remain external to capital, hence they are not reducible to capital, and are potentially troublesome for its movement. The material ontology is merely *combined* with the ideal ontology. But the identitarian system of capital is no philosophical construction but is 'out there' and constellationally embraces the richness of material life.

The speculative identity of the value form, and the formed world, cannot be sustained; for there is the 'excess', escaping the Concept, which is the site of possible contingent disruption, or even – with the class struggle – its overthrow.

Use-value depends upon specific material properties of the commodity, given originally by Nature itself. Since capital as a producer of use-values employs the land as a factor of production, but cannot itself produce it, there is every reason to study how capital treats the land, and the changes (deterioration most likely) in the use-value of land itself. (Likewise, one would look forward to a different relationship to Nature after capitalism.) Thus, aspects to be considered would include industrialisation of agriculture, exhaustion of the soil, patenting of life-forms, environmental 'externalities', the despoliation of natural forests, and the profligate use of finite resources (oil, coal, ores, etc.).

Capital abstracts from the riches of nature, and treats such material production as if it were *capitalist production*; but, in the case of finite resources such as mines, 'value' (meaning here 'price') is not determined by the labour time socially necessary to '*reproduce*' a commodity but simply to '*produce*' it. This change of determination arises because the commodity is not reproducible at all. With natural resources the 'value' of such commodities is in reality determined by their *time of acquisition*. What is crucial where natural resources are concerned is that the labour theory of value does not apply. In many parts of the world, the price of timber is not determined by the time it takes to grow a tree but by the time it takes to cut one down. Indonesia was originally covered in forests. Today an area the size of Belgium is logged out *every year* for wood pulp with catastrophic ecological consequences. Similarly, non-renewables like oil should have infinite value, but the price depends on the trivial cost of sticking a well in the sand.

Capitalism wastes scarce resources in a very profligate manner, because its value measures are blind to such material considerations (this is a point to be pressed at every opportunity). Likewise, never was a proverb more outdated than the saying 'plenty more fish in the sea'. At one time the best food a British worker ate was cheap cod, but nearly all cod banks have now disappeared. The truth is that capital pays no attention to *reproduction* except where it is compelled to do so. With non-reproducibles, like oil, it will be too late when it finally wakes up; and the same goes for the forests it does not bother to reproduce. The change in the use-value of land, including its deterioration, and the likelihood of this being stemmed by state restrictions, and taxes, are somewhat contingent, and demand ecological and historical studies. But it is possible to make certain general points consequential on the peculiar relations of capital to modern landed property. These are that capital in its concept i) is incapable of recognising such externalities, and ii) in its mystification of 'economics' in reality *obscures* the truth by using only value measures.

(It is true that other modes of production are indifferent to nature; nothing is more destructive than the slash and burn agriculture practised by aboriginal tribes. But capital is uniquely invasive and shuffles off responsibility for its so-called 'externalities'. Capital's blindness to environmental destruction points to its collapse to barbarism.)

Use-value is as such an ahistorical category; but now is thoroughly subverted by capital. The most immediate shape of this is when use-value is simply identified with value. One buys very expensive items just for the sake of demonstrating that one can. Of course, the cultural practice of conspicuous consumption predates capitalism; but then it was figured in unproblematically use-value terms: salad of pearls, gold shaving-mug, and so forth. Now, however, the specificity of what it consists in is of little moment. All that counts is the monetary value. That is what you now 'have'.

A consequence of mass production for the market is the homogenisation of use-value, as in the slogan 'one size fits all'. Ideally, capital would produce billions of copies of the same item. In a desperate attempt to individuate the product it is now sold on its brand value, if consumers can be found stupid enough to fall for this. As a counter point to 'one size fits all', the slogan 'just for you' is advanced. On rare occasions this might even be useful as when computerisation allows for some peculiar size to be manufactured or some personal selection of extras purchased. But the parameters of such customisation are few and narrow. The apotheosis of the evacuation of use comes with the replacement of the world with its image; as Debord strikingly showed, today we consume images for the most part. Use-values are the shell of value; but the phantom objectivity of value bleeds across to those use-values, which become empty vessels for impoverished desire, under the cultural regime of capital.

In the next section I treat the role of capital's 'internal other', namely labour, which may even be considered as 'use-value for itself', in this struggle to throw off capital.

§103.2   The Immediate Condition of Existence of Capital: Labour
While the activity of production *is* the activity of capital at one remove, living labour as a peculiar use-value underpins capital accumulation. But labour power does not yield a flow of labour services automatically; for the workers are potentially recalcitrant to their exploitation (they may embody 'counterproductive labour'!). Thus living labour is not merely 'not-capital' in some formal sense but stands *opposed* to capital, it has to be 'pumped out' from workers. Capital cannot simply invest itself in that which is other than it; it can produce value only through negating this negation, winning the class struggle at the point of production. New value is the successful reification of living labour. Dialectically speaking, here the opposition of use-value and value is heightened into an actual contradiction.

Surplus value is a category *of* capital, and its source in surplus labour has to be enforced *by* capital. But the very possibility of surplus labour is a material fact on which the logic of capital depends. Thus a condition of existence of capital is 'doubly free labour'. This is labour which is free from feudal control, but by the same token 'free' from any means of production. It seems to be contingently given as a result of history but when *reproduced* as free by capital it is posited as capital's presupposition by capital itself, and so no longer to be taken as merely contingently available to it, but a moment actively reproduced in its own circuits. It is available to capital because modern landed property excludes it from the soil. However, even if the thesis that modern landed property is necessary for the existence of a class of wage labourers has *historical* merit, this point has equally lost historical relevance in fully developed capitalism for the following reasons.

i)   The reserve army of labour created by enclosures, clearances, etc. is now provided by capital itself in its own rhythm of development.
ii) Even if land were available to individuals, it could not lead to self-employment in the technical conditions of modern agriculture, while pure subsistence farming would be at a lower standard of life than that of waged work.
iii) The principal obstacle to self-employment on the land is not rent but credit. Numerous 'land reforms' only swept the immediate producer into the clutches of banks and merchants.

Thus the *exclusion* of labour from land allows capital to *internalise* it as waged labour. So wage labour as a presupposition of capital is entirely reproduced *within* the capitalist relations of production.

The existence of a value form 'rent' does not necessarily imply a separate class of landowners. All investment trusts, etc., simply include property in land and buildings as part of a balanced portfolio. There is now one single *class* of the propertied facing the propertyless. This merger does not, however, negate the difference in form of the revenues profit, rent and interest.

I argue that the landowners as a separate class have disappeared, being unnecessary to the structure of bourgeois society. It seems then that there are just *two* great classes of modern society. However, the capitalists too are unnecessary to the perfected capital system. The joint-stock company, consequent on the increasing scale of the productive forces, certainly puts in question the need for a class of *capitalists*. It is only necessary to suppose a punitive inheritance tax drove out such *individuals* to release *capital as a social power*. The stocks and shares could all be owned by unit trusts, insurance companies, pension funds and the like; and run (ostensibly) for the benefit of ordinary people enrolled in such institutions. Nothing would change in the *capital relation*. The factories would be managed according to the dictates of capital, not the workers.

Wage labourers form the only class necessary to the existence of capital. I say this because I have a stipulative definition of the capital relation as exploitative; if all workers were replaced by robots we would have a surplus product, but no longer capitalism on this definition; certainly it would be absurd to speak of the hire price of robots as a 'wage'; there would be no reserve army of robots! (See the discussion above in Chapter 13, *Addendum*, 'A Note on the neo-Sraffian System'.)

For methodological reasons, at a certain point in the presentation I 'quiet' living labour's recalcitrance to capital, once capital is comprehended as *constituted* only through winning the class struggle at the point of production, the struggle to negate its negation. Capital lives only by appropriating living labour. Moreover, the value form *has* to be the way living labour appears in *this* specific society. But it is not an inner force that *must appear* thus. Rather the value form is an alien imposition on it, such that the primary movement is that of capital, which responds to determinations from labour by shaping it into an adequate basis. So if labour time is a determinant of value it is itself a determined determinant through which capital, rather than labour, is realised. Labour itself is caught in a crying contradiction because its objective realisation in the product is simultaneously its reification in value, because of the expropriation of its powers by capital. Capitalist production is by no means the specific social form in which *labour* realises itself, it is the form under which *capital* realises itself at the expense of the worker. If the truth of capital is found in labour, labour finds itself falsified in capital.

Summary

Capital perfects itself when incorporated. It faces two others of itself which it subsumes but cannot create *ab initio*. Its internal other is labour; its external other is land.

Labour power is not produced by capital, as if it were a genuine commodity. Rather it is reproduced in the domestic sphere. But domestic labour does not become socially recognised in value. However, if the erstwhile domestic labourer becomes a waged worker in the service sector then such labour does!

Modern landed property is a form of capital itself. However, the disappearance of the class of landed proprietors does not abolish the distinction between rent and other revenues.

The presentation broadens the discussion of the conditions of existence of capital to treat the relation of use-value to value, and of labour to capital. These relations are complicated because they cross the interface between the ideal and material spheres of the economy. To accomplish valorisation capital must invest in suitable use-values, above all, labour power. Here, use-value, at the outset of the presentation bracketed, has its economic effectivity. Yet, as subsumed by capital, it is posited as capital's *own* use-value. But this illusion is undercut by the potential recalcitrance of living labour to its 'use' by capital. Trapped within the capital relation it is yet 'in and against' capital.

CHAPTER 17

The Spectre

This chapter draws the conclusion of my whole presentation, namely that capital is a spectre. As such it demands a thoroughgoing critique to uncover its genesis. This is what the dialectical development of the value form has achieved.

Capital *presents itself* as a system articulated in logical forms. So these must be presented as such by value-form theory in a systematic way. But, also, the capital system must be *interrogated* in order to uncover its origin in the contradiction of association and dissociation embedded in the antinomies of production and trade.

So the *presentation* of the commodity-capitalist system here is *at the same time its immanent critique*. It is so in itself, apart from the bringing to bear of any external criterion of criticism. (Critique is distinguished from criticism in that it locates the source of the imputed error or inadequacy, and explains it, within the object itself.) It is precisely its homology with the forms of logic that shows capital is an inverted reality systematically alienated from its bearers, an object which, in its 'spiritualisation' of material interchange and practical activities into the heaven of pure forms, virtually incarnates the 'Idea'. Capitalism stands condemned *just because* it instantiates an idealist logic. (However, this does not mean 'breakdown' necessarily. Thus far capital has imposed its regime of truth, notwithstanding occasional rebellions.)

Capital's position is both immensely strong and immensely weak. Strong, because its ideality subsumes formally all otherness, weak, because as pure form it cannot comprehend its others (land and labour) in their reality. Capital *thinks* it makes the economic metabolism its own; but in reality subsumption is always radically incomplete, broken backed. In one way capital simply *is* the alienated expression of human powers; nevertheless, on this basis capital has made itself an *autonomous power* through the dialectic traced in this book. The chains that bind are invisible, hence 'weak', but immensely 'powerful' all the same, not least because they *are* invisible.

Capital does not appear as what *it is*; it has to be uncovered. Full-blown fetishism takes value to be intrinsic to the commodity. But even when critique exposes the social origin of the fetish-character of commodities, and capital, this demystification must acknowledge that this absurdity is really *present*. Critique moves now within the object itself. Thus the object of critique should be the *Idea* of capital. This does not mean 'ideas *about* capital', but that the reality confronting us *is* itself Idea in the sense of an identity of concept and reality. If we see the concept at work *in* reality, then we may say definitively that our critique is *immanent* to the object when we point out that value-*as*-concept (not just *our* concept) cannot recognise the real wealth of use-value. Since the fault is in reality theory has to adjust to that by a peculiar form of critique that grants the false its epochal validity, yet seeks to undermine its regime of truth while avoiding simple utopianisms.

The original separation of the ideal and material realms of the economic metabolism is generated *practically* as the ideal arises through a fold in the material. There results a metaphysics of presence: capital has a metaphysical presence – *the spectre* – shaping the material side from which it was detached. This 'presence' is *there* in the value form taken by commodities. Yet it *is not*. It is a spectre. If we treat value as the spiritual essence of the capitalist economy, its range of incarnations all centre on money, the transubstantiated Eucharist of value. 'The spectre' is this hollow armour, at once mute metal and possessor of the magical power to make extremes embrace. The spirit is made metal and stalks among us. The spectre interpellates all commodities as its avatars, an uncanny identity of discernibles, a spectral phenomenology. This negative presence, posited thus, fills itself out through emptying them of all natural being, and forming for itself a spectral body, a body of spectres. In capitalism all is *always* 'another thing' than what it is.

So far, then, from 'value' being some mundane material property or stuff, it is a shape opposed to all materiality, a pure *form* which takes possession of our world in the only way it can, through draining it of reality, an ontological vampire that bloats its hollow frame at our expense. 'Value as presence' *contrasts* immediately with the spheres where it is not, positing them as its non-being. But the result of the systematic development of the value form is to *subsume* them under it. The name of this active negativity is ultimately 'capital'. Only the emergent powers characteristic of this form of value can *effect* the inversion and reduce use-value to a moment of valorisation.

Capital produces *for exchange*, so this (seemingly external) condition of existence of value is then *internal* to its completed concept as it realises itself *through* exchange. Value is a *sui generis* form arising from capitalist commodity exchange, sinking into production, and then reflecting back on exchange so as to accomplish its *self-production*.

This movement, 'Being'–'non-being'–'Being', is capital as absolute negativity; it negates itself, in taking the shape of a material production process, but in the negation of its negation it recovers itself in fuller form. So, even when the value form grounds itself on production, the former is not reduced to the mere appearance form of the latter, a previously empty form seized by this content; rather, the form of self-determination achieved by this ideality maintains itself, takes production *within* its power, thereby *formally determining* production so as to shape it into its adequate ground (real subsumption of labour for example).

But capital confronts production and consumption as alien domains that it must subdue and actively seek to *in*form with its shapes. It must *take charge* of presenting commodities to exchange through shaping industry as capitalist industry so as to guarantee that there *be* commodities for exchange, that there be *new value*. So the forming of existent commodities as values in exchange is not enough; there must be real *positing* of value, occurring in time and space 'prior' to exchange. Then value as *presence* embraces what is outside exchange, subsuming it, 'formally' and then 'really', to the self-valorisation of capital.

If this form has sufficient determinacy to be a power in the world then an ontological *inversion* obtains. But it is important to realise that such ontological inversion does not, and could not, abolish the reality outside exchange, which still stands (on its own feet, so to speak); but it is *haunted* by it; still worse, at the emergent level of ontological complexity achieved by capital (self-valorising value) the spirit of capitalism *takes possession* of the real world of production and consumption. When capital attempts to ground itself *on* production, it runs into economic determinations springing from use-value. This should have dethroned ideality; but instead the opposite happens; the spectre prevails. The spectre 'takes possession' of use-value, estranges its meaning, drains away its truth, and substitutes a new one. Just as those 'possessed' by spirits use their own larynx and tongue but speak in another's voice, so use-values are 'possessed' by capital, in the spiritual as well as the legal sense. Capital speaks through them only of its own concerns, profit and accumulation. What capitalist accumulation is (un)really about is the sublimation of material wealth into a ghost of itself.

Nothingness is the ultimate ground as well as the starting point. There it was a vanishing point but in the shape of self-positing capital it is the movement of absolute negativity. Starting from an empty presence, it has no fixed ground so its ultimate form is simply the absolute negativity of its self-generation. Only in its infinite movement is it actual. On this view, it seems, the movement of 'presencing' is but a ripple on a sea of 'absence'.

Capital is a spectre in that, through it, the originally posited 'Nothing' gains *its determinacy*, subsuming, transforming and negating the 'real being' of the capitalist economy. But is it really *present*? Is it not rather a halo, a mirage, a semblance of actuality? To those who doubt that 'Nothing' can have agency and power I reply: 'It acts therefore it exists'. That it acts is demonstrated by the impossibility of trying to say what is going on in a factory without referring to valorisation; and what is that but increase in money? And what is money but the empty form that not only 'stands for' real wealth but elbows it aside and takes precedence? In money-making the spirit of capitalism is able to enter into commerce with the earthly reality of production and consumption. This 'Spirit' inhabits such material as a secret subject, animating it, and, vampire-like, communicating spectrality to all with which it has intercourse. Under the hegemony of the spirit world of capital, the phenomenal subject is itself a spectre. We exist for each other only as capital's 'personifications', 'masks', and 'supports'. The spectre is therewith incarnate in 'our' activity, and 'our' products.

But the fault is in reality; hence the needed critique is not critique of a false *view* of the world, but one that moves within the *object itself*, granting its objective validity, epochally speaking. In the society of the spectre the false is *out there*. A critique of its categories *is* a critique of the object because the ideal character of the object here allows for its *being* false. But to think against capital's regime of truth requires a peculiar insight: to grasp that in an inverted world 'the true is a moment of the false', as Guy Debord says.[1]

---

1 Debord 1977, § 9.

CHAPTER 18

Review of the Presentation

Here I take an overview of the critique of capital. When I rehearse briefly what has been achieved, I aim to explain once again, and to vindicate the fruitfulness of, the method of systematic dialectic. In my account of the logical genesis of capital I deploy the triad: sociation, dissociation, association. What is important here is that dissociation of social production requires a form of association. But in the system of capital this association takes the shape of an *alienated sociality*. The value form certainly brings together the array of private producers, but only as they are subjected to a system of pure form within which the concrete richness of the wealth produced is absented in the imposition of money measures, as all is counted not as what it is, but as its 'worth' on the market. In a nutshell, the dissociation of production that underpins social alienation is overcome by a 'second alienation', so to speak.

The ideality of capital as subject is purely a matter of its form, which unifies its determinations abstractly; it is quite different, then, from the affective unity of the family, or the conscious subordination of team members to a common goal. While, at the material level, economic activities are complementary, formally the social division of labour is unified through abstract determinations, such as the hidden hand of the market, and the not-so-hidden hand of capital's subordination of everything to the 'bottom line'. The spirit of capital is present everywhere, in the individual enterprise, and also at the level of the totalisation of capital.

This chapter has the following sections: the uses of Hegel; the question of form and content; the architectonic of the presentation.

The Uses of Hegel

I say at the outset that my aim is to see how far a Hegelian reading of capital's logic might illuminate its ontology. I also say that the Hegel to be deployed in this is the metaphysical, pan-logical, Hegel; *this* Hegel is my model.[1] This Hegel holds that the truth of reality exists in, *and only in*, its Idea. Conversely the Abso-

---

1 This is the Hegel Marx took for granted in his work. According to Tony Smith, Marx was guilty of a *misreading* of him. See Smith 2014.

lute Idea, as a self-specifying universal, is identical with all its determinations, which have no independent status, other than sustaining the self-actualising Universal.

Capital is at bottom pure form, even if it acquires in the material metabolism of the capitalist economy a body for itself. This corresponds to Hegel's philosophy only in its 'pan-logicist' reading. A sober reading of Hegel would assert that Logic should not be read as the overlord of Nature and History, but rather that these three spheres form together a 'circle of circles' such that, in principle, each of them is capable of providing a point of entry to the system, and then be completed as the necessary dialectical relations of the three are traced. It might even be said that the purely logical categories are simply abstracted *ex post* from what science reveals of nature and society. I have no reason here to take a position on 'what Hegel really meant'. But I follow the 'pan-logicist' reading of Hegel as my model. For it is a *good model for capital*. I argue capital is a metaphysical being; hence it is modelled on a metaphysical Hegel. Thus capital may be criticised for parallel reasons to those who criticise *this* Hegel.

Such a view of Hegel is contested by 'non-metaphysical' readings. Within Marxism, such a reading has been advanced by Tony Smith.[2] I reiterate that I cannot enter into this debate. It is not to my purpose in any case, because I argue that the critique of capital is parallel to the critique of the metaphysical Hegel. In both cases self-moving form claims to absorb the material inscribed within it. In the case of capital, it is social forms, and, in the case of Hegel, thought forms.

Where the presentation addresses the logic of the value form, narrowly considered, the putative hegemony of form has some plausibility. However, as the presentation develops it becomes clear that, if capital 'subsumes' otherness within its forms, it cannot pass off the irredeemably other simply as a moment of its self-actualisation. At the end of the argument I show this is especially the case with living labour, and with Nature. The 'original sin' of the separation of the ideal realm of value forms, from that of the material metabolism of the economy, is never overcome but rather becomes more painfully obvious.

It is interesting now to recur to Smith's view. He finds that Hegelian categories may well cast light on capital; but he holds that it is not a matter, as with my view, of the logic of the Concept, but of an 'Essence-logic'.[3] This is because con-

---

2 Smith 1990, 2014.
3 Smith 2014, p. 35.

tradition is a feature of Essence-logic, resolved for Hegel in the Concept. (A twist on this view is found in Patrick Murray's work. He too argues that capital is trapped in the logic of Essence. But he suggests that Marx criticises Hegel himself, despite the latter's critique of the Enlightenment in such terms, for failing to transcend it when he resorts to 'self-activating abstraction'.[4])

I cannot agree that capital may be comprehended merely by the categories of Essence. I have shown, in Division I above (§ 3), that it requires the categories of the Concept, for example those of 'teleology' and 'universality'. The issue for me, then, is to find the right terms in which to diagnose the failings of capital. It is all a question of *form*. In form capital follows the logic of the Concept and Idea. But this system of self-moving form is an alien imposition on social production. Labour and Nature are formally subsumed by capital, but they have their own reality outside it.

Hegel's category of Absolute Idea is the final term of his *Logic*. But, in my opinion, this is the *abstract* absolute, for pure form without material content is senseless. But in our case, it is precisely the abstract Absolute that successfully posits itself as Idea, albeit achieved as a totality only through the mediation of 'finite spirits' such as workers and capitalists. For the social whole is not their creation, but the creation of capital of which they are mere agents. The system is a system of self-moving social forms, albeit taking possession of human and natural 'capital'. Given this, it seems the Idea has an all-embracing character. Human relations are encompassed by logical relations. Capital, too, remains within its abstract forms, not knowing real Nature, or real people.

When I assert that capital is characterised by the logic of the Concept, this connects with the question of the *subject* of the dialectic discussed above; for, in Hegel's view, the Concept is the logic appropriate to the constitution of a subject, paradigmatically of the 'I'. I show that capital is such a subject, pursuing its aims at the expense of ours. It follows that my systematic-dialectical presentation of capital has nothing whatsoever to do with human freedom. The latter is, I know, *Hegel's* concern. His social philosophy presents the preconditions for the realisation of *human freedom*. However, my presentation is about the conditions of *capital's freedom*. This change in the 'subject' addressed does not prevent me from adopting the same logic. Thus human freedom is no concern of mine when I present the logic of *capital*, except as a threat to it. It is capital that is the *subject of modernity*.

---

4 Murray 1988, p. 218.

The Question of Form and Content

In my account of capital, I say that its homology with the logic of the Concept is all a matter of *form*. However, my critique of capital draws attention to what lies beyond such a concept. At the outset I align myself with value-form theory. However, *within* my presentation of the dialectic of the value form there are different levels at which a version of the category appears. The exact relation of *form and content* is a subtle, and complicated, question in this respect. The *category* 'content' is itself developed *in* the presentation of the value form, but it has further *applications*. When money forms commodities as values this corresponds to the internal relation of form and content in the logic of Essence. (But, abstractly, the possibility of contentless form must be allowed.) There is also the movement of 'absolute form', taken to stand over against the categories themselves as 'method', generating through absolute negativity the entire array of its determinations, as the 'content' of the system. For the value forms collapse unless they are systematically continuously produced in the *circuit* of capital. Furthermore, as Absolute Idea, capital takes *itself* as its own content when it treats itself as the transformable condition for another twist in the spiral of accumulation: 'K–K'–K" ...'. Capital must always be in movement, never a thing at rest. Finally, there is the case in which the Idea exists only in its process of self-realisation in the world and is fully actual only in its unity with it. This then raises anew the issue of form (the categories) and content (that to which the categories apply). There has to be something *to be formed*.

Money takes the role of synthesising the commodity manifold and giving sense to this mass of heterogeneous products. Capital dynamises money, and, in search of a source of accumulation, seizes on production itself. But it cannot be allowed that capital's dynamic creates the very substance of material production. There remains in it a 'Kantian' moment, in that the *things themselves* are in the last analysis inaccessible to capital, hence its blind destruction of the environment.

I underline that Hegel's dialectic is not understood by him as primarily *meth*odological but as *onto*logical. 'Method' itself in Hegel is simply the rhythm of this unfolding of the Idea by itself. This is *'the fluidity of the Concept'*. Engels thought the discovery of the transformation of energy a triumph for dialectic. In a sense it is, but not for idealist dialectic; it is not the concept of energy that is fluid but the energy itself. However, my position is that value is *itself conceptual* in character. While it is absurd to say the *concept* of energy spells itself out in heat, motion, etc., I argue that when value appears in commodities, money, and capital, it *determines itself* to these shapes because it *is* Concept, not something *we* conceptualise as 'value'. It is not a stable concept like 'energy'. The concept 'value' *itself* fluidly develops logical complexity as it becomes actual through its presentation. *My* presentation of its dialectic follows that of value itself as it exhibits the fluidity of the Concept.

The value-form dialectic in its purity, as a development of *form*, is *ideal* because it is distinct from, although borne by, commodities themselves. However, it is not a system of thought but is *itself real*, distinguished from reality proper by its character as an inverted reality, a fold in the material sphere. The reason why I term the commodity form of the product of labour 'ideal' is that the mediation of social labours here is of an abstract 'logical' character. The value form springs from the abstraction implicit in the exchange process, a *practical* abstraction from the bodily features of a commodity that are the basis of its use-value. My view is that we have in the 'Concept' of capital a self-moving system of pure forms. But the value forms, although they have a 'logical' character, are *out there*. This system of form determinations becomes 'Idea' if it *subsumes* material production. There is a real sense in which the forms *apply themselves* to the material to be formed, rather than the form being the *expression* of the content. This ideal aspect of capital springs from the *inversion* of concrete and abstract characteristic of the system of production for exchange. The result is a peculiar interpenetration of 'ideality' and 'materiality'; capital as an *ideal totality* subsumes within its own form-determinations all otherness, including living labour and natural forces. In situating all otherness merely as a moment of its own absolute reality, capital proclaims itself a self-identical totality. All that is not itself 'conceptual' is degraded to its bearer. The totalising logic of the value form imposes itself in such a manner that all relationships become inscribed within it.

However, the Idea of capital requires that it strive to *acquire* a material basis in order to 'fill itself out' so to speak. This turn is marked by the transition from the general formula for capital to capitalist production. Because the material reality of production is *given* to capital rather than created by it, capital has to transform this material into a suitable shape more or less adequate to it; this I call the 'formal determination' of the 'content'. But this transformation cannot be achieved through 'formal' subsumption alone; it requires real changes to the production process so as to make possible capital's fluidity in its other.

I have just now put 'content' in scare quotes because I do not think use-values, or for that matter objectified labour, are a genuine content. In a dialectical relation of form and content not only does the form posit itself in the content but the content gains its proper existence in the form. However, when use-value is inscribed within the value form this is by no means a form natural and appropriate to it, but an alien form imposed upon it. This is still more the case when living labour objectifies itself in value only to find itself estranged from its product. This is why I speak of capital 'taking possession' of land and labour so as to subordinate them to the purpose of valorisation. Rather than a proper content one might see them as material conditions of value creation.

The presentation at first seems to move forward under a theoretical impulse. But, as capital is itself conceptual in character, *it* must be understood as *presenting itself* through these same forms as the categorial framework presents.

Broadly speaking, transitions between categorial forms have the shape of the diagnosis of a problem followed by a putative solution, which then itself is problematised. What must be observed is that this sequential development of the presentation is not merely a matter of a theoretical device, such that theory 'zeroes in' on truth, so to speak, discarding along the way all the false starts. Rather, the presentation should be seen as identifying problems immanent to capital's *own* presuppositions, and it is capital that has always already solved them through a sequence of new forms that *preserve* the inadequate shapes of the truth, now as sublated interior moments. So, if this dialectic has a drive to solve problems of adequacy, it must not be understood merely as a quest internal to theory. Rather, theory, coming 'late' to the object, hence elucidates the solutions capital has already produced. The identity of the presentation with the inner dialectic of capital itself is all the more plausible in that the sequence of value forms has a certain conceptuality to it in reality. The forms, and the relations between them, have a logical character.

However, there are two categorial forms in which it might seem their material character is undeniable, namely 'value as substance' and 'production of value'. But both these, as with others for that matter, are to be taken in their logical minimum. Thus, with 'substance', this is neither material not spiritual, but purely logical; it is that which subsists on its own account, can change its appearance while remaining the same, and, crucially for us, can accumulate. 'Value as substance' is a form posited only through the development of money, but the *bearer* of money, whether gold or magnetic dots, is contingent; what 'counts', so to speak, is its purely formal functions of presenting value. (It is true to say that so to serve sets limits on what is a suitable bearer.)

As for 'production', that too is to be taken only in its most formal sense, namely that which has a result separable from the activity that posited it. Indeed, concrete positing of value is precisely what 'counts' here, albeit that it must be *carried* by material production, in order for a surplus product to arise.

If I describe the investigation as value-form *analysis*, in truth we just 'look on' while really the restless movement of capital carries out the analysis itself!

Capital makes value actual in the sense that it now has a form that posits itself as its own end. That is to say, with the form of capital we have before us a 'subject' that expressly aspires to the totalisation of its grounding determinations, and to include within its effectivity all its conditions of existence. The motive of the presentation in seeking to ground value finally becomes the motive of capital itself!

The systematic-dialectical presentation is guided by an architectonic allowing the placement of all the categories and forms of the system in a coherent sequence. My architectonic of capital discriminates the pure logic of the value form, from its imposition on the material underpinnings of capital. This architectonic has not only to be convincing as a 'big picture' of how capital presents itself; it has also to be tested by how convincing the 'mapping' of specific categories of logic are with the associated forms of value. However, the architectonic will in large part dictate such putative homologies without immediate consideration of case-by-case plausibility.

(One example is that in my research I was surprised to find that Hegel's modal categories mapped on to the concretisation of a unique universal equivalent simply as a consequence of the architectonic borrowed in large part from him. At other places, however, I introduce novelties; for example, replacing Hegel's *sequence* of measures with my *series* of measures. But, architectonically, both serve as transitions to the domain of Essence.)

The architectonic of the presentation exhibits two features that vindicate its usefulness. First, it orders the categories in a series of *levels* of logical complexity that allows them to be perspicuously structured. Second, it shows that the order of presentation of the levels follows a peculiar logic, namely that of the *retrogressive* grounding of the more abstract by the more concrete.

Overview

I now review the presentation as a whole. When commodity exchange occurs, a commodity that crosses the space of exchange is assumed to be identical in some respect with the other one. Yet (setting aside the phoney category of 'utility') completely heterogeneous goods are thus paired. So there is nothing common to them that provides a ground for their engagement. The obvious response to this, then, is to say that, any notion of 'intrinsic value' being thus excluded, to explain exchange requires reference solely to the aims of the exchangers.

However, my presentation develops determinations *intrinsic* to commodity production and exchange. Yet I start from the unpromising thought that there is indeed *nothing* given in the commodities concerned from which one could begin a theory of exchange-value. But it is precisely the Nothingness at their heart that I dialectically develop through a series of pure forms to the Idea of capital as the solution to the problem of vindicating the presence of value. When exchange imposes its 'infinitely negative judgement' on the commodity, nothing is left of it save the pure *form* of 'presence'; yet nothing *is* present (all materiality being absented). It is the presence of emptiness; but this Nothingness is *made present* in the dialectic of the *logical* form of exchange.

I begin with simple commodity relations. Categories such as quality, quantity, and measure, are deployed in order to analyse what it is to *be* a commodity (§1). The highest point reachable with such 'surface' categories is that of 'specifying measure', which is the series of exchange-values a commodity may acquire (§1.3). The transition to the next logical level is founded on the presupposition that exchange-value is the form in which the *immanent* exchangeability of a commodity appears. It is posited that it has such a thing as its value, distinct from its exchange-values, lying behind them, and retrogressively supporting the imputation that the series of measures gain their truth as expressions of this underlying immanent value.

Yet the presupposition just mentioned cries out for its own grounding movement. How do I *show* that value is 'of the essence' so to speak? So it is required that the presentation explore the level of Essence relations. This is of greater logical complexity than those of 'Being'. The dialectic of essence I trace step by step through a sequence of more concrete expressions until I reach the money form of value (§2).

It is money that posits the ordering of commodities in a value universe centred on the presupposition that money is the actuality of value. But this needs careful analysis. The fundamental function of money is that of the real measure of value. The dialectic posits that all commodities have intrinsically a *magnitude* of value; but since our presentation thus far has followed a dialectic of pure form, such a magnitude is *itself* a matter of pure form; it is posited as *sheer immanence* without the metric that would be present if there were any substance to it. Money, however, posits such a metric in its *own* measure. Thus money provides commodities with measure, because it is the actuality of value. But, even when money allows value to gain phenomenal existence, what money measures is simply pure immanence; there is nothing *to* measure, albeit that money effects such a judgement as that two commodities are 'equal in value'.

It is important to my account of the transition between categories to distinguish *necessary* and *sufficient* conditions. A sore point in this respect is the appearance here of *commodity* money. I introduce gold as *sufficient* to bear the shape of 'unique universal equivalent', which is required to make present value in autonomous form. But it is not itself *necessary* to capital. It is replaceable when it is required by the presentation to develop credit money, as a more perfect actualisation of the money form. The unique universal equivalent requires a bearer, because it cannot be merely the *thought* that all commodities are equivalent as values that effects it. Money has to say so in *practice*, make it present. It is entirely legitimate to pass through the stage of gold money because that is sufficient to ground the requirement that value in autonomous form be presented. However, not only is gold itself *not necessary* for this (but merely a contingent solution), it is demonstrably inadequate to the fulfilment of the Concept. Yet the more adequate form of money, namely *ex nihilo* credit, requires the separation from commodity circulation of a financial system; this is far too concrete a social form to be brought up to the level of abstraction at which the need for money is first posed.

There follows a crucial turn to a further level of complexity that retrogressively establishes that the claim of money to embody value is valid. Although there is no such thing as a substance *of* value, value as money is itself pure substance; for it may be aggregated and accumulated in *sums* of money. The identity of all sums of money with each other as mere divisions of a notionally infinite sum, leads to the claim that this is made explicit in value as Concept. This condenses the indeterminate realm of substance to a *unitary* form, capable of being determined to instances of itself, namely the Capital Concept (§3).

Here the logic of the Concept is articulated in the moments of universality, particularity, singularity. Value is particular as 'amount' and is present in singular shape as '*an* amount' of money. This third level of the dialectic of the value form supports the claim of money to actuality as it actively asserts its truth. The most important single transition here is the argument that immanent exchangeability, 'value', is *posited* when this is made the essence of commodity relations by money. Money functions as the bearer of value in autonomous form *apart* from the commodities, and hence brings them to judgement through their worth in price. The system becomes determinate if it is possible to establish a *valid* judgement of worth (§ 31.2).

Commodities are formally granted recognition as 'values' only in money price. More significantly, through the metamorphoses of commodities and money the latter gains a permanent presence in monetary circulation and then, in the general formula for capital, sets itself as its own aim in a circuit through which it generates an increment over the principal.

Capital is characterised by objective teleology (§ 32.3). (For the complexity of 'teleology' see *Glossary*.) The money form develops to the capital form when it sets itself as its own end, rather than simply mediating circulation. But what 'end' could be set for money? The only such possibility is the generation, through the circuit of capital, of a monetary increment to add to the principal. Indeed, that is the only way in which money *can* affirm itself in opposition to commodities as value in autonomous shape. In its Idea then, capital is bent on its own accumulation. Admittedly, the task of accumulation seems trapped in endlessness. But the truth is that capital's very being is simply that of *accumulating*. This is what makes it capital, and its proper measure is its *rate* of accumulation. Money now measures, not only the worth of commodities, but also of capital as a rate of accumulation of new value (§ 33.31).

Capital measures itself against itself therewith, even if growth is only pure increase for its own sake. (If one points to the growth of factories and labourers, this is of no moment because capital is concerned only with their *value*; capital is the spectral presence that has taken possession of them.)

But there is a crying contradiction in the pure form of capital. It requires continual appropriation of new value, but under the rule of equivalent exchange this is ruled out. When commodities are valued, they are to be found standing in relations of equivalence according to their law, yet must contain non-equivalence to realise capital in its concept. Now the value form logic really has run out of road because of the apparent impossibility of *grounding* a regular surplus value. I have to show how self-valorisation is possible in a world where, putatively, exchange is only of *equivalent values*. The problem of how the relation of commodity *circulation* can result in both identity and non-identity is to be resolved in turning to what is itself both identical and non-identical with it, namely commodity *production* by capital (§§ 4, 5, 6).

The *logical* form of capital is by no means absolute but insufficient to maintain itself, and it requires a transition to a domain of reality regulated by the form but by no means inessential to it; capital is not free to develop in its concept alone; it must confront the problem of its lack of self-subsistence as mere concept of self-valorisation. Capital is defined as 'self-valorising value'; but how can this form maintain itself? The main point here is that while capital has the *form* of self-realisation it still lacks control over its bearers.

With capital we reach a form of circulation of commodities that is its own end, but the self-valorisation process still rests for its possibility on the emergence into being of the goods themselves from some external source. The concept of unconditioned self-development of the value form fails to realise itself if the appearance of goods in the marketplace is utterly contingent. Thus, there is still a large element of conditionedness in the mere possibility of valorisation. It is not *self-grounded*. Circulation in its immediacy is therefore 'pure semblance', a play of forms. Exchange could fade away (as during the decline of the Roman Empire). Hence to make a reality of its concept capital must itself undertake the production of commodities and reduce them to moments in its own circuit. Only on this condition does value in and for itself pass from a mere formal potential to embed itself in a real material process.

Hence another major turning point in the presentation is the turn to production of commodities by capital. In this, the formal determination of *production* itself, by the demands of valorisation, results in the formal, and then the real, subsumption of it to capital, which appears therewith as a unitary totality. The turn to the real world of production and circulation in space and time is one to a world in which pure form is concretised in its engagement with what is other than it. This has two aspects. In the first place, there are developments of form itself, as it becomes articulated by the temporal dimension especially (§4). In the second place, material conditions of capitalist production must be characterised as subsumable by the circuit of capital in such a manner as capital appropriates the surplus product (§5).

Here there begins a new dialectic in that the whole value-form array is to be taken as a self-referring immediacy now having to undertake to mediate itself in the material metabolism of the economy, through informing with its determinations the reality of circulation and production in space and time.

However, I distinguish from such formal determination the material determinations, relevant to the production of use-values, which also have economic determinacy at the value level, e.g. notions such as socially necessary labour time in a purely technical sense. It requires the real subsumption of circulation and production to capital.

I first deal with the reality of circulation, which concretises the rate of accumulation in accordance with an interval, e.g. per annum. More than this, however; the infinity of capital previously presented abstractly is now shown to be temporalised in that its past and future are interior to its Idea. Temporality is intrinsic to the Idea of capital insofar as it is actual only in its becoming. Thus it is fair to say that time is the *existent* concept (§41).

As far as production of commodities by capital is concerned, here, too, time is of the essence; more precisely, the time that passed in their production is the basic determinant of value (§51). I provide also an original argument for a version of the labour theory of value in terms of a dialectic of negativity (§52.3). Living labour is peculiar in that the time of its appropriation by capital is marked by its tendential recalcitrance to capital's dictates. It is true that in value labour appears as 'reified' – as 'dead labour' – but this is merely the *res-*

ult of a process in which labour differs from all other inputs in its *resistance* to capital. It is not merely so-called 'human capital', as if it were a 'resource' to be exploited like others (as bourgeois ideology has it).

The value added is allocated by capital between its profits and the wages it has to disburse to the workers. A working day of sufficient length allows for surplus labour to emerge as the condition that grounds surplus value. Only thus are the empty forms discussed earlier given substance. The mediator of ideal and material is the personification of capital, the character masks of capital are the capitalist and the manager. These human agents operate with a consciousness colonised by capital. The capitalists respond to the demands of the Concept they internalise, by applying it to the empirical material before them.

The turn from the value form to production and circulation does not leave ideality behind; on the contrary, the process of formal determination 'idealises' even such apparently material relations. While originally capital is alienated from the realm of use-value, it restores unity with what it separated from, but it nearly loses itself in the material production process, from which it returns having undergone a dangerous journey, because the other is *not* already given as its presupposition but posited by it as if it were. But, for capital to be self-grounded, it must undertake the *production* of commodities, rather than simply trade in them.

I now come to the central issue of the (initial) determination of value magnitudes. There are two claims. First is that the genesis of value in *time* leads to the understanding of its magnitude as a function of the time of its *positing* (the logical abstraction of production time). Second is the restriction of production time to labour time. Of all the times in which capital is 'tied up' before it sells its product, labour time is peculiar in its recalcitrance to its exploitation. Only this time requires capital to engage in a struggle to 'negate' its opposite. Only if capital succeeds in this 'labour of the negative' is it *constituted*. This is the central determinant of its valorisation therefore (§ 53).

To be self-grounded, value must be produced by value. This means that only those goods produced by capital itself count as values, as true commodities both in form and content. Only capitalistically produced commodities have adequacy in both form and content to value in and for itself. The activity of production is an activity of labour. Hence, capital must set itself to make that activity its own activity. Capital makes that activity its own activity insofar as it thoroughly subsumes living labour as its carrier, penetrated through and through by the value form. The limitlessness of accumulation inherent in the form of capital is given a solid *ground* in productive labour.

Non-produced commodities retain the value form but only, as such, the semblance of value; they are lacking in the substance of value because they do not originate within the value circuit itself as it is driven by valorisation. Products, on the other hand, if capitalistically produced as commodities for sale, gain both determinations of value, being both produced as values and sold as values. Insofar as capital conquers the sphere of production it gains reality and permanence instead of being dependent on external conditions to provide the values on which it feeds. That the presentation only found it necessary to turn to productive labour, when the capital form required a ground, implies that there are inadequate grounds for positing a labour theory of value at the level of commodity exchange alone; that relation is still too indeterminate.

The dialectic of commodity production is best presented, I think, as one in which the form sinks into the matter and then develops it as its own. Within the value form, instead of the content developing itself through the mediation of its form, the form seeks to secure and stabilise itself through subsuming the matter and turning it into a bearer of self-valorisation.

A further important turn in the presentation is that which takes up the *system* of capital, since its Idea is actual only on the condition that there are competing capitals that effect it (§ 8). This is concretised in two interlinked axes. Capital has the moments of its Concept reflected *within* itself, in its circuit for example; at the same time these moments articulate the reflection of capitals *against* each other, in competition and its consequences. The categories here have a 'mixed' character in that the logical scheme is effective only as the material inscribed within it has adequate economic effectivity, for example the interplay between departments of reproduction.

Here the dialectic takes shape in more concrete forms, such as are found in the development of price and profit, until I establish the logical actuality of reproduction price and the general rate of profit (§ 83.3). Value necessarily appears as price. It is a mistake, then, to speak of the transformation *of* value *into* price. Thus my transformation procedure concretises value in the sequence: simple price; production price; reproduction price. Only in the production price is value present in its actuality, as systemically determined. What is conserved, throughout the transformation of value, is the division between wage goods and surplus goods; but these heaps of commodities cannot have determinate measure until capital sets, and reproduces, prices through competition. The existence of a surplus is ontologically prior to its measure, but its value may be measured at different levels of determination. It is finally set as a result of *all* the system's determinations, beginning with exploitation and ending with the reproduction of departments.

At the end of my presentation, I characterise the constellation of Finance, Commerce, and Industry, as the Absolute Idea of capital (§ 9). The most important thing by far here is the *creation* by banks of money *ex nihilo*, for the purpose of credit to industry. This 'comes from nowhere', so to speak, and it is a reinstatement of our original notion of the void at the heart of capital (§ 91).

The capital Idea is a totality systematically encompassing all its moments in the whole. I set out to find a ground for value, surplus value, and capital. There is no foundation for such forms since there is *Nothing* to be made present. Capital, therefore, can only be that permanent process of absolute negativity which sets itself against the transience of the forms it creates. So the *pure* ground of the system as a whole is simple negativity. It is the process of Nothingness affirming itself. But in the end nothing is affirmed. No final resting place is found. Yet the *movement* of presencing sustains itself just in negating all fixity. The spectre of capital is present only as what is *not* there, yet proves its hegemony by denying what *is* there its own truth, and transfiguring all reality into the medium of its becoming in Idea.

However, the Idea remains other than the material metabolism it subsumes. The infinity of capital exists in its continual accumulation of itself. It is here it aspires to 'absolute becoming', before it gets bogged down in unreliable machinery and striking workers. From one point of view this movement follows the path of the ideal *realising itself* in materiality, rather than *giving way* to more concrete shapes – which are *ipso facto* more 'real'. From another point of view the entire movement is possible only insofar as form encounters, and subsumes, material production, notably the ability of labour to produce a surplus. So use-value does have its own economic determinacy, undermining thereby any claim of capital to be all-in-all.

There is a difference between this move of ours and Hegel's transition from the logical forms to those of the real world. Hegel is confident that there is a good 'fit' between the logical forms of reality and that reality itself. In our case, the forms are not forms *abstracted from* reality but *sui generis* self-referring forms radically other than the material metabolism. So the unity effected between logical form and material content here is external, a matter of the *subsumption* of the material by the ideal, of the spirit of capitalism *taking possession* of a world that does not *require* such a form unless, and until, its matter has been so shaped through formal determination as to have the possibility of existing in that shape only as what is expressible in capitalist form.

In production the ideal moves *in* the real, indeed takes possession of it, and acts within it as a *real power*. But this turns the social forms of production into deranged, alienated, ones. Notably labour is subsumed by the capital Concept in such a manner that it is formed as an abstraction of itself. When registered in value, it does not gain an appropriate social form, rather it is 'derealised' there. However, capital contracts an unacknowledged debt for this; in totalising labours only as abstractions of themselves, it cannot account for what is in excess of its concept of itself, the concrete richness of social labour. It is precisely because capital cannot fully incorporate its material foundation that there must be a limit to its ideality. A consequence of this duality of ideal and material is that, if capital is ideally a hegemonic totality, it is also vulnerable because of its dependence on the productive forces of labour power. Capital builds a world for itself, but land and labour at bottom are potentially destabilising of it. This is because its ideality fails to recognise living labour and Nature; instead it pretends to be self-constituting, as if the inverted world is the truth. Nonetheless, capital *exists* as a power over us. So I treat capital as such a *given whole* and demonstrate how it reproduces itself.

The method of rising from more abstract indeterminate notions to the concrete whole, according to an immanent dialectical moment, may well be mistaken for a teleological one. This would only be so if the whole were to be taken as immanent in the movement of the process of its generation. *Once* the presence of the whole is granted, it may be shown how it reproduces itself precisely through its interior dialectic. However, there is no necessity of a quasi-causal type which imposes the transition from simple categories to more concrete ones. Since the systematic dialectic is not historical there is certainly no claim to be made about how capital *must* develop out of its precursors. But even in pure logic the transitions are not to be understood as if they *had* to take hold because the need to reach the whole is effective. The 'need' is purely hypothetical: *if* we are to understand the concrete existent whole, abstract indeterminate shapes of it must be supplanted in the presentation by more concrete ones. Expositionally we rise from abstract to concrete; but while it is *logically* the destiny of the abstract to rise to the concrete this has no bearing on the *real* movement from one to the other. For example, *conceptually* value is not perfected unless it is developed to self-valorising value, but a hypothetical society with commodity circulation has no necessity to develop into a capitalist one, because the immanent logical tendency may not take hold for all manner of reasons.

What is certainly true is that capital itself has an immanent teleology; but the theoretical exposition of its logical '*constitution*' does not rely on this but on the theoretical requirement to show how the system tendentially supports its inner moments. For such a story the development is immanent: at the end capital shows retrospectively how it abstracts from itself its own logical presupposition, namely the commodity.

Capital as subject is not some God-like being imposing value determinations on the economy. It just *is* the activity of absolute negativity through which the form-determinations are posited only to be negated in every twist of the dialectic. Nor is capital as subject a final *result* of its 'presencing'; it exists only in its *movement* from beginning to end. The end of the systematic dialectic itself circles back to the beginning when capital posits products as commodities, the very same commodities with which the presentation began. Capital in its movement in matter directs it to the purpose of its own accumulation. However, I have undermined capital's arrogance by showing that use-value determinations must underpin and support the value forms, and that there is no valorisation without exploitation of living labour.

CHAPTER 19

Beyond Capital and Class

At the outset, the capital system originates through an original separation between the logical forms, and the useful products, of social production. This split is never healed, no matter how much adequation of each side to the other is achieved; so there remains throughout its presentation a context in which the system is always to be understood as alienated from human sociality. Nonetheless, capital *acts as* an autonomous power. It is not just a mistake by us to take it only *as if* it were standing over against us as dictating our possibilities.

Capital becomes fully determinate only in the capital *relation* which is developed into a class relation. However, the relation is properly termed 'the capital relation', not 'the wage labour relation', nor yet the capital-labour relation. Capital is the *principal moment* of this contradiction, because through this relation it *realises* itself. Waged labour, by contrast, *negates* itself in yielding value and surplus value. Capital continually accumulates; labour continually returns to its propertylessness. I suggest that such a striking asymmetry legitimates a presentation of the relation of capital to waged labour as *internal to* the concept of capital, albeit that a special study of waged labour would usefully complement it.

From the capital relation flow subject positions, which articulate it at the phenomenal level, and structure the opposition of classes and their struggle. However, the struggle between such classes is already given in terms of the capital relation which logically pre-exists them. In this sense 'wage labour' is a category of capital itself, but it would be a mistake from this to conclude that capital can only be disrupted from outside. Living labour is always in-and-against the capital relation. So 'class struggle' is a category that undoubtedly has a place at the level of pure theory, despite the fact that the trade union movement, for example, may be left to be discussed at a more concrete and historical level. Yet epochally the working class is *atomised* by capital, so it is at present merely a virtual counter-subject until historical events give rise to a *consciously organised* anti-systemic movement.

Workers have to sell their labour power to capital, but normally are recalcitrant to their exploitation even when the dull compulsion of economic necessity forces them to accept their destiny as wage labourers. Although the capital relation is antagonistic, the principal pole is always capital, which sets the terms for labour's engagement, for the workers are separated from the means and object of labour. But the movement of self-valorisation runs up against the recalcitrance of the working class to being interpellated as a mere resource for capital to use as it thinks fit.[1]

Nonetheless workers fight always on capital's terms, and their victories are largely defensive and partial, e.g. the reduction in the work-day. This is why the workers are the secondary pole of the contradiction. Momentarily they may become the principal pole (workers control) but unless revolution eventuates, capital reasserts its authority. It is true the capital relation can be read in both ways, but the revolutionary variant is the *repressed* truth, while capital is epochally dominant. The task is to *make* the working class the principal moment. Politically, labour is merely a *virtual* counter-subject until it acts to break from capital.

The theory of value presented earlier is not merely political, in that it roots value in struggle at the point of production; at the limit it is internally related to the revolution against self-valorising value. But it is beyond the scope of this work to study the dynamics of revolution. Here the point is to show how capital reproduces itself on a daily basis in unexceptional times.

However, there are two ways in which class comes into pure theory. *First*, the very constitution of capital requires a recognition of the – always problematic – subsumption of labour. Indeed, I have argued this is central to the very *definition* of capital and separates this form of exploitation from others. (Traditional labour theory, descended from classical political economy, speaks of the toil and trouble of labour. But in capitalist production this is irrelevant. What is relevant is the time and trouble of capital as it tries more effectively to pump out labour services from recalcitrant workers.) *Second*, although revolution is not discussed here, pure theory must undercut capital's claim to be the absolute reality, and to find a standpoint from which such a critique is meaningful. This can only mean adopting the standpoint of labour. Capital is a real power in the world. Epochally, it has made itself the ruling idea, and it has imposed its regime of truth. However, there remains the possibility of the working class becoming a counter-subject to capital. All along, from the human point of view, the capitalist system embodies the self-negation, alienation, of the workers.

The dialectic of waged labour is as follows: i) formally it is determined in relation to capital, meaning its conditions of existence are determined for it; ii)

---

1 A good example of recalcitrance in *Capital* is that Marx predicates the switch to machinery in part on the need to overcome the resistance of skilled craftsmen. Although this change is part of capital's own *history*, the point here is that it is to be situated in terms of the achievement of the *logical* perfection of the Capital Idea.

determined for itself in Trade Unions etc. ameliorating conditions, it has some consciousness of itself as a social subject even if defined in capital's terms; iii) in and for itself, labour takes up a critical attitude to *itself*, and re-determines its conditions of existence so comprehensively as to abolish itself.

Capital is blind to the human being of the worker outside its positing as a bearer of labour power, supposedly available for hire to capital like any other input to production. But any *critical* theory of capitalism that grasps the capitalist totality, not only in its own terms but from a perspective beyond its limits, can draw crucial theoretical lessons from the identity and non-identity of wage labour, and landed property, with capital. True, the overriding 'middle' which epochally secures the *identity* of identity and difference is the Idea of capital, which divides, as new value, into itself (profit) and its others (wages, rents). But, from the standpoint of critique, it is the *difference* of identity, and difference, of value, and use-value, that points to historical supersession of the value form.

Wage labour is internal to the very concept of capital because it is under the wage form that living labour, and hence surplus value, is available to capital. That is why capital is epochally the pole which determines the conditions of existence of its other more than the reverse. The struggle for dominance is won by capital, which successfully returns from the sphere of production with surplus value, while living labour returns from the factory exhausted and deprived of its own product.

It is not like a boxing match configured by the interaction of independent agents. Rather, capital makes labour *its* agent when it prevails. Conversely, self-assertion by the working class would involve throwing off the shackles of capital. The world is not big enough for both to fulfil themselves at the same time. For the proletariat to assert itself, in and for itself, is not only incompatible with its definition as a bearer of labour power for capital, it must involve its own abolition as a class. Capital must negate its negation to stay as it is. But wage labour must negate its negation to become something *other* than what it is.

If the main contradiction *of* capital is *between* capital and labour, then 'capital' appears twice, once as whole and once as part. If subject positions are *constituted* by this relational totality, then wage labour as such a subject position is yet *negated* within the capital relation, hence is in and against it as a whole, not just engaged in a partial struggle with the partial capitalist position. The working class is a peculiar, transitory 'subject', posited as a general category only *by capital* as its 'otherness'. The meaning of the struggle against the totality that defines its being is then to liberate individuals from 'classification'.

This capital relation contains an immanent contradiction of each pole with itself; thus:

(1) on the side of labour, it alienates its substance, therewith generating its own oppressor, (2) on the side of capital, it produces the proletariat *as* proletariat, its own gravedigger.

The contradiction, then, involves self-contradiction insofar as each pole posits its own opponent. Capital, as the principal aspect of the contradiction, for the present *affirms* itself even in its other. Wage labour *denies* itself in producing its other, because it has accepted the definition of itself by the other, as internal to capital, hence it affirms its negation. To be *self-critical* requires that it grasp itself as other than what it is in this definition, and destroy itself along with the relationship that defines it. Thus I argue that the standpoint of our critique is that of the *critically adopted* standpoint of labour. The aim is to abolish class and therewith 'labour' itself. However, this demand to abolish class is rooted *immanently* in the dialectic of the real; it is not the product of a critique *opposing* itself to reality. Its presentation is at the same time a critique of capital.

Thus we must not only theoretically engineer the return of the repressed, but anticipate its revolt against capital. However, I do not draw a politics from the theory set out in this work. For that, more mediated forms would have to be developed, notably a theory of the revolutionary subject.

There are two sorts of dialectical movement:

1) the purely affirmative, perfecting itself through the sublation of all contradictions; here the poles are to be preserved but the contradiction is given 'room to move', so to speak, in a higher unity;

2) and the purely negative, the absenting of the emergent contradiction through its dissolution; here the emergent poles are to be superseded in a re-totalisation that 'takes back', so to speak, a misstep.

But the 'taking back' is not a *return* as such but incorporates a learning experience, or else the mistake would be repeated. Within the property system there is to be no going back to a supposed Eden of equal exchange, but the abolition of private property in socialism. The injuries of class cannot be resolved through some class compromise between right and right; without a revolution against class itself there is only a fudge. The very *ground* of the contradiction has to be transformed.

But if the proletariat defines its task *negatively*, as its own abolition, when it abolishes the relationship that defines it, what is the standpoint of the *positive* coming out of this determinate negation? If revolution is not 'the affirmation of the proletariat' the question arises *of what is it an affirmation*? If, negatively, it abolishes class, what, positively, is it about? It can only be about human liberation. In that sense the class struggle is a moment of a larger project, one in which non-proletarians have an interest since the very split into classes is an affront to human community.

Some may claim that the view advanced here substitutes for class struggle some larger socio-historical contradiction, and that it prevents us seeing class struggle as what is 'really productive of history'. If an 'efficient contradiction' refers to a causal impulse rather than a reason for action, in that sense it *is* class struggle that produces change. But the *project of change* is something else.

In order to articulate the need for change, I argue the *speculative* moment cannot be avoided. (I venture this with due trepidation!) Looking forward, however, requires a wager: that communism *will have been* produced from class struggle. In order to articulate the revolutionary project the existent must therefore be grasped from the standpoint of the 'not yet'. Is this a teleological problematic? Certainly not, if this means there is some guarantee inscribed in the heavens that communism will redeem humanity. What it does imply is that the meaning of a historical situation cannot be properly understood in its own terms, but only from the standpoint of what it has in it to become. The speculative moment emerges when reason demands the realisation of this standpoint in a practical project, to act as if this 'not yet' is actually on the agenda. However, from the practical viewpoint, for the proletariat, the promise of classlessness is a *speculative* supersession of the contradictions of its existence as long as it lies in the future.

'Another world is possible' is a speculative proposition, not because we do not have good arguments but in its logical status. This creates a philosophical problem. The speculative moment cannot be eliminated precisely because we live in an alienated society (the asocial sociality of bourgeois life) in which the standpoint of social humanity is unactual, and hence available only in its displacement to philosophy, which wagers on the proletariat to realise it. Scientific socialism conceives itself as the theoretical expression of a revolutionary process. But philosophy remains an alienated science as long as revolutionary practice lacks immediate historical actuality. In sum dialectic is not a science of efficient causation allowing prediction. The future that will become has to be produced by 'us' out of the mire of contradictions, and in anticipating it the speculative moment is unavoidable.

I think it is important to distinguish the peculiar form of sociality underpinning generalised commodity production, and sociality in its truth. From the logically precedent disruption of immediate sociality, by dissociation, arises the untruth of capital. But the opposition of sociation and dissociation is retained when mediated through the association provided by exchange. This is an estranging mediation because it is predicated on the original separation. But sociality as such has no need to appear as something other than itself. If it does so, this is due to a systemic *derangement* of form. Then labour appears, not as what it is, but as what it is not, a part of capital.

However, capital has established the power to *appropriate our powers* in its service. Thus, ontologically, the productive powers of capital are nothing but the collective powers of living labour, in alien form. Capital *needs* our collective heritage of cultural knowledge, including scientific-technical knowledge. Although it successfully appropriates these socially developed powers, they remain external to it in a very real sense, nonetheless. One of the hidden secrets of contemporary capitalism is how it has come to depend increasingly on scientific-technical knowledge, whose development has been funded with public money, because the costs and risks of research at the frontier are too great to be compatible with accumulation. After centuries of capital's mobilisation of the powers of collective social labour, and 'the general intellect', there now arise, more and more, the objective and subjective preconditions of socialism.

The principle of an immanent development of sociality is given in estranged shape in capital's dialectic of negativity. Never content with its sublation of its previous condition, it continually transforms those presuppositions and creates itself anew. Throwing off the estranged form of the development of our powers leaves humanity as the subject of its own 'absolute process of becoming'. However, epochally the Idea of capital has *made itself* real. Capital is the totalising Subject of modernity. Whether that which is in excess of its concept *remains* forever marginal is for the future to determine.

APPENDIX 1

Commentary on the Hegelian Origins of the Logic of the Value Form

Throughout my work, I draw freely on Hegel and Marx, although I do not often supply direct quotations. At the same time, I depart from Hegel and Marx in many respects. Most of my Marxian categories are intended to parallel closely those of his *Capital*. However, they are always matched with a logical category, thus giving them a place in my own system. The main difference between my articulation of the logic of capital, and that of Marx, is largely that of its *ordering*. I believe Marx is precipitate in bringing into his chapter on the commodity the category of labour, which he associates so closely with value that unwary readers may even identify the two. As I explained above, there are good reasons for delaying an account of the labour theory of value until after the general form of capital has been thematised, as I do. This means that, through Division I here, the value form is treated as empty of material content; 'value' itself means no more than the power of exchange possessed by a commodity; the elucidation of its ground in material production is postponed until Division II.

With respect to Marx's *Capital* I am therefore something of a revisionist. The same is true of my appropriation of Hegel. Since my entire system is articulated around Hegel's *Logic*, in this Appendix I go into it, and my use of it, in some depth. This has the advantage that the main text need not be cluttered with asides on the Hegelian provenance of each category.

It is a striking fact that Hegel's two versions of his logic differ, markedly so in the case of the Doctrine of Essence. It is equally striking that very little attention is given to this in the Hegel literature. Some prefer the *Science of Logic*, some the *Encyclopaedia*, but little is done to compare them so as to justify it. It seems that some think the *Encyclopaedia*, as the later version, represents Hegel's final word; others think it a mere popularisation of the more substantial, hence superior, *Science of Logic*. Only McTaggart carefully notes, and discusses, all the discrepancies, in his valuable commentary of 1910. Moreover, the original culprit is Hegel himself! He makes no mention of the discrepancies between the *Science of Logic* and the three editions of the *Encyclopaedia*.[1]

---

1 An extraordinary case of a failure to note a change is that the second edition of the *Encyclopaedia* omits the 'big triad' (Logic/Nature/Spirit) at the end; it appears in the first, and reappears in the third, edition (§§ 575, 576, 577).

Thus in taking a view on the merits of the various versions of the logic we have nothing pertinent from Hegel, and we must rely on our own readings. My presentation embodies in its logic three different reasons for its choices with respect to the categories and their order.

First, the two versions of Hegel's *Logic* force on me a choice between them; after careful study, I prefer the *Science of Logic*, although there are weaknesses in it. If I mainly follow this, I do not hesitate to follow the *Encyclopaedia* where it is of more use.[2]

Second, I think Hegel is sometimes wrong and I revise him for that reason. (An example is my criticism of his treatment of 'Measure'.)

Third, my logic is in the service of my elucidation of the ontology of capital; this is a specific domain of reality. Because of this, not all the wealth of material Hegel provides is required, and where I do draw on it, the precise significance of a category, and its relation to others, is to be read according to my purpose. A trivial instance, in my project, is that under quantity I need 'number' and 'ratio' only, but not 'degree'. (Value does not come in degrees, only in amounts.) Under judgement and syllogism, I neglect most of Hegel's effort to comprehensively situate all the logical paradigms of his day. Only the 'syllogism of equality' is needed for transitive pricing.

Hegel's logic is really an ontology; as such it pertains to the universe in general. The *range* of my dialectic is more restricted, however. Indeed, it is striking that capital has a poverty-stricken ontology, in which quantity predominates over quality; this is the very reverse of Hegel's approach, since he generally slights simply quantitative relations. But, naturally for an *Encyclopaedia*, he includes categories of quantity. Capital has enough unity in its structure to be self-reproducing, but the number and richness of its categorial forms is reduced in comparison with those of Hegel. Moreover, I often simplify the number of categories by ignoring the finer divisions and hoping that a transition is plausible without them. Sometimes, however, I have expanded upon Hegel's list.

I call attention now to a few major disanalogies with Hegel's philosophy, present in my attempt to appropriate it within the framework of my claimed homology between the work of Absolute Spirit and the hegemony of capital. The most striking pertains to the final term of Hegel's *Logic*, the Absolute Idea. The self-perficient concept here reaches its apotheosis. Since contradiction is no longer present in it there seems no ground for a transition from it; Hegel presents therefore a transition to Nature which is *not* 'a transition' – it is an act of prefect freedom. Much could be said, and has been said, about this mysterious leap by the Idea out of itself. But here I underline that the

---

[2] The best English translation of *The Encyclopaedia Logic* is that by Geraets, Suchting, and Harris: Hegel 1991; but I do not always follow it in my own citations of Hegel's paragraphs.

final term of the logic of the value form is that of the concept of capital realising itself only in contradiction with itself. As pure form capital is far from Absolute. A transition to a realm in which this contradiction may be resolved is necessary.

A parallel might yet be retained if Hegel's own account is itself thoroughly revised. I believe that there is an unremarked sleight of hand in Hegel's *Logic* itself. Let us look at how the logic is related to the real world. What is striking is that this is thematised by Hegel in the part *preceding* the Absolute Idea, namely *cognition*. Here there *is* a discussion of how, in theory and in practice, the Idea both discovers, and creates, itself in what seems other than it. Yet by thematising this *before* the logical Absolute, Hegel makes it appear that success is guaranteed in advance. So 'cognition' should come at the end of the Logic, encapsulating the ambition of the concept to make itself Idea through uniting thought and reality, but with the job itself still to be done in the following parts of the *Encyclopaedia*. Cognition is surely the *hinge* of the logical and the real. Thus in my presentation its homologue – formal determination – is at the end of Division I.

The second disanalogy is more subtle. It relates to the understanding of what succeeds pure logic, and how logic is yet supposed to be at work within it. After his logic, Hegel presents his philosophy of Nature. However, from the outset, we are advised that Nature 'has its truth outside itself' – in the Idea, of course. If anywhere in Hegel this is where his official line seems to require simply finding bodily clothing for the moments of the concept, rather than show how Nature moves on its own basis. However, as an attentive student of science, Hegel makes a fair show of this in places, although many transitions appear forced.

If Hegel's Absolute Idea were really absolute then the notion that it 'freely' releases from itself Nature and History may have plausibility. But however strongly the Idea may aspire to such a content it cannot, in truth, create it. Rather, Hegel should have argued that the emptiness of the logic, as a science of pure form, culminates in an *abstract* Idea; its apparent freedom of movement is achieved only because it is abstracted from the realm of finitude. It requires, in order to unite thought and being, a transition to a complementary reality. If this is right, only the 'big triad', Logic/Nature/Spirit, is that which really is an unconditioned whole, that is, Absolute. It is a mark of Hegel's idealism that he insists the logical Idea is perfectly whole. In truth, as merely the logical aspect of the full triad, the Absolute Idea is only the abstract Absolute, the mere thought of an Absolute.

In passing, note that Hegel's prejudice in favour of a logical Absolute is complemented by a disdain for Nature. The status of this realm in Hegel's philosophy is far from glorious. Unlike the philosophical logic, and the philosophy of spirit, it does not culminate in an Absolute, but with 'death'! The reason Hegel has no Absolute at the end of Nature is that its position in the big triad indicates that it is the moment at which the Absolute is different from itself, whereas in Logic the Absolute has identity and in Spirit it is the mediated unity of subjective and objective. If one were to write a 'Philosophy of Nature' today, in a more generous account of it, the culminating category should surely be a quasi-absolute, namely Gaia, the thought of an all-encompassing, homeostatic organism of organisms, even if this is not *known* by Gaia. Gaia survives the rise and fall of all the species on earth, as it develops itself as a truly organic system. It has its own categories, for example 'ecological niche'. It is only a small step from this system of infinite teleology to that of a whole with a comprehensive consciousness of itself, namely self-knowing Spirit.

At the end of his *Encyclopaedia*, Hegel's three 'philosophies', that of Logic, of Nature and of Spirit, are presented in a triad of 'syllogisms', each in turn playing the mediating role, but with philosophy perhaps in the highest place. The transition from logic to Nature has attracted fire. Hegel's Absolute Idea is supposed to be complete in itself, and yet it gives rise to *Realphilosophie* for no obvious reason, but the transition from Nature to Spirit is also very problematic. What is clear is that the relation between logic and reality has a duality to it: on the one hand the logical forms rule because reality lacks all coherence without the structure provided by logic; on the other hand, viewed as a mere abstract skeleton of reality, logic appears ontologically 'thin', lacking in concrete wealth of content. One might say that, taken as a whole of pure form, logic is reduced to an immediacy of mere immanence, unless and until mediated in the content provided by Nature and history.[3]

The point I emphasise is that for him philosophy should have no trouble showing that 'reason', with its logic, is at work in the world, because it is always already guaranteed to find only itself. The case of capital is very different. The world capital comes upon is already shaped by the requirements of its own form; indeed, the existing economic metabolism may even be recalcitrant to its rule by capital. Capital must embark on the serious 'labour of the negative' if it is to succeed in the purpose of *in-forming* its world with its drive for valorisation. This negativity is made the basis for my privileging labour in the theory of value.

A further disanalogy is still more subtle. Although I present capital as the *subject of modernity*, imposing its logic on the epoch, this must be qualified. Most obviously, a subject paradigmatically is an individual consciousness. Is capital an individual? Is capital conscious? Is an analogy between capital and Absolute Spirit more than gestural? At first sight it seems clear capital is an impersonal abstract Absolute, lacking in consciousness. Nonetheless it achieves a form of self-consciousness through its human avatars, the capitalists, character masks of a personified capital, faithful to the proverbial bottom line, because capital has them in its possession, having colonised their consciousness.

---

3 In Arthur 2000, I argue that even in his logic Hegel's philosophy does not escape its bourgeois horizon.

Finally, intrinsic to my project is that capital is presented as having a poverty-stricken ontology. The consequence for the 'homology thesis' is that most of its forms lack the richness of the Hegel category presented as parallel. Nonetheless I hold there is always some substance to the parallel. Moreover, I think the architectonic of both systems is clearly congruent at a general level. (For example, the difficulty capital has in practice in achieving its hegemony over the material sphere of production has some analogy with the philosophical problem Hegel has in making this turn from logic to reality; for in both cases pure form has to show itself active in a variety of contingent circumstances.)

I provide in *Appendix 2* three charts (organised in triads) of logical categories:

(i) Hegel's *Science of Logic*, (ii) Hegel's *Encyclopaedia* Logic, (iii) the immanent *Logic of the Value Form*, drawing on, but reconstructing, these versions of Hegel's system. This reveals my own preferences, and underpins the argument in the text. So, in addition, I provide (iv) one of the value-form categories themselves.

The Treatment of Specific Terms

Below I methodically work through, by paragraph, the reasons for some of the choices I arrived at in my sequence of categories. It is by no means essential to the reading of this book to master this detail. I provide it for the benefit of those familiar with Hegel, who may be curious how I revise him to suit my purpose.

§11.1   Nothing and Being

This order is the reverse of Hegel's 'Being and Nothing'. The argument for it is in the main text, Chapters 5 and 6.

§11.2   Exchangeableness (Being Determinate)

My presentation simplifies Hegel's exposition of 'Determinate Being', which includes a morass of categories that in my opinion do not do any real work. I follow here the *Encyclopaedia* version of this dialectic, but even this is simplified by extracting what I take to be the central categories: Something and other, Spurious Infinity and True Infinity.

§ 11.3 An Exchangeable (Totality)

I replace 'repulsion and attraction' as the head category here with 'totality', which is not given here by Hegel (departing in this respect from Kant), but I believe it is the obvious 'third' as long as it is understood as the merely 'relative' totality not a centred one. But it hangs together through the dialectic of repulsion and attraction, as I show.

§ 12 Quantity

'Pure quantity' Hegel characterises as infinite unity; 'Quantum' is 'limited quantity' that has its 'perfect determinacy' in 'Number', which is part of a triad I end with the 'Number of Units'. The category of 'determinate quantity' Hegel calls 'Magnitude', but I elide that here, to avoid confusion with 'the magnitude of value' which appears much later. My final term of Quantity is 'Ratio' (as in *Science of Logic*; all translations give this for what is literally 'the quantitative relation'). Ratio is a reflexive magnitude. In our case, it is the exchange ratio of commodities.

§ 13 Exchange-Value

My initial treatment of Measure is closer to the abbreviated account in Hegel's *Encyclopaedia* than it is to the longer discussion in his *Science of Logic* in which he distinguishes 'real measure' from 'specifying measure'. (In his *Encyclopaedia*, Hegel drops the distinction between kinds of Measures and goes straight from Rule to the Measureless and thence to Essence.) Hegel develops the category of specifying measure, in which something is measured by something else (in our case the exchange-value of one commodity is given in terms of another). From there he goes to 'real measure'. Now I think Hegel's argument for 'real measure' very dubious. But in any case, I see the term 'Real Measure' as a category of essence; it has the complexity of a relationship manifesting a common substance, because it presupposes there is essential to commodities a value magnitude capable of appearing in a suitable measure. Oddly enough, Hegel himself at the outset of 'Measure' concedes that 'already present in [real] measure is the idea of essence, namely of being self-identical in the immediacy of being determined'. But 'specifying measure' does not presuppose essence because it refers to some external comparison. Hence, I postpone the form of Real Measure to a point at which essence is indeed posited in money. Here at the level of the Being of commodities I consider 'exchange-value' as their 'specifying measure'.

§21.1   Reflection and Show (*Schein*)

Because Hegel is obsessed with the notion of '*Schein*', and its rhetorical and metaphorical possibilities, he elevates it to a higher categorial level than it should be. It is followed by the 'determinations of reflection'. Surely then the precedent category should be 'Reflection', with '*Schein*' as an interior moment of it, standing for a reflection that is not a reflection, so to speak. At all events, in my recasting of the logic I depart from Hegel for the reason just given.

§21.13   Determining Reflection

Although the figure 'positing the presupposition' is used in several places late in the *Science of Logic*, it is originally thematised in the section on Reflection; but not in this exact formulation; however, it is a natural gloss on the result of '*determining reflection*'; and it is used in Mure's commentary accordingly.[4]

However, this figure has general application in systematic dialectic.[5] A good example of it is elucidated by Jairus Banaji: 'Circulation is posited as both presupposition and result of the Immediate Process of Production. The dialectical status of the Sphere of Circulation thus shifts from being the immediate appearance (*Schein*) of a process "behind it" to being the posited form of appearance (*Erscheinung*) of this process'.[6]

The question arises: what does it *mean* 'to posit the presupposition'? 'Posit' is an unusual English word. Here it must be used in the Hegelian sense of 'bringing into relation' or more explicitly 'established'. It is a very common term in Hegel (but note that 'positing the presupposition' is rare). It is worth noticing that Hegel makes a connection between the term 'presupposition' and that of 'condition'. The category 'condition' is used in the explication of that of 'necessity', in *Encyclopaedia* §§148–9. Hegel writes: 'the condition is what is presupposed; as only "*posited*" it is so only in relation to the fact [*Sache*]; but as "pre-" it is by itself: it is a contingent external circumstance that exists without reference to the fact' (§148). I follow this logic in the appropriate place: §23.1.

§21.2   Identity, Difference, and Contradiction

I follow here Hegel's *Science of Logic*. The *Encyclopaedia* Logic omits 'contradiction' and unites identity and difference in 'ground'. There are good reasons to see this as

---

4   See Mure 1950, pp. 95–6.
5   See Bellofiore and Finelli 1998, p. 50.
6   Banaji 1979, p. 28.

an improvement, for identity and difference are opposites but not obviously contradictory. However, in my presentation I have structured identity and difference as fully contradictory. I do not say that the commodity is different from another commodity, I say that, as value, it is *different from itself*. I define value as 'not use-value', so these determinations *exclude* one another. A more subtle issue is: why do I have 'contradiction' as a *form* of the commodity? In dialectical argument, there are a small class of terms that are not themselves forms, but rather supply a characterisation of the movement between forms, for example 'sublation', 'mediation', 'contradiction'.[7] But to grasp the nature of value is to see that the commodity as value *is* existent contradiction, no matter that the value form grounds it through giving it room to subsist.

§ 22.12 Form and Content

Considering the importance of form, it is amazing how uncertain Hegel shows himself as to its placing. It is put far too early, under 'ground', in *Science of Logic*; but although in *Encyclopaedia* it is rightly held back to the logic of Essence and Appearance, Hegel does not explain why it should be in the middle of Appearance. At all events, I revise Hegel by placing Form and Content under 'existence' because a thing exists immediately only as such a duality. Then the dialectic of the 'forms of value' is treated here as the middle category of Appearance.

§ 22.2 The Forms of Appearance of Value

This corresponds to Hegel's logic of 'the World of appearance and the World in itself'. I use the dialectic of 'force and expression' as soon as it seems useful (encouraged by the *Phenomenology* where it is associated with 'thing' and 'law'), whereas Hegel addresses it only under 'essential relationship'. Certainly, the dialectic of forms of value is powered by that of 'force and expression'. For Hegel's discussion of force and expression see *Science of Logic*, Book II, Section 3, Chapter 3; compare *Phenomenology of Spirit*, Chapter 3.

This dialectic introduces relations of *inversion* between value and use-value. For Hegel on the relation of the inverted worlds see *Science of Logic*, 'The World of Appearance and the World-in-Itself' and 'The Dissolution of Appearance'; also *Phenomenology of Spirit*, 'Force and Understanding: Appearance and the Supersensible World'; the pos-

---

7 See on this category McTaggart 1910, p. 116.

sibility of some overlap of content in the two works arises because the *Phenomenology* at this place is elucidating the work of the 'understanding' and, logically, its standpoint is that of Essence.

§ 23.1   The Modalities of the Equivalent Form

In his *Science of Logic*, Hegel begins the final part of the Doctrine of Essence, namely 'Actuality', with a chapter on 'the Absolute', continues with 'Actuality proper', dealing with modal categories, and then concludes with a chapter on 'Absolute Relation'. In his *Encyclopaedia* the Absolute drops out; the modal categories are promoted to categories of Actuality as a whole, and those of 'Absolute Relation' follow from that of Necessity. Here I restore 'the Absolute' in terms of 'money as absolute form of value', but I position it after an initial section treating the modal categories. So this arrangement is somewhat different from both versions of Hegel's logic. However, it suits my purpose to follow the becoming of the Universal Equivalent Form with that of the necessity of a unique bearer of it.

In the discussion of 'modality' I draw upon Hegel's discussion of Necessity in which he uses the sub-categories 'condition' (*Bedingen*); 'fact' (*Sache*); 'activity'. The sub-categories 'condition' and 'fact' are present in both Hegel logics. However, whereas in the *Science of Logic* they are part of the transition to 'existence', in the *Encyclopaedia* they are held back to the treatment of 'necessity'. For Hegel on presupposed 'condition', 'fact', and the grounding 'activity' that mediates them see Hegel *Encyclopaedia* §§ 148–9.

§ 23.2   Money as Absolute Form of Value

It is confusing that Hegel has a section on 'the Absolute' in the Doctrine of Essence, because the Absolute *proper* comprehends the whole wealth of logical determinations. However, as he points out, here it is the Absolute in its *abstract* pure notion, uncontaminated with specific determinations. I follow his lead here.

Hegel terms both the negative and positive movement of the Absolute 'the exposition of the Absolute': '*Auslegung*' is his term. However, I think it is more idiomatic to use 'exposition' for the positive alone, because the literal meaning of *Auslegung* is 'laying out'; so I find another term for the negative moment of self-identification. Hegel follows the Absolute with 'attribute'. But he says 'the absolute attribute' here is its 'form-determination' so I use that category in this section, especially when I discuss the reciprocity of form-determinations.

§ 23.31 Value as Substance

My take on Substance here is somewhat reminiscent of Spinoza's, in that it is all-pervasive. Hegel's *The Science of Logic* is peculiar; in his discussion of 'the Absolute' his use of Spinoza's terms is highly idiosyncratic. Moreover in the *Encyclopaedia* the section on 'The Absolute' in 'Essence' is entirely omitted, and he takes up after 'Necessity' the absolute relationship of substantiality.

§ 23.33 The Infinite Unity of Substance

I do not pass, with Hegel, from Substance to Causality because in the domain I am articulating value is *one* Substance. So there is no call for the presentation to cover 'causality', and the reciprocity of cause and effect, which presupposes two qualitatively distinct substances. In my presentation it is true that value becomes plural, but the relation of values is not causal but internal. As a consequence I model the transition from Essence to Concept on that I used from Being to Essence. Thus in order to make a transition to the Concept I move directly from Substance by means of a category of my own device: 'the infinite unity of substance'.

§ 23.33/1 Interchangeability of Commodities

Here I draw on Hegel's discussion of '*Die Wechselwirkung*'. (See *Encyclopaedia* §§ 155–8.) This is exceptionally easy for us to construe in my terms because the term 'exchange' (*Wechsel*), as well as having a general use, is deployed in specifically monetary contexts. 'Interchange' is my rendering of Hegel's category of *Wechselwirkung*. But it does not refer as with him, to causality, but to the mutuality of forms of the same substance.

§ 31.1 Value as Notion

I term the moments of the Concept or Notion: Universality, Particularity, Singularity, following Hegel's *Encyclopaedia Logic* (not his *Science of Logic*). This is important because I distinguish 'singularity' from 'singular'. It is essential in translating Hegel to render the third moment as 'Singularity', not 'Individuality'. The translations I give in the Bibliography of the *Science of Logic*, and of the *Encyclopaedia*, get it right: Hegel 2010; Hegel 1991.

As to 'Individuality', I show how capital, both as single capitals, and as capital-as-totality, has this specific logical status.

§ 32 Exchange and Circulation (Value in Objectivity)

The move from the 'subjective' conceptuality of value to its positing in real transactions corresponds to Hegel's logic of 'Objectivity' (outlined in the second section of Hegel's 'Doctrine of the Concept'). Hegel's first category of Objectivity is that of an immense collection or heap of things. He then develops the logical order of their interactions such that the heap becomes a universe with an inherent dynamic.

§ 33 Capital as Concept and Idea

The triad of capital derives from that of Hegel's 'Idea', but somewhat re-positioning its logical categories: I have: The Living Individual, Life, and Absolute Idea.

§ 33.2 Money as Capital

Here we trace *The 'Life' of Capital*, so to speak, which divides into:

§ 33.21 Money as Its Own End: Capital as Living Individual; the category of *'Living Individual'* parallels Hegel's *Science of Logic* which also develops the 'singular' into *'Das lebendige Individuum'*: Hegel 1975 II, p. 417;

§ 33.22 *Life Process* of Capital in Its General Formula;

§ 33.23 Capital as Self-Valorising Value entails the *Generation* of an increment of money.

§ 33.23 Generation

I replace Hegel's category of *'Genus'* with that of 'Generation' for I think Hegel goes wrong here. (*'Genus'* should be held back to the philosophy of Nature.) This fits with the notion of money generating more money of course.

§ 33.31 Accumulation

This parallels *'Method'*. The *Absolute Idea* section of Hegel's logic is very brief. Most attention is given to the question of 'method'. But this is not to be taken narrowly as the province of 'methodology'. Rather, it is to be taken ontologically as the pulse of absolute negativity that generates and sublates all categorial forms, the rhythm of the Idea unfolding itself out of itself. Of course, in our value-form homology, it cannot possibly be anything but an ontological category. I identify it with the spiral of accumulation, the production of capital by capital. Note also that I reverse the order of 'method' and 'cognition' as I have explained above.

§ 33.32 Formal Determination

Unusually, Hegel here departs from his preference for triads for he has only *two* divisions of *Cognition*, which are differently named in his *Logics*. I follow the duality of 'Cognition' in my homology of it, but I provide a justification for it, of sorts. The category homologous with Cognition is that of *Formal Determination*. This differs from material determination in that it refers to the way in which the material metabolism is inscribed within social forms that determine its lines of interchange and development.

Hegel's category of 'Cognition' has to do with how the concept unites itself with the reality it conceives. Formal determination is congruent with cognition because cognition is about how logical categories inform the real world; and for me the value form equally takes possession of the real economic process, and then informs it with the purposes of capital when it brings the commodities under the determinations of value.

I term Hegel's two complementary aspects of cognition, theoretical idea (interpreted as valuation) and practical idea (as subsumption), which is a characterisation Hegel gives in both texts. Compare *Encyclopaedia* § 225, § 235. However, I take them in reverse order. Hegel, in *Encyclopaedia* § 235, treats the unity of these two, although it is not given the dignity of a category; thus it must be carried forward to the supposed 'absolute idea'.

§ 33.33 Idea of Capital Realised in Contradiction

The final term of the logical dialectic I term 'realised Idea', which brings out better than 'Absolute' that it 'freely' is to go on to 'logicise' the real. This term also allows me to redraw it at the end of the value form dialectic as 'the Idea realised in contradiction', and it *must* go on to resolve itself in the real world where it is given room to move.

Hegel has perfect confidence that the rule of the Absolute may safely be posited at the end of his Logic. Thus cognition is *self*-comprehension. In the end what the Absolute *finds* in the world is the ideality that it *put* there; and this is true even if at any time there still remains much for the 'will' to achieve in this respect.

It is odd that Hegel says the life of thought in unity with the object *is* absolute at this point, therewith *presupposing* the unity of thought and object. Here this result should be properly seen as merely the *abstract absolute* because it is *not yet* shown to inform the real world, something which *becomes* true historically with the apotheosis of spirit in modern philosophy. In the *Logic*, the Absolute Idea is only *supposed* to be a reality but it is far from *posited*. Even if the Concept is logically concrete, the Idea is still abstract, the mere thought of unity with being. In our case the Capital Concept at this point is contradictory.

Divisions II and III

While Hegel's logical categories are in large part well suited to the purpose of presenting the logic of the capital concept, what corresponds here to Hegel's unity of concept and reality, is very different. He needs to develop in a logical order the categories of Nature and Spirit. But after Division I on form, I look at the production process of capital and its specific categories. At this more concrete level of analysis, therefore, the relation between Hegel's philosophy and my own theory of capital is merely analogical; there is no *homology* of categories, as there is where pure form is concerned. For example, I do not 'deduce' the categories of Space and Time. However, I argue that capital is structured by these 'conditions of existence' in a peculiar way.

§ 93   Absolute Idea of Capital

Hegel's *Encyclopaedia* covers Logic, Nature, and Spirit. But what is its final word? It consists of three 'syllogisms', placed at the end of the Absolute Spirit part. In each of these a different domain is prioritised. I follow Inwood[8] in reading the culmination as prioritising the Absolute Idea, which returns us to the beginning, so the whole system forms a circle of circles. Hence my final term is the Absolute Idea of Capital; Absolute Spirit I identify with the financial system.

---
8 Hegel 2007, pp. 658–63.

APPENDIX 2

Tables

Note: these tables are presented here roughly in the order in which they become relevant to the text; we begin with the Hegel background.

§ 1   *Table of Correspondences*
§ 2   *Hegel's Science of Logic Categories* (in Triads)
       § 2.1   *Hegel's Science of Logic* 1 Being
       § 2.2   *Hegel's Science of Logic* 2 Essence
       § 2.3   *Hegel's Science of Logic* 3 Concept
§ 3   *Hegel's Encyclopaedia Logic Categories* (in Triads)
       § 3.1   *Hegel's Encyclopaedia of Philosophical Sciences*
       § 3.2   *Hegel's Encyclopaedia Logic* 1 Being
       § 3.3   *Hegel's Encyclopaedia Logic* 2 Essence
       § 3.4   *Hegel's Encyclopaedia Logic* 3 Concept
§ 4   *Immanent Logic of the Value Form* (in Triads)
       § 4.1   *Immanent Logic of the Value Form* 1 Being
       § 4.2   *Immanent Logic of the Value Form* 2 Essence
       § 4.3   *Immanent Logic of the Value Form* 3 Concept
§ 5   *Systematic-Dialectical Presentation Table*
§ 6   *Dialectic of the Value Form* (in Triads)
       § 6.1   Commodity
       § 6.2   Money
       § 6.3   Capital
§ 7   *Presentation of Logical Categories of the Value Form*
§ 8   *Presentation of the Categories of the Value Form: Capital in Its Notion*
§ 9   *Tables of Absence and Presence*
§ 10   *The Forms of Value*
§ 11   *Price*
§ 12   *Metamorphoses of Money*
§ 13   *System of Industrial Capital*

1   Table of Correspondences

Hegel *Encyclopaedia* § 18
I.   Logic: The Science of the Idea in and for Itself,
II.   The Philosophy of Nature; the Science of the Idea in Its Otherness,

III. The Philosophy of Spirit; as the Idea Come Back to Itself out of that Otherness.

Arthur
I. Value Form: as the Science of Capital in Its Notion,
II. Capital Relation: Capital and Its Other,
III. Capital as Systemic Unity.

Hegel *Encyclopaedia* § 83
Logic falls into three parts:
I. The Doctrine of Being,
II. The Doctrine of Essence,
III. The Doctrine of the Concept and the Idea.

That is, into the theory of Thought in:
I. Its *Immediacy*: The Concept Implicit and in Germ,
II. Its *Reflection* and *Mediation*: The Being-for-Itself and Show of the Concept,
III. Its *Return* into Itself and Its Developed Being-by-Itself: The Concept In-and-for-Itself.

Arthur
The dialectic of the value form falls into three parts:
I. Commodity,
II. Money,
III. Capital.

That is, into the theory of Exchange in:
I. Its *Immediacy*: Value Implicit and in Germ,
II. Its *Reflection* and *Mediation*: Value for-Itself, the Showing-Forth of Value,
III. Its *Return* into Itself, and Its Development of Itself: Self-Valorisation.

Hegel: *Logic*		**Arthur:** *Dialectic of the Value Form*	
I.	The Doctrine of Being	I.	Commodity
A.	Quality	A.	Exchangeable commodities
B.	Quantity	B.	Quantity of commodities
C.	Measure	C.	Exchange-value of commodities
II.	The Doctrine of Essence	II.	Money
A.	Intro-reflection	A.	Value-in-itself
B.	Appearance	B.	Forms of Value
C.	Actuality	C.	Money
III.	The Doctrine of Concept	III.	Capital (General Formula)
A.	Subjectivity	A.	Price
B.	Objectivity	B.	Metamorphoses of commodities (C–M–C′)
C.	The Idea	C.	Capital (M–C–M′)

2 Hegel's Science of Logic Categories (in Triads)

Hegel's Science of Logic – 1 Being

- Quality
  - Being
    - (Pure) Being
    - Nothing
    - Becoming
  - Determinate Being
    - Determinate Being
    - Finitude
    - Infinity
  - Being-for-Itself
    - Being-for-Itself as such
    - One & Many
    - Repulsion/Attraction
- Quantity
  - (Pure) Quantity
  - Quantum
  - Quantitative Ratio
- Measure
  - Specific Quantity
    - Specific Quantum
    - Specifying Measure
    - Being-for-Itself in Measure
  - Real Measure
    - Relation of Stable Measures
    - Nodal Line of Measure Relations
    - The Measureless
  - The Becoming of Essence (Indifference)

Hegel's Science of Logic – 2 Essence

Essence as Reflection into Self	Show	Essential/Unessential Show Reflection
	Determinations of Reflection	Identity Difference Contradiction
	Ground	Absolute Ground (Form) Determined Ground Condition
Appearance	Existence (The Thing)	
	Appearance	
	(Essential) Relationship	Whole/Part Force/Expression Outer and Inner
Actuality	The Absolute	
	Actuality	Contigency Relative Necessity Absolute Necessity
	Absolute Relation	Of Substance Of Causality Reciprocity

Hegel's Science of Logic – 3 Concept

Subjectivity	The Concept	Universal / Particular / Singular
	Judgement	Judgement of Existence / Judgement of Reflection / Judgement of Necessity / Judgement of the Concept
	Syllogism	
Objectivity	Mechanism	
	Chemism	
	Teleology	
The Idea	Life	Living Individual / Life Process / Genus
	The Idea of Cognition	The Idea of the True / The Idea of the Good
	Absolute Idea	

3 Hegel's Encyclopaedia Logic Categories (in Triads)

Hegel's Encyclopaedia of Philosophical Sciences

Logic
- Being
- Essence
- Concept

Nature
- Mechanics
- Physics
- Organics

Spirit
- Subjective Spirit
- Objective Spirit
- Absolute Spirit

Hegel's Encyclopaedia Logic – 1 Being

Quality
- Being
  - Pure Being
  - Nothing
  - Becoming
- Determinate Being
- Being-for-Itself
  - One
  - Many
  - Repulsion/Attraction

Quantity
- Pure Quantity
- Quantum
- Degree

Measure
- Rule
- Measureless
- True Infinite of Measure

Hegel's Encyclopaedia Logic – 2 Essence

- Ground of Existence
  - Pure Determinations Of Reflection
    - Identity
    - Difference
    - Ground
  - Existence
  - The Thing

- Appearance
  - World of Appearance
  - Content and Form
  - (Essential) Relationship
    - Whole/Part
    - Force/Expression
    - Inner/Outer

- Actuality
  - Possibility
  - Contingency
  - Necessity (Absolute Relationship)
    - Of Substance
    - Of Causality
    - Reciprocity

Hegel's Encyclopaedia Logic – 3 Concept

- Subjective Concept
  - Concept as Such
    - Universality
    - Particularity
    - Singularity
  - Judgement
  - Syllogism

- The Object
  - Mechanism
  - Chemism
  - Teleology

- The Idea
  - Life
    - Living Entity
    - Life Process
    - Genus
  - Cognition
    - Cognition
    - Willing
  - Absolute Idea

4 Immanent Logic of the Value Form (in Triads)

The Immanent Logic of the Value-Form – 1 Being

Quality	Being	Nothing / Pure Being / Becoming
	Determinate Being	Something and Other / Spurious Infinity / True Infinity
	Being-for-Itself	One/Many/Totality
Quantity	Pure Quantity	
	Quantum	Unit / Number / A Number of Units
	Ratio of Quanta	
Measure	Rule	
	Series of Specific Measures	
	Infinite Unity of Measure-Relations	

The Immanent Logic of the Value-Form – 2 Essence

- Intro-reflection
  - Reflection
  - Pure Determinations Of Reflection
    - Identity
    - Difference
    - Contradiction
  - Ground
- Appearance
  - Existence
    - The Thing
    - Form (and Content)
    - Law
  - Worlds of Appearance
    - Force and Expression
  - Correlation
- Actuality
  - Modality
    - Possibility
    - Contingency
    - Necessity
  - Absolute Form
    - Absolute Identity
    - Exposition
    - Reciprocity
  - Substance
    - Substance in Immediacy
      - Oneness
      - Extension
      - Finite Modes
    - Absolute Relation of Form/Content
    - Infinite Unity of Substance

The Immanent Logic of the Value-Form – 3 Concept

- Subjectivity
  - The Notion
    - Universal
    - Particular
    - Singular
  - Judgement
    - Formal Judgement
    - Categorical Judgement
    - Judgement of the Concept
  - Syllogism
- Objectivity
  - "Mechanism"
  - "Chemism"
  - Teleology
- The Idea
  - The Individual
  - "Life"
    - Living Indvidual
    - Life Process
    - Generation
  - Absolute Idea
    - The Idea in Itself
    - The Idea of Cognition
      - Practical Idea
      - Theoretical Idea
    - Realised Idea

5   Systematic-Dialectical (SD) Presentation Table

Systematic-Dialectical (SD) presentation table

	Analytical dialectic	Synthetical dialectic
Starting Point	*Commodity*: its prevalence is a *given* to be posited as result	*Value*: the pervasive totalising form posited as grounded on itself through SD
Movement	*Uncovering* of necessary *conditions of existence* (CoE) then posited	*Development* of *grounds* sufficient to posit the starting point
Sublation	CoEs are sublated when posited as 'idealised' by SD	Presuppositions are sublated through the grounding movement of SD
Positing the Presupposition	CoEs are posited through the SD	*Grounds* posit sequentially the actuality of what they presuppose
Result	All CoEs are *subsumed* in the system as it reproduces itself	The whole grounds its moments when developed in a hierarchical system of determinations

6 Dialectic of the Value Form (in Triads)

Dialectic of the Value Form – 1 Commodity

Quality of Being Exchangeable	{ Being Present in Exchange Exchangeableness An Exchangeable
Quantity of Commodities	{ Infinite Unity of All Exchangeables Number of Commodities to Be Exchanged in a Transaction Ratio of Exchange
Exchange-Value	{ Pro-rata exchange Series of Exchange-Values Infinite Unity of Measures

Dialectic of the Value Form – 2 Money

Value as Immanent Exchangeability	Intro-Reflection of Value	
	Reflex-Determinations of Value	Value Is in the Commodity
		Value Is Not in the Commodity
		Value Is/Is-Not in the Commodity
	Value Grounded in the Value-Form	
Value as Appearance	Value as Existent	(Value as Form & as Content. Value as Law)
	Expression of Value	Simple Form 'Form I'
		Expanded Form 'Form II'
		General Form 'Form III'
	Correlative Totalities of Value	
Value as Actuality Is Money	Modality of Equivalent Form: Total Form 'Form IV'	Possible Any Commodity May Be Money
		Contingency of Money Commodity
		Actuality of Money Is Necessary
	Money as Absolute Form of Value	Exchangeability in Immediacy Money Form of Value 'Form V'
		Immediate Exchangeability Laying Out of Money 'Form VI'
		Reciprocity of Form-Determinations
	Value as Substance	Value as Substance in Immediacy
		– Oneness of Money
		– Dimensionality of Value
		– Money as Measure
		Value as substance of commodities, Money as their Real measure
		Infinite Unity of Value Substance 'Form VII'

Dialectic of the Value Form – 3 Capital

Capital	Price	The Notion	Universality of Value / Amount / An Amount
		Judgement of Worth	
		Transitivity of Price	
	Exchange and Circulation	Immediate Exchange	
		Sale and Purchase	
		Metamorphoses of Commodities and Money	
	Capital	Money as Money	End of Exchange / Means of Payment / Fund
		Money as Capital	General Formula
		Capital as Idea	Accumulation / Formal Determination (Subsumption/Valuation) / Capital Realised in Contradiction

7 Presentation of Logical Categories of the Value Form

These categories are drawn from Hegel's two Logics, but selected, and ordered, with a view to the presentation of the value-form dialectic; the numbering system is my own.

1 Being
    11 Quality
        11.1 Being
            11.11 Nothing 11.12 Pure Being 11.13 Becoming
        11.2 Being (Qualitatively) Determinate Is in Being-for-Other
            11.21 Something and Other
            11.22 Spurious Infinity
            11.23 True Infinity
        11.3 Being-for-Itself
            11.31 One
            11.32 Many
            11.33 (Relative) Totality (Attraction / Repulsion)
    12 Quantity
        12.1 Pure Quantity (Infinite Unity)
        12.2 Quantum:
            12.21 Unit, 12.22 Number, 12.23 A Number of Units
        12.3 Ratio of Quanta
    13 (Specifying) Measure
        13.1 Rule
        13.2 Series of Specific Measures
        13.3 Infinite Unity of Measure Relations

2 Essence
    21 Intro-Reflection
        21.1 Reflection (and 'Show')
        21.2 Determinations of Reflection
            21.21 Identity
            21.22 Difference
            21.23 Contradiction
        21.3 Ground
    22 Appearance
        22.1 Existence
            22.11 Thing (and Property)
            22.12 Form (and Content)
            22.13 Law

        22.2   Worlds of Appearance
        22.3   Correlation
  23   Actuality
        23.1   Modality
                23.11   Possibility
                23.12   Contingency
                23.13   Necessity
        23.2   Absolute Form
                23.21   Absolute Identity
                23.22   Exposition
                23.23   Reciprocity of Form-Determinations
        23.3   Substance
                23.31   Substance in Immediacy
                        23.31/1   Oneness
                        23.31/2   Extension
                        23.31/3   Finite Modes
                23.32   Absolute Relation of Substance as Form and Content
                23.33   Infinite Unity of Substance

3   Concept
    31   Subjectivity
         31.1   Notion (31.11 Universality, 31.12 Particularity, 31.13 Singularity)
         31.2   Judgement
         31.3   Syllogism
    32   Objectivity
         32.1   'Mechanism'
         32.2   'Chemism'
         32.3   Teleology
    33   Idea
         33.1   The Individual
         33.2   'Life':
                33.21   Living Individual
                33.22   Life Process
                33.23   Generation
         33.3   Absolute Idea
                33.31   Idea in Itself
                33.32   Cognition
                        33.33/1   Practical Idea
                        33.33/2   Theoretical Idea
                33.33   Realised Idea

8   Presentation of the Categories of the Value Form:
       Capital in Its Notion

1   Commodity
    1 1   Quality of Being Exchangeable
          11.1 Being Present in Exchange
                Nothing; Being; Nothingness (the Presence of Nothing)
          11.2 Exchangeableness: Something and Other; Spurious Infinity; True Infinity
          11.3 An Exchangeable
                One; Many; (Relative) Totality (Attraction / Repulsion)
    1 2   Quantity of Commodities Exchanged
          12.1 Pure Quantity (Infinite Unity of All Exchangeables)
          12.2 Number of Commodities Exchanged in a Transaction
          12.3 Ratio of Exchange
    1 3   Exchange-Value as the (Specifying) Measure
          13.1 Rule of Pro-rata Exchange
          13.2 Series of Exchange-Values (i.e. of Specific Measures)
          13.3 Infinite Unity of Measure Relations

2   Money
    2 1   Value as Immanent Exchangeability
          21.1 Exchange-Value Reflected into the Commodity
                21.11 Positing Reflection; 21.12 External Reflection; 21.13 Determining Reflection
          21.2 Reflex-Determinations of Value
                21.21 Identity (Value Is in the Commodity)
                21.22 Difference (Value Is Not in the Commodity but Different from It)
                21.23 Contradiction (Value Is and Is Not in the Commodity)
          21.3 Value Grounded in the Value Form
    2 2   Value as Appearance
          22.1 Value as Existent
                22.11 Value as (Relational) Property of a 'Thing'
                22.12 Form and Content
                22.13 Value as Law-like in Its Appearance
          22.2 Forms of Appearance of Value:
                22.21 Form I Simple Form
                22.22 Form II Expanded Form
                22.23 Form III General Form

22.3 Correlation of Immediate and Reflected Totalities of Value
23 Value as Actuality: Money
    23.1 The Modalities of Equivalent Form: Possibility; Contingency; Necessity;
    Form IV: Total Form of Value
    23.2 Money as Absolute Form of Value
        23.21 Exchangeability-in-Immediacy; Form V: Money Form of Value
        23.22 Immediate Exchangeability; Form VI: Laying-Out of Money
        23.23 Reciprocity of Form-Determinations of Money
    23.3 Value as Substance (the Substantiality of Value Exists in Money)
        23.31 Value as Substance in Immediacy
            23.31/1 Substance-in-Itself; Its Oneness (Its Self-Identity)
            23.31/2 Substance-for-Itself as a Dimensionally Extended Body of Value
            23.31/3 Money as Finite Mode of Value:
                23.31/31 Immanent Magnitude
                23.31/32 Monetary Medium
                23.31/33 Measure Proper Is Given in Units of Money
        23.32 Value-Substance Actualised in a Realm of Finitude: Commodities
            23.32/1 Money is the Real Measure of Value of Commodities
            23.32/2 Commodities as 'Values'
                23.32/21 Value as the Substance of Commodities
                23.32/22 The Transubstantiation of the Commodity
                23.32/23 The Commodity Posited as 'a Value'
            23.32/3 Value as Absolute Relation of Form and Content
        23.33 Infinite Unity of Value Substance: Form VII: Substantial Form
            23.33/1 Interchangeability of Commodities as Values Predicated by Money

23.33/2 Money as Comparator (Unitary Measure of Value)
23.33/3 Merging of Values in a Mass of Value Measured in One Sum

3 Capital
   31 Price (Subjectivity of Value)
      31.1 Value as Notion
         31.11 Infinite Value Notion
            31.11/1 Universality of Value
            31.11/2 Particularity as 'Amount'
            31.11/3 Singularity as 'an Amount'
         31.12 Finite Value Notion (Schematised in Money as 'Measure-Making')
         31.13 Value Brought Back to the Infinite: Fungibility of Money
      31.2 The Value Judgement (Money Assumes the Role of Measure-Taking)
         31.21 The Judgement of Worth, 'This Commodity is Worth $x'
         31.22 Standard of Price; Money of Account;
         31.23 The Unfolding of the Judgement of Worth
            31.23/1 The Formal Judgement (Qualitative and Quantitative)
            31.23/2 The Categorical Judgement;
            31.23/3 The Judgement of the Concept
      31.3 Transitivity of Price
         31.31 Syllogism of Abstraction: If A Is Worth $x, and B Is Worth $x, Then A = B
         31.32 Syllogism of Equality: If A = B, and B = C, Then A = C
         31.33 Syllogism of Syllogisms:
If A = B & B = C Then A = C;
If C = A & A = B Then C = B;
If B = C & C = A Then B = A (the System Is Closed).
   32 Exchange and Circulation (Objectivity of Value)
      32.1 Immediate Exchange (Money as Ideal Measure) C–C'
      32.2 Sale Is Purchase (C–M) ≡ (M–C)
      32.3 Metamorphoses of Commodities and Money
         32.31 Sale and Purchase (C–M) + (M–C')
         32.32 Metamorphoses of Commodities C–M–C' (Finite Teleology)

- 32.33 Metamorphoses of Money (Monetary Circulation: Infinite Teleology)
- 33 Capital as Concept and Idea
  - 33.1 Money as Money (Value as 'Individuated')
    - 33.11 Money as End of Exchange
    - 33.12 Money as Means of Payment
    - 33.13 Money as Funds
  - 33.2 Money as Capital
    - 33.21 Money as Its Own End
    - 33.22 'Life Process' of Capital: General Formula for Capital
    - 33.23 'Generation' of Increment of Money
  - 33.3 Capital as Idea
    - 33.31 Accumulation
      - 33.31/1 Transformation of the Monetary Increment into Capital
      - 33.31/2 Rate of Accumulation as a Measure of Capital by Itself for Itself
      - 33.31/3 The Infinity of Capital
    - 33.32 The Formal Determination by Capital of Its Real World Existence
      - 33.32/1 Subsumption
      - 33.32/2 Valuation
    - 33.33 Idea of Capital Realised in Contradiction

9 Tables of Absence and Presence

Absence and presence in exchange

	'production'		exchange		'consumption'
A: real being (use-value)	*present*	⇒	*absented*	⇒	*present*
B: ideal being (in exchange)	*absent*	⇒	*present*	⇒	*absent*

Being-in-exchange and its other

'production'		exchange		'consumption'
(use-value) non-being	⇐	Being ('in exchange')	⇒	non-being (use-value)

Dialectic of Being-in-Exchange

as Absence	as Presence	as Presence of Absence
Nothing ⇌	Being ⇒	Nothingness

10 The Forms of Value

Form I *The Simple Form of Value*
z of commodity A *expresses its value in* y of commodity B

Form II *The Expanded Form of Expression of Value*

z of commodity A *expresses its value in* $\begin{cases} \text{y of commodity B} \\ or \text{ x of commodity C} \\ or \text{ w of commodity D} \\ or \text{ so on and so forth} \end{cases}$

Form III *The General Form of Value*

$\left. \begin{array}{l} \text{y of commodity B} \\ and \text{ x of commodity C} \\ and \text{ w of commodity D} \\ and \text{ so on and so forth} \end{array} \right\}$ *express their value in* z of commodity A

Form IV *The Total Form of Expression of Value*

1) *The total expanded form*
    The value of zA *is* yB or xC or wD etc.
or The value of yB *is* zA or xC or wD etc.
or The value of xC *is* zA or yB or wD etc.
or etc.
2) *The total general form*
    The value of yB and xC and wD etc. *is* zA
or The value of zA and xC and wD etc. *is* yB
or The value of zA and yB and wD etc. *is* xC
or etc.

Form V *The Money Form of Value: Exchangeability in Immediacy*

20 yard of linen
1 coat
40 lbs. of coffee   } *express their value in* an ounce of gold
10 lbs. of tea
Half a ton of iron
etc.

Form VI: *The Form of Immediate Exchangeability* or *the Laying-Out of Money*

an ounce of gold *is immediately exchangeable for* { 20 yards of linen
  and 1 coat
  and 40 lbs of coffee
  and half a ton of iron
  and so on

Form VII: *The Substantial Form of Value*

a units of A	*is worth*	z of money
b units of B	*is worth*	y of money
c units of C	*is worth*	x of money
d units of D	*is worth*	w of money
etc.	*is worth*	...

A & B & C & D ... together   *are worth*   the sum of z + y + x + w ...

NB Thus, A & B & C & D *together* are worth *n*, a single sum of money, where *n* is the *sum* of z + y + x + w ...

11   Price

1. *Value in Its Notion*
   Universality   (value all pervasive)
   Particularity   (= amount)
   Singularity   (= an amount)
2. *Judgement of Worth*: This commodity A is worth $x
   (i)   Formal Judgement
          a) of Quality b) of Quantity

(ii) Categorical Judgement
(iii) Judgement of the Concept
3. Transitivity of Price
  (i) Syllogism of Abstraction
      if A is worth $x
      & B is worth $x
      then A is worth what B is worth
      so A = B i.e. equal in price
  (ii) Syllogism of Equality (of Price)
      if A = B, & B = C, then A = C
  (iii) Syllogism of Syllogisms
      if A = B & B = C then A = C
      if C = A & A = B then C = B
      if B = C & C = A then B = A

12 The Metamorphoses of Money

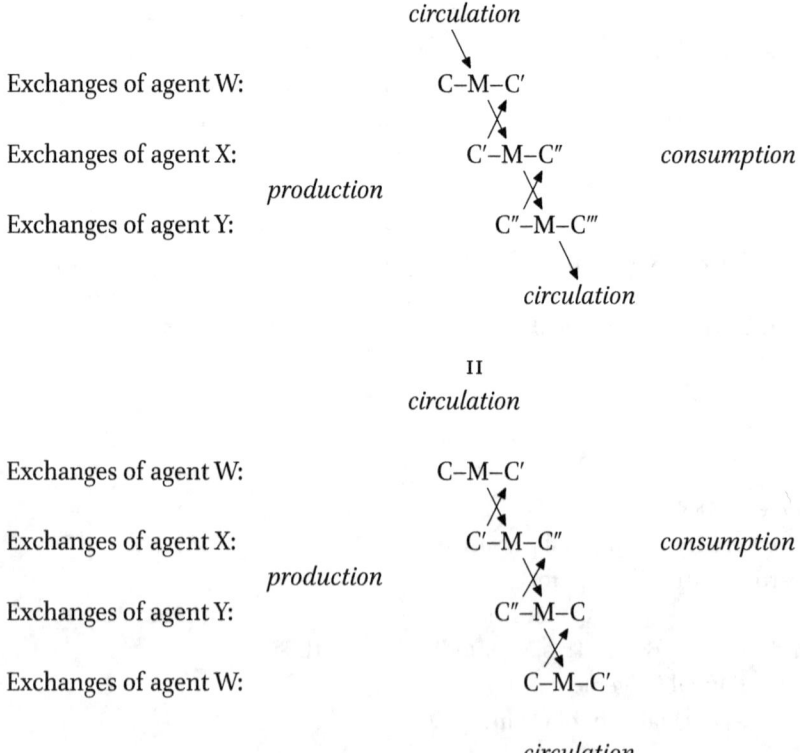

13   The System of Industrial Capital

Reflection into self ⟶

Reflection into other ↓

	Universality (self-identity)	Particularity (difference 'within' capital)	Singularity (self-relation)
Universality (capital as such reflected into itself)	The Rate of Surplus Value	The metamorphoses of capital	Simple price = Cost price plus profit. Rate of profit
Particularity (difference between capitals)	Capitals in competition absolute & relative surplus value	Organic composition of capital	Production price = Cost price plus uniform rate of profit
Singularity (systemic unity of social capital)	General law of capital accumulation	Reproduction of total social capital via Departments of Reproduction	Reproduction price General Rate of Profit

Glossary

Absence This is the founding category of the presentation. Exchange absents entirely the material of the commodity when identifying heterogeneous commodities with each other. The dialectic begins by arguing that this absence is yet present.

Absolute The highest point of a hierarchically organised unitary system, which comprehends it retrospectively *as* unitary.

Absolute Relation The highest form of relatedness, in which the two sides are merely complementary aspects of a single whole; it contrasts with essential relationship, where the poles have their defining relation in common, but are not otherwise unified.

Actuality In the value-form presentation the category of 'actuality' resolves the opposition of essence and appearance; when a form is 'actual' it appears as *what it is*, as fully realised, so to speak. It is also used here broadly as a category ontologically superior to 'being', 'existent', or 'real'. In this sense 'actuality' is not to be equated with contingent empirical facts. Rather, a developed actuality sublates less determinate levels of being to achieve *its own effectivity*. This effectivity may be retained in the face of contingent disturbances of its action. In Hegel's logic it is defined as the unity of essence and existence. Mere 'existences' lacking any essential reason for being, or failing to live up to it, are not actualities. This background explains why I consider my account of total social capital to develop it in its actuality, albeit that such contingencies as supply and demand are disregarded.

Added Value 'Added Value' is generated in the process of production of capital. It is the source of the revenues wages and profit.

Architectonic The dictionary definition of this term as 'the systematic arrangement of knowledge' is very pertinent here. The 'homology thesis' maintains that two orders of categories, those of the logical, and those of the value form, have parallel architectonics.

Being-in-exchange The first concrete category of the value-form dialectic is 'Being present in exchange', so what is present is termed briefly 'Being-in-exchange'.

Circuit and *Circulation* A circuit is run through when value *stays* in the same place, for example, capital is the same throughout its metamorphoses, e.g. M–C–M′. Circulation is the objective movement of commodities and money *between* various hands (for example, as a commodity is bought and sold).

Concept, Moments of The Infinite Moments of the Concept are Universality, Particularity, Singularity. These have finite determinations, e.g.

singulars. (See also *Individual* and *Notion*.)

Concept In Hegel the *Concept* is a purely logical category. An *Idea* (q.v.) is the fully realised, or actualised, Concept. Whereas Hegel completes his Logic with the Absolute Idea, I must refuse this because Capital at the level of pure form (see Division I) is realisable only in contradiction with itself. The Capital Concept therefore is realised only with the turn to production (in Division II), which shows how the contradiction is resolved in the theory of surplus value. For Hegel the Concept is paradigmatically incarnate in the 'I', an individual subject with a self-determining 'will'. Just so, I take every capital to be such a subject, with a drive to accumulate. Albeit there is lacking in this 'subject' consciousness and personality, the character of the capitalist supplies this moment. However, an individual capital achieves truth only in and through the competition of capitals. So the Idea of Capital is treated in the System of Capital (in Division III). This system is itself implicitly *the* Idea, with its general rate of profit. But it is explicitly present with the regulation of industry by the capital markets, the normal rate of interest, etc. (q.v. '*Spirit*').

Concrete universal The term 'concrete universal' is used here in a basic sense and an extended sense. Initially it is contrasted with the 'abstract universal'. That stands opposed to *singulars*, which *fall under*, so to speak, its range of reference. By contrast the concrete *universal* comprehends them as part of its meaning; instead of standing *opposed to* them, it *particularises* itself *in* them. Such a view of concepts (or at least some of them) may be taken by thought considering the nature of concepts. However, a further consideration is that the Concept may be considered as *determining itself* in such a movement from universal, to particular, to singular. A paradigmatic example is embodied in the 'will', which *sets itself* to some particular object. This richer notion is incarnate in living labour, and capital. Both move from universality, more or less fluidly, to particular shapes.

Conditions of Existence Material and social conditions, first encountered, then subsumed, and finally reproduced in a shape adequate to the Idea of Capital.

Derangement Cognate with Marx's *Verrücktheit*. I trade on the double sense: 'disarrange' and 'absurd'.

Dimension of Value When first presented it is figured as *pure immanence lacking in measure*; it is actualised only when a monetary medium provides a ground for it, and its measure.

Exchange-Value The measure of exchangeability given by one commodity to another. This is a form of Being; it is developed *before* 'Value', a form of Essence.

Exchangeableness/Exchangeability
The concept of value has qualitative and quantitative aspects; to reflect this I distinguish between 'exchangeableness' and 'exchangeability'. The former refers to some *quality* intrinsic to the commodity, which allows it to *be exchanged*; the latter refers to the *quantitative proportions* in which it exchanges against others pro rata.

Exchangeability in Immediacy See *immediate exchangeability*

Form This notion occurs at three levels of generality. First, the ideal social form of the commodity contrasts with its material form. This relation is relatively external (but see *formal determination*). Second there are forms *of* value such as the commodity form, the money form, and so forth. The presentation shows how these forms develop out of one another in a systematic order (see *form-determination*). Finally, one of these is 'value *as* form', which might be empty (see § 22.12) or might be united with its content (see § 22.32/3). (Note that 'shape' differs from 'form' in that the latter is pure and abstract but the former is phenomenally perceptible, almost sensuous, so to speak.)

Form-Determination This term I use in my discussion of the money form of value, but it has very general application as there are many *determinations of form* throughout the presentation. (Note that it is distinct from '*formal determination*', q.v.)

Formal Determination The category homologous with Hegel's 'Cognition' is that of 'Formal Determination'. This differs from material determination (e.g. causal determination) in that it refers to the way in which the material metabolism is inscribed within social forms that determine its lines of interchange and development. It is congruent with cognition because cognition is about how logical categories inform the real world; and the value form equally takes possession of the real economic process and informs it with the purposes of capital. Since each moment (formal and material) informs the other, the task is to study how each complements the other, e.g. on the material side, the potential for labour power to be exploited is certainly given, but how and why it is, and how the result is socially registered, all comes from the value form side, as if that were of the essence of the economy. Formal Determination occurs both in formal valuation and in practical subsumption. In sum, it is to impute something with form. Note that it is distinct from '*form-determination*' (q.v.) which is precisely a form a thing has.

Generalised commodity production
A mode of production in which the vast majority of products are commodities destined for the market. It is a condition of existence of capitalism.

Ground As a specific category, it is introduced in order to resolve by the *value form* the contradiction in commodity value in which the value of one commodity is given in another exchangeable for it. However, both terms (*ground* and *value form*) are used very generally also, in order to characterise any form of value required to actualise another, e.g. money grounds the immanence of value.

Idea This is the unity of the Concept and Reality; it does not refer to ideas in the head. (q.v. *Concept.*) The Idea is presented as resulting from the idealisation of the reality apparently other than it, but then seen as an indivisible aspect of it.

Ideal and Real Initially the presentation follows Hegel in first treating the Ideal (in our case the logic of the value form) as opposed to the real (in our case the material metabolism of the economy). However, when the Ideal subsumes the real, 'idealises it', so to speak, the Ideal *makes* itself real. In its unity with the real, the Ideal shapes it according to its own logic. So the Idea, as the unity of the two aspects, is objectively present, not merely a thought in the head. But our presentation is complicated by the fact that the homology of form relies on commodities and money to *bear* the Ideal. These are perfectly real themselves, whether their putative ideal aspect is, or is not.

Immediate Exchangeability This is a feature of money, not shared by commodities. It is distinguished from *Exchangeability-in-Immediacy*. The latter is given in the reality of the unique universal equivalent, which shows the value of a commodity, while itself not requiring a value expression, because it *is* the actuality of value. Form V assigns this power of incarnating *Exchangeability-in-Immediacy* to the money commodity. Form VI is the reverse and shows that money, as immediate exchangeability, has the power of laying itself out on commodities insofar as, unlike commodities themselves, it is always acceptable for them.

Individual I use this in a technical sense to comprehend the whole triad of the Notion: Universal/Particular/Singular.

Infinitely Negative Judgement I speak metaphorically of this when I originally define value as 'not use-value'. It is the practice of exchange, not thought, that effects this 'judgement' on commodities when *constituting* them therewith as beings-in-exchange.

Judgement The infinity of the Notion determines itself to finitude in the judgement. Thus the Judgement of Worth is an ontological move and money passes therewith from the form of abstract wealth to finite existence in coins etc. capable of exchanging with commodities. The *formality* of the Judgement says that a thing is of worth and, indeed, worth so much money. The *categoricality* of the Judgement takes the thing to be a genuine commodity, having value as its substance (there is no category mistake involved). The Judgement in its *conceptual* perfection asserts that the true worth of the commodity is registered (but this is determined systemically in the whole relatedness of commodities). (For a distinct sense of 'Judgement' see *Infinitely Negative Judgement*.)

Labour Power   Labour capacity as a concretely universal potential is formally determined as labour power by capital, posited as a mere resource yielding labour in the abstract. However, living labour is required for production of goods, and is the carrier of abstract labour.

Measure   I distinguish: *specifying* measure registered by exchange-value, *proper* measure incarnate in a monetary medium, and *real* measure as the money which expresses the magnitude of value immanent in a commodity. When treating money as the incarnation of the homogenous value substance, I recognise its necessary quantitative extension by its proper measure in units of the monetary medium, just as the proper measure of spatial extension is a standard metre ruler. When treating the relation of money to commodities it is a question of the taking of the real measure of their value in this money, already determined as the proper measure of value.

Moment   This is cognate with the moments of a lever, not with a moment in time. A moment is an essential feature of a whole; it is informed in its movement by complementary moments to effect the subsistence of the whole; yet they are all *sublated* within it, so it is the whole that is precedent.

Necessary labour   This is that labour *yielded* by the worker in order the receive the wage; it contrasts with the surplus labour appropriated by capital in the form of surplus value. It is distinct from the labour *required to produce* the means of subsistence purchased with the wage. It is also distinct from two other notions: (i) the labour time socially necessary to produce a commodity; (ii) modes of labour which may be deemed socially necessary in other contexts, such as domestic labour, that of civil servants, and so forth.

Nothing and *non-being*   Nothing is that immediacy opposed to Being but indistinguishable from it; these moments are sublated in *Nothingness*. Non-being is the mediated result of the positing by Being-in-exchange of what is outside it, originally the absented use-value sphere, as indeterminately other than Being.

Notion   This has here both a formal use with 'N' and an informal use with 'n'. The Notion is my coinage for the first section of Hegel's Doctrine of the Concept (i.e. the *formal* concept). This corresponds in the 'homology' to the price form. (In this I take advantage of the traditional variant translations of *Begriff* as 'Concept' and 'Notion'. I prefer 'Concept'; but this leaves 'Notion' free to mark the above subtlety.) The informal use of 'notion' refers to a merely mental or subjective representation, which is to some extent caught by the connotations of English usage, especially in the adjective 'notional'.

Numerical Difference Two things identical in every respect are said to be two as a matter of only numerical difference. It is an important proposition of this book that two commodities of the same value are *as values* merely numerically different, and not individuated in any other way.

Posit This is the process of making explicit what is implicit. Also it is what is understood as arising from its presuppositions. It is not merely that thought affirms the posited entity is logically consequent, but that it arises from an objective relation or movement. Positing the presupposition occurs when the posited element is shown to ground its own presupposition. At the level of Division I, the relation of positing is merely formal. At that of Division II, there is a 'concrete positing'.

Presence Cognate with Hegel's *Dasein* (Being-There); when speaking of 'the presence of absence' it is also presence in the sense of 'a Presence'.

Presentation Cognate with Marx's '*Darstellung*'. The term *presentation* has two referents. My presentation of the logic of capital follows in the tracks of capital's own presentation of itself. With regard to the latter, it has the sense 'making present'.

Presupposition This is not the same as 'assumption', because it is to be posited in the course of the dialectic developed from it.

Price I distinguish *Simple price* (= Cost price + notional profit), *Production price* (= Cost Price + uniform rate of profit), and *Reproduction Price* (= Cost Price + general rate of profit).

Quality As a general heading this characterises 'Being' in the most indeterminate sense, namely that without which it would not *be*; here this is the exchangeableness of the commodity. It is also used more specifically under 'determinate being' as defined by its limit in another quality; but here there are no contrastive qualities, so the determination is secured by otherness as such, namely another commodity identical to the first.

Separation, original This refers to the constitutive parting of the material and ideal realms, more specifically to the use-value and value determinants of the commodity.

Space In this work, space refers to the notional separation of produced commodities synchronously commensurated in exchange.

Spirit This is my usual rendering of Hegel's *Geist*. (Note that modern translators prefer to use 'Mind' for it.) It is the self-knowing moment of the Idea. 'The spirit of capitalism' (Weber) is here taken as objective not subjective (q.v. *Idea*), which has its explicit moment in finance.

Subject Since the presentation is restricted to the logical form of capital, its presentation as subject draws primarily on the logic of the concept. There are three levels to its development: Notion; Teleology; and Life. Logically the category of subject can hardly be distinguished from that of the 'self-acting Concept', which determines itself from universality to singularity. The universality of a fund is capable of being determined to many different investments. Next comes the consideration that it selects means towards realising its projects. It engages in 'teleological positing' in the form M–C–M'. Finally, the capital subject takes *itself* as its own project, when self-developing as infinite accumulation. (See also 'substance'.)

Sublate Cognate with Hegel's '*aufheben*'. This comprehends three linked determinations: abolition, elevation, and preservation. It is the characteristic figure of a dialectical transition, in which a form is not abolished outright but is preserved in a new shape when elevated to a moment of a higher form.

Substance Its substance is what allows something to preserve its existence independent of that of others. It is the bearer of attributes, which themselves may change while the substance itself endures. The substantiality of value is posited by money (§ 23.3). It follows that there is no 'substance *of* value' because value is *itself* a substance, albeit appearing simply as the *logical form* of substance. (It is the *ideal* product of social practice, so it has nothing to do with any physical substances.) When I term money 'the value substance', then, it is the elucidation of substance as *pure form*. Spinoza held that there is only *one* substance. This is a good analogy for *value*, since commodities, however various, are, *as values*, of the same ideal substance. Because value is *one* substance, different values are not different substances, hence they are as much identical (except in magnitude) as different. As products, commodities have some *material* substance in addition. So there is consubstantiation. From capital's point of view, it is value substance that counts, so implicitly it assumes transubstantiation occurs with commodification. When I use the Hegelian figure 'substance becomes subject' this does not refer to the *material* substance of the commodity but to money as the *value substance* becoming capital.

Subsumption This has three contexts. (i) At the end of Division I on the value form it refers formally to commodification; (ii) the process of formal determination of production subsumes it under the rule of capital; (iii) and consequently reshapes it as it is *really* subsumed by capital in its service.

Surplus Value This is a residual once wages are deducted from added value. It is the source of such revenues as entrepreneurial profit, interest, rent, etc.

Teleology This characterises a form having immanent purposiveness. It comes in three sub-categories in my usage. *Finite Teleology* has agent, means, and end, external to one another. I use this term to characterise C–M–C′ where the C–M is a means to the M–C′. *Infinite teleology* arises when what is an end for one agent is a means for another, and also means are ends. It is used here to characterise the entire system of sales and purchases, collating all the movements concerned in what I call the metamorphosis of money, which continually sustains monetary circulation. *Immanent teleology* is how I characterise M–C–M′. Here the origin of the movement, the money thrown into circulation, is qualitatively identical with the end aimed at, the money that returns to itself with its increment.

Tendency A tendency is that which generates evolving forms of something, or directional quantitative variation in it. It is predicated on the presence of certain forces within it, or acting upon it. A tendency may be counteracted by other tendencies in a system. Thus it may well not give rise to an empirical 'trend'. (This distinction I owe to Reuten 2019.) The question whether the so-called 'Tendential Fall in the General Rate of Profit' (see § 83.3 *Addendum*) may nonetheless predominate has been a vexed issue.

Thing As a moment of the category 'value as existent' it is cognate with Kant's 'thing in itself'; under 'value as substance' I characterise the commodity as a 'thing of value' or – simply – 'a value'.

Time In this work 'time' has two referents. First: the notional *interval* between two readings of accumulated value underlies the temporality of capital accumulation as a movement interiorising time; in this sense time is the '*existent* concept' because it concretises the virtual time of *succession* in the formal notion of capital accumulation. Second: the *duration* of the production periods which are transformed into values; in this sense time turns into space (q.v.).

Totality A totality, organised around two poles, has the following character: a) both poles are *essential* to each other as a matter of their very definition; b) each produces its *opposite* through its own movement; c) each reproduces *itself* through the mediation of its opposite; d) the totality is constituted out of its moments, but the totality *reproduces* itself in and through its moments even when the material reduced to such moments existed in some sense prior to the constitution of the totality (not merely prior to it in the exposition by science of its constitution).

Unique Universal Equivalent Because value is a homogeneous all-pervasive substance its autonomisation in a universal equivalent must be a unique one. There are many possible *bearers* of the universal equivalent, but they are not compossible. The demand of the Concept is that there is actual only one such.

Use-Value While value is posited in this work as 'not-use-value', use-value is not therewith permanently set aside; it comes back in as economically effective in its own right.

Valorisation 'Valorisation' is a neologism prevalent in the English literature to render Marx's '*Verwertung*', as a result of Ben Fowkes's translation of *Capital*. The valorisation of capital is the generation of surplus value, ideally to be added to capital.

Value Form This form contrasts with other forms such as 'natural form'. It is historically specific, being actual only in capitalism. It is distinct from 'form *of* value' which is used within the presentation to refer to the various forms that value takes on such as 'money form of value' (see '*Form*').

Variable Capital I use the abbreviation 'v' for consistency with Marx's notation, but for me it is a revenue paid to the wage worker and *not* 'variable capital'. Since workers produce their own wages, having given credit to capital, there is no logical reason to speak of capital advanced in this respect (regardless of contingent discrepancies of wage period and production period). In any case labour power has no value even if there is a price for hiring it. So the added value is a single mass and the v returned to labour power normally less than it. So this 'v' is a result, not an input like constant capital.

Select Bibliography

As well as the sources to which explicit reference is made in the text, I include some other works that I found germane to my concerns here.

Adorno, Theodor W. 1976, 'Sociology and Empirical Research', in *The Positivist Dispute in German Sociology*, by Adorno et al., translated by G. Adey and D. Frisby, London: Heinemann.
Arthur, Christopher J. 1986, *Dialectics of Labour: Marx and his Relation to Hegel*, Oxford: Basil Blackwell.
Arthur, Christopher J. 1993, 'Hegel's *Logic* and Marx's *Capital*', in Moseley (ed.) 1993.
Arthur, Christopher J. 1997, 'Against the Logical-Historical Method: Dialectical Derivation versus Linear Logic', in Moseley and Campbell (eds) 1997; as revised in Arthur 2002a, Chapter 2.
Arthur, Christopher J. 1998, 'The Fluidity of Capital and the Logic of the Concept', in Arthur and Reuten (eds) 1998.
Arthur, Christopher J. 2000, 'From the Critique of Hegel to the Critique of Capital', in *The Hegel-Marx Connection*, edited by T. Burns and I. Fraser, Basingstoke: Macmillan.
Arthur, Christopher J. 2001, 'The Spectral Ontology of Value', *Radical Philosophy*, 107.
Arthur, Christopher J. 2002a, *The New Dialectic and Marx's 'Capital'*, Leiden: Brill.
Arthur, Christopher J. 2002b, 'Capital in General and Marx's Capital', in *The Culmination of Capital*, edited by Martha Campbell and Geert Reuten, Basingstoke: Palgrave.
Arthur, Christopher J. 2003, 'The Problem of Use-Value for a Dialectic of Capital', in *New Dialectics and Political Economy*, edited by Robert Albritton and John Simoulidis, Basingstoke: Palgrave.
Arthur, Christopher J. 2004, 'Money and the Form of Value', in Bellofiore and Taylor (eds) 2004.
Arthur, Christopher J. 2005a, 'Reply to Critics', *Historical Materialism*, 13, no. 2.
Arthur, Christopher J. 2005b, 'The Myth of Simple Commodity Production', in *Marx Myths and Legends*, edited by R. Lucas and A. Blunden, http://marxmyths.org; also on http://www.chrisarthur.net/
Arthur, Christopher J. 2006, 'The Inner Totality of Capitalism', *Historical Materialism*, 14, no. 3.
Arthur, Christopher J. 2010, 'Capital in General' from 'Historical-Critical Dictionary of Marxism', *Historical Materialism*, 18, no. 1.
Arthur, Christopher J. 2013, 'The Practical Truth of Abstract Labour', in Bellofiore et al. (eds) 2013.

Arthur, Christopher J., and Geert Reuten (eds) 1998, *The Circulation of Capital: Essays on Volume Two of Marx's 'Capital'*, Basingstoke: Macmillan Press.

Backhaus, Hans-Georg 1992, 'Between Philosophy and Science: Marxian Social Economy as Critical Theory', in *Open Marxism: Volume 1 Dialectics and History*, edited by Werner Bonefeld et al., London: Pluto Press.

Banaji, Jairus 1979, 'From the Commodity to Capital: Hegel's Dialectic in Marx's *Capital*', in *Value: The Representation of Labour in Capitalism*, edited by Diane Elson, London: CSE Books.

Bellofiore, Riccardo 2004, 'Marx and the Macro-Monetary Foundation of Micro-Economics', in Bellofiore and Taylor (eds) 2004.

Bellofiore, Riccardo 2014, 'Lost in Translation: Once Again on the Marx-Hegel Connection', in *Marx's Capital and Hegel's Logic*, edited by Fred Moseley and Tony Smith, Leiden: Brill.

Bellofiore, Riccardo 2018, 'Forever Young? Marx's Critique of Political Economy', *PSL Quarterly Review*, 71, no. 287.

Bellofiore, Riccardo 2019, 'The Adventures of *Vergesellschaftung*', in *Marx Inattuale*, edited by Riccardo Bellofiore and Carla Maria Fabiani, Roma: Edizioni Efesto.

Bellofiore, Riccardo, and Roberto Finelli 1998, 'Capital, Labour and Time', in *Marxian Economics: A Reappraisal, Volume 1, Method, Value and Money*, edited by Ricardo Bellofiore, Basingstoke: Macmillan.

Bellofiore, Riccardo, and Roberto Fineschi (eds) 2009, *Re-reading Marx: New Perspectives After the Critical Edition*, Basingstoke: Palgrave Macmillan.

Bellofiore, Riccardo, Guido Starosta, and Peter Thomas (eds) 2013, *In Marx's Laboratory: Critical Interpretations of the Grundrisse*, Leiden: Brill.

Bellofiore, Riccardo, and Nicola Taylor (eds) 2004, *The Constitution of Capital: Essays on Volume One of Marx's Capital*, Basingstoke: Palgrave.

Bensaïd, Daniel 2002, *Marx for Our Times*, translated by Gregory Elliott, London: Verso.

Bhaskar, Roy 1993, *Dialectic: The Pulse of Freedom*, London: Verso.

Bidet, Jacques 2005, 'The Dialectician's Interpretation of Capital', *Historical Materialism*, 13, no. 2.

Bidet, Jacques 2007, *Exploring Marx's* Capital: *Philosophical, Economic and Political Dimensions*, trans. David Fernbach, Leiden: Brill.

Bonefeld, Werner 2014, *Critical Theory and the Critique of Political Economy*, London: Bloomsbury Academic.

de Brunhoff, Suzanne 2015, *Marx on Money*, 2nd edition, translated by M.J. Goldbloom, London: Verso.

Callinicos, Alex 2014, *Deciphering Capital: Marx's Capital and Its Destiny*, London: Bookmarks.

Campbell, Martha 2002a, 'The Credit System', in Campbell and Reuten (eds) 2002.

Campbell, Martha 2002b, 'Rent and Landed Property', in Campbell and Reuten (eds) 2002.

Campbell, Martha 2017, 'Marx's Transition to Money with No Intrinsic Value in *Capital*, Chapter 3', in *Continental Thought and Theory*, 1, no. 4: 150 Years of *Capital*.

Campbell, Martha, and Geert Reuten (eds) 2002, *The Culmination of Capital: Essays on Volume Three of Marx's 'Capital'*, Basingstoke: Palgrave Macmillan.

Debord, Guy 1977, *Society of the Spectacle*, Detroit: Black and Red.

Dussel, Enrique 2001, *Towards an Unknown Marx*, London: Routledge.

Eldred, Michael, Marnie Hanlon, Lucia Kleiber, and Mike Roth, 1982/85, 'Reconstructing Value-Form Analysis 1–4', *Thesis Eleven*, 4, 1982; 7, 1983; 9, 1984; 11, 1985.

Elson, Diane (ed.) 1979, *Value: The Representation of Labour in Capitalism*, London: CSE Books.

Hegel, Georg Wilhelm Friedrich 1969, *Enzyklopädie der Philosophischen Wissenschaften* (1830), edited by F. Nicolin and O. Poggeler, 7th edition, Hamburg: Verlag von Felix Meiner.

Hegel, Georg Wilhelm Friedrich 1975, *Wissenschaft der Logik*, 2nd edition, 2 Vols, edited by G. Lasson, Hamburg: Verlag von Felix Meiner.

Hegel, Georg Wilhelm Friedrich 1991, *The Encyclopaedia Logic*, translated by T.F. Geraets, W.A. Suchting, and H.S. Harris [translation of *Enzyklopädie der Philosophischen Wissenschaften im Grundrisse I, Die Wissenschaft der Logik* (third edition 1830)], Indianapolis: Hackett.

Hegel, Georg Wilhelm Friedrich 2007, *The Philosophy of Mind*, translated by M. Inwood, Oxford: Oxford University Press.

Hegel, Georg Wilhelm Friedrich 2010, *The Science of Logic*, translated by G. di Giovanni, Cambridge: Cambridge University Press.

Heinrich, Michael 2012, *An Introduction to the Three Volumes of Karl Marx's Capital*, translated by A. Locascio, New York: Monthly Review Press.

Inwood, Michael 1992, *A Hegel Dictionary*, Oxford: Blackwell.

Kant, Immanuel 1934, *Critique of Pure Reason*, translated by J.M.D. Meiklejohn, London: Dent.

Kay, Geoffrey, and James Mott 1982, *Political Order and the Law of Labour*, Basingstoke: Macmillan.

Lebowitz, Michael A. 1992, *Beyond 'Capital'*, Basingstoke: Macmillan.

Lotz, Christian 2014, *The Capitalist Schema*, Lanham: Lexington Books.

McCarney, Joseph 2000, *Hegel on History*, London: Routledge.

McTaggart, John McTaggart Ellis 1910, *A Commentary on Hegel's Logic*, Cambridge: Cambridge University Press.

Marx, Karl 1976, *Capital*, Volume I, translated by Ben Fowkes, Harmondsworth: Penguin.

Marx, Karl 1978, *Capital*, Volume II, translated by David Fernbach, Harmondsworth: Penguin.

Marx, Karl 1981, *Capital*, Volume III, translated by David Fernbach, Harmondsworth: Penguin.

Marx, Karl 1994, 'Economic Manuscript of 1861–63', in *Marx and Engels Collected Works*, Volume 34, London: Lawrence & Wishart.

Mohun, Simon (ed.) 1994, *Debates in Value Theory*, Basingstoke: Macmillan.

Moseley, Fred 2016, *Money and Totality*, Leiden: Brill.

Moseley, Fred (ed.) 1993, *Marx's Method in Capital: A Reexamination*, Atlantic Highlands, NJ: Humanities Press.

Moseley, Fred (ed.) 2005, *Marx's Theory of Money: Modern Appraisals*, New York: Palgrave Macmillan.

Moseley, Fred, and Martha Campbell (eds) 1997, *New Investigations of Marx's Method*, Atlantic Highlands, NJ: Humanities.

Moseley, Fred, and Tony Smith (eds) 2014, *Marx's* Capital *and Hegel's* Logic: *A Reexamination*, Leiden: Brill.

Murray, Patrick 1988, *Marx's Theory of Scientific Knowledge*, Atlantic Highlands, NJ: Humanities Press.

Murray, Patrick 2017, *The Mismeasure of Wealth: Essays on Marx and Social Form*, Chicago: Haymarket Books.

Mure, G.R.G. 1950, *A Study of Hegel's Logic*, Oxford: Oxford University Press.

Ollman, Bertell, and Tony Smith (eds) 2008, *Dialectics for the New Century*, Basingstoke: Palgrave Macmillan.

Osborne, Peter 2005, *How to Read Marx*, London: Granta Books.

Pashukanis, Evgeny 1978, *Law and Marxism: A General Theory*, translated by Barbara Einhorn, London: Ink Links.

Postone, Moishe 1993, *Time, Labor, and Social Domination*, Cambridge: Cambridge University Press.

Rattansi, Ali (ed.) 1989, *Ideology, Method and Marx*, London: Routledge.

Reichelt, Helmut 2005, 'Social Reality as Appearance: Some Notes on Marx's Conception of Reality', in *Human Dignity: Social Autonomy and the Critique of Capitalism*, edited by Werner Bonefeld and Kosmas Psychopedis, Aldershot: Ashgate.

Reuten, Geert 1998, 'The Status of Marx's Reproduction Schemes: Conventional or Dialectical Logic', in Arthur and Reuten (eds) 1998.

Reuten, Geert 2005, 'Money as Constituent of Value: The Ideal Introversive Substance and the Ideal Extroversive Form of Value in Marx's Capital', in Moseley (ed.) 2005.

Reuten, Geert 2017, 'The Productive Powers of Labour and the Redundant Transformation to Prices of Production', *Historical Materialism*, 25, no. 3.

Reuten, Geert 2019, *The Unity of the Capitalist Economy and State*, Leiden: Brill.

Reuten, Geert, and Michael Williams 1989, *Value-Form and the State: The Tendencies of Accumulation and the Determination of Economic Policy in Capitalist Society*, London: Routledge.

Rosdolsky, Roman 1977, *The Making of Marx's 'Capital'*, translated by Peter Burgess, London: Pluto Press.
Rubin, Isaak Illich 1972, *Essays on Marx's Theory of Value*, translated from 3rd edition [1920] by Fredy Perlman, Detroit: Black and Red.
Saad-Filho, Alfredo 2002, *The Value of Marx*, London: Routledge.
Seaford, Richard 2004, *Money and the Early Greek Mind*, Cambridge: Cambridge University Press.
Sekine, Thomas T. 1984, *The Dialectic of Capital*, 2 Volumes, York University: Yushindo Press. (New edition 2020, Leiden: Brill.)
Sekine, Thomas T. 1997, *An Outline of the Dialectic of Capital*, 2 Volumes, Basingstoke: Macmillan.
Shortall, Felton C. 1994, *The Incomplete Marx*, Aldershot: Avebury.
Smith, Tony 1990, *The Logic of Marx's Capital; Replies to Hegelian Criticisms*, Albany: State University of New York Press.
Smith, Tony 1993, *Dialectical Social Theory and its Critics*, Albany: State University of New York Press.
Smith, Tony 2014, 'Hegel, Marx and the Comprehension of Capitalism', in Moseley and Smith (eds) 2014.
Smith, Tony 2017, *Beyond Liberal Egalitarianism: Marx and Normative Social Theory in the Twenty-First Century*, Leiden: Brill.
Sohn-Rethel, Alfred 1978, *Intellectual and Manual Labour*, Basingstoke: Palgrave Macmillan. (New Edition 2020, Leiden: Brill.)
Sparby, Terje 2015, *Hegel's Conception of Determinate Negation*, Leiden: Brill.
Sraffa, Piero 1960, *Production of Commodities by Means of Commodities*, Cambridge: Cambridge University Press.
Steedman, Ian 1985, 'Robots and Capitalism (Comment)', *New Left Review*, 1/151, May–June.
Steedman, Ian, and Paul Sweezy et al. 1981, *The Value Controversy*, London: Verso.
Toscano, Alberto 2019, 'Last Philosophy: The Metaphysics of Capital from Sohn-Rethel to Žižek', *Historical Materialism*, 27, no. 2.
Uno, Kōzō 1980, *Principles of Political Economy*, translated by Thomas T. Sekine, East Sussex: Harvester Press.
Willett, Cynthia 1990, 'The Shadow of Hegel's *Science of Logic*', in *Essays on Hegel's Logic*, edited by G. di Giovanni, Albany: State University of New York Press.

Index of Names

Albritton, Robert   15
Adorno, Theodor W.   25
Aristotle   24, 179
Arthur, Christopher   ixn1, n2, xi, 1n1, 4–5, 17n, 53n, 101n, 246n, 268n, 285n, 330n, 398n, 409

Banaji, Jairus   36n, 401
Bellofiore, Riccardo   xi, 1n, 38n, 106n, 232, 244n, 297, 322n, 332, 343n4, n5, n6, 401n
Bhaskar, Roy   47n
Bidet, Jacques   246n
de Brunhoff, Sylvia   344n

Campbell, Martha   xi, 147n, 340n
Carson, Rebecca   186n

Debord, Guy   364, 371

Eldred, Michael   ixn
Engels, Frederick   329n, 375

Finelli, Roberto   58n, 401n
Fineschi, Roberto   xi
Fowkes, Ben   440

Hegel, G.W.F.   ix, x, 1–5, 19–24, 25–34, 37, 46, 48, 51, 53–55, 57, 69–71, 74, 75, 77, 80–81, 87, 121, 130, 152, 153, 156, 176, 183, 190, 196, 201, 269, 272–3, 374–75, 378, 385, 395–407, 432–438

Inwood, Michael   407

Kant, Immanuel   24, 81, 107, 158, 375, 400, 439
Kay, Geoffrey   352n, 359n

Lebowitz, Michael   242n

Marx, Karl   1, 2, 9, 11, 12, 16, 17n, 31, 33, 36, 56, 101n2, 105, 138, 147, 164, 178, 186, 222, 243, 245, 249, 250–51, 253, 254, 257, 267, 276, 278, 280, 285, 318n, 324, 328, 332, 333n, 340n2, 343n, 355n, 372n, 374, 379n, 395, 433, 437, 440
McTaggart, J.M.E.   402n
Moseley, Fred   xi, 297, 321, 324, 333n
Mott, James   352n, 359n
Mure, Geoffrey   401
Murray, Patrick   xi, 158n, 233n, 374

Pashukanis, Evgeny   359n

Reuten, Geert   ix, xi, 9n, 13n, 44n, 47n, 130n, 147n, 148n, 163n, 222n, 311n, 312n, 317, 318n, 327n, 333n, 339n, 340n, 343n4, n6, 344n8, 355n, 359n, 439

Saad-Filho, Alfredo   265n
Schrödinger, Erwin   220
Seaford, Richard   116n
Sekine, Tom   1n2, 15, 172n
Smith, Adam   239
Smith, Tony   ixn2, xi, 1, 29, 31, 372n, 373
Sohn-Rethel, Alfred   13
Sraffa, Piero   320, 321
Steedman, Ian   323n

Taylor, Nicola   xi

Uno, Kōzō   xn, 15, 172n

Weber, Max   23, 437
Willett, Cynthia   53n
Williams, Michael   ixn2, 9n, 13n, 44n, 47n, 327n, 343n4, 344n8

Index of Subjects

Absence   14, 47, 49, 50, 53, 72, 221, 427–8, 432
Absolute   23–4, 29, 54, 69, 348, 432
  form   118, 184
  Idea   70, 191, 338, 342, 344, 349, 374, 384, 407
  negativity   93, 190, 369–70, 375, 385–6
  relation   140, 341, 432
  Spirit   351, 407
Abstraction   12–13, 21, 22, 23, 24, 36–7, 46, 88, 207, 226–7, 269
Actuality   109–14, 277, 319–20, 432
Architectonic   ix, 1, 378
Aufheben   438

Banks
  ante-validation by   343
  Central   164, 339
  money creation by   339–40
Begriff   152, 436
Being-in-exchange   47, 52, 74

Capital   9, 186–7, 189, 202, 235, 352
  commercial   344, 384
  financial   342–4, 384,
  general formula of   185–8
  industrial   213–5, 217, 265–8, 274–9, 342, 344, 354, 360, 384, 431
  merchant   212–3, 214, 342
  money-lending   212–3, 214, 342
Capital relation   223–4, 236–45, 358
Charaktermasken   56, 223, 383
Circuit   28, 190, 281–9, 342, 432
Circulation   202–6, 209–12, 253–4
Class   32, 245, 272, 322, 349, 365–6, 388–94
Commodity   9, 12, 17, 20, 33, 36–7, 40, 42, 43, 77–89, 113–5, 136, 170–72, 206–208, 209–12, 254, 379
  metamorphoses of   172, 175, 380
Commodity production   9, 41, 215, 217, 238, 248, 253, 258, 381
  generalised   9, 434
  petty   265
  simple   17–18, 258
Concept   x, 20–21, 24, 25, 145, 151, 153, 156, 175, 177–8, 182, 184, 244, 373, 375, 433

Concrete universal   229, 433
Condition of existence   27, 38, 39, 43, 45, 195, 202, 356–66, 433
Consubstantiation   132, 138
Contradiction   30, 83, 401,
  in commodity money   180
  in exchange at value   193–4, 381, 406
  in the commodity   95, 116
  of capital relation   391
  of labour   16, 366
  of labour and capital   243
  of use value and exchange value   365
  quality and quantity   182–4

Darstellung   437
Dasein   53, 74, 437
Derangement   347, 385, 393, 433

Exchange-value   16, 84–8, 92
  and use-value   11, 13, 37
Exploitation   20, 239, 241, 251, 279, 291, 305, 334

Fetishism   106–7, 139, 232, 240–41
Form and content   11, 16, 22, 31, 54, 98–100, 140, 191, 214, 223, 234, 350, 375–8, 402, 434
Form-determination   107, 119–25, 201, 434
Formal Determination   11–12, 119, 192–3, 201, 223, 275, 349, 359, 406, 434
Forms of value   38, 40, 100–9, 115, 117–25, 357, 428–9

Gaia   398
Geist   437
Ground   38, 43–4, 95, 194, 385, 434–5

Hegelian-Marxism   1
Hegel's logic   ix, 1, 3, 20, 22, 23, 34, 37, 69, 395–407
  Encyclopaedia Logic   2, 4–5, 395n., 396, 398, 407, 408–9, 413–4
  Science of Logic   2, 27, 396, 410–12
Homology   ix, 1, 19, 22, 368, 399

Idea   ix, x, 23, 32, 187, 193, 271, 355, 435
  practical and theoretical   192, 406

Immediate exchangeability 122–3, 435
Individual 153, 268, 269–72, 344–6, 350, 404, 435
Infinitely negative judgement see Judgement
Infinity of capital 190–1

Judgement 435
  infinitely negative 47, 435
  of worth 151, 161–2, 435

Labour 11, 14, 225, 229, 249
  abstract 15–6, 224–34, 238, 248
  alienated 230, 243
  domestic 354–61
  intensity 294–5
  power 237, 250–5, 353–5, 436
  recalcitrant 237–8, 245–6, 383
Labour theory of value 2, 15, 16, 229, 239, 248, 300, 304, 321, 324, 384
Land 355, 365

Marx's *Capital* 2, 27, 36, 389n., 395
Measure 34, 128–9, 189, 220, 222, 227, 379, 400, 436
  nodal line of 87
  proper 125, 131,
  real 132 ff.
  series of 86–7
  specifying 84–9, 131
Method 9, 17, 19, 27, 29–30, 33, 34, 36, 297, 372, 375, 405
Moment 28, 38, 95, 99, 275, 347, 432–3, 436
Monetary medium 130–31
Money 20, 34, 91–2, 112
  as capital 184–5, 283, 339
  as commodity 113, 146–8, 180, 183, 338–9, 380
  as end of exchange 179
  as fund 179, 257
  as means of payment 179
  as money 178–81, 339, 343
  ex nihilo 339–41, 380
  form of value 11, 25, 91, 120–5, 403
  fungibility of 159–60
  metamorphoses of 171–7, 430
  myth of origin 115–6

Negative theology 75
Non-being 52, 219, 243
Nothing 52–4, 72–5, 219–20, 340, 436
Nothingness 54–5, 73–7, 370, 379
Notion 152, 154–9, 201, 436

Positing the presupposition x, 34, 37–8, 40, 43–4, 94, 114, 135, 401, 437
Pre-commensuration 344
Presence ix, 50, 51, 53, 55, 72, 74, 205, 369–70, 379, 437
Presentation 12, 25–6, 28, 33, 36, 39, 40, 46, 54–6, 178, 181, 361, 377, 437
Price
  simple 281, 290–2, 329–30
  production 296–309
  reproduction 299, 318–23
  standard of 162–4
  transitivity of 167–70

Rate of profit 301, 305, 309–13, 318–9, 321–3, 331
  fall of 325–7
Reflection 92–5
Repulsion and attraction 79–81, 120, 267, 315

Schein 401
Schematisation 157–8
Space 217–9, 437
Spectre ix, 56, 75–6, 221, 350, 366–71
Sraffian system 321, 323–5
Subject ix, 24, 187, 192, 236, 242, 243, 268, 345, 350, 358, 374, 387, 390, 393, 438
Sublate 31, 43, 45, 114, 242, 287, 438
Substance 25, 125–31, 136–46, 240, 377, 404, 438
  becomes subject 145, 150, 187–8
Subsumption 193–4, 201, 234–6, 253, 438
Surplus value 249–51, 279–80, 292–4, 305, 311–3, 325–7, 438
Systematic dialectic 9, 27–35, 37, 43, 69, 335, 339, 372, 418

Teleology 381, 439
  finite 172, 177
  immanent 175, 177
  infinite 173, 177

INDEX OF SUBJECTS

Time   18, 202, 217, 218, 219–23, 382, 439
   and accumulation   203–6
   and production   226, 242, 246–9
   Marx on   222
Transformation problem   2, 297, 311, 329
Transubstantiation   132, 137–8

Universal equivalent   105–11
   its uniqueness   109–15, 439
Use-value   12, 13, 14, 21, 46, 50–3, 130, 195, 214, 355, 359–64, 370, 440
   and exchange-value   11, 13, 22, 37, 96, 108, 359–64

Valorisation   245–6, 250, 287–90, 440
Value form   11, 13, 19, 26, 37, 52, 95–7, 440
Value-form theory   ix–x, 2, 11, 13, 227, 368
Variable Capital   249, 279–80, 283–4, 295, 303, 440
Verrücktheit   433

Wages   230, 250–5, 279–81, 322, 354–5

www.ingramcontent.com/pod-product-compliance
Lightning Source LLC
Chambersburg PA
CBHW071227070526
44583CB00017B/2077